South Asian Security

The South Asian security complex refers to security interdependencies between the states in the region, and also includes the effect that powerful external actors, such as China, the US and Russia, and geopolitical interests have on regional dynamics. This book focuses on the national securities of a number of South Asian countries in order to discuss a range of issues related to South Asian security.

The book makes a distinction between traditional and non-traditional security. While state-centric approaches such as approaches to bilateral relations between India and Pakistan are considered to be traditional Realist approaches to security, the promotion of economic, environmental and human security reflect global concerns, liberal theories and cosmopolitan values. The book goes beyond traditional security issues to reflect the changing security agenda in South Asia in the twenty-first century, and is a useful contribution to studies on South Asian Politics and Security Studies.

Sagarika Dutt is a Senior Lecturer in International Relations at Nottingham Trent University, UK. She has published several articles and a book on Indian politics and foreign policy.

Alok Bansal is Senior Fellow at the Centre for Land Welfare Studies (CLAWS), New Delhi, India, and Visiting Professor in the Pakistan Studies Programme at Jamia Millia Islamia, India.

Routledge contemporary South Asia Series

South Asian Security

21st century discourses

Edited by Sagarika Dutt and Alok Bansal

Routledge
Taylor & Francis Group

LONDON AND NEW YORK

First published 2012
by Routledge
2 Park Square, Milton Park, Abingdon, Oxfordshire OX14 4RN

Simultaneously published in the USA and Canada
by Routledge
711 Third Avenue, New York, NY 10017

First issued in paperback 2015

Routledge is an imprint of the Taylor & Francis Group, an informa business

British Library Cataloguing in Publication Data
A catalogue record for this book is available from the British Library

Library of Congress Cataloging in Publication Data
South Asian Security: 21st century discourses/edited by Sagarika Dutt and
Alok Bansal.
    p. cm. – (Routledge contemporary South Asia series; 51)
    Includes bibliographical references and index.
    1. Security, International–South Asia. 2. South Asia–Foreign relations.
    3. South Asia–Politics and government–21st century. I. Dutt, Sagarika,
    1958– II. Bansal, Alok.
    JZ6009.S64S67 2011
    355′.033054–dc22   2011016985

ISBN13: 978-1-138-11930-7 (pbk)
ISBN13: 978-0-415-61891-5 (hbk)

Typeset in Times
by Wearset Ltd, Boldon, Tyne and Wear

To the citizens of South Asia

Contents

Illustrations

Map

Tables

Contributors

Sita Bali is Senior Lecturer in International Relations at Staffordshire University, UK.

Alok Bansal is Senior Fellow at the Centre for Land Warfare Studies (CLAWS), New Delhi and Visiting Professor in the Pakistan Studies Programme at Jamia Millia Islamia, India.

Ashok Behuria is Research Fellow at the Institute for Defence Studies and Analyses, New Delhi, India.

Nicolas Blarel is a Ph.D. candidate in the Department of Political Science, Indiana University, USA.

Tridib Chakraborti teaches in the Department of International Relations, Jadavpur University, Kolkata, India.

Mohor Chakraborty is Assistant Professor in the Department of Political Science, South Calcutta Girls' College, Kolkata, India.

Shebonti Ray Dadwal is Research Fellow at the Institute for Defence Studies and Analyses, New Delhi, India.

Sreeradha Datta is Director, Maulana Abul Kalum Azad Institute of Asian Studies, Kolkata, India.

Sagarika Dutt is Senior Lecturer in International Relations at Nottingham Trent University, UK.

Namrata Goswami is Research Fellow at the Institute for Defence Studies and Analyses, New Delhi, India.

Kunal Mukherjee has recently obtained his Ph.D. from the Department of Politics and International Relations, University of Nottingham, UK.

Martin Mulligan is Deputy Director, Globalism Research Centre, RMIT University, Melbourne, Australia.

B.C. Upreti is Director of the South Asian Studies Centre, University of Rajasthan, Jaipur, India.

TURKMENISTAN

CHINA

Jammu
and
Kashmir

Kabul ⊙

AFGHANISTAN

Islamabad ⊙

PAKISTAN

New Delhi ⊙

NEPAL

BHUTAN

Kathmandu ⊙

Dhaka ⊙

INDIA

BANGLADESH

Arabian Sea

Bay of Bengal

Laccadive Sea

Andaman Sea

SRI LANKA

⊙ Sri Jayawardenapura-Kotte

MALDIVE
ISLANDS

Indian Ocean

South Asia

Introduction

There has always been an interest in national and international security within the discipline of International Relations. The devastation caused by the two World Wars led to the establishment of the League of Nations in 1919 and the United Nations in 1945 to 'maintain international peace and security' (Preamble, UN Charter) by urging states to make a commitment to resolving their disputes through peaceful means. The World Wars also led to the emergence of the academic discipline of International Relations. While war is a timeless theme, interest in the study of the causes of war and of different types of conflict, both between states and within states, has grown over the years and produced an impressive body of academic literature on the subject. With the emergence of post-World War II regions following decolonization and their potential to become theatres of 'proxy wars' following the onset of the cold war, research has also been conducted on regional security complexes as an intermediate level between national and international security.

This book is about the South Asian security complex, which refers to security interdependencies between the states in the region but also includes the effect that powerful external actors (e.g., China, the US and Russia) and geopolitical interests have on regional dynamics. South Asia comprises India, Pakistan, Bangladesh, Sri Lanka, Nepal, Bhutan, the Maldives and Afghanistan, all of whom are members of the South Asian Association for Regional Co-operation (SAARC). The Indian subcontinent was under British colonial rule until 1947, and security was defined in terms of the challenges and threats faced by the British Indian empire and the priority accorded to the protection of British interests.[1] The successor states, i.e., the sovereign states of India, Pakistan and Sri Lanka, inherited the emphasis on defense (understood in traditional terms) from the British and adopted a state-centric approach to security. To this day the states in the region have maintained their defensive postures vis-à-vis one another.

The history of the region has also contributed to the development of its security discourses. The creation of Pakistan, which was an unpopular move in Indian political circles, and the unresolved status of Kashmir led to hostile relations between the two largest countries in the region and several wars, one of which helped Bangladesh to secede from Pakistan, with a heavily militarized border between the two countries. In fact, one of the demands made by the Kashmiri nationalists, as recently as summer 2010, relates to the demilitarization of the region. But according to Indian government sources there will be 'no withdrawal of security forces from J&K' in the foreseeable future.[2] By the 1980s a civil war was also raging in Sri Lanka, highlighting the issue of ethnic identities and ethnic conflict. This war ended in 2009, but the Tamil issue has not really been resolved satisfactorily. In more recent years, especially since India and Pakistan became nuclear powers in the late 1990s, the issue of nuclear security has also become one of the most serious aspects of the regional security complex in South Asia, while Taliban insurgency in Afghanistan and terrorist bases in the region have given external actors (ISAF/NATO) a major role in the region. Yet environmental vulnerabilities and human insecurity are two of the most pervasive and widespread problems in South Asia.

The South Asian region is important for many different reasons. Close to 1.5 billion people (which is over 20 percent of the world's population) live in South Asia. There is a lot of potential in the region as demonstrated by India's economic success in recent years. However, the region is also characterized by mass poverty, conflict and environmental problems. Efforts to deal with these problems at the regional level are still taking shape. This volume attempts to discuss a selection of issues that relate to South Asian security including the national securities of various countries in the region. It makes a distinction between traditional (military) and non-traditional security (the 'New Security Agenda'), drawing on Buzan's conceptualization of security (among others). While state-centric approaches such as examining bilateral relations between India and Pakistan are considered to be traditional Realist approaches to security, the promotion of economic security, environmental security and human security reflect and are congruent with global concerns, liberal theories and cosmopolitan values. The book is divided into three sections to reflect this distinction as well as the interconnections between the different levels of security. The second section focuses on the theme of identity, democracy and order. This problématique is crucial to the internal security of the states in the region, although it may manifest itself as a clash between national security and individual or group security, and will be explored in several chapters. A summary of each chapter is given below.

Chapter 1 presents a theoretical framework for this book. Security is an important (albeit contested) concept in the study of international relations. Buzan opines that it offers a better approach to the study of international relations than those provided by the concepts of power or peace. 'It points to a prime motive for behavior which is different from, but no less significant than, that provided by power.' Even though the Realist school of thought is based on the concept of power, and uses the concept as an analytical tool, security is a universally accepted concept; most states in the world give some thought to a national security strategy and have national security advisers and national security councils and committees (e.g., the US and India). Buzan writes that 'states are the principal referent object of security because they are both the framework of order and the highest source of governing authority. This explains the dominating policy concern with "national" security.' The focus on regional security complexes is helpful in examining security interdependencies between geographically contiguous states in a region. However, security is not an objective condition. A process of securitization takes place as a result of political and social discourse. Chapters in this volume will examine this process in the South Asian context. They will also apply Buzan's sectoral approach to security, explained in his book *People, states and fear*. The five sectors are military security, political security concerning the stability of states and systems of government, economic security which includes access to the resources, finance and markets necessary to sustain acceptable levels of welfare and state power, societal security which includes the issue of cultural, religious and national identity, and finally environmental security. Buzan argues that there are linkages between these sectors but other scholars such as Howarth and Stavrakakis have a different ontological approach to social practices. They argue that social practices are embedded in a discourse about something and may be mutually exclusive. For example, discourses of economic modernization may not go well with environmentalist discourses as they represent different 'systems of meaningful practices that form the identities of subjects and objects.'[3]

Chapter 2 focuses on post-2001 Afghanistan. It overviews the arrangements put into place by the international community after the Americans put the Taliban to flight, including the Bonn Conference, ISAF, and UNAMA. It then examines the reasons for the deterioration in security and stability over the last decade or so. It highlights the American lack of commitment in terms of troops on the ground, and some of the policies they followed, such as reliance on and resurrection of the warlords, as important reasons for the decline. Further it considers the inadequacy of global financial assistance and the weakness of the Kabul government led by Hamid Karzai in fueling the strengthening Taliban insurgency. It then examines the interests of neighboring countries, including Pakistan, India, Iran and the Central Asian Republics and Russia, in Afghanistan in the last decade, and the extent to which involvement by these countries contributes to the instability and ongoing conflict in there. The chapter concludes by looking at the potential of the US surge and of negotiations with the Taliban as ways out of the current quagmire.

Chapter 3 argues that since the Indian and Pakistani nuclear tests in May 1998, there has been an emerging and prolific literature on the origins of nuclearization in South Asia but also on the new implications this enduring rivalry between two nuclear powers will have for existing theories of nuclear deterrence. This growing literature is multi-faceted, as it concentrates on different aspects of South Asia's nuclearization. A first wave of scholars focused mostly on explaining the external and internal mechanisms and reasons behind the decisions to become openly nuclear for India.[4] Other scholars have studied the impact of nuclearization on strategic stability in South Asia.[5] This debate over the effects of nuclear proliferation in South Asia is an extension of the broader theoretical debate between the 'optimistic' and 'pessimistic' camps.[6] Finally, some scholars have looked more closely at India's and Pakistan's evolving nuclear doctrines.[7] Some have discussed the merits of India's declaratory policy and how it was implemented in the last ten years, notably in times of crisis.[8] This chapter suggests it is also necessary to go beyond models and concepts derived from the cold war experience and that are applied to all emerging nuclear dyads and will attempt to determine how such factors as nuclear triads and non-state actors have influenced nuclear stability in the region.

Chapter 4 gives a historical overview of relations between India and Pakistan since these two states were created in the late 1940s. The issue of Kashmir, a Muslim majority state, led to the first war between the two states in 1948 and remains unresolved to this day, but it is mainly Pakistan that is unhappy with the status quo. Each country sees the other as a security threat and this has impacted on their defence budgets. Additionally, their possession of nuclear weapons has focused world attention on this region and led to Western efforts to defuse crises that threatened to spiral out of control. Also, terrorism emanating from Pakistan has blighted relations between Pakistan and India, as the Mumbai attacks of November 2008 have shown, and derailed the peace process. This chapter analyzes the securitization of Indo-Pak relations and assesses the efforts that have been made at the political level by virtually every government on both sides of the border to improve relations. A pattern emerges from this discussion about the competitive nature of regional politics in South Asia and the influence of domestic politics on bilateral relations, as well as national insecurities.

Chapter 5 argues that as China has a common border with South Asia and other strategic interests in the region, relations between China and the South Asian states are determined by geopolitics. The border dispute and the Tibet issue have strained relations between India and China ever since India became an independent state and inherited from the British Raj the borders demarcated by the MacMahon line. During the cold war years Pakistan and China became allies, and to this day Pakistan is receiving military and economic assistance from China. Chinese investment in and trade with the smaller South Asian countries is growing day by day, and in recent years so is its presence in the Indian Ocean. Despite the assurances from China that India and China can have co-operative relations with each other (and there are some good examples of co-operation between the two countries), China's growing strategic influence in South Asia has caused feelings of national insecurity which are reflected in both the statements made by the Indian government and the views expressed in the Indian media.

Chapter 6 was written prior to the ending of the civil war in Sri Lanka in 2009. However, as the 'Tamil issue' has not been completely resolved, the author's arguments are still relevant.[9] He writes that after nearly thirty years of civil war and the collapse, in 2006, of a fragile yet promising cease-fire agreement, confidence in the future of Sri Lanka was at an all-time low. The tsunami – which killed over 30,000 people and left a further 100,000 homeless – added to the nation's woes. Yet this natural disaster triggered a rare moment of unity in a nation divided along ethnic lines. To understand why morale-sapping divisions have become so endemic in Sri Lanka we need to begin by reviewing the process of nation formation that followed independence from Britain in 1948. The chapter then aims to put the failings of nation-building into a broader historical and geo-political context, drawing on a 'new wave' of Sri Lankan scholars who have been offering some fresh perspectives on Sri Lankan identity that could become circuit-breakers for the debilitating and self-perpetuating conflict. The author uses the Hambantota story to argue that a history of co-existence at the local level can be undermined by national conflicts and national political agendas. Decisions made primarily in Colombo do not take into account local realities and sensitivities, nor do they value the proud history of co-existence that offers hope to more divided local communities. In the wake of the tsunami Hambantota's 'civil society' acted resolutely to prevent new and damaging divisions, but a lack of attention by national and district authorities to the social impacts of proposed new developments could undermine their efforts in the longer term.

Chapter 7 argues that the ruling elites in Pakistan, in their quest for nationalism and national unity, have always tried to suppress any spirit of genuine federalism, perceiving it as a prelude to separatism. The main challenge to their efforts to foster a unitary structure can be attributed to the extreme ethnic consciousness and the sense of strong socio-cultural identity of most of the ethnic groups residing inside Pakistan. From the very beginning, the central government has had problems in appreciating the requirements of a federal arrangement, and it has assumed powers to run the provincial governments that did not rightfully belong to it. The problem was further aggravated by the fact that the Muslim League itself had very little support in the areas that came to constitute Pakistan. To counter the ethno-national aspirations of the populace, the Pakistani state, right from the beginning, promoted an all-inclusive Islamic identity to subsume various ethnic identities. The process was fairly successful in some parts of the country but in due course gave rise to a bigger Frankenstein, that of radical Islam. As the menace of Talibanization – a manifestation of radical Islam – threatens the very existence of Pakistan, an attempt is being made to de-emphasize this Islamic identity. This is giving a fillip to ethno-nationalism and has revived ethnic fires in regions that had hitherto remained quiet.

Chapter 8 tries to give an all-encompassing and balanced picture of Islamism in South-Central Asia, first by looking at the various facets of Islamism and then by analyzing the various factors that have given rise to it in the region. Islamism is studied by security officials within the broader framework of the New Security Agenda and is seen as one of the 'new threats' in the post-cold war period. After some background information in relation to Islamism, and some definitions, the chapter looks at the various factors that have given rise to this violent form of religiosity in Pakistan by looking at internal as well as external factors. The external factors which have contributed to the rise of Islamism in Pakistan encompass the spillover effects of the Taliban and its ideology from neighboring Afghanistan, the influx of Islamist groups from Central Asia, and the impact the Iranian Revolution had on Islamism in the region. Some of these factors are slightly more historical whereas others are more contemporary and are still contributing to Islamism in South-Central Asia. The second part of the chapter looks at the various internal causes of Islamism in Pakistan which include the program of Islamization by General Zia, the role of the seminaries and *madrasas* and the role played by the Jamat-i-Islami. Again, as far as these internal factors are concerned, some of them are slightly more historical and some are still contributing to the strengthening of Islamist forces in Pakistan. Thus, the chapter takes a very analytical approach towards the study of Islamism and tries to give an all-embracing and comprehensive picture by capturing both the internal causes as well as external factors that have given rise to Islamism in contemporary Pakistan.

Chapter 9 is about Nepali politics following the successful revolution in the country that led to the abolition of the monarchy. The Nepalese political system entered a new phase of transformation after the successful completion of the elections to the Constituent Assembly in April 2008 and the declaration of Nepal as a republican state based on federalism and secularism. This new phase has been characterized as the beginning of a new democratic Nepal. The chapter argues that the 1990 movement for democracy (Janandolan) was a major landmark in the political history of Nepal. It brought the authoritarian *panchayat* system to an end and initiated a process of democratization. The 1990 movement was a collective movement bringing together political parties, civil society and the masses. It led to high expectations regarding the socio-economic and political transformation of the country. However, the governments elected in subsequent years failed to deliver. Not only did they fail to fulfil the expectations of the people, they also failed to provide political stability and maintain order in the country. While the traditional political elites exercised power, the Nepali economy and society continued to be based on feudalism and social hierarchies. The fulfilment of popular aspirations and the socio-economic transformation of the country became secondary to political maneuvering and the politics of power. These conditions led to a critical phase in Nepali politics towards the second half of the 1990s in the form of a Maoist insurgency. It gradually covered nearly two-thirds of the country, challenged the basic premises of the Nepalese society and state, and called for a protracted guerrilla war and a new and democratic Nepal. This chapter discusses the new politics of the country following the abolition of the powerful institution of monarchy and in which the Maoists (as well as other marginalized groups such as *dalits*, ethnic minorities and women) are playing an important and constructive role, and the challenges and opportunities facing the country.

Chapter 10 is on insurgencies in the North East of India, one of the most picturesque yet troubled regions of the Indian subcontinent. The indigenous population consists of more than 220 major tribes and various other sub-tribes as a result of mass migration over the centuries from Southeast and East Asia. One of these tribes is the Ahoms, who reigned over Assam for more than 600 years and were successful in forging tributary relations with various other tribes like the Dimasas and the Nagas. However, British colonial rule created political and territorial divisions between the hills and the plains by the adoption of the Inner Line Regulation Act of 1873 and the Excluded Areas Act of 1880. A combination of political, economic and cultural factors have led to insurgencies in the region which the Indian government has tried to deal with using a variety of methods ranging from state repression to negotiations. The Northeast is strategically important to India as it is located between four neighboring countries of India, namely, Bangladesh, Bhutan, China and Myanmar. Apart from the fact that insurgencies in this region have an impact on relations between India and its neighbors (as insurgents often have bases in these countries and operate from across the border), the author argues that India's 'Look East' policy is dependent on the Northeast for an optimal opening to the countries of Southeast Asia via Myanmar. As insurgencies in the Northeast have become one of the dominant security discourses in India and South Asia, this chapter discusses some of the major insurgencies in Assam, Manipur and Nagaland like the United Liberation Front of Asom (ULFA) and the Dima Halam Daogah in Assam; the United National Liberation Front (UNLF) in Manipur and the National Socialist Council of Nagalim led by Thuingaleng Muivah and Isak Chisi Swu (NSCN-IM) in Nagaland.

Chapter 11 argues that the concept of human security is people-centered and is about protecting individuals from various kinds of threats ranging from war and internal conflict to hunger, disease and repression. The concept is associated with the post-cold war discourse about security and was first articulated in the 1994 UN Human Development Report. In recent years high-profile terrorist attacks and natural disasters have also helped to widen and deepen the security agenda. The chapter discusses the relationship between development and human security and the UN's role in promoting human security in developing countries, for example by promoting the Millennium Development Goals. Since the Rwandan genocide the debate has moved on from the 'right to intervene' towards the 'responsibility to protect.' The chapter examines some of the most important aspects of human security in South Asia such as economic security, health security, food security, environmental security and gender-related issues. It argues that state intervention is necessary in South Asia as there are demographic, social, economic and political structures in all the countries of South Asia and across the region, and indeed at the global level, that are often the root causes of human insecurity in those countries. International institutions, Western donors and international non-governmental organizations can also play a role by providing funding and expertise for particular projects as well as humanitarian assistance during a crisis. More importantly, the UN provides a framework for global governance based on international norms that can assist states in developing countries in various ways to improve human security. The tentative conclusion of this chapter is that the problem of human insecurity needs to be tackled at many different levels.

Chapter 12 is on climate change in South Asia. There is a plethora of serious environmental problems in South Asia, such as deforestation, soil erosion, floods, droughts, the impacts of population growth, and pollution. There is also a strong relationship between these problems and global warming/climate change. The Copenhagen Accord adopted on 18 December 2009 underlined that 'climate change is one of the greatest challenges of our time.' Its impacts are visible in melting glaciers, rising sea levels, more violent storms and extreme weather events. The impacts of climate change are being felt most acutely in the poorest countries of the world.[10]

According to a DFID source frequent floods and rising sea levels are devastating the South Asian region and affecting the lives of millions of people. At the present rate, by 2100 the sea level would rise by up to 1.4 meters and would engulf island nations such as the Maldives in the Indian Ocean and devastate coastal cities such as Kolkata and Dhaka (*The Times*, 1 December 2009, p. 1). Scientists claim that the glaciers of the greater Himalayan region (in China and South Asia) are melting faster than those of the north and south poles. The Himalayan region straddles six countries, China, Nepal, India, Afghanistan, Bhutan, and Pakistan and is the source of ten major river basins, which supply water to around 1.3 billion people. This chapter discusses national action plans and regional initiatives to combat and adapt to climate change. For example, in August 2009 the government of Nepal hosted the South Asian Regional Climate Change Conference. The conference released a statement recognizing that countries of South Asia need to work together and with partners globally to develop the infrastructure and knowledge base required to support their ongoing battle against climate change. They agreed to focus this effort around their shared river basins.

In Chapter 13 the author argues that the demand for energy in the South Asian region is growing and will continue to grow in the coming decades. Economic growth in the region will, to a large extent, be determined by access to adequate, secure and affordable supplies of energy resources outside the region, as domestic energy resources are inadequate for meeting the requirements of most of the largest countries in the region. As these countries are under increasing international pressure to cut their greenhouse gas emissions, and as renewable energy has its limitations, more and more countries are turning to natural gas as the cleanest fossil fuel available, particularly for the power and industrial sectors. However, most of this natural gas will have to be imported from outside the region and from distant countries. The author discusses the proposals for constructing pipelines that will transport natural gas to the countries of South Asia, principally India and Pakistan. The chapter focuses on three pipeline projects, the Iran–Pakistan–India (IPI) project, the Turkmenistan–Afghanistan–Pakistan–India (TAPI) project and the Israel–Turkey–India project, and explains why they have not been successful so far.

Chapter 14 is on nuclear energy co-operation between India and the US. The rapid growth of the Indian economy has prompted the Indian government to address the issue of energy security. On 10 October 2008, India and the United States signed the 123 Agreement for co-operation between the two countries in the field of the peaceful uses of nuclear energy. This was the culmination of a process that began over three years ago and gave rise to intense diplomatic and political debate. The agreement will allow India access to nuclear reactors, fuel and technologies from the US after a gap of 34 years. Washington had terminated nuclear co-operation with India back in 1974 after New Delhi had conducted a nuclear test in the Pokhran desert in Rajasthan. The agreement makes India the only country in the world able to pursue civil nuclear trade with other willing nations even though it has not signed the Nuclear Non-proliferation Treaty (NPT) of 1968. The US–India nuclear deal has given rise to controversy in both India and the US, although for different reasons. While the opposition parties in India argue that the deal is a continuation of the pro-US shift in Indian foreign policy and a deviation from the policy of non-alignment, the nuclear non-proliferation lobby in the US expressed its disapproval of the discussions taking place between the US and India and opposed the legislation that had been introduced in the US Congress to amend US laws to enable co-operation between the two countries, arguing that civil nuclear co-operation with a country that has not signed the NPT would seriously undermine the global nuclear non-proliferation regime. However, based on an examination of various documents including the Hyde Act (2006), the author of this chapter comes to the conclusion that the agreement does not only promote strategic co-operation between the two countries, it also strengthens the nuclear non-proliferation regime, which is an ongoing concern in the US.

Chapter 15 adopts a regional perspective and examines efforts to promote multilateral economic co-operation in South Asia. Compared with regions in the developed world such as Europe and even Southeast Asia, South Asia is not a well integrated region and has low levels of intra-regional trade, and political considerations often override economic considerations, thwarting efforts to bring about greater co-operation between the countries in the region. The chapter discusses the history of the South Asian Association for Regional Co-operation (SAARC), the regional organization created in 1985, and attempts to explain why it has not been very successful in promoting regional integration. The emergence of other multilateral groupings such as BIMSTEC and Mekong–Ganga Co-operation (MGC) is also considered and their contribution to economic co-operation between relevant countries is assessed. As the largest country in the region, India's role in regional integration is important and is the main focus of this chapter.

Notes

1 Even today Britain's focus is on threats to British interests. See, for example, Green Paper on defense and BBC interview with Professor Michael Clarke (defense expert) on Wednesday 3 February 2010.
2 According to a newspaper report there is little likelihood of the 'thinning of security forces' in Jammu and Kashmir. A senior security officer who attended a meeting of the Union home ministry in New Delhi in early January 2011 said that there were more than 500 active militants across the state and there were indications that fresh batches of militants were coming from across the border. As a result, security forces were strengthening their vigil along the borders to check infiltration. They were also expecting another bout of street protests in the summer of 2011. There had been a reduction of 30,000 troops in Jammu and Kashmir in 2009 but the security forces later warned against any further reductions. See 'No Withdrawal of Security Forces from J&K', *The Statesman* (Kolkata), 3 January 2011.

3 D. Howarth and Y. Stavrakakis, 'Introducing Discourse Theory and Political Analysis' in D. Howarth, A.J. Norval and Y. Stavrakakis (eds), *Discourse Theory and Political Analysis*, Manchester: Manchester University Press, 2000, pp. 1–5.
4 See for example George Perkovich, *India's Nuclear Bomb*, New Delhi: Oxford University Press, 1999; Ashley J. Tellis, *India's Emerging Nuclear Posture*, Santa Monica, CA: RAND Corporation, 2001.
5 Sumit Ganguly and Devin T. Hagerty, *Fearful Symmetry: India-Pakistan Crises in the Shadow of Nuclear Weapons*, Seattle: University of Washington Press, 2005; S. Paul Kapur, *Dangerous Deterrent: Nuclear Weapons Proliferation and Conflict in South Asia*, Stanford: Stanford University Press, 2007.
6 Jeffrey Knopf, 'Recasting the Optimism–Pessimism Debate', *Security Studies*, 12:1, 2002; Sumit Ganguly and S. Paul Kapur, *Nuclear Proliferation in South Asia: Crisis Behavior and the Bomb*, New York: Routledge, 2009.
7 Scott D. Sagan (ed.), *Inside Nuclear South Asia*, Stanford: Stanford University Press, 2009; and Jason A. Kirk, 'The Evolution of India's Nuclear Policies' in Sumit Ganguly (ed.), *India's Foreign Policy: Retrospect and Prospect*, New Delhi: Oxford University Press, 2009.
8 Rajesh M. Basrur, *Minimum Deterrence and India's Nuclear Security*, Stanford: Stanford University Press, 2006.
9 A report of the United States Senate Committee on Foreign Relations entitled 'Sri Lanka: Recharting US Strategy After the War' and dated 7 December 2009 states that 'the war in Sri Lanka may be over, but the underlying conflict still simmers … a culture of fear and paranoia permeates society.'
10 Recently, however, the Intergovernmental Panel on Climate Change (IPCC) has been discredited by leaked emails from the University of East Anglia. Claims made about human made/induced climate change are being disputed. It now seems that a claim that the glaciers of the Himalayas might melt by 2035, which has been endorsed by the IPCC, was unfounded (*The Independent on Sunday*, 7 February 2010, p. 43). This is a good example of the relationship between environmentalist discourses and the formation of epistemic communities.

1 Theorizing regional security

Sagarika Dutt

The purpose of this chapter is to discuss the concept of security in the study of international relations and the importance of regional security complexes in post-cold war analyses. Scholars such as Buzan opine that the concept of security offers a better approach to the study of international relations than those provided by the concepts of power or peace. 'It points to a prime motive for behaviour which is different from, but no less significant than, that provided by power.'[1] Even though the Realist school of thought is based on the concept of power and uses that concept as an analytical tool, security/national security is a universally accepted concept, and most states in the world give some thought to a national security strategy and have national security advisers and national security councils or committees (for example, the US, the UK and India). Buzan writes that 'states are the principal referent object of security because they are both the framework of order and the highest source of governing authority. This explains the dominating policy concern with "national" security'[2]. Campbell observes that traditional scholarship has, as a result, treated foreign policy as 'an internally mediated response to an externally induced situation of ideological, military and economic threats.'[3] Campbell argues that this approach does not problematize the nature of the state or the nature of security. Security is understood as freedom from threats to the survival and well-being of human collectivities. Wolfers makes a helpful distinction between an objective and a subjective sense of security. The former 'measures the absence of threats to acquired values' while the latter may be defined as 'the absence of fear that such values will be attacked.'[4] But, as Campbell argues, the articulation of danger involves more than the determination of the seriousness of risks. 'An important site of interpretation is the way in which certain modes of representation crystallize around referents marked as dangers.'[5] These insights are broad enough to accommodate a widening security agenda.

However, as Buzan points out, security is an essentially contested concept. Since the end of the cold war the classical approach to security has been critiqued by many authors, most of whom have argued that 'a broader, multisectoral approach to security is preferable to the traditional understanding of seeing security concerns as relating only to issues of militarized relations between competing states.'[6] This is reflected at both academic and policy levels. However, the multisectoral approach can give rise to contradictions, for example, between defense and security, individual security and national security, national security and international security and between violent means and peaceful ends.[7] Definitions, indeed theories of security, are contingent on the referent object of security (i.e., what is it that is to be made secure?). There is also an attempt in the literature to address the reification of the state. Buzan asks 'What exactly is the referent object of security when one refers to national security? If it is the state, what does that mean?'[8] Realist discourses are able to answer this question without reducing national security to the security of individuals who make up the state, partly by concentrating on military security. The billiard ball model[9] simplifies but also clarifies the conceptualization of security. In the absence of a world government or central authority regulating the behavior of states, states interact in an anarchical system and have to look out for themselves. Conflict between states is inevitable and states need to invest in their own defense, often leading to the classic security dilemma.[10]

According to Realists there is no natural harmony of interests between states (in the international system). State action is required to harmonize 'common interests' and this has implications for regional co-operation and integration. According to Morgenthau, the key to understanding international politics is the concept of interest defined in terms of power.[11] Thus, the national interest which ought to be the sole pursuit of statesmen is always defined in terms of strategic and economic capability. Perhaps anticipating the debates about 'hard' power and 'soft' power,[12] Realists argue that the forms of power states choose to exercise will be determined by the political, cultural and strategic environment. Furthermore, universal moral principles do not guide state behavior (notwithstanding 'ethical' foreign policies associated with former British foreign secretary Robin Cooke). When states proclaim these universal principles they are merely projecting their particular national or cultural codes onto the world as a whole. For Realists 'interest is the perennial standard by which political action must be judged and directed.'[13]

Realists allow for the unequal distribution of power in the international system but posit that it is the root cause of conflict. As the analysis of the history of the Peloponnesian war suggests, weak states are always at the mercy of powerful ones. The only way to minimize the incidence of war (and also ensure the survival of weaker states) was to ensure that a rough balance of power existed between states. The balance of power theory[14] is, therefore, an important part of Realist policy prescriptions. But power may also be structural, allowing the dominant states to shape and 'enshrine an existing economic and political order' which is favorable to them. Marxist and neo-Marxist theories are more inclined to pursue this line of argument.[15]

But are states a means to an end or an end in themselves? Statist discourses suggest that the security and territorial integrity of states are of paramount importance (this is reflected in the rhetoric of governments/heads of governments). The *raison d'être* of the state is often lost sight of: to protect the individual/the citizen. On another level the rise of nation-states and the spread of democracy around the world has shifted the focus of the debate to 'the people.' Hay, Lister and Marsh argue that 'no concept is more central to political discourse and political analysis than that of the state. Yet, whilst we all tend to think we know what we're talking about when we refer to the state, it is a notoriously difficult concept to define.'[16] As an institution it has developed over time and is an integral part of the modern world. Of course political sociologists such as Anthony Giddens argue that modernity is inherently globalizing and that the development of global social relations could weaken nationalist feelings linked to nation-states, but that at the same time it could also strengthen pressures for local autonomy and regional cultural identity as the state becomes too big to deal with local issues and the 'small problems of life.'[17] However, the Weberian understanding of the state continues to exert a powerful influence in the modern world, and the modern state may be defined as 'an institutional complex claiming sovereignty for itself as the supreme political authority within a defined territory for whose governance it is responsible.'[18] While a distinction may be made between a Hobbesian state, a Lockean state and a Kantian state, for our purposes it is more useful to remain focused on the Weberian model. That being said, Hay *et al.* write that Weber's definition of a state 'displays considerable similarities with that of Hobbes.' A state, according to Weber, 'is a compulsory political organization with continuous operations ... insofar as its administrative staff successfully upholds the claim to the monopoly of the legitimate use of physical force in the enforcement of its order.'[19] The differentiation of the state from civil society has allowed states to consolidate their power independently of societal factors. Neo-Weberian perspectives have also often relegated political forces that are outside and beyond the state, such as social movements and pressure groups, to a marginal role. The preoccupation with national security can lead to authoritarianism, as Buzan points out: 'excessive use of security justifications cannot but shift the process of government away from constitutional practices and towards what are, in effect, authoritarian methods.'[20] The situation becomes compounded by the fact that security is not an objective condition. As Ole Waever points out, 'the labelling of an issue as a security problem by the government automatically legitimizes the use of exceptional means.'[21] In the study of international relations, state-centric theories based on a Weberian understanding of the state have been challenged by other theoretical perspectives such as Post-structuralism and Feminism. Taking these critiques on board is important and both theoretical and empirical research need to address 'the complex and ever changing relationship between the state and society, the public and the private'[22] (a distinction often made in Anglo-Saxon thinking).

However, Ayoob has his own take on state-centric theories. Writing from a 'subaltern realist' perspective, he argues that International Relations theories, especially in the field of security studies, portray states as unitary actors responding to external threats or posing such threats to other states. Ayoob prefers to go beyond this 'ethnocentric obsession with external threats to state security' and focus on the security concerns of the subalterns – those that are weak and of inferior rank. The majority of the states in the world/international system are third-world states, and their security preoccupations are primarily internal in character and are a function of the early stages of state-making at which they find themselves. State-building often involves the use of violent means by the state to extend and consolidate its control over contested demographic and territorial space.[23] Populations resisting the extension and consolidation of state power will also resort to the use of violence. Ayoob writes that 'this is the stuff of which civil wars and secessionist movements are made, and they pose much greater, and more immediate, threats to the security of the large majority of states than do external adversaries.'[24] However, he accepts that internal instability can lead to inter-state conflict between geographically contiguous states such as India and Pakistan. The growth of a form of irredentist nationalism in Indian-administered Kashmir is an example of how an 'internal issue' can become a source of inter-state conflict. Ayoob argues that a definition of the concept of security that has adequate explanatory power must go beyond the traditional Realist definition of security and overcome its external orientation and military bias, and must remain firmly rooted in the political realm while being sensitive to variables in the societal sector because of their potential capacity to influence political outcomes.[25] The most helpful framework for analyzing the different dimensions of security is provided by Buzan's regional security complex theory.

Regional security complex theory

In his earlier work entitled *People, states and fear*, Buzan defined a security complex 'as a group of states whose primary security concerns link together sufficiently closely that their national securities cannot realistically be considered apart from one another.'[26] Security complexes are about the interdependence of rivalry, emphasizing that security is a relational phenomenon but also embraces shared interests. As such, states with shared interests can form security communities as developed in Europe in the post-World War II era and also the post-cold war period. Buzan explains the significance of this concept and the contribution it makes to the study of security in international relations.

Regions form an intermediate level of analysis between individual states and the international political system as a whole. Buzan argues that comprehensive security analysis requires a study of regional security complexes and how they mediate the interplay between states and the international system. Regions comprise geographically contiguous states which may feel threatened by their neighbors. However, Buzan theorizes the security of regions not in terms of a balance of power but in terms of patterns of amity and enmity among the states in the region. Furthermore, regions form a subsystem and are often affected by the policies of extraregional powers. Hence the engagement of great powers/extraregional powers with regional powers has implications for regional stability as well as international stability/peace and security. As Buzan argues, 'because of their susceptibility to external influences, balances of power are a much less reliable guide to security relations in the periphery than they are at the centre.'[27] A security complex is characterized by security interdependence, and it is mainly on this basis that Buzan considers South Asia to be a security complex, as it is characterized by a high level of threat/fear which is felt mutually among two or more major states. Security interdependency can also involve a high level of trust and friendship, i.e., patterns of amity rather than enmity. Buzan also suggests that where there are low levels of economic exchange, security interdependence is defined mainly in terms of military security. In fact the military, political and societal dimensions/sectors of security 'are the most relevant to the patterns of threat and amity/enmity'[28] in a region. Yet economic factors may motivate extraregional powers to intervene in regional politics 'as in the case of the US and the oil producing countries of the Gulf.'[29]

Buzan does not, however, attempt an ahistorical analysis of regional security complexes. He writes that the international system was structured around four great civilizational areas before Europe's rise to global dominance: Europe, the Middle East, India and China. 'The rise of the European powers from the fifteenth century steadily subjected nearly all of this ancient system to overlay.'[30] By overlay he means the direct presence of outside powers in a region, which suppresses the normal operation of security dynamics among local states and subordinates them to the larger pattern of major power rivalries.[31] During the colonial era patterns of global security were simply an extension of European great-power rivalry; later, during the cold war, rivalry between the superpowers.[32]

Decolonization made the regional level of security both more autonomous and more prominent in international politics. The end of the cold war has accelerated this process.[33] At the same time major military threats, such as a nuclear confrontation between the two superpowers, have faded away. Focus has, therefore, shifted to other kinds of threats to security. While the global security agenda is still set primarily by the major powers, each region has its own regional (security) dynamics. A better understanding of global security, therefore, needs an analysis of the interaction between these two levels of security concerns.

The 'securitization' of regional security

In *Security: A new framework for analysis* (1998), Buzan *et al.* present security as a discourse.[34] It takes the form of identifying an existential 'threat' to a referent object of security, to an audience that accepts the case being made by the securitizing agent/actor. They write that 'in security discourse, an issue is dramatized and presented as an issue of supreme priority; thus by labelling it as security, an agent claims a need for and a right to treat it by extraordinary means.'[35] The process of securitization is 'what in language theory is called a speech act.'[36] But it is not simply the utterance of the term security that matters but also the existence of a group (audience) that is receptive to what is being said. Thus 'security ... has to be understood as an essentially intersubjective process.'[37]

Buzan *et al.* attempt a constructivist analysis of security and argue that security/insecurity is not an objective condition. Referent objects of security are socially constructed and the process of securitization, including the identification of threats to the referent objects and the adoption of extraordinary measures to deal with those threats, are 'a part of a discursive, socially constituted, intersubjective realm.'[38] However, just because an issue is socially constructed does not mean that it is possible to bring about change by, for example, exposing relationships of power, as discourse analyses within Post-structuralist studies are often apt to do. Buzan *et al.* argue that 'the socially constituted is often sedimented as structure and becomes so relatively stable as practice'[39] that one treats it almost as a 'given.' Buzan *et al.* subsequently/consequently redefine a regional security complex as 'a set of units whose major processes of securitization, desecuritization or both are so interlinked that their security problems cannot reasonably be analysed or resolved apart from one another.'[40] This definition can be applied to South Asia.

As mentioned above, with the ending of the cold war the security agenda has changed. This has led to the widening of the concept of security to include non-military threats in the economic, societal, environmental and political societal sectors. The definition of the nature of these threats may be left to individual scholars and will partly be determined by the referent object of security. Buzan defines them in the following terms: economic security concerns access to the resources, finance and markets necessary to sustain acceptable levels of welfare and state power; societal security concerns the sustainability, within acceptable conditions for evolution, of traditional patterns of language, culture and religious and national identity and custom; environmental security concerns the maintenance of the local and the planetary biosphere as the essential support system on which all other human enterprises depend; and political security concerns the organizational stability of states, systems of government and the ideologies that give them legitimacy.[41] There are linkages between these sectors and potential contradictions: for example, if economic security is interpreted in such a way that it leads to environmental degradation on account of rapid industrialization and unsustainable use of natural resources etc, it will not meet the (universal) goal of sustainable development (although Buzan *et al.* seem to suggest that the contradictions occur within rather than between sectors[42]). But in the developing world the state continues to be the most important referent object of security. The ruling elites of states are the main securitizing actors, and the military and political sectors of security tend to be given more importance than other sectors, although 'emerging economies' are beginning to give more importance to economic security than they did in the past.

Buzan *et al.* argue that South Asia's main security concerns have occurred in the political-military sector organized by the struggle between India and Pakistan.[43] But societal factors such as religious differences, ethnicity and identity in general are equally important. It may be recalled that Pakistan came into existence on the basis of the two-nation theory[44] that rejected India's secular model. The Kashmir conflict has been aggravated by religious differences between the Muslims and the Hindus of the subcontinent, yet Bangladesh (also a Muslim nation) seceded from Pakistan on the basis of ethno-nationalism. Buzan *et al.*

argue that 'the dominant single-conflict dynamic, which integrated many dimensions in one conflict formation, is potentially giving way to a much more general, complicated and confusing security scene in which societal conflicts within the states have become more prominent.'[45] The tensions between different ethnic groups in Pakistan are discussed in Chapter 7 of the present book, while Chapter 6 discusses the conflict between the Sri Lankan state dominated by the Sinhalese and the Tamil minority. The rise of Hindu nationalism could threaten the secular foundations of the Indian state, and insurgencies in various parts of the country have affected the internal security of the Indian state. In addition, 'each government regularly accuses the other of aiding and arming its internal dissidents, but the societal dynamics also have a dynamic of their own.'[46]

The South Asian regional security complex

It is interesting to note that South Asia was the foundational case study Buzan *et al.* used to develop their regional security complex theory.[47] They argue that the South Asian regional security complex, like other 'postcolonial security regions,' came into being as 'a conflict formation.'[48] India and Pakistan are the main rivals in the South Asian regional security complex. The rivalry led to three wars (1947–8, 1965, 1971), several serious crises any of which could have escalated into a full-blown war (1984, 1987, 1990, 1999, 2002), and numerous lesser military incidents.[49] But the process of securitization started before independence and continues to this day. Both states are now nuclear powers; the issue of nuclear security is discussed by Nicolas Blarel in Chapter 3. The smaller (and weaker) states in the region such as Bangladesh, Bhutan, the Maldives, Nepal and Sri Lanka are tied into the regional security complex 'because of their economic and societal entanglements with India.'[50] Nepal and Bhutan are dependent on India for trade and transit, and Sri Lanka's Tamil minority has links with the Tamil population in southern India. Bangladesh seceded from Pakistan with India's help but has many bilateral issues to resolve with India such as illegal migration across the Indo-Bangladesh border, sharing river waters and access to the Indian market. During the cold war South Asia was 'penetrated' by the superpowers to a certain extent, and their influence served to maintain the existing patterns of amity/enmity and preserve the status quo. Pakistan became part of the US network of containment alliances, especially during the Soviet occupation of Afghanistan during the 1980s, and received American military aid.[51] India, on the other hand, found an ally in the USSR, although it should be noted that India was a non-aligned state and its foreign policy was based on this concept.[52] Pakistan's relations with China also affected the South Asian regional complex, increasing the mistrust between India and Pakistan, especially after the Sino-Indian war of 1962. In 1998 when India conducted nuclear tests, its defense minister, George Fernandes, justified them on the grounds that China posed a serious threat to India's security. The Chinese government vehemently denied these charges.[53] There has never been a mediator in the region and the principal regional organization, the South Asian Association for Regional Co-operation

(SAARC), established in 1985, has never had much impact on the security politics of the region.

The ending of the cold war did not lead to any dramatic transformations in the security dynamics of South Asia. Each state had its own internal security issues that had their roots primarily in ethnic conflict, ethno- (and ethnoreligious) nationalism and identity politics, although socio-economic factors were also important.[54] At the regional level the India–Pakistan rivalry dominated the security agenda. Factors on both sides contribute to the process of securitization: a heavily militarized border between the two countries; insurgency; alleged state repression in Kashmir; and communal violence, partly exacerbated by the rise of the Bharatiya Janata Party (BJP), a Hindu right-wing political party, in India. Indo-Pak relations and the Kashmir issue are discussed in Chapter 4. Buzan and Waever argue that 'the intense domestic rivalry during the 1990s between Benazir Bhutto and Nawaz Sharif fuelled competitive anti-Indian rhetoric over Kashmir, escalating the two states' mutual accusations of interference in each other's domestic affairs.'[55] The pattern of an improvement in relations and dialogue between the two countries followed by a breakdown of diplomatic relations/peace process, often on account of a security threat such as the Kargil war of 1999 and the Mumbai terrorist attacks of 2008, has continued to this day.[56] As regards the Mumbai attacks, while Pakistan's foreign minister, Shah Mahmood Qureshi, is reported to have said in November 2010 that Pakistan was committed to bringing those responsible for the terrorist assault to justice, the Indian government's opinion is that the Pakistan government has failed to do so.[57] India's external affairs minister S.M. Krishna said recently, during an interview with the press, that 'our only expectation from Pakistan is' that it will 'dismantle the terror infrastructure that operates from the territories under its control,' adding that 'a serious and sustained dialogue can thrive only in a peaceful and terror free climate.'[58] However, the irony is that terrorist violence is a much more regular occurrence in Pakistan and has claimed the lives of more than 6,000 civilians and security personnel in 2008–9 alone, according to some sources. A recent assessment by Pakistan's Inter-Services Intelligence (ISI) has concluded that 'Islamic militants pose a greater internal security threat to Pakistan than the Indian army.'[59]

As exchanges between the governments of India and Pakistan indicate, the securitization rhetoric is still strong at the interstate level, but challenges to the Pakistani state also come from within, as discussed by Alok Bansal in Chapter 7. Even sympathetic observers have noted that 'widening ethnic, regional and religious-sectarian cleavages, the after effects of the Afghan War, and weapons proliferation all pose serious challenges to the government' of Pakistan.[60] With the end of the first decade of the twenty-first century the focus may be shifting from military security to economic security. High economic growth rates in India, the policy of economic liberalization that it has pursued since the 1990s and a more proactive foreign policy could bring about transformation in the region. As Buzan et al. note, 'despite the ongoing confrontation with Pakistan, there is evidence both that the South Asian regional level is diminishing in importance to India and that India's significance within the Asian supercomplex is increasing.'[61] Chapter 15 on regional co-operation in South Asia makes a similar suggestion. Pakistan has been reduced to an 'irritant' in Indo-Pak relations and this finding was corroborated by research conducted by the present author in India in 2007–8. Not many people in India see Pakistan as a serious threat and some even feel that focusing too much on Pakistan is a waste of time.[62]

Finally, while the war in Afghanistan continues, Pakistan cannot afford to get involved in a major war with India and is cultivating China in order to maintain a balance of power in the region. In December 2010, during Mr. Wen Jiabao's visit to Pakistan, the two countries signed agreements worth between $10 billion and $30 billion 'aimed at deepening strategic and economic relations between the two countries.'[63] However, China has made it very clear that it is not interested in getting involved in the conflict between India and Pakistan. During a media briefing, a Chinese foreign ministry spokesperson said that Mr. Wen Jiabao's visit to India and Pakistan had been 'fruitful' and would contribute to good neighborliness, mutually beneficial co-operation and peace and stability in the region. She described the Kashmir issue as a 'left over from history' and expressed the hope that it would be resolved, by India and Pakistan, through 'dialogue and consultations.'[64] The Chinese premier's visit to India was handled quite delicately. The joint statement did not mention Tibet, and to divert attention from contentious bilateral issues, the focus of the trip was kept firmly on economic issues. Several agreements were signed and bilateral trade is set to rise to over $100 billion by 2015 from $60 billion in 2010.[65] The visits of other heads of states to South Asia (President Obama and President Medvedev in November and December 2010, respectively) also further strengthened relations between the South Asian states and the extraregional powers.[66] Co-operation between India and the US in the field of nuclear energy is discussed in Chapter 14 by Sagarika Dutt, highlighting the link between nuclear power and nuclear weapons, but it should also be noted that Russia is helping India to build more nuclear reactors in Kudankulam in Tamil Nadu.[67]

Conclusion: widening and deepening security

A review of the literature on the study of security in international relations reveals the nature of the debates that have been taking place within the discipline. As Buzan and Hansen note in their recent book, *The evolution of international security studies*, International Security Studies (ISS) has 'both undergone some radical changes and maintained some core continuities.'[68] It is mainly a western subject with its roots in western political theory. During the cold war it was defined by 'a largely military agenda of questions surrounding nuclear weapons and a widely embedded assumption that the Soviet Union posed a profound military and ideological threat to the West.' As the relationship between the superpowers matured, the international security agenda expanded to include economic and environmental security and then during the 1990s societal security, human security, food security and so on. This was accompanied by more critical and radical challenges to state-centrism. In addition to the more traditionalist, military-centered Strategic Studies and Peace Research, other branches of ISS have emerged, including Critical Security Studies, Feminist Security Studies, the Copenhagen School, Post-structuralist and Constructivist Security Studies.[69]

The events of 9/11 and the global war on terrorism could have strengthened the Realist, traditional agenda, and the American response, especially the invasion of Afghanistan, was 'state-centric.' But 'the prominence of globally networked non-state actors raised questions about both state-centrism and the rationality assumptions that underpinned traditionalist thought.'[70] Al-Qaeda and Osama bin Laden were shadowy figures and could not be treated as 'rational actors.' This new phase in the study of international security also revived concerns about the use of force. At the same time it emphasized the indivisibility of security and this is best demonstrated by NATO's strategic concepts and involvement in Afghanistan. On the other hand, as Buzan *et al.* point out, many developing states like India attempted to link their own struggle against insurgents to the US war on terror.[71]

Nevertheless, Buzan's core ideas about regional security complexes provide a suitable theoretical framework for analysing South Asian security. His sympathy with 'an explicit post-colonial ISS perspective' is also helpful. Other scholars such as Krause (1996) have drawn on Charles Tilly to also argue that the state-centric concept of security advocated by traditional Realist approaches was based on a particular European history of state formation.[72] However, Buzan's earlier works have been critiqued by scholars such as Booth. Booth writes that the deepening and broadening of security are interlinked and the broadening of the security agenda is a function of deepening. Security in the political realm is above all a derivative concept. Booth writes:

> Deepening, in other words, reveals the political theory in which conceptions of security are anchored, and so the priorities that will shape the associated political agenda. By uniting security with political theory, the deepening move also provides a basis for a synthesis of critique and reconstruction – the process of creating a politics of emancipation.[73]

Booth also critiques the Copenhagen school's thesis that 'threats to security do not exist outside discourse.'[74] There are two problems with the Copenhagen thesis. The first is that it is based on a fallacy: there is empirical evidence of threats that are independent of any discourse that has developed about them, for example, climate change. Bansal and Datta discuss this issue in the context of South Asia in Chapter 12. Similarly, threats to human security may go unrecognized. Secondly, because securitization is discourse-centric, those without discourse-making power are disenfranchised. So those (people) who are threatened by rising sea levels, for example, are at the mercy of scientific/epistemic communities that shape discourses about global warming and climate change (on which international action to deal with the issue might depend). A third problem is that desecuritization can disempower: for example, 'the ordinary politics of institutional racism can flourish if racism is desecuritized.'[75] So, while desecuritization is in the interests of the power-holders, it is not in the interests of the 'victims.' But it should be clarified here that Buzan *et al.* do acknowledge that the securitization approach 'points to the responsibility involved in talking about security (or desecuritization) for policymakers, analysts, campaigners, and lobbyists.' The choice and consequently the decision to securitize or desecuritize an issue has to be justified by the appropriateness and the consequences of the decision.[76] This chapter, therefore, concludes that there are both strengths and weaknesses in Buzan's theoretical approach and that it needs to be applied cautiously to regional case studies. While an understanding of the interplay between different levels of security is useful, a deeper understanding of security is also necessary.

Notes

1 B. Buzan, *People, states and fear*, 1991, p. 3.
2 Ibid., p. 22.
3 D. Campbell, *Writing security*, 1992, p. 42.
4 A. Wolfers, *Discord and collaboration*, Baltimore: John Hopkins University Press, 1962, cited in Buzan, *People, states and fear*, p. 17.
5 Campbell, *Writing security*, p. 2.
6 M. Sheehan, *International Security*, 2005, p. 3.
7 Buzan, 1991, *People, states and fear*, p. 15.
8 Ibid., p. 15.
9 See J. Burton, *World society*, 1972.
10 According to Herz, as states acquire more military capabilities for strengthening their defense, rival states begin to feel more insecure thus 'compelling both sides to engage in a "vicious circle of security and power accumulation"'; see J. Herz, 'Idealist internationalism and the security dilemma', *World Politics*, 2:2, 1950, pp. 157–80, cited in B. Buzan and L. Hansen, *The evolution of international security studies*, 2009, p. 12.
11 See R.O. Keohane, 'Theory of world politics – structural realism and beyond' in R.O. Keohane (ed.), *Neorealism and its critics*, 1986, p. 164; H.J. Morgenthau, *Politics among nations*, 1948; S. Burchill, 'Realism and neorealism' in S. Burchill and A. Linklater (eds), *Theories of international relations*, 1996.
12 See for example, J.S. Nye, *Soft power*, 2006.
13 Burchill, 'Realism and neorealism', pp. 75–6.
14 See M. Sheehan, *Balance of power*, 1996.
15 See A. Linklater, 'Marxism' in Burchill and Linklater (eds), *Theories of International Relations*.
16 C. Hay, M. Lister and D. Marsh, *The state*, 2006, p. 1.
17 A. Giddens, *The consequences of modernity*, 1990; A. Giddens, 'The consequences of modernity' in P. Williams and L. Chrisman (eds), *Colonial discourse and postcolonial theory, a reader*, Hemel Hempstead: Harvester Wheatsheaf, 1993, pp. 181–2.
18 Hay *et al.*, *The state*, p. 5.
19 Ibid., p. 8.
20 Buzan, *People, states and fear*, p. 116.
21 Quoted in Buzan, *People, states and fear*, pp. 115–16.
22 Hay *et al.*, *The state*, p. 3.
23 M. Ayoob, 'Defining security, 1997, p. 133.
24 Ibid.

25 Ibid., p. 134.
26 Buzan, *People, states and fear*, p. 191.
27 Ibid., pp. 188–9.
28 Ibid., p. 201.
29 Ibid., p. 202.
30 Ibid., p. 203.
31 Ibid., p. 198.
32 Ibid., p. 204.
33 P. Katzenstein, cited in B. Buzan and O. Waever, *Regions and powers*, 2003, p. 3.
34 Campbell defines the term 'discourse' as 'the representation and constitution of the "real"' or as a managed space in which some statements and depictions come to have greater value than others so that the idea of an 'external reality' has a particular currency that is internal to a discourse. Discourse analysis 'starts from the position that social and political life comprises a set of practices in which things are constituted in the process of dealing with them.' This mode of analysis seeks to ascertain how certain terms and concepts have historically functioned within discourses and the kind of power discourses have over the structuring of social relations. (Campbell, *Writing Security*, pp. 4–6).
35 B. Buzan, O. Waever and J. de Wilde, *Security*, 1998, p. 26.
36 Ibid.
37 Ibid., p. 30.
38 Ibid., p. 31.
39 Ibid., p. 35.
40 Ibid., p. 12.
41 Ibid., p. 8.
42 They write that while the discourse on economic security is now shaped largely by the dominance of the liberal agenda, the relentless pursuit of free trade could have an adverse impact on society leading to reactions against the basic principles of the system. Or financial deregulation may give certain kinds of economic actors so much freedom to pursue their interests that they overreach the carrying capacity of the system and bring it down (see Buzan *et al.*, *Security*, p. 108).
43 Ibid., pp. 133–4.
44 See for example, F. Robinson, 'Islam and nationalism' in J. Hutchinson and A.D. Smith (eds), *Nationalism*, 1994.
45 Buzan *et al.*, *Security*, pp. 133–4.
46 Ibid., p. 134.
47 Buzan and Waever, *Regions and power*, p. 93.
48 Ibid., p. 101.
49 Ibid., p. 102.
50 Ibid.
51 Ibid., p. 104.
52 See R. Thakur, *The politics and economics of India's foreign policy*, 1994; V.P. Dutt, *India's foreign policy in a changing world*, 1999; S. Dutt, *India in a globalized world*, 2006.
53 See for example, M. Ehsan Ahrari, 'Growing strong', 1999. However, Brahma Chellaney, Professor of Security Studies at the Centre for Policy Research, New Delhi, writes that

> India must tackle its vulnerability against China at the earliest possible opportunity. A deterrent against Pakistan was never the central mission of India's nuclear strategy. The subcontinent's nuclearisation only blunts New Delhi's conventional military advantage over Islamabad, since it allows Pakistan to deploy nuclear forces as an equaliser.

See B. Chellaney, 'After the tests', Winter 1998–9, p. 107.

54 See for example, R. Ganguly and U. Phadnis, *Ethnicity and nation-building in South Asia*, London: Sage, 2001; I. Macduff and R. Ganguly (eds), *Ethnic conflict and secessionism in south and southeast Asia: Causes, dynamics, solutions*, New Delhi, London, Thousand Oaks: Sage, 2003; P. Sen Gupta, 'Ethnic discontent and India's unity', 1995.

55 Buzan and Waever, *Regions and powers*, p. 108.

56 Ibid., p. 109.

57 'Need to validate Kasab's statement, says Pak', *The Statesman* (Kolkata), 28 November 2010; 'India using terror as propaganda tool: Pak', *The Statesman* (Kolkata), 19 December 2010. However, Prime Minister of Pakistan Yousuf Raza Gilani said that there was a 'lack of trust' between India and Pakistan and that the bilateral dialogue/peace process should not be held hostage to the 2008 Mumbai incident, but also added that the resolution of the Kashmir issue is 'vital for regional stability;' No communication gap between India-Pak over Kashmir: Gilani', *The Statesman* (Kolkata), 29 December 2010, p. 3.

58 'Pak must discard compulsive hostility: Krishna', *The Statesman* (Kolkata), 3 January 2011. However, there is a view in India that the Prevention of Terrorism Act (POTA 2002) should not have been repealed by the Congress government. It was replaced by the Unlawful Activities (Prevention) Amendment Act, 2004, which is not as stringent as the former. POTA included punishment for and measures for dealing with terrorist activities and terrorist organizations. It categorically stated that 'whoever commits a terrorist act, shall ... if such [an] act has resulted in the death of any person, be punishable with death or imprisonment for life and shall also be liable to fine', available www.satp.org/satporgtp/countries/indi/document/act. It is also interesting to note that according to Wikileaks, the then US ambassador to India, David Mulford, pointed out that in almost every incident of terrorist or communal violence, the then home minister of India, Shivraj Patil, was found 'asleep on the watch.' After 26/11, the US felt that the removal of the 'spectacularly inept' Shivraj Patil was inevitable. See 'US felt removal of Shivraj Patil was inevitable after 26/11', Yahoo News, 18 December 2010, available http://in.news.yahoo.com/us-felt-removal-shivraj-patil-inevitable-26–11–20101218–00410.

59 T. Wright and S. Gorman, 'Militants overtake India as top threat', *The Wall Street Journal*, 16 August 2010.

60 H.-A. Rizvi, 'Civil–military relations in contemporary Pakistan', *Survival*, 40:2, 1998, p. 110.

61 Buzan and Waever, *Regions and powers*, p. 120.

62 Interviews conducted by the author in New Delhi, Kolkata and Mumbai in August and December 2007 and August 2008.

63 'Pak, China to sign $10b pacts', *The Statesman* (Kolkata), 19 December 2010.

64 'Indo-Pak talks to solve Kashmir row?', *The Statesman* (Kolkata), 22 December 2010.

65 'Joint statement skips Tibet, UNSC mention', *The Statesman* (Kolkata), 17 December 2010. Also see 'India, China not rivals: Wen Jiabao', *The Statesman* (Kolkata), 16 December 2010; S. Haidar, 'When Wen comes calling', *The Statesman* (Kolkata), 23 December 2010, p. 4.

66 V. Bajaj and H. Timmons, 'Obama to visit India', *The New York Times*, 4 November 2010; 'Obama backs India UNSC seat to counter China: US media', *The Times of India*, 9 November 2010.

67 'Medvedev talks tough on terror', *The Statesman* (Kolkata), 22 December 2010, p. 1; also see 'India, Russia firm up deal for fifth generation fighters', *The Statesman* (Kolkata), 22 December 2010; 'India, Russia sign nuclear deal', *The Times of India*, 7 December 2009; 'Putin in deal to build nuclear reactors for India', *guardian.co.uk*, 12 March 2010.

68 Buzan and Hansen, *The evolution of international security studies*, p. 3.

69 Ibid., pp. 2–3.
70 Ibid., p. 229.
71 Buzan and Waever, *Regions and powers*, p. 115.
72 Buzan and Hansen, *The evolution of international security studies*, pp. 200–1.
73 K. Booth, *Theory of world security*, 2007, p. 149.
74 Ibid., p. 164.
75 Ibid., p. 168.
76 Buzan *et al.*, *Security*, p. 211.

Bibliography

Ayoob, M., 'Defining security: A subaltern realist perspective' in K. Krause and M.C. Williams (eds), *Critical security studies*, London: UCL Press, 1997.

Bajaj, V. and H. Timmons, 'Obama to visit India, and both sides hope to expand ties', *New York Times*, 4 November 2010.

Baral, L.R. (ed.), *Non-traditional security: State, society and democracy in South Asia*, New Delhi: Adroit Publishers, 2006.

Booth, K., *Theory of world security*, Cambridge: Cambridge University Press, 2007.

Burchill, S. and A. Linklater (eds), *Theories of international relations*, Basingstoke: Macmillan, 1996.

Burton, J., *World society*, Cambridge: Cambridge University Press, 1972.

Buzan, B., *People, states and fear*, New York, London, Toronto etc.: Harvester Wheatsheaf, 1991.

Buzan, B. and L. Hansen, *The evolution of international security studies*, Cambridge: Cambridge University Press, 2009.

Buzan, B. and O. Waever, *Regions and powers: The structure of international security*, Cambridge: Cambridge University Press, 2003.

Buzan, B., O. Waever and J. de Wilde, *Security: A new framework for analysis*, Boulder and London: Lynne Rienner Publishers, 1998.

Campbell, D., *Writing security*, Manchester: Manchester University Press, 1992.

Chellaney, B., 'After the tests: India's options', *Survival*, 40:4, Winter 1998–9, pp. 93–111.

Dahal, D.R. and N.N. Pandey (eds), *Comprehensive security in South Asia*, New Delhi: Manohar, 2006.

Dutt, S., *India in a globalized world*, Manchester: Manchester University Press, 2006.

Dutt, V.P., *India's foreign policy in a changing world*, New Delhi: Vikas Publishing House, 1999.

Ehsan Ahrari, M. 'Growing strong – the nuclear genie in South Asia', *Security Dialogue*, 30:4, 1999, pp. 431–44.

Fierke, K.M., *Critical approaches to international security*, Cambridge: Polity Press, 2007.

George, J., *Discourses of global politics: A critical (re)introduction to international relations*, Basingstoke: Macmillan, 1994.

Giddens, A., *The consequences of modernity*, Oxford: Polity Press, 1990.

Hay, C., M. Lister and D. Marsh, *The state: Theories and issues*, Basingstoke: Palgrave, 2006.

Howarth, D., and Y. Stavrakakis, 'Introducing discourse theory and political analysis' in D. Howarth, A.J. Norval and Y. Stavrakakis (eds), *Discourse theory and political analysis*, Manchester: Manchester University Press, 2000.

Hutchinson, J. and A.D. Smith (eds), *Nationalism*, Oxford: Oxford University Press, 1994.

Johnstone, B., *Discourse analysis*, Oxford: Blackwell, 2008, 2nd edition.

Katzenstein, P. (ed.), *The culture of national security*, New York: Columbia University Press, 1996.

Keohane, R.O. (ed.), *Neorealism and its critics*, New York: Columbia University Press, 1986.

Krause, K., 'Insecurity and state formation in the global military order: The middle eastern case', *European Journal of International Relations*, 2:3, 1996, pp. 319–54.

Morgenthau, H.J., *Politics among nations*, New York: Knopf, 1948.

Nye, J.S., *Soft power: The means to success in world politics*, New York: Public Affairs, London: Perseus Running, 2006.

Rajagopalan, S. (ed.), *Security and South Asia*, New Delhi: Routledge, 2006.

Sen Gupta, P., 'Ethnic discontent and India's unity' in A. Banerjee (ed.), *Integration, disintegration and world order*, Kolkata: Allied Publishers, 1995.

Sheehan, M., *Balance of power: History and Theory*, London: Routledge, 1996.

Sheehan, M., *International Security, an analytical survey*, Boulder and London: Lynne Rienner Publishers, 2005.

Thakur, R., *The politics and economics of India's foreign policy*, London: Hurst and Co., New York: St. Martin's Press, 1994.

Wright, T. and S. Gorman, 'Militants overtake India as top threat, says Pak's ISI', *The Wall Street Journal*, 16 August 2010.

Part I

State-centric approaches to security

2 Afghanistan and the war on terror

Sita Bali

Afghanistan stands at the crossroads of empires, and has rarely been a peaceful, united and stable unit for any length of time in its long history. It has been fought over by competing powers, and seen soldiers of the Persian, Greek, Mauryan, Hun, Mongol, Moghul, British, and Soviet empires marauding through, establishing themselves for varied lengths of time. When there have been no outside influences, Afghans have often fought each other for control of the country. In the aftermath of the events of 11 September 2001, Afghanistan found itself thrust into the forefront of world affairs and it is here, in one of the poorest, least developed and most war-debilitated countries of the world, that the consequences of the 'war on terror' have been most long lasting and perhaps most damaging.

9/11 led to the US invasion of Afghanistan, and the toppling of the Taliban regime as part of the pursuit of Al-Qaeda, who had established themselves as long-term 'guests' of the Taliban government. When the Taliban refused to hand over Osama bin Laden, the US, with the assistance of the Northern Alliance, drove them from power. But they failed to capture bin Laden and other key Al-Qaeda leaders who managed to escape into the tribal areas of Pakistan, where they are currently believed to be living. The Taliban leadership also fled to Pakistan and soon began to reorganize and re-establish themselves in that country.

The international community has been involved in trying to rebuild and develop Afghanistan since the Bonn Conference of 2001, which charted the process for establishing a new government in Afghanistan. An interim government was established under Hamid Karzai, a Durrani Pashtun leader from the Popolzai tribe, who had spent years in exile in India and Pakistan. Based on an agreement between various Afghan groups, under the auspices of the United Nations (UN) in Bonn, an independent commission was constituted to decide the composition of a *loya jirga* or grand assembly, which was held in June 2002. The *jirga* of nearly 1,600 members, about a thousand of whom were elected, and which allocated 160 seats to women, selected a new transitional government headed by Hamid Karzai, and the process of creating a constitution was begun. The new constitution was ratified in January 2004;, elections under this constitution were held in June the same year, and Hamid Karzai was elected President. He was then re-elected in 2009, in a very flawed election.

The Bonn Declaration also called on the UN to establish a security and assistance force for Afghanistan, which was done by the passage of Resolution 1368 in 2001. The International Security and Assistance Force (ISAF) became a North Atlantic Treaty Organization (NATO)-led operation in 2003 and currently involves the deployment of around 130,000 troops from 48 countries including most of the 28 NATO members (NATO, 2011, online). Its purposes are to help provide security for the Afghan people and their government, and thus to enable governance and development. Towards achievement of the latter task ISAF works with the United Nations Assistance Mission in Afghanistan (UNAMA), which supports the Afghan government on a range of governance issues from running elections to human and women's rights.

The international community has further supported Afghanistan since 2001 through provision of aid, and there have been eight donor conferences since the first one in Tokyo in 2002, which pledged $4.5 billion of assistance. In the nine conferences, substantial funds have been promised, but these have not always been delivered, and increasingly donors are becoming reluctant to continue to pour money into Afghanistan, due to allegations of corruptions and misuse. Despite the grand promises and the great needs in Afghanistan, the international community's generosity has been limited, especially when compared to the largesse doled out in other reconstruction and nation-building situations. For example, it was calculated that in the first two post-conflict years, the 'United States and its allies have put 25 times more money and 50 times more troops on a per capita basis into post-conflict Kosovo than into post-conflict Afghanistan.'[1]

In late 2001 the Afghans had high hopes that their 21-year-long nightmare of civil war, warlordism and repressive Taliban government was about to end with the 'coming of a Pax Americana.'[2] There was real optimism and goodwill towards the Americans in particular and the international community in general. Unfortunately, this window of opportunity, which lasted a good few years, has been wasted. The situation in Afghanistan has been deteriorating since about 2003, and today there are serious challenges with regard to peace and security, stability, institution-building, economic development and governance. The Taliban is once again a force to be reckoned with in Afghanistan and the Afghan government is increasingly ineffective and weak. NATO and the international community face an uphill task, especially given an ever more hostile Afghan population that has seen little improvement in daily life. Conditions remain difficult for the Afghan people and the country has once more become a haven for opium and cannabis producers and traffickers.

This chapter will examine the nature of, and reasons for, this decline and the impact it has on Afghans, on the region and on the wider world. The decisions, actions and attitudes of the American-led international approach to Afghanistan; the problems of ineffectual and corrupt government from Kabul; the strengthening insurgency, and the role of Pakistan and other neighboring countries, are the main reasons for the prevailing crisis, and will be explored in detail first.

What has gone wrong in Afghanistan?

The US military campaign in 2001 involved mainly the CIA, Special Operations Forces and air power. Supported by the Afghan Northern Alliance fighters, it successfully removed the Taliban in less than three months at the cost to the US of only a dozen or so American lives.[3] But the US had gone into Afghanistan without a clear idea of what or who would succeed the Taliban regime, of the US role in the aftermath, or of any agreed goal except the capture of Al-Qaeda leaders and the destruction of their organization.

The Bonn process, influenced by UN special representative Lakdar Brahimi and Afghan–American Special Presidential Advisor on Afghanistan Zilmay Khalilzad among others, created an interim leadership and government, and laid out a path to a new constitution and elections. However, there was considerable debate in US policy-making circles regarding the necessary level of troop deployments and the role of ISAF in stabilizing and providing security in post-Taliban Afghanistan. The more neo-conservative elements in the US administration, led by Defense Secretary Rumsfeld who prevailed, felt that a 'light footprint' was advisable, both because US troops did not do nation-building or peacekeeping, and given the context of the Afghans' historical aversion to foreigners in their land.[4] At that point the decision was made to deploy some 8,000–10,000 American troops in Afghanistan, primarily for hunting down remnants of Al-Qaeda and the Taliban, and about 4,000 ISAF troops were deployed to provide security around Kabul. It was also decided that it was better to build rapidly a strong Afghan Army to provide security, and this task fell to the Pentagon. Further, Brahimi felt that the UN presence in Afghanistan should be limited, and should seek to build capacity among Afghans themselves to take responsibility for their own governance. In this view he was reacting against the UN's experience in Bosnia and Kosovo, where the missions had involved large international security and civilian deployments with the UN taking control of governance for some time, a pattern he clearly did not want repeated in Afghanistan.[5]

It should be noted that all these discussions were taking place and decisions being made against the backdrop of a changing focus in US policy, which was turning to planning the Iraq war. Once the Taliban were routed, Afghanistan was seen as a nation-building and stabilization operation, and it was 'considered a sideshow by a White House that had gotten its priorities seriously wrong.'[6] The decisions taken on low-level of troop deployments in this period were thus very hard to overturn, as American troops, equipment, Special Forces and intelligence operatives, as well as attention and priorities, all became increasingly engaged in Iraq and were not available for Afghanistan. The speed with which the US government shifted its attention to Iraq after the defeat of the Taliban was breathtaking. Before the end of 2001, even before the battle of Tora Bora, US assets were being withdrawn from Afghanistan and reassigned to planning for Iraq.[7]

As Rashid notes, the consequences of Washington's lack of commitment to state-building in Afghanistan and its focus on Iraq were catastrophic:

For Afghanistan the results have been too few Western troops, too little money, and a lack of coherent strategy and sustained policy initiatives on the part of Western and Afghan leaders. The Bonn conference created the scaffolding to build the new Afghan structure, but what was consistently missing were the bricks and running water. Inside the scaffolding there is still only the barest shell.[8]

Jones adds weight to this, arguing that when compared with a series of post-war stabilization and reconstruction programs including Germany (where 89.3 troops per 1,000 inhabitants were deployed), Bosnia (17.5), Kosovo (19.3), and East Timor (9.8), in Afghanistan the US and the international community only had 1.6 troops per 1,000 Afghans, making this 'one of the lowest levels of troops, police and financial assistance in any stabilization operation since the end of World War II.'[9]

Moreover, on the matter of financial assistance to rebuild Afghanistan, things were not going as planned, and mixed messages did nothing to help manage the expectation of an Afghan nation desperate for investment and economic development. In the aftermath of the easy victory, President Bush raised hopes of substantial financial assistance to Afghanistan by referring to the Marshall Plan in a speech about the future of Afghanistan at the Virginia Military Institute, *alma mater* of George C. Marshall; but he gave no specific details or promises.[10] In reality his administration did little to assess the level of need in Afghanistan or to channel substantial assistance for reconstruction and rebuilding, as opposed to security and defense, until early 2004, wasting two crucial years and much goodwill.[11] The US generally appeared to have little time and money to expend on Afghanistan, because despite all the public promises and raised expectations, their focus was on Iraq. Other countries were also less forthcoming with assistance, probably because of the invasion of Iraq. Jones remarks, 'At $60 per Afghan, foreign assistance over the first two years of nation-building operations was lower than most operations since World War II'[12]; and this for a country that had seen more than 20 years of civil war, and systematic looting and destruction, at the hands of various Mujahidin commanders and warlords.

One consequence of this neglect of Afghan needs, and the emphasis on hunting Al-Qaeda, was the re-emergence of those hated figures from the past, the Afghan warlords. These warlords were Mujahidin commanders of the anti-Soviet jihad era, who fought each other and carved up the country after the Soviet withdrawal, rendering unfeasible any chance of the emergence of a united and stable Afghanistan. Their rapacious activities, including drug trafficking, extortion, and exploitation of the poor and war-ravaged Afghan population, had made them widely despised, and had been a factor in allowing the Taliban to gain some measure of support when they initially took power from them in 1996. In the absence of sufficient international, US and Afghan troops, and given the continuing urgency of the battle against Al-Qaeda and the pursuit of bin Laden, the CIA began to rely on the existing militias of the warlords. US funds began to flow to these predatory old war-horses, allowing them to rebuild their power bases and re-establish themselves. Ishmael Khan of Herat, Gul Agha Sherzai of Kandahar and others of the same greedy and ruthless ilk were provided with arms and money to raise and maintain their private militias once again, and were enlisted to help track Al-Qaeda, to guard American installations and to provide escorts to supply convoys etc. They also became the suppliers of choice to the American troops, providing them anything they needed at vastly inflated prices, and enriching themselves enormously in the process.[13] They were even incorporated into the new governmental structures, and appointed as Provincial Governors as they became strong enough to present a significant threat to the Karzai order if relegated to the sidelines. The strengthening of the warlords weakened the central government, especially its ability to establish institutions and exercise its authority at provincial and district levels. It continued the tradition noted by Chayes: 'in Afghanistan, the exercise of power remains personal. There are no institutions; there are only powerful men.'[14] The Afghan people were horrified to see this reinvigoration of their erstwhile oppressors and it began to erode their faith and optimism in the new order, as well as in the Americans and the international community who seemed to be supporting them.

The empowering of the warlords was a dangerous development, particularly given the slow progress being made in establishing a properly trained Afghan National Army (ANA). The new ANA was intended to reflect the ethnic mix of Afghanistan, but the Defense Minister Mohammed Fahim, an ex-warlord, wanted it composed only of his Tajiks, and the US had to bypass him and recruit directly from the population. The whole Afghan Ministry of Defense, dominated by Fahim and his Panjshiris, had to be restructured and its composition rebalanced to reflect the ethnic mix of Afghanistan.[15] Simultaneously, UNAMA was pressing ahead with the disarmament of the private militias of warlords, and trying to move the country towards a situation where there was only one legal army, the ANA. But the US was still hiring warlords and their militias, so the UN and the US were working at cross-purposes with each other. Despite this the US, guided by Khalilzad, who was appointed the US ambassador to Afghanistan in November 2003, was beginning to take the building up of the ANA seriously, investing $797 million in 2004, $788 million in 2005 and $830 million in 2006. The first units of the ANA began to deploy in 2003, and by 2006 the ANA was 37,000 strong. This was a rare US success, even though problems of desertion and illiteracy plagued the new Afghan Army.[16]

The US was not alone in its neglect of Afghanistan. The Germans, who were given the key task of training the new Afghan national police (ANP) in 2002, did not do much better. The role of the police in a post-conflict state is widely acknowledged as crucial. They contribute to the demilitarization of society and the restoration or establishment of the rule of law.[17] The police represent the government and provide security in its name, and can thus play a pivotal role in legitimizing the government. The Germans put minimal resources and effort into building up the ANP, sending only '41 trainers to train 3,500 Afghan officers over three years.'[18] No proper plan to implement training across the country was ever put in place, minimal equipment was made available to the ANP, and the whole effort was described as 'pathetic and next-to-useless' by a veteran observer of Afghan affairs.[19] Eventually police training was taken over by Washington, who sub-contracted the job out to DynCorp, but their efforts were also less than satisfactory. The delay in establishing a proper police force has proved costly and is a continuing problem, as a RUSI/FPRI report from mid 2009 outlines:

> Unprofessional, riven by alternative – often unsavoury – loyalties, and largely ineffectual against crime, they remain the Achilles heel of the state building effort, an important component which is not living up to its potential in providing civil security and the space for social, political and economic development to flourish. More dangerously, the ANP are a widespread source of crime and insecurity, synonymous with corruption and widespread human rights violations. Consequently they exacerbate public dissatisfaction with the political order, undermine government legitimacy, and ultimately stoke the embers of violence and insurgency.[20]

All this meant that there have never been sufficient security forces (either army or police), whether American, international or Afghan, to truly stabilize the country post-2001. Further, the warlords continued to have militias that were locally stronger than state security forces. Although numbers of both ISAF and American troops increased from the low base in 2001 to about 12,000 ISAF and 18,000 American forces, supported by 25,000 ANA, 55,000 ANP and some Afghan militias, in 2004,[21] this was still an untenably low level given the nature of the task. Even today, when troop levels stand at much higher levels, the security threats are commensurately greater.

Weak governance was another key problem in post-Taliban Afghanistan, and one that has contributed enormously to the deteriorating situation there. Effective governance involves the government establishing control of the country, and being able to enforce law and order, guarantee the security of its citizens and provide them with public services. In a post-conflict situation such as Afghanistan it should include controlling and holding the territory of the state, building new, strong institutions, and rejuvenating the economy so as to provide civilian employment to demobilizing fighters. The inability of the Karzai governments (interim, transitional and then elected) to deliver on these matters, due to a range of reasons from insufficient support in institutional capacity-building from the international community, to ethnic rivalries within his governments and the inclusion of warlords in his cabinets, to his indecisiveness and increasing capriciousness, as well as the endemic corruption in the country, has been a source of disappointment and frustration for the Afghan and world communities alike.

Two factors in particular have been highlighted by Jones as contributing to the fragility of the Afghan government and the susceptibility of Afghanistan to the Taliban insurgency. The first of these is the failure of the government to provide public services such as schools, courts etc., and this failure is compounded by corruption.[22] Surveys show that substantial numbers of Afghans identify corruption within the government and police as one of the major problems facing the country, and this perception is on the increase.[23] Corruption undermines the ability of the government to deliver and erodes the trust of the people. And when it is alleged to involve provincial governors such as Sher Mohammed Akhundzada, Governor of Helmand until 2005, and others close to the Karzai family, it damages the legitimacy and standing of the President himself.[24] The second is the inability of the state's security forces, both ANA and ANP, to establish law and order or to offer the citizens any modicum of security. If the state in a post-conflict society cannot guarantee its citizens peace and stability, it fails in its most basic task, and this is clearly the case in Afghanistan.

Linked to both these factors is the role and impact of opium production in Afghanistan. Growing poppies and producing opium is the most lucrative and well-organized economic activity in Afghanistan. The United Nations Office on Drugs and Crime (UNODC) reports that in 2009 Afghanistan produced 5,900 to 7,900 metric tonnes of opium, which was 89 percent of global production; in 2010 production fell to 3,000 to 4,200 tonnes (due to plant disease), which was 77 percent of global production.[25] Peters argues that the Taliban insurgents and drug traffickers of Southern Afghanistan and Pakistan have achieved global market dominance by creating a farm support and export network that manages to give farm loans to small growers, import chemicals needed in the industry, and securely ship the product across rugged terrain to the wider world, describing this as 'an organizational feat of the very highest order' and all without the use of modern communications, machines or even high levels of literacy.[26]

Through a well-established and efficiently managed system, the Taliban insurgents collect a 10 percent tax (*ushr* or *usher*) from farmers, which is sufficient to meet the day-to-day needs of village-level Taliban commanders, including fighters' wages, weaponry and ammunition, petrol and food.[27] They further collect tax on units processing and refining the drug, and on shipments passing through their territory. A proportion of the money (or opium, as often they are paid not in cash but in kind) collected is handed over to Taliban commanders at district level, who in turn hand over to commanders and 'shadow governors' at provincial level, who in turn pass on some to the highest leadership echelons of the Taliban.

Major drug traffickers and traders, who control the trade and movement of tonnes of opium, pay a 'donation' or a 'tax' directly to the top echelons of the Taliban leadership. This can take the form, for example, of provision of four-by-four and pick-up truck type vehicles. It can also come in the form of the drug trafficker building a *madrasa* or guesthouse where Taliban fighters can go for R&R, and in one case includes the running of a clinic for the treatment of wounded talibs, all in neighboring Pakistan.[28]

Peters estimates that the Taliban earn approximately half a billion dollars a year (in cash and goods) from all these drug-related activities, with about $54 million coming from *ushr*, $133 million from the tax on drug factories, and about $250 million from protecting and taxing shipments.[29] UNODC points out that the most insecure areas of Afghanistan are also the areas that produce the most opium:

> Eighty two per cent of opium cultivated in 2010 was concentrated in Hilmand, Kandahar, Uruzgan, Day Kundi, and Zabul provinces in the Southern region. These are the most insecure provinces in the country, where security conditions are classified as high or of extreme risk by the United Nations Department of Safety and Security.
>
> (UNDSS)[30]

The link between opium production, poor governance and insurgency comes from the fact that corrupt officials within the Afghan government also assist this drugs-and-insurgency relationship. Indeed some have argued that post-2001, some of the erstwhile warlords incorporated into the Karzai regime were in fact big players in this drug production and trafficking industry. There are regularly stories in the press, sourced to Afghan counter-narcotics officers, regarding the involvement of senior Afghan government officials in the ongoing drug-smuggling industry.[31]

The Taliban suffered some serious losses in the 2001 war, particularly at Kunduz, and among prisoners taken by Northern Alliance in the north. But their leadership council and high-level commanders as well as most of their dedicated foot-soldiers escaped into Pakistan, in part as a result of a high-level intervention by Pakistani President General Musharraf. In a phone call to President Bush, Musharraf requested a temporary suspension of hostilities to enable Pakistan to fly out their ISI (Inter-Services Intelligence) and Frontier Corps personnel who were in Afghanistan assisting the Taliban. Bush agreed and the Pakistanis flew planeload upon planeload of their people, Taliban fighters and Arabs and Uzbeks associated with Al-Qaeda, out of harm's way.[32] Others crossed into Pakistan over the porous border and were soon regrouping and planning their response. The Taliban's leadership council settled in Quetta, Al-Qaeda members settled in North and South Waziristan, and Taliban fighters and lower-level commanders spread out over the rest of the Federally administered Tribal Areas (FATA), among their fellow Pashtuns. They received help and support from their mentors, Pakistan's ISI, and from various jihadi groups such as the Jamat-ulema-e-Islami (JUI) and the Tehreek-e-Nafaz-e-Shariat-e-Mohammadi (TNSM) in Pakistan.

By April of 2002, the Taliban were sufficiently recovered to begin attacks across the border in Afghanistan, and they have gone from strength to strength since. The year 2005–2006 saw a huge explosion of violence: the number of suicide attacks increased from 21 in 2005 to 139 in 2006, to 140 in 2007; remotely detonated bombings more than doubled from 783 to 1,677 and armed attacks nearly tripled from 1,558 to 4,542. In 2007 insurgent attacks rose another 27 percent from 2006 levels, with Helmand province (where British troops were deployed in 2006) seeing a 60 percent rise in violence in the same period.[33] In 2007, Afghanistan experienced 12.4 attacks per day, in 2008, it was 18.4.[34] Put another way, in 2007 there were around 5,000 'violent incidents' in the 20 worst-affected districts of the country, and in 2008 that figure was 7,000.[35] The situation continued to deteriorate in 2009 and 2010, and in the period between September and December 2010, the number of security incidents was 66 percent higher than during the same period in 2009.[36] The Taliban today dominate in the Pashtun areas, south and east of the country, with Kandahar, their traditional stronghold, and Helmand, the center of opium production, being the most insecure provinces.

All the conditions necessary for a successful insurgency are present in Afghanistan. First, there are highly motivated and ideologically driven insurgents (Taliban, Hizb-i-Islami and Haqqani network), who have never accepted their overthrow and the legitimacy of the current government, and who are determined to reinstate themselves and their Deobandi/Wahabi-inspired view of Islam and Sharia across their country. These committed insurgents are operating among a local population that fears them, with whom they blend easily and from whom they either attract or extract support. They can also appeal to those Afghans who may not share their extreme and narrow interpretation of Islam, by invoking the age-old Afghan aversion to the presence in and control of the country by foreign troops. Further, there is a weak and corrupt government, propped up by foreigners, whose security forces, whether ANP or ANA, cannot guarantee the security of the citizens, particularly in rural areas. The government lacks real support because of its inability to provide public services, including justice, to the population. And it is subverted by corrupt officials who have connections and dealings with the insurgents. Crucially, there is a neighboring state, Pakistan, supporting the insurgency politically and economically as well as providing strategic and tactical assistance, whose territory provides a safe haven where insurgents can retire and regroup. And finally, the insurgents have access to substantial funds through their involvement in every aspect of opium production and trafficking. In these circumstances their success and ability to control large swathes of rural southern and eastern Afghanistan should come as no surprise.[37]

The Taliban expanded the areas under their domination by taking advantage of the lack of penetration of the Kabul government in rural areas of the Pashtun belt. They moved into areas calling on tribal connections or disillusionment with the Government, they threatened, intimidated and if necessary dealt brutally with those who worked for or supported the Kabul government or the foreigners, and anyone else who opposed them. In the absence of any response from the ANA or ANP, these people had to flee into cities to escape the Taliban, thus emptying rural areas of government supporters and leaving the Taliban a free hand to move in and begin to establish parallel or alternative administrations, which provide elements of governance, including taxation and their own brand of rough justice. This effectively amounts to a slow takeover of the Afghan state, starting from the south and east, and expanding northwards to Kabul and the West; this has been most effective in the Pashtun areas of the country.[38]

At the end of his first year in office, and after conducting a painfully long review of the situation he inherited in Afghanistan (documented by veteran reporter Bob Woodward),[39] President Obama announced in 2009 that the US would send 30,000 more troops into Afghanistan in a last surge to try and pull the situation back from the abyss into which it had descended. These troops are now in Afghanistan, and the surge is on. The US has been more aggressively taking the battle to the Taliban in their strongholds of Kandahar and Helmand. While there have been successes, the old problems remain: actually holding the territory that they clear of Taliban presence, and avoiding civilian casualties. While the ANP and ANA have been considerably strengthened, huge problems remain, including competence, desertions, and the fact that non-Pashtuns dominate the officer classes of both organizations. The final judgement on the surge will be some time coming. NATO's Lisbon Conference discussed 2014 as a possible start date for the draw-down of forces in Afghanistan.

Regional issues and implications

From 1979 to the present, a number of regional powers have been intimately involved in the affairs of Afghanistan, with Pakistan being the main player. It was Pakistan that co-ordinated help to the Mujahidin to reverse the Soviet invasion; Pakistan that played king-maker, empowering Islamic extremist groups rather than secular or nationalist opposition to the Communist presence and when their proxies failed to deliver a stable Afghanistan after taking control of the country in 1992, it was Pakistan that helped create the Taliban to do what the Mujahidin had been unable to do.

Pakistani policy in Afghanistan must be seen as a part of its wider anti-India strategy in the regional context. Pakistan believes it has a vital security interest in a pliant and friendly Afghanistan, giving it the 'strategic depth' it needs versus India. After three unsuccessful wars with India since Independence in 1947, the last of which resulted in the secession of Bangladesh, conventional war with India had proved to be devastating and unwinnable, so Pakistan developed an alternative strategy for its key security objectives of resisting Indian hegemony and control of Kashmir. The new policy emerged from the genuinely Islamic orientation of key Army and intelligence officers of the time, from President General Zia to the then chief of the Inter-Services Intelligence (ISI), Hamid Gul. It involved seeking to control Afghanistan to ensure a friendly and anti-India government there, by supporting and arming the more Islamist of the Afghan Mujahidin groups. The alliance with the US, which put Pakistan into a commanding position with regard to Afghanistan, facilitated and financed its implementation. This strategy also had the vital consequence of making it easier to similarly train and despatch ideologically committed Islamic extremists to destabilize Kashmir and India.[40]

Pakistan's entire strategy vis-à-vis Afghanistan and Kashmir was called into question after 9/11. The Americans put Pakistan on the spot, asking them to choose between their proxies, the Taliban and the US. President General Musharraf did the only sensible thing possible and assured the Americans that Pakistan stood with them, granting the US unprecedented access to Pakistani ports, airbases and territory from which they could launch and supply their 2001 assault on the Taliban. But Pakistan then embarked on a hazardous tightrope walk, balancing their alliance with the US with continued support for 'their' Taliban. Pakistan once again played host and mentor to the Taliban as they fled Afghanistan in disarray, helped them regroup, and supported them in their renewed assault on Afghanistan. But Pakistan simultaneously satisfied the Americans with the facilities extended to them, and with the capture and handing over of Al-Qaeda members, along with Arabs and other associated foreign militants. This Janus-faced strategy was not particularly difficult to sustain during the early years of the Bush administration, when Bush indulged Musharraf, in his gratitude and recognition of the assistance Pakistan was providing. It became more dangerous latterly, when the Taliban began to have success in military operations and caused US and NATO casualties.

Pakistan's adherence to the policy of spawning, nurturing, training and using Islamists as proxies has had devastating consequences within the country too. The various Islamist groups, and the Islamic political parties that spring from them such as the Muttahida Majlis-e-Amal (MMA), a hardline Islamic six-party alliance, the JUI, TNSM, and anti-Shia outfits like the Sipah-i-Sahaba as well as the Kashmir-oriented anti-India groups like the Lashkar-e-Toiba, have all begun to interact and merge, creating a substantial, vocal and violent force in the country. There has also emerged a Pakistani Taliban, made up of individuals from some of these groups and others.

Since the episode of the *Lal Masjid* in Islamabad, and even more so after Pakistani army actions against Islamists in Swat and parts of FATA, many of the Islamic militants have turned on their erstwhile mentors, targeting the Pakistani government and army in a series of daring and spectacular attacks on targets including the Marriott Hotel in Islamabad, the Army Headquarters in Rawalpindi, a mosque in Rawalpindi cantonment used by senior Army officers and their families, the police training establishment, the visiting Sri Lankan cricket team and even an ISI building, as well as carrying out frequent attacks on ordinary civilians in marketplaces up and down the country. There have also been numerous assassinations of politicians seen as inimical to the Islamist cause, including Benazir Bhutto in December 2007, and most recently Governor of Punjab Salman Taseer in January 2011.

Pakistan itself is now in danger of being 'Talibanized.' Its people are reeling from the onslaught, and given the substantial support Islamists enjoy, particularly in the most deprived parts of the country like FATA, parts of the North West Frontier Province and Baluchistan, Pakistan may well be facing its deepest crisis yet. But even this grave peril has not been enough to make the ISI abandon this policy, they persist on this desperate trajectory, now making distinctions between 'good' Taliban (Afghan or anti-India) and 'bad' Taliban (anti-Pakistan), continuing to support the former while fighting the latter. And they go on using Islamists against India, as evidenced by attacks like those on the Indian Embassy in Kabul in October 2009.

'Afghanistan holds strategic importance for India as New Delhi seeks friendly allies in the neighborhood, and because it is a gateway to energy-rich Central

Asian states such as Turkmenistan and Kazakhstan.'[41] India had supported all Afghan governments until the Taliban took control in 1996, presaging the end of Indian influence. India had every reason to oppose the extremist Taliban, as it has been on the receiving end of Islamic extremist terrorism for many years in Kashmir and beyond, and does not want any group that subscribes to this ideology to reach a position of power in South Asia. Further, in a graphic demonstration of the links between ISI's Kashmir and Afghan policies, India was humiliated in 1999 by the hijacking of an Indian Airlines aircraft from Kathmandu to Lucknow by Islamic extremists, who had it flown to Kandahar, from where, under Taliban protection, they secured the release of key terrorists captured in Kashmir in exchange for the hapless Indian passengers.

India seized the opportunity presented by the defeat of the Taliban to reestablish a good relationship with Afghanistan, opening consulates in several Afghan cities, and embarking on a generous and surprisingly effective development program. Since 2001 India has spent over a billion dollars in Afghanistan, building the new Zaranj–Delaram road giving Afghanistan access to the sea via Iran, constructing a new Parliament building in Kabul, erecting the Salma dam for the hydroelectric plant in Herat, as well as being involved in the health, education, governance capacity-building and telecommunications sectors.

India also has considerable soft power in Afghanistan due to the popularity of its Bollywood films and music, and most Afghans have a positive view of India and the Indian contribution to reconstruction in Afghanistan. Indian's excellent relations with Afghanistan are noted with growing alarm in Pakistan, to the extent that the ISI have persisted with old habits, using Islamic militants to launch two deadly attacks on the Indian Embassy in Kabul in July 2008 and October 2009 respectively, as well as several others on Indians working on development projects and in Indian consulates. An important reason why Pakistan refuses to abandon the Taliban is because it still sees them as the best instrument for retaining influence in Afghanistan and denying such influence to India, after the US and NATO leave Afghanistan, as they must. Some have argued that there is an India–Pakistan proxy war dimension to the war in Afghanistan, and while there is an element of truth in this, with these parties being on opposite sides of the dispute, it does not appear to be the determining feature of the conflict itself.[42] It does however embed Afghanistan irrevocably into the regional security equation in South Asia.

Iran is another significant actor in the politics and conflict in Afghanistan. It has a deep historic and cultural connection with Afghanistan, which has often been part of various Persian empires through the ages; and the Persian-speaking Tajiks and Hazaras have a particular affinity with Iran. Iran had taken in nearly two million Afghan refugees during the Soviet invasion, and assisted the Mujahidin against the Soviets. Iran has no wish to see the Sunni extremist Taliban come to power in Afghanistan, and had supported the Northern Alliance, along with India, Russia and the Central Asian republics, to that end. During the conquest of Mazar-e-Shareif in September of 1998, Taliban fighters entered the Iranian Consulate, and killed all 11 diplomats present there, along with an

Iranian journalist. This act of provocation nearly triggered war between the two countries, and Iran sent a 200,000-strong force to its border with Afghanistan, but war was avoided by a UN intervention.[43] The Iranians were therefore no doubt very pleased to see the back of the Taliban in 2001.

Iran has substantial interests in Afghanistan. The most important of these is the reining-in of drug production and trafficking, which has serious consequences, including the 2.8 percent of its population aged between 15 and 65 being opiate addicts.[44] Drug trafficking regularly causes clashes between Iranian security forces and criminals on the Afghan–Iran border, and constitutes a serious security problem. Further Iran has a significant trade relationship with Afghanistan, and has been contributing to reconstruction efforts in post-Taliban Afghanistan, concentrating on the Tajik and Hazara dominated areas, including better transport links between those parts and Iran itself. It also enjoys significant soft power advantages in Afghanistan because of linguistic and cultural ties.

In recent years, much of what Iran does in Afghanistan has been viewed in the context of its competitive relationship with the US for power and influence in the region. Thus, some have argued that Iran has taken to helping its erstwhile enemies the Taliban in their offensive against US troops with the objective of keeping the US hurting and bogged down in Afghanistan. But prior to and during the 2001 US offensive in Afghanistan, as well as during the Bonn process, Iran co-operated positively with the Americans and the international community, only retreating after Bush's 'axis of evil' speech.[45] It is clear that Iran is an influential force in Afghan politics, providing assistance (sometimes in the form of bags of cash) to Karzai,[46] as well as helping finance Tajik and Hazara candidates in the recent parliamentary elections.

The Central Asian Republics (CARs) Turkmenistan, Uzbekistan and Tajikistan (all with common borders with Afghanistan), and to some extent the Soviet successor state Russia, also have historic connections to and interests in the situation in Afghanistan. There are Turkoman, Uzbek and Tajik minorities in Afghanistan, making these connections a live and pertinent factor in Afghan politics. All three of the CARs have authoritarian post-Communist governments, and all feared the rising tide of Islamic extremism that the Taliban represented. Tajikistan had a five-year-long civil war between 1992 and 1997, in which Islamists played a substantial role, and Uzbekistan, with perhaps the most repressive government, faces a significant challenge from the Islamist Movement of Uzbekistan, a group affiliated with Al-Qaeda and the Taliban, many of whose members are based in FATA, and have fought alongside the Taliban against ISAF forces in Afghanistan.

Turkmenistan has the 11th highest reserves of natural gas in the world, and needs to find a way of transporting this out to the world, and of breaking its dependence on Russia. It has built a pipeline connecting with Iran, and this is the only route for the export of gas that does not involve Russia, and the only pipeline built in the post-Soviet era in the whole region.[47] Turkmenistan, together with UNOCAL, was negotiating with the Taliban in 1997 to build a pipeline through Afghanistan and into Pakistan, but that never came to fruition, because the American government withdrew support for the project after Al-Qaeda's activities caused it to completely disassociate itself from the Taliban regime. There was an attempt to resurrect this project in the early years of Karzai's regime, but the deteriorating situation in Afghanistan has put paid to that too.

For the CARs, the arrival of the US in Afghanistan represented an opportunity to move out of Russia's sphere of influence and to begin to build independent relationships with the West. But the US only saw them as staging posts on a supply line, and no relationship has emerged, leaving them firmly in Russia's, and to a lesser extent China's, domain. Their chief interests in Afghanistan today lie in supporting their fellow ethnic groups, and stopping the instability and extremism in Afghanistan from crossing the Amu Darya, which forms their border. Plans for pipelines have turned into mere pipe dreams.

Conclusion

After the US invasion of 2001, the fate of Afghanistan became inevitably and intrinsically linked to eventual American success or failure in Iraq. The US decision to have a 'light footprint' in Afghanistan, both to enable them to focus on Iraq, and as a preferred policy, has cost Afghans dear, creating conditions, including weak governance, that have allowed the Taliban insurgency to flourish. It was thus only after General Petraeus's surge in Iraq, when the situation in that country was thought to have been pulled back from the brink, that the Americans refocused their attention on Afghanistan, by which time the Taliban insurgency was too well established and much harder to fight.

Perhaps more importantly, the initial lack of commitment to nation-building and the slow arrival of assistance gave rise to the perception both within and outside Afghanistan that the US and the international community were not, as promised, in it for the long haul: that their intentions were limited to neutralizing Al-Qaeda, and that they had no real interest in staying the distance and building a secure and stable Afghanistan. The consequence of this plausible assessment of American intent was the weakening of the whole Afghan project at its very inception, eroding faith in the prospects for the current order. This left Afghans wary of whole-hearted support for Karzai, and that, along with the inadequacies of his government, created the space for the Taliban to once more exercise influence over the Afghan people.

The flawed 2009 presidential election, the reports of Karzai's increasingly erratic behavior, and the deteriorating relationship between him and some American senior officials, have made the last year or two very frustrating for the international community and for Afghans. The Taliban now dominate in the south and east of the country. Thus, after nearly ten years of international involvement in Afghanistan, the situation is now more or less back to square one, where the Taliban once again controls a considerable proportion of the territory and the people's lives have barely changed, particularly in the Pashtun areas (though things are appreciably better in the North).

We are currently in the early stage of the American 'surge' in Afghanistan, and it is too early to tell whether it will dramatically change the landscape of the conflict. Arguably the position in Afghanistan is irretrievable now, and lofty ambitions to create a stable, secular and democratic Afghanistan must be scaled down to something more achievable and realistic; and so in recent months all parties have begun to talk about opening negotiations with the Taliban as a way of bringing the conflict to some sort of end.

In this process, as in the turbulent history of the last 30 years in Afghanistan, the role of her neighbors will be crucial, even decisive. The biggest problem is Pakistan, with its fear of hostile encirclement and its desire to play king-maker in Afghanistan. Pakistan needs to shift its threat perception away from India and to where the dangers really lie – in nurturing Islamists. This will be difficult for an army that has always justified colonizing the lion's share of the country's resources and maintaining a grip on power, directly or indirectly, by reference to the perceived threat from India. But if Pakistan accepts the reality that India has no expansionist ambitions towards it, this should help it arrive at a more flexible approach to the power configuration in Afghanistan.

India, which now conceives of itself as having not merely a regional but a global role, may have to take unpopular steps, such as lowering its profile in Afghanistan, to reassure Pakistan. But it will still want to ensure that the Taliban do not have free reign, and Afghanistan cannot again become a haven for Islamic extremism, or export Islamic terrorists and terrorism to India. And it would help the situation a great deal if both India and Pakistan could move towards serious attempts at resolving the Kashmir dispute. But this would only be possible if Pakistan were to desist completely from any involvement in Islamist terrorism in India, so that the process would not be constantly derailed by some new terrorist outrage, as in the past.

Iran is less likely to present a stumbling block, as long as it has some credible guarantees that an Afghan governing configuration, even if it is inclusive of the Taliban, will not present a direct threat to itself or to the Hazaras and Tajiks it supports. It will also want to see any future Afghan government do more to curtail opium production and trafficking. But it will probably want to use its position in Afghanistan as leverage with the Americans on a wider range of extra regional issues of concern, including the duration of the US presence on its borders, both east and west. The CARs and Russia do not want the US indefinitely in Afghanistan, but nor do they want the Taliban to dominate.

The US and the international community have probably already achieved their main goal, which was to deny Al-Qaeda the use of Afghan territory,[48] but this is not as yet irreversible. The surge is about that final push to try and weaken the Taliban enough that they come to the negotiating table. While the Afghan Taliban were creations of Pakistan, there is some evidence now of their wanting to break free and act independently in any negotiations about their future in the politics of their country.[49] If this is indeed what their leadership now want, and if they are able to negotiate with the Karzai government and the Americans without the involvement of Pakistan, this would offer the real possibility of a genuine Afghan accommodation that could perhaps stand a chance of medium to long term survival. But serious considerations of trust and credibility must still hang over the Taliban in the context of negotiations, particularly because of the dismal record of their friends and allies like Sufi Mohammed of TNSM and the deal he made with the Pakistani government with regard to Swat.

As ever, the Afghan people find themselves at the mercy of forces they cannot control. It is their need for stability, security and development, all of which have been strangers to their country for over 30 years, that Afghans, regional players and the international community as a whole need to prioritize. The situation of ongoing conflict that they have endured for so long cannot, surely, continue indefinitely.

Notes

 1 J. Dobbins, 'Nation-building', Summer 2003.
 2 S. Chayes, *The Punishment of Virtue*, 2007.
 3 S.G. Jones, *In the Graveyard of Empires*, 2009, p. xxii.
 4 Ibid., pp. 116–19.
 5 Ibid., p. 118.
 6 A. Rashid, *Descent into Chaos*, 2008, p. 196.
 7 Jones, *Graveyard of Empires*, pp. 126–7.
 8 A. Rashid, 'Afghanistan on the brink', 22 June 2006.
 9 Jones, 2009, *Graveyard of Empires*, pp. 118–19.
10 Ibid., pp. 116–17.
11 Rashid, *Descent into Chaos*, pp. 173 and 189.
12 Jones, *Graveyard of Empires*, p. 121.
13 Rashid, *Descent into Chaos*, p. 136.
14 Chayes, *Punishment of Virtue*, p. 163.
15 Rashid, *Descent into Chaos*, pp. 201–2.
16 Ibid., pp. 202–3.
17 R. Mani, 'Policing in Post-Conflict Situations', 2003.
18 Rashid, *Descent into Chaos*, p. 204.
19 Ibid.
20 RUSI/FPRI, *Reforming the Afghan National Police*, 2009.
21 S.G. Jones, *Averting Failure in Afghanistan*, p. 119.
22 S.G. Jones, *The Rise of Afghanistan's Insurgency*, pp. 16–18.
23 The Asia Foundation's survey shows 27% of Afghans identified corruption as a major problem in 2010, an increase from 2009 when 17% identified it as such. See The Asia Foundation, *Key Findings*, 2010. The survey conducted in 2010 for ABC News, the BBC and ARD by the Afghan Center for Socio-Economic and Opinion Research (ACSOR) shows that when asked directly if corruption was a problem, 76% of people said that it was, which was an increase from 2009 when 63% had answered positively.
24 Rashid, *Descent into Chaos*, pp. 322–5.
25 UNODC, *Afghanistan Opium Survey*, 2010.
26 G. Peters, 'The Taliban and the Opium Trade', 2009, pp. 7–8.
27 Ibid., pp. 8–10 and G. Smith, 'What Kandahar, Taliban Say', 2009, p. 202.
28 Peters, *The Taliban and the Opium Trade*, p. 13.
29 Ibid., p. 19.
30 UNODC, *Afghanistan Opium Survey*, p. 60.
31 L. Paoli, V. Greenfield and P. Reuter, *The World Heroin Market*, 2009, p. 114.
32 Rashid, *Descent into Chaos*, pp. 90–2.
33 Jones, *Graveyard of Empires*, p. 207.
34 C. Radin and B. Roggio, 'Afghanistan: Mapping the Violence', 2008.

35 J. Burke, 'NATO Figures show Surge in Afghan Violence', 31 January 2009.
36 UN Secretary-General's Report on Afghanistan, December 2010, A/65/612-S/ 2010/630.
37 Jones, *Rise of Afghanistan's Insurgency*, pp. 7–40; *Averting Failure*, pp. 111–18 and *Graveyard of Empires*, pp. 151–62.
38 S.G. Jones, *Graveyard of Empires*, pp. 190–3.
39 B. Woodward, *Obama's Wars*, 2010.
40 S. Ganguly and N. Howenstein, 'India–Pakistan Rivalry in Afghanistan', 2009, pp. 132–4.
41 J. Bajoria, *India–Afghan Relations*, 2009.
42 W. Dalrymple, 'The Military and the Mullahs', *New Statesman*, 23 August 2010.
43 A. Rashid, *Taliban*, 2001.
44 UNODC, *World Drug Report 2008*.
45 L. Beehner, *Timeline: Iran–US Contacts*, 2007.
46 M. Torfeh, 'Iran is Buying Influence in Afghanistan', 26 October 2010.
47 A. Rashid, *Taliban*, pp. 144–51.
48 It is another issue that Al-Qaeda has found other congenial sanctuaries in Pakistan and Yemen.
49 A. Rashid, 'The way out of Afghanistan', 13 January 2011.

Bibliography

Afghan Center for Socio-Economic and Opinion Research, (2010) *Survey for ABC News, the BBC and ARD*, online, available on http://news.bbc.co.uk/1/shared/bsp/hi/ pdfs/11_01_10_afghanpoll.pdf

Bajoria, Jayashree, (2009) *India–Afghan Relations (Backgrounder)*, Council on Foreign Relations, online, available on www.cfr.org/india/india-afghanistan-relations/p17474

Beehner, Lionel, (2007) *Timeline: Iran–US Contacts (Backgrounder)*, Council on Foreign Relations, online, available on www.cfr.org/iran/timeline-us-iran-contacts/p12806

Burke, Jason, (2009) 'NATO Figures show Surge in Afghan Violence', *Guardian/ Observer*, 31 January 2009, online, available on www.guardian.co.uk/world/2009/ jan/31/afghanistan-nato-violence

Chayes, Sarah, *The Punishment of Virtue*, London: Portobello Books, 2007.

Dalrymple, William, (2010) 'The Military and the Mullahs', *New Statesman*, 23 August 2010, online, available on www.newstatesman.com/asia/2010/08/india-pakistan-afghanistan

Dobbins, James, (2003*) Nation-building: The Inescapable Responsibility of the World's Only Superpower*, Rand Review, Summer 2003, online, available on www.rand.org/ publications/randreview/issues/summer2003/nation1.html

Ewans, Martin, *Afghanistan: A Short History of its People and Politics*, London, Harper Perennial, 2002.

Ganguly, S. and N. Howenstein, 'India-Pakistan Rivalry in Afghanistan', *Journal of International Affairs*, Autumn/Winter, 63:1, 2009, pp. 127–40.

Giustozzi, Antonio, *Koran, Kalashnikov and Laptop: The Neo-Taliban Insurgency in Afghanistan*, London: Hurst and Co., 2007.

Jones, Seth G., 'Averting Failure in Afghanistan', *Survival*, 48:1, 2006, pp. 111–28.

Jones, Seth G., 'The Rise of Afghanistan's Insurgency: State Failure and Jihad', *International Security*, 32:4, 2008, pp. 7–40.

Jones, Seth G., *In the Graveyard of Empires: America's War in Afghanistan*, New York and London: Norton and Company, 2009.

Mani, Rama, (2003) 'Policing in Post-Conflict Situations', Concept Paper for Whitehall Policy Seminar London, online, available on www.ssronline.org/edocs/manir_policing_in_post-conflict_2003.pdf

NATO ISAF Website available on www.isaf.nato.int/

Paoli, L., V. Greenfield and P. Reuter, *The World Heroin Market: Can Supply be Cut?* Oxford: Oxford University Press, 2009.

Peters, Gretchen, 'The Taliban and the Opium Trade', in Antonio Giustozzi (ed.), *Decoding the New Taliban: Insights from the Afghan Field*, London: C. Hurst and Company, 2009, pp. 7–22.

Radin, Christian and Bill Roggio (2008) 'Afghanistan: Mapping the Violence', *The Long War Journal* website, online, available on www.longwarjournal.org/archives/2008/08/afghanistan_mapping.php

Rashid, Ahmed, *Taliban: The Story of the Afghan Warlords*, London: Pan Books, 2nd edition, 2001.

Rashid, Ahmed, (2006) 'Afghanistan on the Brink', *New York Review*, 22 June 2006, online, available on www.ahmedrashid.com/publications/afganistan/articles/

Rashid, Ahmed, *Descent into Chaos: How the War against Islamic Extremism is being Lost in Pakistan, Afghanistan and Central Asia*, London: Allen Lane, 2008.

Rashid, Ahmed, (2011) 'The Way Out of Afghanistan', *New York Review of Books*, 13 January 2011, online, available on www.nybooks.com/articles/archives/2011/jan/13/way-out-afghanistan/?pagination=false

RUSI/FPRI, (2009) *Reforming the Afghan National Police*, online, available on www.rusi.org/downloads/assets/ANP_Nov09.pdf

Smith, Graeme, 'What Kandahar's Taliban Say' in Antonio Giustozzi (ed.), *Decoding the New Taliban: Insights from the Afghan Field*, London: C. Hurst and Company, 2009, pp. 191–210.

The Asia Foundation, (2010) *Key Findings: A Survey of the Afghan People 2010*, online, available on http://asiafoundation.org/resources/pdfs/KeyFindingsAGSurvey2010.pdf

Tidsall, Simon, (2010) 'India and Pakistan's Proxy War puts Afghanistan Exit at Risk', *Guardian*, 7 May 2010, online, available on www.guardian.co.uk/commentisfree/2010/may/06/india-pakistan-afghanistan-exit

Torfeh, Massoumeh, 'Iran is Buying Influence in Afghanistan', *Guardian*, 26 October 2010, online, available on www.guardian.co.uk/commentisfree/2010/oct/26/iran-cash-payments-to-afghanistan

UN Secretary-General's Report on Afghanistan, (December 2010) A/65/612–S/2010/630, online, available on http://unama.unmissions.org/Portals/UNAMA/SG%20Reports/SG%20REPORT_10DEC2010.pdf

UNODC, (2008) *World Drug Report 2008*, online, available on www.unodc.org/documents/wdr/WDR_2008/WDR2008_Statistical_Annex_Consumption.pdf

UNODC, (December 2010) *Afghanistan Opium Survey*, online, available on www.unodc.org/documents/crop-monitoring/Afghanistan/Afghanistan_Opium_Survey_2010_web.pdf

Woodward, Bob, *Obama's Wars: The Inside Story*, London: Simon & Schuster, 2010.

3 Nuclear weapons in South Asia

Theoretical implications

Nicolas Blarel

The notion of deterrence and its theoretical foundations emerged from the experience of the US-Soviet nuclear confrontation during the 50 years of the cold war. Much of this literature has focused on bipolar opposition and the implications for reducing large-scale wars, ignoring the operation of nuclear deterrence in limited wars in a more regional context.[1] The end of the cold war and the spread of nuclear weapons to new players encouraged scholars to reassess the conventional wisdom which had prevailed around deterrence as a leading theoretical and policy framework. Much of the cold war deterrence literature had indeed relied on abstract formulations and deductively interesting and parsimonious models derived from microeconomic theories.[2] Taking into account the growing complexity in deterrence relationships, new studies have concentrated on conflicts between regional adversaries, as in South Asia, to resume their debate on the effects of nuclear deterrence on stability as well as to find new theoretical insights.[3]

However, do these stylized models fare well in the light of specific case studies? With the exception of the broad cold war confrontation, has deterrence theory ever properly been tested? This chapter argues that the South Asian security environment offers an interesting context to revisit, evaluate and refine the existing conceptualizations of deterrence theory. Despite the absence of direct and large-scale conflicts in the past 20 years,[4] there has been a series of crises between India and Pakistan that could have potentially turned nuclear.[5] These repeated crises are all cases where nuclear weapons' impact on regional stability and crisis management can be assessed. Instead of using arguments derived from the cold war history to explain the behavior of newly nuclearized states, South Asia's recent history with nuclear weapons may offer more pertinent lessons.

Since the Indian and Pakistani nuclear tests in May 1998, there has been an emerging and prolific literature on the origins of nuclearization in South Asia but also on the new implications this enduring rivalry between two nuclear powers will have for existing theories of nuclear deterrence. A first wave of scholars focused mostly on explaining the external and internal mechanisms behind India's decisions to become openly nuclear.[6] Other scholars have studied the impact of nuclearization on strategic stability in South Asia.[7] This debate over the effects of nuclear proliferation in South Asia was an extension of the broader theoretical debate between the 'optimistic' and 'pessimistic' camps.[8] Finally, some scholars have looked more closely at India's and Pakistan's evolving nuclear doctrines since 1998.[9]

This chapter begins by reviewing this rich literature, which empirically tested existing deterrence theories in the South Asian context. The aim of the first part of this chapter is not to take a particular stand in the existing theoretical debates. The objective of a selective synthesis of the existing literature is to demonstrate that there is in fact considerable overlap in different efforts to explain stability and instability in the region. What mainly distinguishes the various approaches is the phase of the nuclear crisis they concentrate on. While most optimist accounts are outcome-based and emphasize the ultimately stable resolutions of past nuclear crises, pessimists will be more attentive to initiation and escalation phases leading to crises.[10] This difference of focus in their analyses explains their diverging perspectives on the nuclear future of South Asia. Bridging these exaggerated differences and encouraging further dialogue between these scholars is necessary to fully account for nuclear behavior in the region.

The second part of this chapter will then discuss the necessity to go beyond models and concepts derived from the cold war experience that are applied to all emerging nuclear dyads. Existing deterrence theories might produce totally different and even opposite effects in varying contexts. Hence, this chapter describes how new nuclear considerations have interacted with regional-specific factors. This chapter emphasizes two important differences. First, Indo-Pakistani strategic behaviors and nuclear doctrines can also be influenced by external nuclear powers that have interests in the region like the US and China. There is no precedence in the literature on such complex, multi-level nuclear triangular (or quadrangular?) relations, and on how they actually impact both Indian and Pakistani security and deterrence calculations.[11] Second, the role of non-state actors, whether proxies or not of Pakistan, are another factor neglected by traditional studies. Both crises of December 2001 and November 2008 were attacks from non-state actors that could have led to an escalation to a large-scale conflict with potential nuclear consequences.[12] The aim of this chapter is therefore to point towards new avenues of analysis which could contribute to the broader theoretical debate.

Deterrence in South Asia: moving beyond the optimist–pessimist debate

A prolific scholarship has been interested in testing old deterrence concepts using the South Asian context. This section will concentrate on this emerging literature, which has evolved from an inductive approach, testing the central premises of rational deterrence theory in the South Asian context, to a more fertile debate sensitive to the specific features of the South Asian security environment.

Deterrence and strategic stability in South Asia

Deterrence theory remains one of the most prolific bodies of literature in international relations. Since the 1940s, scholars have argued that a 'nuclear revolution' had made large-scale conventional conflicts between great powers all but obsolete.[13] Nuclear optimists, such as Kenneth Waltz, have even argued that the continued proliferation of nuclear weapons had the potential to help stabilize regional conflicts as well.[14] The argument was that the possession of nuclear weapons raised the costs of conventional conflicts and therefore increased the risks of escalation. Nevertheless, other scholars have been more skeptical, and even actively pessimistic, about the alleged stabilizing effects of nuclear weapons.[15] These pessimists stressed other factors to account for cold-war peace, such as painful memories of World War II and increasing economic interdependence. The optimist–pessimist debate on deterrence has been translated to the South Asian context.

There are two periods in this literature. Earlier scholarship was more interested in simply testing old theoretical debates on deterrence using the South Asian context. The most famous example of this trend was the 2003 exchange between Scott Sagan and Kenneth Waltz opposing the traditional (i.e., cold war-based) ways of thinking about nuclear South Asia. The authors disagreed on the consequences of nuclear weapons for stability on the subcontinent, with Sagan expressing a generally pessimistic perspective, and Waltz advancing a nuanced optimism.[16] In spite of the Kargil and 2001–2 crises, Waltz observed no differences between nuclearized India and Pakistan and other traditional nuclear powers that would make him think nuclear weapons would not have the same stabilizing effects.[17] In fact, he argued that Kargil essentially proved his point about stability: it was a much more limited and concentrated conflict than the previous Indo-Pakistani wars, which spiraled into full-fledged wars involving more casualties and which were spread out along most of the border.

By contrast, Sagan emphasized organizational factors such as the absence of effective policy coordination and nuclear safeguards (especially in Pakistan where the nuclear arsenal is under de facto military control), as well as other background factors that existed independently of the nuclearization of South Asia, such as India and Pakistan's shared history of conflict and the dispute over Kashmir.[18] Sagan more recently described how strong personalities, domestic politics, accidents, organizational compulsions and mistakes could lead to a breakdown of deterrence.[19] Sagan notably criticized one of the main assumptions of the deterrence model which presumed that all nuclear-armed states are rational unitary actors. Because of these fragmented decision-making processes in the nuclear domain, India and Pakistan are anything but unitary actors. However, Sagan still argued that there were some reasonable comparisons to be made between the South Asian and cold war contexts. Sagan had made similar pessimist organizational arguments about US and Soviet decision-making during the cold war. His conclusion was that such organizational pathologies are equally present in India and Pakistan.

Following this introductory debate, the literature was considerably improved and qualified by more recent work by Sumit Ganguly, Devin Hagerty and Paul Kapur which combined theoretically-informed analysis with extensive empirical description.[20] This new scholarship encouraged a healthy debate between deterrence optimists and proliferation pessimists.

Ganguly and Hagerty became the leading proponents of this camp of deterrence optimists. Similarly to Waltz, they believed that 'there is no more ironclad law in international relations theory than this: nuclear weapon states do not fight wars with one another.'[21] However, they also qualified this argument by admitting that nuclear weapons could constitute one of the many factors inciting actors to undertake low-intensity conflicts.[22] Because new nuclear powers needed to learn the opportunities and limits their nuclear arsenals provided them, there has been a learning process over the last 20 years. The occurrence of four major crises within this period proved that South Asia had not been the stable and peaceful region it should have become according to classical deterrence theories. The authors nevertheless remained optimistic that India and Pakistan would learn from their own mistakes and successes.[23] Nuclear weapons have helped stabilize an otherwise volatile region which witnessed three major conflicts in 1947, 1965 and 1971. According to Ganguly, the contrast with the pre-nuclear era confirmed the robustness of the nuclear deterrence argument, as no crisis in the last 20 years escalated to a major war.[24]

Optimists argued that India's restraint in different crises such as Kargil and the December 2001 attack on Parliament reflected its overriding concern to limit escalatory potential so as not to provoke a nuclear Pakistan.[25] For instance, though India considered sending its ground forces across the Line of Control (LoC) to attack Pakistani positions in less difficult terrain, it ultimately refrained from doing so.[26] Nuclear weapons could also explain why India limited itself to coercive diplomacy in the aftermath of the terrorist attack on the Indian Parliament in 2001.[27] Finally most deterrence optimists argued that nuclear learning has occurred between Indian and Pakistani policy-makers since 2003. Both sides have developed doctrines and stronger command-and-control mechanisms to ensure that future crises could be defused in a less dangerous manner. Additionally, optimists believed that nuclear weapons played a decisive role in encouraging new dialogues to resolve the Kashmir dispute and to adopt confidence-building measures following the 2001–2 crisis.[28] Basing themselves mainly on the relatively peaceful outcomes of these crises and the non-use of nuclear weapons, deterrence optimists argued that a shared fear of nuclear escalation and its disastrous consequences had prevented major war and dangerous escalation on the subcontinent.

In opposition, pessimists maintained that more nuclear weapons will result in more dangers and perhaps nuclear confrontation. However, this new wave of deterrence pessimists moved away from the dominant school of proliferation pessimism represented by Sagan. Because of the rational-actor assumption, most deterrence scholars had indeed neglected as irrational all deviant behavior from new nuclear powers that could create conditions for nuclear confrontation.[29] For instance, Sagan argued that shortcomings and fragmentation within the organizations controlling nuclear weapons in India and especially in Pakistan made nuclear escalation more credible in the South Asian context. As organizational problems interfered with the rational process of strategic policy formulation, there were no guarantees that nuclear weapon states would not act dangerously.[30] While there were many merits in analyzing the many irregularities in the nuclear decision-making processes in the subcontinent, this type of argument implied that both Pakistan and India had no rational or strategic motivations when provoking nuclear standoffs in the last 20 years.

This is why new studies have tried to explain how the possession of nuclear weapons actually facilitated limited or proxy wars. A new critical concept nuancing the 'strategic stability' argument of deterrence came to be known as the stability-instability paradox.[31] Some scholars argued that this situation has been witnessed in South Asia: the nuclearization of the subcontinent could be perceived as an insurance policy against the most dangerous types of escalation, thereby encouraging war-making below the nuclear threshold.[32] Kapur equally observed a direct causal relationship: as Pakistan's strategic elite became more confident of their country's limited nuclear capability, they began to perceive it as a kind of shield.[33] This new scholarship posed a stronger challenge to the optimist's core logic by arguing that the acquisition of nuclear weapons in the South Asian context had adverse effects. Since the Indo-Pakistani conflict of 1971, India had a conventional military superiority over its adversary. This military imbalance was correlated with almost 30 years of relative absence of major conflicts.[34] After 1998, nuclear weapons actually reversed this military balance and emboldened a more secured Pakistan to engage in aggressive behavior.[35]

Kapur went further than most pessimists in arguing that given certain conditions, the possession of nuclear weapons actually created 'strong incentives for rational states to adopt aggressive, extremely risky policies.'[36] The acquisition of nuclear capabilities was interpreted as an opportunity for Pakistani leaders to pursue their revisionist territorial goals. Despite the relative calm that prevailed in the region following the 1971 Bangladesh war, Kashmir remained an unresolved issue for the Pakistani elites. As a result, nuclear weapons altered the traditional cost-benefit calculations and emboldened Pakistan to lead a more activist and risky policy in Kashmir, first by indirectly supporting militant groups in the 1990s and then by sending troops into Indian-held territory in Kashmir in 1999.[37] Pakistani decision-makers predicted that lower-level military operations would restrict India's options as escalation up the nuclear ladder would be too dangerous. Similarly, in 2001–2 and in spite of the failure of the Kargil operation, Pakistani leaders still felt confident they could sustain a proxy war against India by supporting militant attacks against targets in India.[38] As a result, Kapur argued that not only did nuclear weapons not deter Pakistan from pursuing military operations, but that overt nuclear capacities actually created favorable conditions for Pakistan to pressure India. According to this very pessimist appraisal of the new strategic situation in South Asia, which has been termed 'strategic pessimism,' nuclear weapons have facilitated the outbreak of lower-level conflict after years of stability.[39]

Bridging the divide

Recent studies have certainly brought the optimism/pessimism debate to a stimulating new level of conceptual nuance and sophistication. However, for this literature to continue to provide some important insights to the broader nuclear deterrence research program, scholars contributing to this debate need to revisit the theoretical bases of their arguments in order to clarify their differences and similarities. If both theoretical camps develop their arguments in isolation and refuse to engage in a systematic and substantial fashion, it will be difficult to appraise progress in deterrence theory. Both theoretical perspectives will unabatedly support their respective arguments in parallel and with limited dialogue.

For instance, optimists and pessimists see the ambiguous evidence provided by the recent nuclear crises in diverging lights. Both camps used the conflict in Kargil as a major example supporting their theses.[40] For the pessimists, Kargil served as an ominous warning that conventional conflicts would persist in nuclear South Asia, as nuclear weapons enabled Pakistan to pursue its revisionist ambitions with greater security guarantees. By contrast, optimists observed Kargil as essentially proving their point about stability. Kargil was the most limited of all India–Pakistan wars to date, fought on a limited scale and dimension. Furthermore, the crisis was resolved before it could escalate to a full-fledged war. On what criteria can we evaluate which is the most convincing argument? Do these opposing scholars share some minimum theoretical and empirical standards?

This chapter argues that these over-exaggerated theoretical disagreements are not completely unreconcilable. There is in fact considerable overlap between these different studies and there are many agreements on certain strategic developments in the region. What mainly divided the various approaches is that they focused on different phases of the nuclear crisis process. Optimist accounts have concentrated on the outcome of the crisis and therefore appropriately highlighted the 'relatively benign nature of past history.'[41] On the other hand, pessimists have traced the initiation and escalation processes. This has led them to view the recurring nuclear crises as increasingly more dangerous.[42] Scholars have to move beyond the opposing outcome-based and process-based approaches which focus on different dependent variables (conflict initiation vs. conflict resolution) and which follow very opposite dynamics. Instead, encouraging dialogue between these scholars looking at different phases of nuclear crises would help to fully account for nuclear behavior in South Asia.

There are some areas of agreement between optimists and pessimists. One of the main accepted standards is that the deductive models of deterrence that were developed during the cold war cannot be applied to the South Asian context without some important caveats. Traditional deterrence arguments interact with contextual factors specific to the South Asian case such as territorial disputes, asymmetry of conventional forces, and other histories of animosity.[43] Such non-nuclear factors can explain how nuclear weapons have impacted differently the Indo-Pakistani nuclear rivalry. The Pakistani elite's revisionist goals over the

Kashmir dispute can for example explain why Pakistan has remained committed to an aggressive behavior in spite of nuclear risks.[44]

Another area of convergence among deterrence scholars in South Asia is the sentiment that it was because of nuclear weapons that the past crises did not escalate to major wars. Nuclear deterrence induced some level of caution among decision-makers after each crisis was initiated. Optimists and pessimists still disagreed on the actual significance of the nuclear weapon factor in relation to other important variables like American diplomatic intervention or the asymmetry of conventional forces. But in the end, most agreed that nuclear weapons have played some role in the relatively stable outcome of past nuclear crises.[45] Optimists and pessimists also seemed to agree that there had been some level of nuclear learning in the region following the different crises. However, while optimists became more confident about South Asian strategic stability in the aftermath of the various crises, pessimists remained cautious about the future possibility of crossing nuclear 'red lines' if India and Pakistan misperceived the lessons from past disputes.[46]

Finally, both optimists and pessimists are conscious that the growing role of non-state actors in provoking these nuclear standoffs adds an element of complexity to the traditional deterrence framework.[47] Future studies will therefore have to take into account the learning processes from the previous crises, as well as the interference of non-state actors, in a more systematic manner.

Beyond theory-testing: what can South Asia bring to the broader theoretical debate?

Looking beyond the debate on the success of nuclear deterrence, the South Asian history and context have also introduced new contextual variables which have problematized deterrence logic in different ways. According to historical deterrence studies, the cold war saw a simplified opposition between two unitary and rational states.[48] The US and the USSR were the two sole superpowers which were incorporated into the deterrence dynamic. Most deterrence-based concepts such as mutual assured destruction almost exclusively assumed a two-state opposition. Consequently, earlier scholarship analyzing the nuclearization of the India–Pakistan rivalry has neglected the triangular (or quadrangular?), as opposed to bipolar, security architecture that has emerged in South Asia.[49]

The opposition between nuclearized India and Pakistan has attracted international attention and most especially interventions, from China as a neighboring nuclear power, as well as the US as the preeminent extra-regional power. China still has an unresolved border dispute with India and has been providing assistance to Pakistan's nuclear program.[50] Additionally, the US shares certain interests with both South Asian states and has the potential to exert significant diplomatic, economic, and even military influence in the region.[51] The implication of these two other actors' interests in the region is that strategies in Delhi and Islamabad are elaborated anticipating the possibility of an external power's intervention. This often neglected factor is crucial to understanding the dynamic leading to the different South Asian nuclear crises over the last 15 years. A growing scholarship led by regional specialists has analyzed this tendency toward trilateral 'compellent' strategies by both India and Pakistan, notably putting the US in the challenging position of trying to play the 'pivot.'[52]

Another important factor neglected by earlier deterrence studies in the South Asian context is the rising role of non-state actors in the outbreak and/or escalation of Indo-Pakistani nuclear crises. Classical deterrence theories have notably failed to explain the recurrence of Indo-Pakistani crises since 1998. If one sticks to the traditional deterrence logic, the Pakistani and Indian governments would have found conflict prohibitively risky. Furthermore, the November 2008 terrorist attack in the city of Mumbai committed by Pakistan-based militants presented Indian policy-makers with an important strategic dilemma: how can India deter such attacks?[53] Can groups like Lashkar-e-Taiba be deterred by a threat of nuclear retaliation? Because of India's conventional military superiority and the nuclearization of the subcontinent, Pakistani strategists have increasingly relied on these unconventional means to keep New Delhi off-balance and to tie down large numbers of Indian forces in the Kashmir region. Such non-state actors have been at the origin of the 2001–2 and 2008 crises and could play an even greater role in future standoffs as they move away from state control and take on a life of their own. Terrorist groups add one more layer of complexity to the deterrence framework in the South Asian context, and the role of proxies in a nuclear rivalry needs to be further analyzed.

The irrelevance of the nuclear dyad framework and the role of third-party actors

Most scholarly studies on deterrence in the South Asian context have neglected the possibility that states such as India and Pakistan may employ different strategies of nuclear diplomacy than the cold war rivals did. Since the nuclearization of South Asia pushed external actors such as the US to monitor regional developments more closely, India and Pakistan have used their nuclear capacities to provoke crises in order to draw external powers into the conflicts. Sagan was the first to elaborate on the possibility that external nuclear powers (such as the United States) could intervene in crises in South Asia as a constraint or an incentive for escalation.[54]

More recently, Ganguly and Hagerty accorded an important role to US diplomacy in defusing tensions in 1990 and 1999, and preventing the outbreak of major war in 2001–2.[55] Kapur later argued that the possibility of external intervention actually encouraged the governments of India and Pakistan to engage in risky behavior, provoking crises and/or making limited uses of force.[56] After the US intervened to de-escalate tensions in 1990 and especially during the Kargil crisis of 1999,[57] regional nuclear powers became convinced they could resort to military standoffs in anticipation of US mediation to their advantage. Such strategies could have led to unintended escalation, because of miscalculation of the other side's reaction. For instance, an Indian action intended as a signal to the international audience might inadvertently have crossed a 'red line' for Pakistan, or vice versa. Similarly to nuclear weapons in the optimist-pessimist debate, US diplomatic interventions had a double effect: first, they did prevent military escalation as an outcome, but they also had a second perverse effect in that they created diplomatic incentives for frustrated states to engage in aggressive military behavior.[58]

In most of these works, however, American involvement was mainly described and remained under-theorized. Studies attempting to account for the third-party factor have only included it as a secondary variable and remained silent on the role of China in exacerbating regional nuclear tensions. Lately, there have been a few attempts to theorize third-party intervention. Basrur was the first to note that 'South Asia's nuclear rivals have added a new dimension' to the generally bilateral politics of nuclear weapons 'by involving a third country.'[59] He also labeled the strategy, in which one principal actor aims simultaneously to affect the behavior both of its adversary and of the extra-regional power, 'trilateral compellence.'[60] Originally, a compellent strategy meant one seeking to alter the status quo, by using force or the threat of force to 'compel' another state to change its behavior. Compellence therefore differs from deterrence, which seeks to maintain the status quo.[61] Basrur argued that both India and Pakistan at different times had sought to compel one another to follow a particular diplomatic course, by provoking crises with potential escalatory potential in the nuclearized region in order to compel diplomatic intervention by a stronger extra-regional power such as the US, in a way that would advance their preferences.[62]

Jason Kirk equally pointed out that the only constant variable in the three nuclear-era crises (1990, 1999, and 2001–2) was that all three were brought to a pacific outcome under the arbitration of American diplomacy.[63] Kirk argued that this dimension of external intervention and its strategic implications could be a new theoretical insight to the deterrence literature, the novel dimension being that 'a stronger, extra-regional power with its own interest in preventing a regional nuclear war might intervene diplomatically in a crisis – and that the very expectation of such high-level intervention might lead South Asian leaders to manipulate the threat of nuclear war.'[64] Kirk described deterrence in this context as 'pivotal' with the US as external power (a 'pivot') having an interest in deterring India and Pakistan from attacking each other.[65] In other words, using its considerable diplomatic and economic resources, the US has exercised effective 'pivotal deterrence' over the course of several serious crises in nuclear South Asia, while avoiding long-term military commitments or offering full political support to either side.[66] As there is no record of such outside pivotal intervention in cold war nuclear calculations, this is a purely South Asian dynamic which could eventually be explored in other contexts. The mere possibility of such external interventions has deeply shaped nuclear strategies for India and Pakistan in ways that conventional deterrence theories could not anticipate.

While there have been some interesting attempts to theorize the impact of the US factor on the Indo-Pakistani nuclear rivalry, there has been much less theoretical and even empirical work on the Chinese factor.[67] Chinese influence is covert and therefore less visible and directly observable than US mediation in Indo-Pakistani crises. For example, already in 2004, Lowell Dittmer intentionally included China as part of a 'triangular' security architecture in South Asia, even more so than the US.[68] Although there could be disagreements on the actual significance of the Chinese factor in the nuclear rivalry, there is a history of conflict with India and a highly documented history of nuclear co-operation with Pakistan. The opacity of actual exchanges between Pakistan and China and of Chinese intentions in the region makes any attempt to theorize the Chinese factor a more complex enterprise.

In coming years, a rising China could become a decisive factor in either or both of the states' strategies. As with the US factor, both states are progressively learning what China's intentions and potential capabilities are in the regional security environment.[69] For instance, the expansion of India's military industry (both of its conventional military capabilities and of its missile programs) has not been directed solely at Pakistan but has also developed in order to counter a rising China. India's military buildup has had negative effects on Pakistan's nuclear calculations.[70] The growing imbalance in conventional military capabilities in the region has been encouraging Pakistan to rely more heavily on its nuclear deterrent as well as on its unconventional assets such as militants operating in Kashmir. The missile defense program has also alarmed Pakistani decision-makers and created incentives for aggressive regional behavior.[71] Facing an India with even a modest missile defense capacity, Pakistan could perceive its arsenal as no longer sufficient to deter any Indian attacks. It would therefore need to strike before India possessed such capabilities, or at least it would need to invest in expanding its nuclear arsenal in order to have an extended chance to reach enemy territory.[72] While India has been focusing on nuclear deterrence with China, justifying larger military and nuclear forces to compete with Beijing, the expansion of Indian forces has also indirectly driven the continued growth of Pakistan's nuclear arsenal and encouraged an arms race in the region.

Another indirect and under-theorized aspect of the Chinese factor is the historic Sino-Pakistani nuclear co-operation. China has long supported Pakistan's nuclear and military programs to check Indian power.[73] Sino-Pakistan ties gained particular momentum in the aftermath of the 1962 Sino-Indian war when the two states signed a boundary agreement recognizing Chinese control over portions of disputed Kashmir.[74] Beijing has also provided extensive economic, military and technical assistance to Pakistan over the years. In this partnership, China has had a crucial role in the development of Pakistan's nuclear infrastructure.[75] In general, most of China's nuclear exports and co-operative projects have been for non-weapons purposes, but the father of Pakistan's nuclear weapons program, A.Q. Khan, has acknowledged the crucial role China played in his nation's nuclear weaponization by offering 50 kilograms of weapons-grade enriched uranium, nuclear weapons blueprints and uranium hexafluoride for Pakistan's centrifuges.[76] Sino-Pakistan nuclear collusion has continued despite the fact that

China is a Non-Proliferation Treaty (NPT) signatory. For example, China announced in late April the sale of two nuclear reactors to Pakistan. This deal was clearly against the guidelines of the Nuclear Suppliers Group (NSG) and the spirit if not the letter of the nuclear Non-Proliferation Treaty.[77] By providing crucial assistance to Pakistan's nuclear capabilities, China intends to constrain India's rise as a competitor.[78]

This new literature must not make the mistake of identifying American and Chinese interventions as the sole and most decisive factors explaining escalation or de-escalation of nuclear crises, but it will be important to evaluate its inter-action with existing traditional arguments emphasizing bilateral nuclear deter-rence. There is obviously a correlation between the nuclearization of the subcontinent and increasing diplomatic intervention. Active US mediation had never occurred at this level until the de facto nuclearization of South Asia in the early 1990s. The fear of nuclear escalation first attracted US attention in 1990. The Gates mission to de-escalate tensions between India and Pakistan in this first nuclear crisis created a decisive precedent in Indian and Pakistani strategists' calculations.[79] The indirect and opaque Chinese factor has also added more com-plexity to the traditional bilateral deterrence framework.

Findings about the US role in South Asian nuclear stability have remained ambiguous. While officially rejecting US intervention, both India and Pakistan relied on the US in the different crises to guide bilateral and regional discus-sions. Pakistani and Indian trilateral compellence has so far focused on the US as the 'pivot' power and there is no a priori reason for either side to expect a very different reaction in the next crisis. As a result, there still exists a potential for future crises in which both actors would want to refine their strategies in accordance with their own expectations of US arbitration. However, in any future crisis, there is little assurance that Washington would always be able to offer face-saving ways for the participants to back down and de-escalate the crisis. Such complex triangular and/or quadrangular deterrence relationships will most probably be the norm of the future in East Asia and the Middle East. In this context, the study of the South Asian situation delivers important insights.

The disturbing impact of non-state actors

Another factor in South Asia which challenged the traditional deterrence logic was the rise of new kinds of actors whose organizational structures, motivations and strategies differed sharply from those of states. Most studies looking at ter-rorism with nuclear implications in the post-cold war period have concentrated on the possibility of a terrorist attack using a nuclear bomb.[80] Many analysts have also been concerned about the potential risk of a Pakistani nuclear weapon falling into the hands of terrorists.[81] While the domestic situation in Pakistan remains volatile, this concern has often been exaggerated.[82] In fact, the most immediate threat in the South Asian context is the role of non-state groups in instigating major diplomatic crises with escalatory potential. Terrorist groups, whether they are official proxies or not, have had a strong impact on the Indo-Pakistani nuclear rivalry.

There has been a long history of Pakistani-sponsored militancy in the Kashmir region. First, feeling threatened by India's conventional military superiority, Pakistan has armed, trained and given sanctuary to terror organizations such as Lashkar-e-Taiba, using them as tools of asymmetric warfare to tie down large numbers of Indian armed forces in Kashmir.[83] Second, the nuclearization of the subcontinent has further encouraged the Pakistani military to pursue this unofficial and opportune strategy of asymmetric warfare on Indian territory.[84] In the traditional deterrence logic, India could have signaled credible nuclear threats which would have made Pakistani-sponsored attacks against India prohibitively costly. Instead, the fear of nuclear escalation has limited India's strategic options for retaliation.[85] Furthermore, because the Pakistani state has progressively lost control over the militants, classical nuclear threats have not deterred terrorists. This highlights the need for future scholarship to analyze the implications of terrorism under the shadow of nuclear weapons.

Indeed, Pakistan's historic support for anti-Indian militancy in the Kashmir region has created an array of terrorist groups that Islamabad is no longer able to control.[86] These groups have further moved away from Pakistani sponsorship as they have obtained funding from international networks.[87] These increasingly independent non-state actors are not affected by deterrence or mutually assured destruction considerations. As future crises can erupt without any deliberate decisions taken by Pakistani leaders, risks of nuclear escalation have become more probable.[88] While the terrorist campaign may not have been part of any official Pakistani strategy, it has led India to react in order to preserve the credibility of its nuclear deterrent. India's refusal to accept Pakistan's nuclear blackmail led to two major diplomatic crises with a potential for nuclear escalation, in 2001–2 and 2008.[89]

As some of these terrorists groups operated in Pakistan, one potential solution has been for India to threaten to punish Pakistan directly, rather than the terrorists themselves. Indian decision-makers have warned the Pakistani government of possible direct retaliation if it allowed terrorist groups to continue operating from its soil. This solved the problem of attribution which is a determinant for successful deterrence. However, the failure of operation Parakram in 2001–2 to obtain Pakistani guarantees to fight terrorism within its own territory demonstrated the practical difficulties of deterring such low-level and unconventional threats with coercive diplomacy. Since the December 2001 terrorist attack, Indian strategists have been actively working to find an operational answer to cope with this new threat. One recent attempt to deal with this strategic challenge was the development of India's 'Cold Start' doctrine.[90] The objective of this new doctrine would be to take hold of an important part of Pakistani territory, sufficiently large to harm Pakistan, but not so large as to threaten the Pakistani state's survival.[91] The problems with the operationalization of the Cold Start doctrine were that it could still create conditions for nuclear war and that it did not solve the long-term problem of Pakistan-based anti-Indian militancy.[92]

As this situation involving rogue non-state groups in a nuclear rivalry could be reproduced in other contexts such as the Middle East, findings from the South Asian region provide important insights.

Conclusions

Even though the proliferation of nuclear weapons by India and Pakistan has been one of the most significant strategic developments of the post-cold war period, and even though South Asia exhibits many contextual features that might make the India–Pakistan nuclear relationship considerably different from the US–Soviet rivalry, the analysis of nuclear behavior in the subcontinent has been too strongly conditioned by theoretical frameworks inherited from the cold war experience. It is only recently, after the publication of new theoretically-informed analyses of the past India–Pakistan crises, that scholars have begun to take note of the triangular, coercive diplomacy dynamics and the role of non-state actors that distinguish this region from other security environments. There are two important implications for the study of nuclear proliferation coming from the South Asian context.

First, the fact that regional nuclear weapons states might engage in triangular coercive diplomacy, using the threat of conflict escalation to compel intervention by an outside power, is an important finding with potential implications both for the future of South Asia itself, and for great-power diplomacy beyond the region. For example, there could be theoretical lessons for another troubled region such as the Middle East. Israel is already believed to possess an opaque nuclear capability, and Iran is an important proliferation concern for the US. It might be suggested that the US could engage in a similar exercise of 'pivotal deterrence.' However, specific contextual factors could also alter these calculations, as the US has had a more decisive historic alliance with Israel as well as crucial economic interests in the region.[93]

Second, different theories of deterrence have shown their limited explanatory leverage in accounting for or predicting the outbreak of crises between newly nuclearized states. In fact, in order to obtain better explanations and predictions of conflict in South Asia, the literature seems to turn to non-nuclear related and more idiosyncratic explanations. Factors such as domestic politics,[94] Pakistan's irredentist claim to Kashmir, the imbalance in conventional military capabilities or the increasing use of asymmetric warfare and proxy militant groups have been equally important or even more decisive in explaining the initiation and resolution of crises.[95] Since political instability in South Asia existed before and independently from nuclear weapons, the nuclearization of the subcontinent has not profoundly modified the Indo-Pakistani rivalry. Nuclear forces can be interpreted more as intervening variables, interacting with other preexisting non-nuclear factors, either increasing or limiting their salience. Although nuclear forces have induced some level of caution in crisis management, recent crises also demonstrated an increased confidence for both actors to conduct conventional war under the nuclear shadow. If New Delhi does develop its 'Cold Start' doctrine of air strikes combined with the capture of non-vital Pakistani territory in response to the rising threat of asymmetric warfare, the next crisis on the subcontinent could even spiral into a new type of conflict.

Notes

1 T.V. Paul, P.M. Morgan and J.J. Wirtz (eds), *Complex Deterrence*, 2009.
2 T.C. Schelling, *The Strategy of Conflict*, 1960; R. Lebow and J.G. Stein, 'Rational Deterrence Theory', 1989.
3 See for example the new edition of S.D. Sagan and K.N. Waltz, *The Spread of Nuclear Weapons: A Debate Renewed*, New York: W.W. Norton, 2003, with a specific new chapter on India and Pakistan.
4 Although the Kargil conflict could be interpreted as full-scale war, as there were more than a thousand fatalities: S.D. Sagan (ed.), *Inside Nuclear South Asia*, 2009, pp. 3–4.
5 This chapter will not delve into the empirical details of the different South Asian security crises of the last 20 years, encompassing both the 'opaque' or de facto nuclear period of the 1980s and 1990s before the nuclear tests, and the more recent post-test conflicts, but will instead focus on their theoretical implications for the study of deterrence. For more detailed accounts of these standoffs, see S. Ganguly and D.T. Hagerty, *Fearful Symmetry*, 2005; P.R. Chari, P.I. Cheema and S.P. Cohen, *Four Crises and a Peace Process*, 2007; S. Ganguly and S.P Kapur (eds), *Nuclear Proliferation in South Asia*, 2009.
6 See for example G. Perkovich, *India's Nuclear Bomb*, 1999; A.J. Tellis, *India's Emerging Nuclear Posture*, 2001.
7 Ganguly and Hagerty, *Fearful Symmetry*; S.P. Kapur, *Dangerous Deterrent*, 2007.
8 J. Knopf, 'Recasting the Optimism-Pessimism Debate', 2002; Ganguly and Kapur (eds), *Nuclear proliferation in South Asia*, 2009; Ganguly and Kapur, *India, Pakistan and the Bomb*, 2010.
9 R.M. Basrur, *Minimum Deterrence and India's Nuclear Security*, 2006; S.D. Sagan, 'The Evolution of Pakistani and Indian Nuclear Doctrine', 2009; J.A. Kirk, 'The Evolution of India's Nuclear Policies', 2009.
10 Ganguly and Kapur, *India, Pakistan and the Bomb*, p. 5.
11 K. Booth and N.J. Wheeler, *The Security Dilemma*, 2008, pp. 284–8.
12 S.P. Kapur, 'Deterrence and Asymmetric Warfare', *Seminar* 599, July 2009.
13 R. Jervis, *The Meaning of the Nuclear Revolution*, 1989.
14 K.N. Waltz, *The Spread of Nuclear Weapons: More May be Better*, 1981.
15 Sagan and Waltz, *The Spread of Nuclear Weapons*, pp. 90–108.
16 Ibid., pp. 88–124.
17 Ibid., pp. 123–4.
18 Ibid., pp. 90–108.
19 Sagan (ed.), *Inside Nuclear South Asia*, pp. 219–63.
20 Ganguly and Hagerty, *Fearful Symmetry*; Kapur, *Dangerous Deterrent*.
21 D.T. Hagerty, *The Consequences of Nuclear Proliferation*, 1998, p. 184.
22 Ganguly and Kapur (eds), *Nuclear Proliferation in South Asia*, p. 101.
23 Ganguly and Kapur, *India, Pakistan and the Bomb*, pp. 25–6.
24 Ganguly and Kapur, *India, Pakistan and the Bomb*, p. 33.
25 D.T. Hagerty, 'The Kargil War', 2009.
26 Ganguly and Kapur, *India, Pakistan and the Bomb*, pp. 47–9.
27 P. Swami, 'A War to End a War', 2009.
28 Ibid.
29 J.G. Stein, 'Rational Deterrence against "Irrational" Adversaries?', 2009, pp. 60–1.
30 Sagan and Waltz, *The Spread of Nuclear Weapons*, pp. 90–108.
31 In *The Illogic of American Nuclear Strategy*, 1984, Robert Jervis defined the paradox:

'to the extent that the military balance is stable at the level of all-out nuclear war, it will become less stable at lower levels of violence,' p. 31.

32 M. Krepon, *The Stability-Instability Paradox*, 2003.
33 Kapur, *Dangerous Deterrent*, p. 93.
34 Ganguly and Kapur, *India, Pakistan and the Bomb*, pp. 15–16.
35 Kapur, *Dangerous Deterrent*, pp. 115–40.
36 Ganguly and Kapur, *India, Pakistan and the Bomb*, pp. 29–30.
37 S.P. Kapur, 'India and Pakistan's Unstable Peace', 2005.
38 Kapur, *Dangerous Deterrent*, pp. 131–9.
39 Ibid.
40 P.R. Lavoy, *Asymmetric Warfare in South Asia*, 2009.
41 Ganguly and Kapur, *India, Pakistan and the Bomb*, p. 84.
42 Ganguly and Kapur, *India, Pakistan and the Bomb*, pp. 85–7.
43 Kapur, *Dangerous Deterrent*, pp. 32–63.
44 Ganguly and Hagerty, *Fearful Symmetry*, p. 82; Kapur, *Dangerous Deterrent*, p. 93.
45 Ganguly and Kapur, *India, Pakistan and the Bomb*, pp. 80–1.
46 T.D. Hoyt, 'Pakistani Nuclear Doctrine and the Dangers of Strategic Myopia', 2001; D. Mistry, 'Tempering Optimism about Nuclear Deterrence in South Asia', 2009.
47 Ganguly and Kapur, *India, Pakistan and the Bomb*, pp. 91–5.
48 Lebow and Stein, 'Rational Deterrence Theory.'
49 Sagan and Waltz, *The Spread of Nuclear Weapons*, pp. 109–24; B. Karnad, 'The Irrelevance of Classical Nuclear Deterrence Theory', 2007.
50 T.V. Paul, 'Chinese-Pakistani Nuclear/Missile Ties and Balance of Power Politics', 2003.
51 D. Mistry, 'Diplomacy, Domestic Politics and the U.S.–India Nuclear Agreement', 2006.
52 Basrur, *Minimum Deterrence*, pp. 90–3; J.A. Kirk, 'From "Tilt" to "Pivot"?', unpublished manuscript.
53 Ganguly and Kapur, *India, Pakistan and the Bomb*, pp. 91–5.
54 Sagan and Waltz, *The Spread of Nuclear Weapons*, p. 107.
55 Ganguly and Hagerty, *Fearful Symmetry*, op. cit.
56 Kapur, *Dangerous Deterrent*, pp. 124–5,135–6, 179.
57 B. Riedel, *American Diplomacy and the 1999 Kargil Summit at Blair House*, 2002.
58 Ganguly and Kapur, *India, Pakistan and the Bomb*, pp. 30–1.
59 Basrur, *Minimum Deterrence*, p. 90.
60 Ibid., pp. 90–3.
61 Ibid., pp. 88–90.
62 Ibid.
63 Kirk, 'From "Tilt" to "Pivot"?.'
64 Ibid.
65 T. Crawford, *Pivotal Deterrence*, 2003.
66 Kirk, 'From "Tilt" to "Pivot"?.'
67 With the notable exception maybe of T.V. Paul, 'The Causes and Consequences of China–Pakistan Nuclear/Missile Collaboration', 2004.
68 Dittmer, *South Asia's Nuclear Dilemma*.
69 Although this could become an issue if China becomes a superpower with interests in limiting nuclear escalation in a neighboring region.
70 'India Rejects Pakistani's Call on Defence Budget Freeze', *Indian Express*, 11 June 2008.
71 Ganguly and Kapur, *India, Pakistan and the Bomb*, p. 81.
72 Ganguly and Kapur, *India, Pakistan and the Bomb*, pp. 87–91.
73 Paul, 'Chinese–Pakistani Nuclear/Missile Ties.'
74 J.W. Garver, *Protracted Contest*, 2001, pp. 227–8.
75 Paul, 'Chinese–Pakistani Nuclear/Missile Ties.'

76 H. Pant, 'China, Pakistan Boost Nuclear Ties', 6 May 2010.
77 M. Hibbs, 'Pakistan Deal Signifies China's Growing Nuclear Assertiveness', *Nuclear Energy Brief*, Carnegie Endowment for International Peace, 27 April 2010; A.J. Tellis, 'The China–Pakistan Nuclear "Deal": Separating Fact From Fiction', *Policy Outlook*, Carnegie Endowment for International Peace, 16 July 2010.
78 Paul, 'Chinese–Pakistani Nuclear/Missile Ties.'
79 In May 1990, US Deputy National Security Adviser Robert Gates was sent to South Asia to pressure both India and Pakistan to pacifically resolve their diplomatic dispute.
80 For a review of this literature, see S.P. Kapur, 'Deterring Nuclear Terrorists' in Paul *et al.*, *Complex Deterrence*, p. 109.
81 S.P. Kapur, 'Nuclear Terrorism: Prospects in Asia', 2008, pp. 333–6.
82 D.E. Sanger and W.J. Broad, 'U.S. Secretly Aids Pakistan in Guarding Nuclear Arms', *New York Times*, 18 November 2007.
83 S. Ganguly and S.P. Kapur, 'The Sorcerer's Apprentice', 2010.
84 Kapur, *Dangerous Deterrent*, Chapter 6.
85 Ganguly and Kapur, *India, Pakistan and the Bomb*, pp. 79–80.
86 Ganguly and Kapur, 'The Sorcerer's Apprentice.'
87 Ibid.
88 S. Coll, 'The Stand-Off: How Jihadi Groups Helped Provoke the Twenty-First Century's First Nuclear Crisis', *New Yorker*, 13 February 2006.
89 Kapur, 'Deterrence and asymmetric warfare.'
90 W.C. Ladwig III, 'A Cold Start for Hot Wars?, Winter 2007–8.
91 Ganguly and Kapur, *India, Pakistan and the Bomb*, pp. 76–8.
92 Kapur, 'Deterrence and Asymmetric Warfare.'
93 Kirk, 'From "Tilt" to "Pivot"?.'
94 K. Bajpai, 'The BJP and the Bomb', and S.D. Sagan, 'The Evolution of Pakistani and Indian Nuclear Doctrine', both in Sagan, *Inside Nuclear South Asia*, 2009.
95 Kapur, 'Revisionist Ambitions, Conventional Capabilities, and Nuclear Instability', 2009.

Bibliography

Bajpai, K., 'The BJP and the Bomb' in S.D. Sagan, ed., *Inside Nuclear South Asia*, Stanford: Stanford University Press, 2009.

Basrur, R.M., *Minimum Deterrence and India's Nuclear Security*, Stanford: Stanford University Press, 2006.

Booth, K. and N.J. Wheeler, *The Security Dilemma: Fear, Cooperation and Trust in World Politics*, New York: Palgrave Macmillan, 2008.

Chari, P.R., P.I. Cheema and S.P. Cohen, *Four Crises and a Peace Process: American Engagement in South Asia*, Washington, DC: Brookings Institution Press, 2007.

Crawford, T., *Pivotal Deterrence: Third-Party Statecraft and the Pursuit of Peace*, Ithaca, NY: Cornell University Press, 2003.

Dittmer, L. (ed.), *South Asia's Nuclear Dilemma*, New York: M.E. Sharpe, 2004.

Ganguly, S. and D.T. Hagerty, *Fearful Symmetry: India–Pakistan Crises in the Shadow of Nuclear Weapons*, New Delhi: Oxford University Press, 2005.

Ganguly, S. and S.P. Kapur, *India, Pakistan and the Bomb: Debating Nuclear Stability in South Asia*, New York: Columbia University Press, 2010.

Ganguly, S. and S.P. Kapur, 'The Sorcerer's Apprentice: Islamist Militancy in South Asia', *The Washington Quarterly* 33:1, January 2010.

Ganguly, S. and S.P. Kapur (eds), *Nuclear Proliferation in South Asia: Crisis Behaviour, and the Bomb*, London: Routledge, 2009.

Garver, J.W., *Protracted Contest: Sino-Indian Rivalry in the Twentieth Century*, Seattle: University of Washington Press, 2001.

Hagerty, D.T., *The Consequences of Nuclear Proliferation: Lessons from South Asia*, Cambridge, MA: MIT Press, 1998.

Hagerty, D.T., 'The Kargil War: An Optimistic Assessment' in S. Ganguly and S.P. Kapur (eds), *Nuclear Proliferation In South Asia: Crisis Behaviour and the Bomb*, London: Routledge, 2009.

Hoyt, T.D., 'Pakistani Nuclear Doctrine and the Dangers of Strategic Myopia', *Asian Survey* 41:6, 2001.

Jervis, R., *The Illogic of American Nuclear Strategy*, Ithaca: Cornell University Press, 1984.

Jervis, R., *The Meaning of the Nuclear Revolution: Statecraft and the Prospect of Armageddon*, Ithaca: Cornell University Press, 1989.

Kapur, S.P., 'India and Pakistan's Unstable Peace: Why Nuclear South Asia is Not Like Cold War Europe', *International Security* 30:2, 2005.

Kapur, S.P., *Dangerous Deterrent: Nuclear Weapons Proliferation and Conflict in South Asia*, Stanford: Stanford University Press, 2007.

Kapur, S.P., 'Nuclear Terrorism: Prospects in Asia' in M. Alagappa (ed.), *The Long Shadow: Nuclear Weapons and Security in 21st Century Asia*, Stanford: Stanford University Press, 2008.

Kapur, S.P., 'Revisionist Ambitions, Conventional Capabilities, and Nuclear Instability: Why Nuclear South Asia is Not Like Cold War Europe', in S.D. Sagan (ed.), *Inside Nuclear South Asia*, Stanford: Stanford University Press, 2009.

Karnad, B., 'The Irrelevance of Classical Nuclear Deterrence Theory' in E. Sridharan (ed.), *The India-Pakistan Nuclear Relationship*, Delhi: Routledge, 2007.

Kirk, J.A., 'The Evolution of India's Nuclear Policies', in S. Ganguly (ed.), *India's Foreign Policy: Retrospect and Prospect*, New Delhi: Oxford University Press, 2009.

Kirk, J.A., 'From "Tilt" to "Pivot"?: U.S. Intervention in India–Pakistan Nuclear Crises and Implications for Deterrence Theory', unpublished manuscript.

Knopf, J., 'Recasting the Optimism–Pessimism Debate', *Security Studies* 12:1, 2002.

Krepon, M., *The Stability–Instability Paradox, Misperception, and Escalation Control in South Asia*, Washington, DC: The Henry Stimson Center, May 2003.

Ladwig III, W.C., 'A Cold Start for Hot Wars? The Indian Army's New Limited War Doctrine', *International Security* 32:3, Winter 2007–8.

Lavoy, P.R., *Asymmetric Warfare in South Asia: The Causes and Consequences of the Kargil Conflict*, Cambridge, MA: Cambridge University Press, 2009.

Lebow, R., and J.G., Stein 'Rational Deterrence Theory: I Think, Therefore I Deter', *World Politics* 41:2, 1989.

Mistry, D., 'Diplomacy, Domestic Politics and the U.S.–India Nuclear Agreement', *Asian Survey* 46:5, 2006.

Mistry, D., 'Tempering Optimism about Nuclear Deterrence in South Asia', *Security Studies* 18:1, 2009.

Pant, H., 'China, Pakistan Boost Nuclear Ties', *International Relations and Security Network (ISN) Security Watch*, 6 May 2010.

Paul, T.V., 'Chinese–Pakistani Nuclear/Missile Ties and Balance of Power Politics', *The Nonproliferation Review* 10:2, 2003.

Paul, T.V., 'The Causes and Consequences of China–Pakistan Nuclear/Missile Collaboration' in L. Dittmer (ed.), *South Asia's Nuclear Dilemma*, New York: M.E. Sharpe, 2004.

Paul, T.V., P.M. Morgan and J.J. Wirtz (eds), *Complex Deterrence: Strategy in the Global Age*, Chicago: University of Chicago Press, 2009.

Perkovich, G., *India's Nuclear Bomb*, New Delhi: Oxford University Press, 1999.

Riedel, B., *American Diplomacy and the 1999 Kargil Summit at Blair House*, Philadelphia: Center for the Advanced Study of India, University of Pennsylvania (Policy Paper Series), 2002.

Sagan, S.D., 'The Evolution of Pakistani and Indian Nuclear Doctrine' in S.D. Sagan (ed.), *Inside Nuclear South Asia*, Stanford: Stanford University Press, 2009.

Sagan, S.D. (ed.), *Inside Nuclear South Asia*, Stanford: Stanford University Press, 2009.

Sagan, S.D. and K.N. Waltz, *The Spread of Nuclear Weapons: A Debate Renewed*, New York: W.W. Norton, 2002.

Schelling, T.C., *The Strategy of Conflict*, Cambridge, MA: Harvard University Press, 1960.

Stein, J.G., 'Rational Deterrence against 'Irrational' Adversaries? No Common Knowledge' in T.V. Paul, P.M. Morgan and J.J. Wirtz (eds), *Complex deterrence: Strategy in the Global Age*, Chicago: University of Chicago Press, 2009.

Swami, P., 'A War to End a War: The Causes and Outcomes of the 2001–2 India–Pakistan crisis' in S. Ganguly and S.P. Kapur (eds), *Nuclear Proliferation in South Asia: Crisis Behaviour, and the Bomb*, Routledge, 2009.

Tellis, A.J., *India's Emerging Nuclear Posture*, Santa Monica, CA: RAND Corporation, 2001.

Waltz, K.N., *The Spread of Nuclear Weapons: More May be Better*, Adelphi Papers 171, 1981, London: International Institute for Strategic Studies.

4 India–Pakistan relations and the Kashmir issue (1947–2009)

A historical perspective

Ashok Behuria

We wished to normalize our relationship with Pakistan and live as friendly neighbours ... our territorial integrity is not negotiable. For the rest, we have the political will and a publicly stated commitment to establish friendly and co-operative relations with Pakistan.

(I.K. Gujral, 2003)

The India–Pakistan relationship is a pessimist's paradise. That is how it is often characterized by seasoned onlookers who have watched the swings in Indo-Pak relations ever since the two countries came into being in 1947. It has also been described as a relationship of enduring rivalry. However, despite their inhibitions about talking to each other and the trust deficit between the two countries, they have demonstrated a precipitate will to engage with each other and settle their differences through peaceful means.

This chapter attempts to uncover the pattern of the Indo-Pak bilateral relationship – periods of hostility followed by periods of often unfruitful dialogue – which cannot be separated from the domestic politics of both countries or from international pressures. The centrality of the Kashmir issue has been evident from the beginning, as this historical account of Indo-Pak relations and the analysis of the complexities involved therein will demonstrate.

Initial interactions

The Partition of the Indian subcontinent was followed by the worst communal carnage and human displacement in the recorded history of South Asia,[1] even though it was undertaken to prevent any such eventuality. As such, the issue of communal riots had to feature as a major referent in the relationship between the two countries in the initial years. Meanwhile, the issue of Kashmir cropped up as a major irritant in India–Pakistan relations from October 1947, when armed tribesmen from Pakistan attacked Kashmir with the active support of the Pakistan government. Indian troops entered the state only after the Maharaja of Kashmir asked for help and signed the instrument of accession on 26 October 1947. The people of Kashmir (especially from the valley) fought the tribal *lashkar* bravely along with the Indian army and repulsed them from the valley.

However, the confrontation between the Indian troops and the armed tribesmen, supported by the Pakistani regular army, continued in other areas in the western part of the state, where the intruders had captured some territory and declared it as independent or Azad Kashmir.

The talks between Mountbatten and Jinnah held in November 1947 were inconclusive, and the Kashmir issue was referred to the United Nations by the Indian government in January 1948. In April 1948 the Security Council adopted resolution 47 which clearly stated that Pakistan should 'secure the withdrawal from the State of Jammu and Kashmir of tribesmen and Pakistani nationals' who had entered the state for the purposes of fighting. However, India became disillusioned with the UN's efforts after the latter began to accommodate Pakistan's concerns and stopped calling for the total withdrawal of Pakistani forces from Kashmir.

During the 1950s the Indian Prime Minister, Jawaharlal Nehru, had informal talks with his Pakistani counterpart, Mohammed Ali Bogra (June–August 1953), to sort out the issue of a plebiscite in Kashmir.[2] The discussions between the two suggest that Nehru had even agreed to appoint a Plebiscite Administrator by April 1954. However, by early 1954, the news of American military aid to Pakistan was published, and this was cited by Nehru as an instance of Pakistan's insincerity about resolving the Kashmir issue and of its adoption of a hostile position vis-à-vis India. The Pakistani decision to join CENTO[3] provided reasons for the Indian decision to cancel the talks and reject the idea of a plebiscite in Kashmir. Nehru argued that Pakistan's membership of CENTO took away any right to appeal for the solution of the problem through peaceful means. However, in 1955 (14–18 May), Nehru had discussions with his counterpart Mohammed Ali during which he underlined his willingness to settle the Kashmir issue on the basis of a Partition of the state along the Cease Fire Line (CFL). Nehru's cable to Krishna Menon in 1957 suggests that he favored a readjustment of the CFL based on 'geographical, strategic and the like grounds.'[4] From the mid-1950s, India was lukewarm to the idea of a UN-mediated plebiscite, and held that the duly elected (in September 1951) Constituent Assembly of Jammu and Kashmir state had ratified the accession of the state to India on 15 February 1954 through a unanimous vote, and therefore, no further plebiscite was necessary to confirm the wishes of the people of Kashmir.[5]

The advent of the cold war brought another important dimension to the Kashmir issue; India perceived that there was an Anglo-American move to use the Kashmir issue to pin down India, which refused to join any alliance and decided to stay non-aligned. From this time onwards, India looked away from the UN as a neutral forum which could resolve the Kashmir issue impartially.[6] From the 1960s, therefore, there was an international effort to encourage bilateral dialogue between India and Pakistan to resolve the Kashmir issue.

It is interesting to note that in spite of Indian opposition to third-party mediation on Kashmir since the late 1950s, India did not object to third-party mediation on the Indus Waters dispute with Pakistan. In fact, the Indus Water Treaty of September 1960 stands out as an isolated example of a successful treaty between India and Pakistan in spite of the deep and abiding sense of mistrust between them.

The sixties: Bhutto and Swaran Singh talks

India–Pakistan talks on Kashmir started in earnest again in 1962. These talks are better known as the Bhutto–Swaran Singh talks. The two met six times between December 1962 and May 1963. The talks focused on the Partition of Kashmir and drawing an international boundary through the state.[7] While India was ready to go beyond the CFL and offer some territory on its side (Handwara area in the north west of Srinagar), Bhutto claimed 'Jammu, Uddhampur, Kishtwar, the Valley and Ladakh leaving only a few hundred square miles around Kathua,' which was certainly unacceptable to India.[8] The talks broke down after six rounds of meetings within a span of five months. It has to be remembered here that the talks were taking place against the backdrop of India's military reversals in the Sino-Indian war of 1962. In fact, this was the time when Pakistan's relationship with China made a quantum leap, resulting in a border settlement whereby Pakistan ceded almost 2,500 square miles of territory in northern Jammu and Kashmir to China, exactly at the time when the first round of Bhutto–Swaran Singh talks was about to begin. India protested against this move, but agreed to the talks, hoping to resolve the issue through dialogue. However, the talks hit a dead end with the Indian government unwilling to accept Bhutto's maximalist demands.

The war of 1965

India and Pakistan fought over an infertile stretch of marshland in the Rann of Kutch in early 1965. On 9 April 1965 Pakistan launched Operation Desert Hawk in the Rann of Kutch. After three months of intermittent engagement, India and Pakistan signed an agreement to settle the Kutch dispute through international arbitration by the International Court of Justice on 30 June 1965. However, the Pakistani leadership had, by then, prepared itself for another round of military engagement in Kashmir.

Pakistan started the war in the Bhimber–Chhamb sector on 6 September 1965 and it lasted for 17 days. It was not confined to Kashmir and spread along the entire India–Pakistan border. By the time the UN Security Council called for a ceasefire on 22 September 1965, the war had resulted in a stalemate. Both the countries had some success story to offer to their people. Subsequently, a truce was mediated by the former Soviet Union, and both the countries reached an agreement at Tashkent to withdraw their troops to pre-war positions. However, the agreement was dismissed by Pakistani public opinion, and was rejected by the groups opposed to General Ayub Khan as a hasty and injudicious move by his government. Ayub's one-time trusted foreign minister, Z.A. Bhutto, who outmaneuvered him in the art of politics, accused him of betraying the Pakistani nation.

The seventies: the Simla agreement

The 1970s started with popular unrest in East Pakistan. Pakistani efforts to enforce a military crackdown had unforeseen spill over effects in India, as it forced people to flee across the border into India. This steady inflow of refugees gave India reason to interfere and engage the Pakistan army in a close fight. The Pakistan army lost the war and had to surrender ignominiously. East Pakistan became independent and was named Bangladesh. The division of Pakistan was complete. The early 1970s saw the golden years of Indian supremacy. The Simla agreement of June 1972 was significant because it committed both the countries to resolve all their outstanding disputes including Kashmir through peaceful means. However, as events have demonstrated ever since, such a commitment could not dispel the sense of mutual hostility that has grown over the years. More importantly, despite Bhutto's personal assurances to Indira Gandhi that he would work towards converting the Line of Control (LOC)[9] into a de facto international border, Pakistan continued to claim Kashmir and tried to take the issue beyond the bilateral track and raise it in international forums.

Enter the eighties: Zia and Indo-Pak relations

The overthrow of the Bhutto government by the military came as a major surprise in June 1977. Zia-ul-Haq picked up from where the earlier government had left off on Kashmir. He proclaimed his 'eagerness to normalize relations with India,' 'extension of support to the right of self-determination of the Kashmiris,' and accused India of a 'big-brother-attitude' or 'hegemonism,' all in the same breath.[10] Meanwhile, the ritual of Indo-Pak diplomatic exercises continued.

However, confidence-building exercises through talks at the governmental level suffered a setback in the wake of the Soviet invasion of Afghanistan in December 1979, when Pakistan's elevation to a frontline state facilitated a flow of arms from the US. This gave rise to concerns in Indian political circles. American assurances would not convince Indian statesmen that the arms would not be used against India and thus the approach to bilateral relations from the Indian side hardened.[11] Reports of China and Pakistan pooling their resources in the nuclear field with financial help from oil-rich countries so that they could stand up against Israel and India also added to the sense of uneasiness in New Delhi. All this led to an inevitable slump in Indo-Pak relations. Meanwhile, against the backdrop of an increasing trail of communal riots in India, Pakistan started harping on the minority issue in international forums. Agha Shahi, the Pakistani Minister for Foreign Affairs, while speaking before the UN Committee on Elimination of Racial Discrimination on 4 August 1979, observed that the minorities in India were being discriminated against and said the Indian government should take steps to preserve the autonomy of educational institutions of various communities, particularly the Muslims.[12]

Under Zia, Pakistan started focusing more on the issue of Kashmir and connecting it with Islamic identity. The reactions from Zia's side seemed to echo the posture adopted by Bhutto on the issue of a no-war pact: 'If there are problems like Kashmir ... no-war pacts and no-aggression pacts are worth nothing, not even the paper on which they are written.'[13] The First Extraordinary Session of the Islamic Conference of Foreign Ministers met in Islamabad on 27–29 January 1980 and adopted a resolution for the 'restoration of the rights of Kashmiris' (and Palestinians), and Zia urged the Muslim Ummah to resolve such issues.[14]

Meanwhile India became concerned about Pakistan's uninhibited pursuit of military strength through its purchase of sophisticated weapons from the US. During 1982–83, India also raised its concerns about the construction of the Karakoram Highway that connected Pakistan with China along the strategic border in Pakistan Occupied Kashmir (POK). The issue of Sikh terrorists being trained in Pakistan in guerrilla camps also began coming up as a major irritant in Indo-Pak relations.

Rajiv Gandhi and Operation Brasstacks

Mrs. Gandhi was assassinated in October 1984 and was succeeded by her son Rajiv Gandhi who won the elections of 1984. The secretary-level talks re-started in early February 1985. Zia and Rajiv met in Moscow, New York and Muscat in 1985, leading to optimism about the improvement of relations between the two countries. During this period, Zia made some overtures that included proposals regarding mutual inspections of nuclear facilities and a bilateral nuclear non-proliferation treaty. But the Indian government was not impressed.

From mid-January 1986, the issue of the Siachen glacier assumed center-stage. The troops of India and Pakistan had been fighting each other since 1984, on the highest altitude in the world, negotiating the worst possible hostile weather. The talks held about Siachen were inconclusive and both the parties were reluctant to surrender their respective positions. However, the official contacts were allowed to continue. Following the foreign-secretary-level talks in April 1986, Pakistan made full-scale preparations to raise the issue of Kashmir at the NAM Summit in Harare. The President of POK, K.H. Khursheed (who was earlier private secretary to M.A. Jinnah), was taken to Harare and introduced to delegates as a leader of Kashmir liberation, which annoyed India. However, the meeting between Rajiv Gandhi and M.K. Junejo (the then prime minister of Pakistan) in the South Asian Association for Regional Co-operation (SAARC) forum eased matters a little and revealed mutual eagerness to pursue the talks.

During November 1986 and March 1987, the Indian army conducted its routine army exercises along the India–Pakistan border. It was one of the largest mobilizations by the Indian armed forces, code-named Operation Brasstacks. This led Pakistan to mass its troops on a large scale all along the border, which brought the two countries to the brink of a war. In this atmosphere, home-secretary-level talks (between C.G. Somaya and S.K. Mahmood) were held to set up a joint committee of respectable persons at the official level to meet periodically to evolve common strategies in matters concerning defense and security. The December talks between the foreign secretaries (A.P. Venkateswaran and Abdul Sattar) sought to explore new avenues for friendship. Yet these talks did not achieve a great deal.

On 31 January 1987, the Indian Foreign Secretary, Alfred Gonsalves, had meetings with Abdul Sattar, and India agreed to moderate the scale of Brasstacks maneuvers in response to Pakistani requests. After the Rajiv–Zia talks in February 1987 Rajiv Gandhi agreed to further pull out Brasstacks forces from the border. The Rajiv–Zia talks were followed up by foreign-secretary-level talks. The talks were continued in May 1988 at secretary level (K.P.S. Mennon and Abdul Sattar) where vital issues were identified as: Siachen, Afghanistan, Punjab, and the drafting of a friendship and non-aggression treaty. But the response from the Indian side was not too encouraging.

Return to democracy

Zia's death in an accident on 17 August 1988 was followed by a return to democracy in Pakistan. On the sidelines of the SAARC summit in Islamabad (29–31 December 1988), Rajiv Gandhi went to Pakistan and held friendly discussions with the newly elected leader, Benazir Bhutto. After the summit, Rajiv and Benazir signed an agreement to promote co-operation between India and Pakistan and the continuation of regular foreign-secretary-level talks. In May 1989, the home-secretary-level talks (between J.A. Kalyani Krishnan and S.K. Mahmud) looked positive. They covered Punjab, Jammu and Kashmir, Sindh, the question of illegal border crossings and drug trafficking. However, in October 1989, the Pakistan army launched its exercise along the Punjab border, code-named Zarb-e-Momin. It was India's turn to feel alarmed and it expressed its concerns to the Pakistani government.

The nineties: turmoil in Kashmir

From January 1990, the turmoil in Kashmir affected domestic politics in both the countries and the relationship between them was gravely affected. Towards the end of January, thousands of men tried to march into India from POK. The Pakistani government stopped the demonstrators before they came into the firing range of Indian troops. However, the Pakistani foreign minister was emphatic about his country's stand on Kashmir, which he expressed during his tour of India: 'It is impossible for Pakistanis not to raise their voice in support of the Kashmiris. Pakistan cannot be cowed down by any pressure or threats and it will continue to support the right of self-determination.'[15]

Thus the issue of Kashmir was responsible for the sudden slump in Indo-Pak relations. The upsurge in the valley, believed by Indian authorities to be substantially incited by Pakistan, assumed a more violent form. The reactions from the Pakistan side took a qualitative turn in that the nature of the upsurge was linked with the fate of Muslims in general in India, and Kashmir was floated as an Islamic issue of enormous importance to the Ummah. Benazir also joined the Islamist bandwagon, saying that Muslim bloodshed in Kashmir would duly outrage the Muslim Ummah the world over.[16] In India, meanwhile, the right-wing Bharatiya Janata Party (BJP) had managed to secure a sound electoral victory, feeding on the communal polarization created by the Ayodhya issue, and its irreverent posture vis-à-vis Pakistan affected the policy of the coalition government of V.P. Singh, whose statement in the Indian Parliament also reflected an uncompromising mood: 'We make it abundantly clear that if any misadventure is attempted (by Pakistan) we will react not only swiftly but decisively. We have the will and the capacity.'[17]

From April 1990, Pakistan showed readiness for talks, but continued with the same belligerent mood over Kashmir. In one of her most uninhibited statements, Benazir took a cue from her father, and gave a call for 'waging a one thousand years war' for Kashmir.[18] The Indian Foreign Minister, I.K. Gujral, reacted to this in a short and crisp manner, stating that her bellicose talk was 'her own way of conceding that Pakistan will not be able to grab Kashmir even in one thousand years.'[19] The Kashmir situation worsened in the meantime and there were anti-Hindu riots in the valley, bomb blasts on Hindu processions, and even the head of a cow thrown at a place of worship, clearly to incite communal passion in the entire country. The Indian government took the hint. V.P. Singh was very blunt in his accusations: '[These are] heinous acts committed under directions from across the border... Pakistan is giving directions to the subversives to communalise the situation in Punjab and Kashmir.'[20]

It was around this time that the US clarified its stand on Kashmir and held that India and Pakistan should settle the Kashmir issue according to the Simla Agreements on a bilateral basis. John Kelly, the then US Assistant Secretary of State, visited India and Pakistan and urged the governments to normalize their relations. But from the Indian side it was conveyed clearly that no summit meeting with Benazir was possible, and V.P. Singh was adamant: 'The ground language today is that of AK-47, rocket launchers... The flowery language of the Pakistan foreign office does not impress me... It was no good shaking hands across the table and kicking your shins under, at the same time.'[21] Still Pakistan's offer of talks at the foreign-secretary level was considered by India. The opposition and the ruling party alike were not averse to opening up a dialogue with Pakistan. A senior politician of the Congress, K.R. Narayanan, who later became the President of India, wrote: 'For India the issue at stake in Kashmir is not territory but the whole concept of India, the secular concept of India without which the nation will fall apart.'[22]

In July, the foreign-secretary-level talks started (between Muchkund Dubey and Tanvir Ahmed Khan), but POK leader Sardar Abdul Qayum Khan was opposed to Indo-Pak talks at any level and expressed his displeasure vehemently on the issue. The opposition in Pakistan was suspicious and urged the government to be cautious in its dealings with India. Nevertheless, the talks continued at the secretary level, and the agreements on non-violation of air space and advance intimation of military maneuvers along the border sought to avert the chances of any accidental war. The talks aimed more at reducing the prospects of war than creating conditions for friendship to grow in.[23]

Nawaz Sharif's first term

Nawaz Sharif's government came to power in Pakistan on a pro-Zia, Islamic Jamhoori Ittehad (Islamic Democratic Alliance) platform, in November 1990. There was a change of government in India too, with Chandra Sekhar replacing V.P. Singh as Prime Minister. Sharif reportedly compared his electoral victory with 'the historic decision in favour of the Pakistan movement and the struggle of the Muslim League under the dynamic and bold leadership of Quaid-i-Azam.'[24] He also pledged to provide moral, political and diplomatic support to the Kashmiris.[25] Typically, while Nawaz Sharif gave a call for observing solidarity with the secessionists in Kashmir, the dialogue at the foreign-secretary level was kept up nonetheless.

In October 1992, the Jammu and Kashmir Democratic Alliance, a sister wing of the ruling IJI, disclosed its plan of launching Operation Zarb-e-Haider, in which they would attempt border crossing on a massive scale. Tension mounted on either side of the LOC but ultimately the Pakistan army managed to keep the marchers within limits. Around this time Pakistan raised the issue of human rights violations in Kashmir, which plagued the relationship further. The Pakistan National Assembly passed a resolution on the human rights situation in India and urged the UN to send a fact-finding team to India to investigate the problem. The Pakistani attempt to raise the Kashmir issue under the agenda item of self-determination within the United Nations Human Rights Commission (UNHCR) in Geneva was countered by India's permanent ambassador, Satish Chandra, as unnecessary interference on the part of Pakistan in the internal affairs of India. From December 1992 Indo-Pak diplomatic interaction was de-intensified.

Benazir's second term

Benazir seemed very enthusiastic about reviving the talks after coming back to power in 1993. In October, Manmohan Singh (the then Indian Finance Minister) met Benazir in Cyprus on the sidelines of a Commonwealth Heads of Governments Meeting (CHOGM), and the need for restoration of dialogue was emphasized. But the Pakistan Foreign Minister, Farooq Ahmed Leghari, made a scathing criticism of the army siege at Hazratbal Mosque in Kashmir (which the Indian army undertook in order to nab terrorists hiding there) and said that India's commitment to bilateral talks could be considered only when the siege at Hazratbal was lifted. Pakistan tried unsuccessfully to rally the Islamic countries behind it and raise the issue of the violation of human rights in Kashmir in the UNHCR (in Geneva) in March 1994. Meanwhile the January 1994 talks at the foreign-secretary level in Islamabad did not make much progress and neither country wanted to make any concessions to the other.

Kashmir as 'the' bilateral issue

From 1994, Pakistan made it clear that any Indo-Pak talk should start with the substantive issue of Kashmir, and India toughened up its stance that India would rather seek to reclaim POK. Benazir started echoing the old verbiage, in a tele-vised address to the nation: 'Kashmir is Pakistan's jugular vein and we will not allow our jugular vein to be trampled under the feet of repression. God willing, the day is not far off when Kashmir will be with us.'[26]

However, despite Pakistan's bid to raise the Kashmir issue at the international level, foreign-secretary-level talks went on (J.N. Dixit and Shahyr Khan) during 1994–95. Benazir, in order not to be outdone by the opposition on the Kashmir issue, sought mediation by the US. Militancy was at its peak in Kashmir, and Pakistan tried its best to leverage it for greater international attention. By January 1996, Benazir announced that Pakistan was ready for 'purposeful talks on Kashmir with India.' India was not too anxious to accept the offer. Pakistan's insistence on Kashmir as 'the' issue to be addressed in the talks was the major stumbling-block in Indo-Pak bilateral talks. When India offered to discuss Kashmir along with other issues, Pakistan was hesitant. In July 1996 Benazir made another attempt to involve a third-party mediator. Undeterred, India expressed its willingness to talk to all its neighbors on all issues of bilateral concern from this time onwards. By December 1996, the then Indian Foreign Minister, I.K. Gujral, had already evolved his characteristic style of providing small concessions to buy lasting friendship with neighboring states in the region. This policy helped India in concluding a thirty-year Ganga Water Treaty as well as new trade and tariff agreements with Bangladesh, co-operation agreements on hydel projects with Nepal, and agreements granting tariff concessions to Sri Lanka. Gujral also tried to improve India's relationship with the countries of West Asia, especially Iran, which showed that India was really picking up on the diplomatic front. The media named such a pragmatic approach in foreign policy the 'Gujral Doctrine.'

Nawaz Sharif's second term

Meanwhile, the President of Pakistan, Mr. Farooq Leghari, dismissed the Benazir Bhutto government, on charges of corruption and inefficiency in dealing with the worsening law-and-order situation. Elections led to the victory of Nawaz Sharif, who swept the polls with a thumping majority (securing 135 seats out of 207) in the Pakistan National Assembly. After coming to power, Nawaz Sharif promised to base his foreign policy on the principle of 'friendship with all and enmity with none.' He expressed his desire to reopen the dialogue with India, which had been in cold storage since 1994, during his election campaign. Ironically, however, his pledge to work for improved bilateral relations always went hand-in-hand with his pledge to his countrymen to intensify Pakistan's moral and diplomatic support for the eventual liberation of Kashmir.

India's acceptance of the Pakistani proposal for a foreign-secretary-level meeting set the ball rolling for an India–Pakistan dialogue, even though at a low key. This culminated in three days of talks in March (28–30) between the foreign secretaries of the two countries, Mr. Salman Haider for India and Shamshad Ahmed for Pakistan, in New Delhi.

The Islamabad talks: steps towards adopting confidence-building measures

The Islamabad dialogue, held on 19–22 June 1997, between the foreign secretaries of the two countries identified the issues that needed to be resolved and laid emphasis on the need to develop Confidence Building Measures (CBMs), and for this purpose the countries agreed to set up separate Joint Working Groups (JWGs) on the separate issues, which were supposed to work simultaneously in an integrated manner. Apart from Kashmir the outstanding issues identified included the demarcation of the boundary around the Sir Creek line, the bilateral settlement of the Wullar Barrage/Tulbul Navigation Project, pulling out of troops from Siachen, easing of restrictions on visas, and the release of civilian detainees.

The outcome of the talks was hailed in the Pakistani media as an edifice for peace. The opposition leader in Pakistan, Benazir Bhutto, however, started voicing her concern about the openness with which Sharif was seeking to befriend India and observed that the outcome of the talks did not signal any perceptible shift in the Indian position. A section of the Pakistani business class was also not too sanguine about the prospect of Indo-Pak trade that would come close on the heels of an agreement. They cautioned that opening the Pakistani market to Indian producers would mean swamping the market with cheap Indian products. Then there was another section in Pakistan which felt that the Indian decision to accord priority to Kashmir would mean reconsideration of the status of POK too. Reactions in India were also not too heartening. The main opposition party, the BJP, urged the government to be cautious in its Kashmir policy.

Kashmir: the sticking point

During his second tenure (1997–99) as Prime Minister, Nawaz Sharif, a businessman by instinct, perhaps realized the necessity of moving ahead on the dialogue track with India. The international community was uneasy about the covert nuclear capability of Pakistan, and there was pressure on Pakistan to start a dialogue with India. The jihad in Kashmir had weakened, and as a result he was under less pressure on that front. He also hoped that trade with India would have a positive effect on the sagging economy of Pakistan. Furthermore, it was increasingly recognized in Pakistan that the jihadis had had a serious impact on the internal security situation, and Nawaz Sharif even appointed a committee to find the reasons for it in November 1997, which submitted its report in May 1998. The report held that it was imperative for the intelligence agencies to keep track of the possible linkages between the militant training imparted by various political groups for jihad in Kashmir and Afghanistan, and acts of terrorism committed in Pakistan.[27] The Kashmir issue thus presented itself as a challenge.

On the Indian side too there was an inclination to restart a meaningful dialogue because by the mid-1990s, with economic liberalization taking root, the problem of Kashmir was increasingly viewed as a constraint on India's rise as a leading regional and global player. The only way out was to settle it through dialogue. In this context, Pakistan's rigid stand on Kashmir posed a serious challenge for Indian diplomacy. Since there was a precipitate will on both sides to restart the talks, the diplomats of both the countries finally managed to negotiate their differences and find a mechanism through which they could accommodate each other's views and proceed on the path of dialogue.

In their meeting on 23 June 1997, the foreign secretaries produced a tentative agreement that outlined eight issues, including Kashmir, to be discussed separately through joint working groups. But both countries stuck to their respective positions. Moreover, India said Kashmir was not a dispute and it would not discuss the status of Kashmir with Pakistan. If anything was to be discussed, it would be Pakistan Occupied Kashmir (POK) and the Northern Areas (NA), which was illegally annexed by Pakistan.

The next round of talks in September 1997, over the composition of the working groups and the methodology to be adopted for discussions, also proved inconclusive. Pakistan favored the idea of according priority to the working group on Kashmir; this was not acceptable to India.[28] The Indian Prime Minister, I.K. Gujral, suggested simultaneous discussions on all issues, including Kashmir, while Pakistan went on pressing for separate and exclusive discussions on Kashmir.

Crossing the Rubicon: we are nuclear powers now

It was at this juncture in March 1998 that the BJP-led coalition formed a government in New Delhi with Atal Bihari Vajpayee as prime minister. This coalition decided to test nuclear bombs in May 1998. Pakistan responded by conducting its own series of nuclear tests. This was viewed as a critical challenge for the non-proliferation lobby in the US and elsewhere. South Asia was described as a nuclear flashpoint. In his address to the Non-Aligned Movement (NAM) meeting at Durban, even Nelson Mandela urged all nations to lend their strength to resolving the Kashmir issue.[29] But the nuclear tests gave Pakistan greater confidence and it appeared resolute in its determination to push its Kashmir-first agenda through diplomatic dialogue.

Pakistanis argued that the primary thrust of Pakistan's policy should be to keep the West's attention fixed on Kashmir and that settlement of the Kashmir issue should precede the process of normalization with India and not the other way round. However, some of the major English-language dailies advised caution and argued that Pakistan should be happy with India climbing down from its earlier position that the Kashmir issue was non-negotiable and that it would not discuss Kashmir with Pakistan, and move on. There were other saner voices that advocated peace with India following the Sino-Indian model of rapprochement. There was also pressure from the international community to start the process of dialogue, given the nuclear dimension of the conflict.

At this juncture, the leaderships of the two countries showed maturity and decided to refresh their relationship after the nuclear tests. The Prime Ministers of India and Pakistan held a bilateral meeting on the sidelines of the UN General Assembly in New York on 23 September 1998 and 'reaffirmed their common belief that an environment of durable peace and security was in the supreme interest of both India and Pakistan, and of the region as a whole.'[30] Vajpayee, the Indian Prime Minister, leader of a right-wing party perceived to have hardline views on Pakistan, agreed to go to Lahore for a high-level bilateral dialogue in February 1999. The euphoria surrounding the visit hid the wave of antipathy that rose against Nawaz Sharif's efforts to start a meaningful dialogue with India.[31] His unpopularity certainly affected his India policy. More importantly, the then army chief Pervez Musharraf stayed away from the reception at the Wagah border. Opposition political parties, even if they did not directly oppose the initiative for dialogue, were skeptical about its consequences.

The Lahore Summit of 20–21 February 1999 resulted in an agreement which contained a pledge from both governments to intensify their efforts to resolve all outstanding issues, including the issue of Jammu and Kashmir. This was the middle path that the diplomats of the two countries had settled for during their long deliberations since 1991. For Pakistan, this was the maximum concession it could extract from India. The Nawaz Sharif government hailed the Lahore agreement as a success and promised to keep India engaged on the Kashmir issue. Sharif also activated back-channel diplomacy, following the agreement, through ex-Foreign Secretary Niaz Naik, to make some meaningful advance on Kashmir.

The Kargil war

However, the Pakistan army's Kargil adventure, barely three months after the Lahore Agreement, came as yet another surprise for India. It proved that there was a lack of consensus among the power-elites in Pakistan on the issue of a dialogue with India. That the army had its own agenda on Kashmir, and would not abide by anything that a civilian government might advocate on Kashmir, became more obvious after Kargil. A discredited Sharif was forced to seek a way out of the Kargil crisis on 4 July 1999, upon pressure from the US, which made him even more unpopular. The Washington Declaration was issued by US President Bill Clinton and Prime Minister Sharif. It stated that it was vital for the peace of South Asia that the LOC be respected by both parties, in accordance with the 1972 Simla Agreement, and that bilateral dialogue between India and Pakistan was the best way forward for resolving issues. The army found in it an opportunity to deflect popular attention from its misadventures in Kargil towards Nawaz Sharif's ignominious surrender to Washington, even if it had approved of the Washington route as the only alternative for Pakistan.

Enter Musharraf: between a rock and a hard place

The media in Pakistan also played into the hands of the army and went hammer-and-tongs against Nawaz Sharif. The pro-Kashmiri religious and militant groups spewed venom against him for playing with the blood of the martyrs. Sharif's

Kashmir policy was interpreted as a shameful surrender of vital national interests. Only a few commentators interpreted the Washington declaration as a welcome internationalization of the Kashmir issue. The army very conveniently passed on the blame for the Kargil operations to Nawaz Sharif, and his unpopularity soared. Opposition politicians like Benazir Bhutto and Qazi Hussain even invited the army to step in and unseat him. Nawaz Sharif facilitated his own ouster by trying to sack Musharraf while the latter was on a tour of Sri Lanka in October 1999. The inevitable happened and the army asserted itself and sacked him instead. Musharraf's takeover was hailed by a majority of the people as deliverance from Sharif's dictatorship.

In his maiden speech, in the seven-point agenda he set before himself, General Musharraf studiously avoided any mention of Kashmir and focused on ushering in a true democracy. He only emphasized pursuing peace with India with honor and dignity. It was natural for Musharraf to disregard the Lahore Agreement in view of the circumstances in which he came to power. Instead, he thought of securing greater concessions from India. Reeling under sanctions and a crisis of legitimacy, and under pressure from the US to start talks with India, he had to turn to dialogue with New Delhi to show his good intentions to the international community. Thus, the Pakistan-controlled militant conglomerate declared a ceasefire in June 2000. Musharraf offered to talk at any place, any time and any level, and even proposed a no-war pact with India in August 2000.

Finally, upon Indian insistence, he agreed to abide by the terms of the Lahore agreement and tried to convince his audience that 'one has to realise that there are bigger issues [than Kashmir?] of economic development, of poverty and the wellbeing of the people.' Even then he came to Agra in July 2001 and tried his best to extract more concessions from India on Kashmir. In Agra, he insisted that India should recognize Kashmir as the core dispute while refusing to accept Indian concerns about terrorism in India being sponsored by forces across the border. The dialogue broke down over this issue even after 10 rounds of intense discussions, including four between Vajpayee and Musharraf. India called it the beginning of a journey. The Pakistani foreign secretary avoided calling it a failure and said it was inconclusive.

Musharraf sought to endear himself to the Kashmiris with a view to restoring the confidence of the Kashmir groups in Pakistan. Two months later, under threat from the US in the wake of the 9/11 terrorist attacks, Musharraf made the most strategic decision of his life with an excuse that by joining the war on terror he could save Pakistan's Kashmir policy. Within less than a month, India had its own version of 9/11 in the attack on the assembly in Jammu and Kashmir on 1 October 2001, followed by an attack on the Indian Parliament on 13 December 2001. Musharraf was quick to send his message of sympathy to Vajpayee and the Indian people as the US recognized India's legitimate right of self-defense, and the then Indian Army Chief, General Sunderajan Padmanabhan, sought to use the window of opportunity to launch hot pursuit and sharp and surgical attacks beyond the LOC. Vajpayee and Jaswant Singh, his foreign minister, however, settled for Operation Parakram and deployed the army along the

Indo-Pak border to convey their sense of disappointment with the Pakistani establishment. Musharraf tried to reassure India through his speech on 12 January 2002 to the Pakistani nation. He banned Kashmiri jihadi groups like the Lashkar-e-Toiba and Jaish-e-Muhammad, seized their offices and denounced their jihad as terrorism, and argued that even as Kashmir runs through the blood of Pakistan, no organization would be allowed to indulge in terrorism in the name of Kashmir. Analysts in India termed it as slowing down rather than turning off the jihadi tap. Jihadis expressed their frustration by attacking Musharraf twice in 15 days during November–December 2003.

Musharraf made several efforts to convince India of his good intentions in early 2003 and these efforts led to Vajpayee extending the hand of friendship in April 2003 during his trip to Srinagar. This was followed by a bilateral ceasefire on the LOC in November 2003. Musharraf tried his best to revive the peace process with India by seeking to project a flexible approach towards Kashmir. In a November 2003 interview with the BBC Radio Urdu service (in its program Talking Point) he called for patience, sincerity, and flexibility, and reintroduced his four-step approach to Kashmir, one he had tentatively put across during the Agra talks which offered to eliminate all options unacceptable to India, Pakistan, and the people of Kashmir, and then evolve a consensual solution. The four-point formula envisaged was:

1   commencement of official talks;
2   acknowledgement of the centrality of the Jammu and Kashmir dispute;
3   agreement that any proposal unacceptable to any party or the Kashmiris is taken off the table;
4   adoption of the best solution acceptable to the parties and the Kashmiris.[32]

Vajpayee and Musharraf signed a joint statement on the sidelines of the SAARC Summit in Islamabad on 6 January 2004. The joint statement stressed that in order to take forward and sustain the dialogue process, violence, hostility and terrorism must be prevented. Musharraf also reassured Vajpayee that he would not permit any territory under Pakistan's control to be used to support terrorism in any manner. The joint statement also said that the two leaders agreed to commence the process of a composite dialogue, and expressed their confidence that it would lead to the peaceful settlement of all bilateral issues, including Jammu and Kashmir, to the satisfaction of both sides. Later that year, there was a change in the government in India. Musharraf met the new Prime Minister, Dr. Manmohan Singh, in New York on 24 September 2004, and both the leaders signed a joint statement indicating that they would take the process forward and start looking into various options on Kashmir.

As the source of all authority in Pakistan, Musharraf put forward several proposals during the next three years to resolve the Kashmir issue. However, he offered most of the proposals through the media. During a visit to India in April 2005 he agreed to drop the option of converting the LOC into an international border and accepted Manmohan Singh's argument that borders cannot be redrawn. However, Musharraf also took care not to alienate pro-Pakistan Kashmiri elements, and a month later in May 2005, he held that any final solution on Kashmir had to be acceptable to Pakistan, India, and the Kashmiris. Manmohan Singh responded on 29 May 2005, by saying that 'the sky is the limit' – once the Indian position about what was not possible – had finally been understood by Pakistan. On 5 December 2006, Musharraf further polished his proposal and reiterated that without changing boundaries, the borders and the LOC could be made irrelevant through staggered demilitarization and autonomy or self-governance, with a joint-supervision mechanism in Kashmir. Towards the end of his time in power Musharraf commented: 'Kashmir is ripe for resolution... Courage is needed to reconcile and shake hands and forget and forgive rather than go for confrontation. Both sides have to swallow their pride and step back.'[33]

Parallel to the three-year-long (2004–07) official process of a composite dialogue, an unofficial back channel was activated (very much like the Niaz Naik– R.K. Mishra talks during 1997–98) to discuss issues in an informal and more nuanced manner. There were 12 rounds of such talks between Musharraf's secretary and his college friend, Tariq Aziz, and senior security advisors to the Indian government considered close to the Indian prime minister. Retired career diplomats of repute like Brajesh Mishra, J.N Dixit, and S.K. Lamba represented the Indian side in these talks. There were speculations in the media about the status of India–Pakistan negotiations on Kashmir and other issues, but no official information was available.

With Musharraf's diminishing importance in Pakistan and the internal situation deteriorating rapidly, he had no time to pursue his Kashmir policy 'to its logical conclusion.' The new government led by Yusuf Raza Gilani, which came to power in March 2008, adapted his India policy after his removal from power in August 2008. The first visit by the Pakistani Foreign Minister to Delhi unfortunately coincided with the heinous terrorist attacks in Mumbai on 26 November 2008. These attacks convinced India of the complexity of the Pakistani situation and the government decided to cancel the talks. The Pakistan government's unwillingness to accept that the terrorists were from Pakistan and its non-committal approach to reining in jihadi elements operating out of its soil made it difficult for India to restart the dialogue.

In 2009, especially after Manmohan Singh and Asif Ali Zardari met in Yekaterinburg on the sidelines of the Shanghai Cooperation Organisation (SCO) summit, the two countries again expressed their willingness to restart the process of dialogue. However, India has made its continuation conditional on the Pakistan government's willingness to take firm action against the perpetrators of the Mumbai attacks.

Conclusion

The above discussion clearly demonstrates that the India and Pakistan relationship has been characterized by a deep sense of mutual distrust and suspicion. There is a tendency to misinterpret each others' intentions. India has a genuine reason to be suspicious of Pakistani intentions because it has been a victim of both overt and covert aggression, while Pakistan's distrust of India primarily emanates from its insecurities and its weaker position vis-à-vis India. It regards Kashmir as an unfinished agenda of Partition and hatred against India as a rallying point to overcome the fissiparous tendencies within its own polity and society.

At a certain level, there is a realization among the elites that enmity has to be overcome and that there should be a movement towards greater trade and economic co-operation and cultural exchanges between the two countries. However, the inability of the Pakistani state to generate a consensus on the issue has stood in the way of designing a consistent policy towards India. Moreover, from the very beginning, the Kashmir issue has been built into the identity of Pakistan, and made the centerpiece of its foreign policy vis-à-vis India.

However, while the jihadi constituency has discouraged any understanding with India, the governments of India and Pakistan have at least agreed to talk to each other about contentious and deeply political issues even though the talks have not yielded any results as yet. If the direction of the talks during 2003–07 were to be analysed properly, the conclusion is likely to be that the two countries were getting closer to an understanding on Kashmir based on the idea of open borders, autonomy and self-government on both sides of the LOC, and the evolution of a joint co-operative framework for security. This trend has to be encouraged once Pakistan decides to rein in the militant groups operating out of its soil against India and seek a solution to the Kashmir issue through meaningful dialogue with India.

Notes

1 The 1951 Census of displaced persons showed that 7,226,000 Muslims went to Pakistan from India while 7,249,000 Hindus and Sikhs moved to India from Pakistan in the aftermath of the partition. As per conservative estimates the total number of deaths was around 500,000. See P.M. Visaria, 'Migration between India and Pakistan, 1951–61', August 1969, pp. 323–334 and R. Symonds, *The making of Pakistan*, 1950, p. 74.

2 They exchanged 27 letters and telegrams between 10 August 1953 and 21 September 1954.

3 The Central Treaty Organization (CENTO) was adopted in 1955 by Iran, Iraq, Pakistan, Turkey, and the United Kingdom.

4 S. Gopal (ed.), *Selected works of Jawaharlal Nehru*, 1992, vol. 36, p. 400.

5 The Constituent Assembly went on to draft a Constitution for the state which came into force on 26 January 1957. It was also incorporated in the Constitution that the 'State of Jammu and Kashmir is and shall be an integral part of the Union of India' (Part II, Section 3 of the Constitution).

6 Jawaharlal Nehru, the Indian Prime Minister, had expressed the Indian sense of dismay in his interactions with many Western diplomats, which is mentioned in D. Kux, *India and the United States: Estranged democracies*, 1993.

7 Y.D. Gundevia, *Outside the archives*, 1984, p. 248.

8 D.K. Palit, *War in the high Himalaya: Indian army in crisis*, 1992, p. 397.

9 CFL was thus renamed after the Simla Agreement.

10 *The Times*, London, 7 February 1978.
11 The US Ambassador Robert F. Goheen said in Delhi '… Indian superiority is so great that a limited supply of arms to Pakistan should not cause as much consternation in India … No doubt Pakistan feels more endangered since the leftist take over in Afghanistan.' Reported in *The Indian Express*, New Delhi, 5 February 1980.
12 Reported in *The Indian Express*, New Delhi, 5 August 1979.
13 Zia in his interview with Kuldip Nayar, quoted in *The Indian Express*, New Delhi, 31 January 1980.
14 See the text of the Final Declaration at www.oic-oci.org/english/conf/fm/All%20Download/frmex1.htm
15 Quoted in *International Herald Tribune*, 1 February 1990.
16 Quoted in *The Indian Express*, New Delhi, 13 February 1990.
17 Quoted in *The Indian Express*, New Delhi, 14 April 1990.
18 Reported in *The Indian Express*, New Delhi, 10 April 1990.
19 Reported in *The Indian Express*, New Delhi, 10 April 1990.
20 V.P. Singh in Amritsar quoted in *The Times of India*, New Delhi, 14 April 1990.
21 Reported in *The Times of India*, New Delhi, 1 June 1990.
22 K.R. Narayanan, *The Times of India*, New Delhi, 1 May 1990.
23 *The Times of India*, New Delhi, 7 August 1990.
24 Cited in S.D. Muni's article in *The Hindu*, Madras, 22 November 1990.
25 Nawaz Sharif to P.S. Suryanarayan of Express News Services in Male, where he was attending the SAARC summit. Reported in *The Indian Express*, New Delhi, 26 November 1990.
26 Reported in *The New Strait Times*, Kuala Lumpur, 26 January 1994.
27 E. Haider, 'Price of Kashmir-Afghanistan Policies', *The Friday Times*, Lahore, 3–9 June 1998.
28 Even at the top leadership level, the then Prime Minister, I.K. Gujral, was not in favor of applying the 'Gujral' doctrine to Pakistan and was not serious about any talks on Kashmir.
29 While South Africa tendered an apology for this mention, there were pressures from the US and the UK on India to talk to Pakistan.
30 See the text of the joint statement at www.indianembassy.org/pic/PR_1998/September98/prsept2498.htm
31 Jamait-i-Islami argued that it would dilute the cause of Kashmir. The jihadi constituency, represented by the Lashkar-e-Toiba, held that jihad, not dialogue, was the need of the hour. Even his populist policy of introducing Sharia could not woo these Islamist forces to his side. Reported in *The News*, 7 July 1998.
32 The Pakistan Ministry of Foreign Affairs mentioned it in its official brief in 2005. See www.mofa.gov.pk/Pages/Brief.htm
33 See reports on General Musharraf's address in a conference titled 'Voices from Asia: Towards a process of cooperation and security', in *Tribune*, 16 February 2007, at www.tribuneindia.com/2007/20070216/world.htm.

Bibliography

Behuria, A. (ed.), *India and its neighbours: Towards a new partnership*, New Delhi: IDSA, 2008.
Dixit, J.N., *Across Borders – 50 Years of India's foreign policy*, New Delhi: Picus Books, 1998.
Dutt, V.P., *India's foreign policy in a changing world*, New Delhi: Vikas Publishing House Pvt. Ltd., 1999.
Gauhar, A., 'Four wars and one assumption', *The Nation*, 10 September 1999.

Gopal, S. (ed.), *Selected works of Jawaharlal Nehru*, Delhi: OUP, 1992.

Gundevia, Y.D., *Outside the archives*, Hyderabad: Sangam Books, 1984.

Gujral, I.K., *Continuity and change: India's foreign policy*, New Delhi: Macmillan, 2003.

Kux, D., *India and the United States: Estranged democracies, 1941–1991*, Washington, DC: National Defense University Press, 1993.

Mansingh, L. *et al.*, *Indian foreign policy: Agenda for the 21st century*, Foreign Services Institute, New Delhi in association with Konark Publishers Pvt. Ltd., 1998.

Palit, D.K., *War in the high Himalaya: Indian army in crisis*, New Delhi: South Asia Books, 1992.

Razvi, M., *Musharraf: The years in power*, New Delhi: HarperCollins Publishers India, 2009.

Shivam, R.K., *India's foreign policy, Nehru to Vajpayee*, New Delhi: Commonwealth Publishers, 2001.

Singh, J., *Defending India*, Basingstoke: Macmillan, New York: St. Martins Press, 1999.

Symonds, R., *The making of Pakistan*, London: ASIN, 1950.

Visaria, P.M., 'Migration between India and Pakistan, 1951–61', *Demography*, 6:3, August 1969.

5 China's growing strategic influence in South Asia

The impact on national securities and insecurities – a comment

Tridib Chakraborti

Throughout the cold-war years, which started soon after India and Pakistan became independent states in South Asia, China remained an important extra-regional power. China's foreign policy during that time was shaped by a desire to participate in the bipolar international system only to the extent necessary to preserve and enhance its autonomy. As a result China leant on one side and subsequently tilted to the other to cultivate new friends, as and when necessary, with the objective of preserving its security and keeping its sovereignty and territorial integrity intact. India, on the other hand, adopted a policy of non-alignment, indicating that it did not wish to be drawn into any alliance. New Delhi's response to the bipolar world was different from that of other South Asian countries, most of which were getting entangled in cold-war military alliances.[1] Yet many of them were attracted to Jawaharlal Nehru's vision of a 'Resurgent Asia,' further strengthened by New Delhi's main policy imperative in the region – the exclusion of foreign interference. This chapter discusses China's growing presence and influence in the South Asian region, which has been problematic because of India's desire to keep extra-regional powers at bay, and the effect it has had on Indian perceptions and relations between the two countries.

China and South Asia: cold-war geopolitics

China's foreign policy during the cold-war years was based on territoriality and sovereignty, and it never allowed any country to challenge its territorial integrity as perceived by it. Against the backdrop of anti-India feelings in South Asia, Chinese military assistance to Pakistan made it a regional strategic balancer against India. But China had its own unresolved issues with India. At the bilateral level, the Tibet issue cast the main cloud over India–China relations, and this remained one of the major bones of contention during the cold-war years. Geo-politically, China enjoyed a certain natural advantage as it almost looked down upon the hills and plains of India from its higher mountain ranges in Tibet and Sinkiang. It always placed greater efforts in fortifying its position in both the Western and Eastern sectors of the boundary, in building roads and networks of communication, establishing check-posts and strengthening its military positions in many areas on the borders claimed by it. Subsequently, its construction of the

Karakoram Highway linking Sinkiang with Pakistan through Indian-claimed areas of Kashmir largely tilted the geo-political advantage in favor of Beijing. Cognizant of China's strategic advantage and India's inability to compete/over-come it, Nehru advocated a policy of befriending the Chinese leadership. But China's military deployment in Tibet and the adverse reactions in India weak-ened India–China ties, as did the Sino-Indian war of 1962. Nehru was helpless in this situation due to India's weak military strength, and India had to be bailed out by extra-regional powers. Furthermore, India's evolving strategic and polit-ical association with the former Soviet Union, which was not on good terms with Beijing especially after the Ussuri River clash in 1969, further alienated the Chinese leadership. Thus China failed to realize its potential in the South Asian region as a rational balancer that could properly handle its relations as a respons-ible neighbor, in order to reduce the rift between the two great regional powers – India and Pakistan.

China's transformation from a socialist to a market oriented economy

The transformation of China from a socialist to a market-oriented economy was initiated by Deng Xiaoping in 1978, under the 'four modernizations' program (agriculture, industry, science and technology, and the military) with the ambi-tious plan of opening up and liberalizing China's economy. He was considered 'the architect' of a new brand of socialist thinking, having developed socialism with Chinese characteristics and led Chinese economic reform through a synthe-sis of theories that became known as the 'socialist market economy.' Deng opened China to foreign investment, the global market, and limited private com-petition. He is generally credited with developing China into one of the fastest-growing economies in the world. From the late 1980s this led the Chinese leadership to try to create a benign image of itself among all countries including those in the South and Southeast Asian regions, in order to expand its interna-tional trade, source raw materials, invest in infrastructural facilities beyond its borders and pursue its economic interests.

China and South Asia in the post-cold war years

From the early 1990s, China's relations with India improved slowly but steadily, and this resulted in the exchange of a number of high-level visits. For example, the Chinese premier Li Peng's visit to India in December 1991 and the Indian president R. Venkataraman's visit to China in May 1992 were important events. Besides this, from 1992 to 1994, President Venkataraman, Prime-Minister Nar-asimha Rao, and Vice-President K.R. Narayanan made successive visits to China. During Narasimha Rao's visit agreements were signed on various matters including cross-border trade, which led to the resumption of border trade after a hiatus of more than 30 years. Further, from 1991 to 1996, Li Peng, Chairman Li Ruihuan of the CPPCC National Committee, Chairman Qiao Shi of the NPC

Standing Committee, and President Jiang Zemin made a sequence of return visits. During Sharad Pawar's July 1992 visit to Beijing – the first ever by an Indian Minister of Defense – the two defense establishments agreed to develop academic, military, scientific, and technological exchanges and to schedule an Indian port call by a Chinese naval vessel. Moreover, consulates reopened in Bombay (Mumbai) and Shanghai in December 1992, and in June 1993, the two sides agreed to open an additional border trading post. An important event took place in 1994 when China and India agreed to reduce troops along the Himalayan frontier, and in January of that year, Beijing announced that it not only favored a negotiated solution on Kashmir, but also opposed any form of independence for the region. This decision of the Chinese leadership was actually taken after the 1993 visit of a Chinese military delegation to India, which was reciprocated by the Indian Army Chief of Staff, General B.C. Joshi, in July 1994. During his talks with his Chinese counterpart in Beijing, the two sides agreed that border problems should be resolved peacefully through 'mutual understanding and concessions.'

Nuclear tests and the Chinese 'other'

However, the state of improving relations lost its rhythm in 1998, when India conducted nuclear tests in response to a perceived 'Chinese threat,' and this resulted in a serious setback in bilateral relations. The process of deterioration of ties between them actually started when, on 4 May 1998, the Indian Defense Minister George Fernandez accused Chinese patrols of intruding into Indian territory. In that speech, he said that 'China was encircling India with alliances with Pakistan and Myanmar, as well as missile and naval deployments of suspicious intent. Its nuclear weapons are stockpiled in Tibet right along India's borders.' He mentioned that Chinese military airfields in Tibet had been extended in the last six months, and 'there was a lot of naval activity off the coast of Myanmar. To underplay the situation across the Himalayas is not in the national interest; in fact, it can create a lot of problems for us in the future.'[2] Similarly, quoting from a 1996 report by the Indian Parliamentary Standing Committee on Defense, he stated

> Despite warming relationships with China, China is and is likely to remain the primary security challenge to India in the medium and long-term. Its enhancement of its missile capability and its immense help to Pakistan in its missile program are serious security concerns for India.

He identified China as India's 'other' and 'potential threat number one', and asserted that if a strategic review of India's situation merited it, India should 'exercise the nuclear option.'[3] Following this statement, on 11 May 1998, India conducted five nuclear tests at Pokhran in the remote Thar Desert. However, the Indian Prime Minister, Vajpayee, and other political leaders repeatedly and publicly said that the 1998 tests were a matter of national security and that India had no wish to consider China as an enemy or a threat, expressing, to the contrary, its desire for a revival of friendly relations with China, thereby trying to balance the statement made by the Indian Defense Minister earlier.

The immediate reaction of the Chinese government to the Indian nuclear tests was extremely negative. It condemned them vehemently and called on the international community to 'adopt a unified stand and strongly demand that India immediately stop development of nuclear weapons.' China also rejected as 'totally unreasonable' India's stated rationale that it needs nuclear capabilities to counter a Chinese threat,[4] and strongly urged the Indian government to immediately stop all unwarranted accusations against China and act concretely to improve relations.

Meanwhile, within a few days, the Pakistan government conducted nuclear blasts and thereby gave a fitting reply to India's monopolistic nuclear status in the South Asian region. However, this event shocked the Chinese government. China viewed the India and Pakistan nuclear tests as a direct threat to regional stability and Chinese security. The Chinese officials blamed India more than Pakistan for initiating the crisis in South Asia, since China was a natural ally of Pakistan as well as the main supporter of Pakistan's nuclear program. However, despite China's harsh rhetoric, Beijing diplomatically did not side openly with Pakistan against India. Rather, China stated that its main concern was the negative impact of the tests on global nuclear non-proliferation efforts, urged India and Pakistan to abandon nuclear weapons development programs, and described these tests as a direct threat to regional peace and stability. Although China criticized India sharply, its actions were more moderate. While the US and Japan led the international community in imposing sanctions on India in response to its nuclear test, China did not impose any sanctions on India or Pakistan, although it threatened that it could stop nuclear fuel sales to India's four nuclear power reactors at Tarapur.[5] Moreover, the then Chinese president, Jiang Zemin, asserted that although India 'targeted' China with its nuclear tests, China would not resume its own nuclear testing program. These tests also prompted China to revisit its nuclear and missile co-operation with Pakistan.

Despite the changed environment since the end of the cold war and the improvement in bilateral relations, a number of issues have continued to affect Sino-Indian bilateral ties. They include China's pro-Pakistan tilt, the issue of Tibet, the pending border dispute, the increasing Chinese strategic presence in India's neighborhood, and the Brahmaputra river water issue. These issues will now be discussed.

The border issue

Historically, the McMahon Line boundary dispute is at the heart of the border issue between China and India. The root cause of the border problem lies in Beijing's position that a large chunk of its territory, especially the 90,000 sq km area in the eastern sector, was illegally taken away by British India after the 1914 Simla Convention, and that that area was inherited by India after the British left in 1947. This historical legacy has provided the rationale for Beijing's rejection of the McMahon Line, a product of the Convention, and prompted it to claim the entire Arunachal Pradesh state of India as part of Chinese territory, called by them 'Southern Tibet.' Recognition of the McMahon Line would be tantamount to Chinese admission of the 1962 conflict as a 'war of aggression,' as well as an implicit acknowledgement that Tibet was once independent. The border between China and India has never been officially delimited. China's position on the eastern part of the border between the two countries is consistent. No Chinese government has recognized the 'illegal' McMahon Line. For China, the McMahon Line is branded as a symbol of imperialist aggression on the country. The so-called 'Arunachal Pradesh dispute' is China's most intractable border issue, because the gap between the positions of China and India is wide and it is difficult for the two nations to reach a consensus.

Arunachal Pradesh is the only issue that has a potential for military conflict between India and China at the present juncture. India holds that the Line of Actual Control (LAC) demarcates the boundary separating Arunachal Pradesh and China's Tibet Autonomous Region. However, China claims that most of Arunachal Pradesh is Chinese territory as an extension of southern Tibet. Since the 1962 war, each side has continued to improve its military and logistical capabilities in the disputed regions. China has continued to occupy the Aksai Chin area, through which it has built a strategic highway linking Xizang and Xinjiang autonomous regions. China has a vital military interest in maintaining control over this region, due to security considerations. Against this background, since 1981, the two countries have held annual talks on the border issue.

On 7 September 1993, an Agreement on the Maintenance of Peace and Tranquility along the Line of Actual Control in the India–China Border Areas was signed in order to foster 'confidence-building measures' between the defense forces of India and China. Thus in November 1995 the two sides dismantled the guard posts in close proximity to each other along the borderline in the Wangdong area, making the situation in the border areas more stable. During President Jiang Zemin's visit to India at the end of November 1996, the governments of China and India signed another 'Agreement on Confidence Building Measures in the Military Field' along the LAC as an important step for improving mutual trust. These agreements provided an institutional framework for the maintenance of peace and tranquility in the border areas and tacitly signaled on the one hand that the two sides could resolve border disputes peacefully without resorting to violence, and on the other, that border disputes would not inhibit the development of bilateral relations.[6]

During the Indian Prime Minister Atal Behari Vajpayee's visit to China in June 2003, the two countries signed a Memorandum on Expanding Border Trade. At this meeting, the Government of India acknowledged that Tibet was an integral part of Chinese territory (although not for the first time), and China recognized Sikkim as part of India. In April 2005, the Chinese Premier Wen Jiabao visited India, and at the end of this visit, the two sides signed an Agreement on Political Parameters and Guiding Principles for the Settlement of the

India–China Boundary Question. In the agreement, China and India affirmed their readiness to seek a fair, reasonable and mutually acceptable solution to the boundary issue through equal and friendly negotiations,[7] and any resolution of the border issue was termed as a 'strategic objective' in the development of India–China relations.[8] However, so far, no tangible result in finalizing a 'framework' for a boundary settlement in accordance with the 'Agreement on Political Parameters' has been achieved, despite the holding of nine rounds of negotiations between the two sides.

Meanwhile, to counter the 'Chinese threat,' New Delhi has decided to take various military measures to defend its borders including the deployment of three Airborne Warning and Control Systems along with Agni-III missiles with a range of 3,500 km. Besides this, the Indian Navy plans to strengthen its fleet on the eastern seafront, including the basing of an aircraft carrier in the Bay of Bengal.

The Tibet issue

When Tibet was under British rule (up to 1947), the Chinese felt insecure and threatened. But now that Tibet is under Chinese control (since 1950), India feels that its whole northern security system is being threatened. The recent Chinese developmental and strategic activities in Tibet have thus created deep anxiety in India. In recent years China has been rapidly improving the infrastructure in Tibet, especially by connecting Lhasa with the interior provinces by railway with effect from 1 July 2006, which is now being extended to Xigaze and Nyingchi in southwestern and southeastern Tibet respectively, close to the Indian border. Beijing is also visualizing a Tibet–Indian Ocean trade route via India through Yadong. In July 2010, the highest civilian airport in the world was opened at Gunsa in Tibet's Ngari Prefecture, and an airport in Xigaze is scheduled to open soon. Besides this, India is also concerned over unexplained Chinese constructions on the Yarlung Tsangpo River, which becomes the Brahmaputra. In late 2009, it emerged that China had begun to build a dam at Zangmu, but China reassured India that this would have no impact on the downstream flow of the river through Arunachal Pradesh. All these events undoubtedly have strategic implications for India, and New Delhi expressed its concerns over the build-up of Chinese military capabilities and the stepped-up construction of infrastructure such as roads and railway lines near the LAC, which provided China's armed forces with greater communication and access to the region.

The most important reason behind India's concern regarding the Tibetan plateau was the stationing of various sophisticated nuclear missiles there. This deployment of armaments on the Tibetan plateau affects South Asian security in general and India's security in particular. In view of this precarious situation, New Delhi may still be seen to have a definite stake in the politics of the Tibet region, though it remains exclusively an internal matter for China. Strategically, Tibet's stability is of importance for neighboring India, in the interest of which it would like the exiled Tibetan community resident in India ultimately to return to Tibet with a proper leadership position for the Dalai Lama there.

The hydropower dispute

The Tibetan plateau is the site of the headwaters for many of Asia's rivers including the Yellow, Yangtze, Brahmaputra, Indus and Sutlej. These rivers are a lifeline for China and India as well as for Bangladesh, Myanmar, Bhutan, Nepal, Cambodia, Pakistan, Laos, Thailand and Vietnam. These countries make up 49 percent of the global population. Chinese efforts to divert the water resources of the Brahmaputra River away from India has been a source of tension between the two countries. The Brahmaputra River flows 2,900 km from its source in the Kailas range of the Himalayas to its massive delta in the Bay of Bengal in Bangladesh. It falls precipitously from the heights of the Tibetan plateau through the world's deepest valley (5,075 m) into northeast India where the river eventually joins with the Ganges and Meghna rivers to form the largest river delta in the world. The Brahmaputra basin covers 651,334 km, 58 percent of which lies in India and 20 percent in China.[9] In 2000, India accused China of not sharing hydrological data on the flow of the Brahmaputra River through the Chinese territory, resulting in widespread devastation due to floods. Following this event, a Memorandum of Understanding (MoU) was signed in 2002 to coordinate data-sharing pertaining to water level, discharge and rainfall. The data provided by China has helped in flood forecasting and given the Indian Water Ministry a better understanding of the river system. Any plan to divert the Brahmaputra will have to be made known to the Indian Water Ministry beforehand as mentioned in the MoU. The Indian concerns over plans to divert the Brahmaputra were not unjustifiable. In early 2003, scientists from the China Water Conservancy and Hydropower Planning and Designing Institute initiated a feasibility study for a major hydropower project along the section of the Brahmaputra River which flows through China, on behalf of the Chinese government, to fulfill its goal of instituting a massive South–North water diversion project, which would affect millions of people downstream in India, Bangladesh and other countries.[10]

China has two major plans on the Tsangpo River (Brahmaputra River in India). One is the Zangmu project in Tibet, which is basically a 'run of the river' hydroelectric power generation project, and not a threat to India. The real concern for New Delhi is Beijing's second major plan of diverting water from the south to the arid north along three major routes. One of the routes is from the Brahmaputra and involves building a dam on the 'great bend' of the Brahmaputra, which would impact India, Bangladesh and millions of people who depend on the waters of this river for their livelihood. This would also have an impact on India's own National River Linking Project (NRLP), which entails diverting the waters of the north to the south. The Brahmaputra accounts for 29 percent of the total run-off of all India's rivers, and its waters are central to the success of the NRLP.[11] In 2006, India observed through satellite images that China was planning to construct the dam, which Beijing denied time and again. Subsequently, the Chinese government officially affirmed the fact but categorically dismissed claims that Beijing plans to divert the Brahmaputra River that flows from Tibet into India.[12] The Chinese plan to construct the dam officially came to light in 2009, when China declared its plan to build a dam upstream on the Brahmputra River–Tsangpo River in Tibet. The construction will be situated in a place called Namcha Barwa on the eastern plateau of Tibet, and will be the world's largest dam, with 26 turbines, expected to generate 40 million kilowatts per hour of hydroelectricity.[13] This hydroelectrical project was inaugurated on 16 March 2009, with a total investment of 7.9 billion yuan ($1.2 billion), and remains the key project for Tibet in China's eleventh Five-Year Plan. The Indian government expressed deep concern regarding the planning of this dam. It was feared by New Delhi that the dam would decrease the flow of the river in India and lead to the destruction of the Himalayan ecosystem. Above all, the agriculture and industry of the northeastern states of India, which depend heavily on the Brahmaputra River, would suffer hugely. In addition, with this project China will directly control more than 90 thousand square meters of land, the sovereignty over which is still disputed. In response to India's anxiety, China asserts that the dam will allow it to develop clean energy and reduce carbon dioxide emissions resulting from coal-fired power plants.[14] This dam issue has raised questions in the Indian Parliament more than once. On 22 April 2010 India's Foreign Minister, S.M. Krishna, told the Upper House of Parliament: 'It is a fact that when I met my Chinese counterpart recently, the question of the hydroelectric project over the Brahmaputra river being built by it in Zangmu did come up. However, the Chinese foreign minister assured me that it is a small project which will not have any impact on the river's downstream flow into North-east India.'[15]

China has finally acknowledged for the first time that it has begun damming the Yarlong Tsangpo River in Tibet in order to break ground on a 510-megawatt hydropower project. The first six generating units are likely to be commissioned by 2014. China has said that the dam will not have any impact on the downstream flow of the river into India. Formal construction of it started on 12 November 2010. While defending the Chinese dam project, foreign ministry spokesman Hong Lei said that China took 'full consideration of the potential impact on the downstream area, and in the development of cross-border water resources, China has always had a responsible attitude and places equal emphasis on development and protection.'[16] China also stressed that its projects were only for hydropower generation, and were neither storage projects nor designed to divert the water. However, the government of India voiced its frustration over China's general lack of willingness to share information. The Union Minister of Environment and Forests, Jairam Ramesh, said in a statement, 'The great fear in India has been that China would divert waters from the Brahmaputra to feed its arid southwest region, thereby impacting India as middle riparian. Politically and even ecologically it would be unacceptable for India. If the project is in fact just a run of the river hydro power project, and doesn't involve plans for storage or diversion, it should not be cause for great concern.'[17] Moreover, as pointed out by Ramaswamy R. Iyer, former Water Resources Secretary of the Government of India, 'Since India has not signed any treaty with China regarding water-sharing … it does not allow India to either qualify or address Chinese claims regarding specific projects.' He further added, 'Between India and Pakistan, we have a treaty which specifies what we should do. We're not supposed to retain a drop, and even during a stated period of construction, inflow is equal to outflow. But with China, we have no treaty. So what they will do, we have no idea.'[18] Indians fear that the water resources of the Brahmaputra could be used to black-mail India. If China blocks the flow of the Brahmaputra, it will lead to famine in the whole northeast region. India needs to take this issue seriously and should initiate a totally different tactic to tackle China.

The Pakistan factor in India–China relations

Despite the fact that the US has been the main source of financial and military aid to Pakistan since 1954, China continues to be the only power that has invested substantially in Pakistan's nuclear program. The recent sale of conventional weapons to Pakistan by China includes JF-17 aircraft, JF-17 production facilities, F-22P frigates with helicopters, K-8 jet trainers, T-85 tanks, F-7 aircraft, small arms and ammunition. Beijing has also built a turnkey ballistic missile manufacturing facility near the city of Rawalpindi and helped Pakistan develop the 750-km-range, solid-fueled Shaheen-1 ballistic missile.[19] China has helped Pakistan to build two nuclear reactors at the Chasma site in the Punjab Province and continues to support Pakistan's nuclear program, although it has been sensitive to the international condemnation of the A.Q. Khan affair and has calibrated its nuclear assistance to Pakistan accordingly. During Pakistani president Zardari's visit to Beijing in mid-October 2008, China pledged to help Pakistan construct two new nuclear power plants at Chasma, but did not propose or agree to a major China–Pakistan nuclear deal akin to the US–India civil nuclear agreement. US congressional members have expressed concern about China's failure to apply Nuclear Suppliers Group (NSG) 'full-scope safeguards' to its nuclear projects in Pakistan. China is also helping Pakistan develop a deep-sea port at the naval base at Gwadar in Pakistan's province of Balochistan on the Arabian Sea. The port would allow China to secure oil and gas supplies from the Persian Gulf and project power in the Indian Ocean. China financed 80 percent of the $250 million for the completion of the first phase of the project, and agreed to fund the second phase as well.[20] This complex, once finished, will provide a port, warehouses and industrial facilities and will eventually have the capability to receive oil tankers with a capacity of 200,000 tons. India is deeply concerned that China may turn its investment in Gwadar Port into access for its warships.[21]

As regards China's Kashmir policy, Beijing initially supported Islamabad's position on the Kashmir issue, but from the early 1990s, China's position became unequivocal that the Kashmir issue is a bilateral matter to be resolved by India and Pakistan through peaceful means.[22] Following the 1999 Kargil crisis, Beijing made clear its position that the two sides should resolve the Kashmir conflict through bilateral negotiations, not by military force. India was pleased with China's stance on the Kargil crisis, and this allowed Beijing and New Delhi to overcome the tensions in their relations that had developed over India's 1998 nuclear tests. However, despite the Chinese position on Kashmir and nuclear testing, Beijing maintains a robust defense relationship with Pakistan. In April 2005, the 'China–Pakistan Treaty of Friendly Cooperation and Good Neighbourly Relations' was signed by Beijing and Islamabad, and both countries considered it a legal foundation for a strategic partnership. This was the first such treaty between China and any South Asian country. Interestingly, the treaty is being looked upon in China as a 'symbol of Sino-Pakistan alliance against foreign invasion,'[23] and it has been felt that Pakistan will use the treaty as leverage against the perceived threat from India. China may also feel that Pakistan will be treaty-bound to come to its aid in the event of any serious China–US competition in South Asia.

Other developments

As nations import more energy and develop their trade, protecting their interests in the Indian Ocean has become increasingly important. Already, close to 70 percent of India's imported oil comes from the Persian Gulf through the Indian Ocean; China is expected to reach this level by 2015. The Indian Ocean is a key arena for US–India co-operation, including periodic joint military exercises. India currently has the strongest Asian naval presence in this region. To counter the Indian Navy's movements extending from the Bay of Bengal to the South China Sea, China has according to many scholars started the process of encircling India through a 'String of Pearls' strategy by building up facilities and access arrangements in the Indian Ocean, from its investment in a new port on the Pakistani coast at Gwadar in the West, to Chittagong in Bangladesh, Hambantota in Sri Lanka and the Cocos Islands in Myanmar in the East. Another issue, which deeply distressed India, was the recent drive in China's military modernization programs. In a Defense White Paper Beijing published in December 2006, it was mentioned that China was concerned about the 'grave threat' coming from 'Taiwan Independence forces,' the situation created by the North Korean missile and nuclear tests in 2006, and the US–Japan efforts to build a defense shield for use in any conflict over Taiwan. Against this background, in 2007, China increased its defense budget by nearly 18 percent.[24] The Indian government did not look upon this increase favorably and New Delhi stressed the need to monitor the situation, since China had already strengthened its military infrastructure in the vicinity of the border areas, which is related to the hike in its defense budget. Along with this issue, China's weaponization of outer space and its anti-satellite testing from January 2007 was another determinant in disturbing bilateral ties.[25]

Meanwhile China's trade with South Asia has been growing, as shown in Table 5.1. The total trade figure of China with the SAARC countries increased from US$3.19 billion in 1995 to US$12.08 billion in 2003, and this figure increased by more than five times to US$65.86 billion in 2008, after China joined the SAARC as an Observer member. However, the balance of trade has always tilted in favor of China. This proportion went down slightly due to the financial crisis of 2008, but more recently, China has made substantial economic and financial investments in Pakistan, Bangladesh, Sri Lanka and Nepal. Its investment strategy has helped open up these nations for Chinese goods as well. The Indian government was reluctant to grant China Observer status in the SAARC. In April 2007, at the 14th SAARC Summit, China became an Observer member of the organization. The inclusion of China as an Observer is seen by some SAARC member states as a counterbalance to India. The 15th SAARC Summit was held in Sri Lanka from 27 July to 3 August 2008. At this meeting, China expressed its enthusiasm for playing a meaningful, proactive and constructive role in addressing regional concerns, such as poverty alleviation, food security, energy crisis, terrorism and climate change.

While China's trade with South Asia has been growing, India's trade figures for the same period have been dismal by comparison. The total trade figure of India with the SAARC countries was a mere US$1.96 billion in 1996–97, increased to US$5.00 billion by 2003–04, and more than doubled by 2008–09. The balance of trade has always tilted in favor of India.[26] It is clear through the trade figures examined here that China is developing all-round co-operation with India's SAARC partners in a structured way in the economic, political and even military spheres. Thus the twenty-first century cannot be an 'Asian Century' unless India plays a more proactive role in the South Asian economic process. In fact in recent times, under the leadership of Prime Minister Manmohan Singh, India has for the first time in its foreign policy agenda exhibited a friendly mindset and interest in prioritizing its neighbors. This became clear when New Delhi made a commitment to providing a credit line of US $1 billion to improve Bangladesh's infrastructure (similar to commitments in Afghanistan) during Bangladesh Prime Minister Sheikh Hasina's four-day official visit to India from 10 to 13 January 2010.

Conclusion

China's strategic influence in South Asia has been growing over the years. As this chapter argues, it is mainly India that feels threatened by China. The border dispute and the issue of Tibet have caused severe strains in relations between the

Table 5.1 China's trade relations with SAARC countries (US$ billion)

Year	Exports	Imports	Total trade	Balance of trade
1995	2.51	0.68	3.19	1.83
2000	3.80	1.89	5.69	1.91
2003	7.19	4.89	12.08	2.30
2005	15.96	10.72	26.68	5.24
2008	44.39	21.47	65.86	22.92

Source: Compiled by the author based on World Integrated Trade Solutions, World Bank Online Data, cited in T. Chakraborti, 'Charting Out the SAARC Destiny: Perambulating its Way Forward,' *World Focus* (New Delhi), 31:7, July 2010, p. 249.

two countries. The Indian government would like to see both the issues resolved amicably and to mutual satisfaction, but they are dragging on; and in recent years other issues have added to India's concerns, such as the construction of hydropower projects in Tibet and dams on the river Brahmaputra. Furthermore, China's military assistance to Pakistan does not take India's sensitivities into account, and neither does the construction of ports, highways and other infrastructural projects there. In recent years China's attempts to become a full member of SAARC have been resisted by the Indian government. As China's trade with South Asia continues to grow, India is feeling encircled and is under pressure to improve relations with its neighbors, to step up its economic performance, and possibly to form strategic alliances with other extra-regional power such as the US and Russia, so as to neutralize China's growing influence in the region. On the other hand, the Chinese Premier, Wen Jiabao, was quite positive about the future of China's relations with India, and during his visit to New Delhi in December 2010 made it quite clear that he felt that there is enough room in the world for both India and China to develop and co-operate with each other. 'The dragon and the elephant should tango,' he said; they are not rivals but 'partners in co-operation.'

Notes

1 Chakraborti, 'India's Southeast Asia Policy in the 21st Century', 2007, p. 155.
2 'India Tests Destabilize Peace', *China Daily*, 20 May 1998.
3 'Fernandez Sounds Warning on China', *The Hong Kong Standard*, 5 May 1998; see also 'China "Greatest Threat to India,"' *Financial Times*, 5 May 1998; 'India's New Defense Chief Sees Chinese Military Threat', *New York Times*, 5 May 1998.
4 'India's Nuclear Tests Show Fear of China', *Wall Street Journal*, 15 May 1998, p. A13.
5 'Reaction of US Allies', *ABC News*, 13 May 1998.
6 C.V. Ranganathan and V.C. Khanna, *India and China: The Way Ahead*, 2004, pp. 171–172.
7 See www.globalsecurity.org/military/world/war/indiachina_conflicts.htm (accessed on 4 December 2010).
8 M. Singh, 'PM's Statement in the Lok Sabha on the Visits of Chinese Premier and Pakistan President', 20 April 2005, New Delhi, online, available http://pmindia.nic.in/speeches.htm (accessed on 4 December 2010).
9 For details see P. Vignesh, 'Brahmaputra River: Dispute between India and China', online, available www.jeywin.com/blog/brahmaputra-river (accessed on 12 January 2011).
10 Ibid.
11 For details see P. Malhotra, 'China's Dam on the Brahmaputra: Cause for Concern?', IPCS no. 3174, 30 June 2010, online, available www.ipcs.org/article/india/chinas-dam-on-the-brahmaputra-cause-for-concern-3174.html (accessed on 10 January 2011).
12 'China Building Dam on Brahmputra River: Report', Zee News Bureau, 15 October 2009, online, available www.zeenews.com/news570993.html (accessed on 10 January 2011).
13 'China Plans World's Biggest Dam on Brahmaputra River', 2 June 2010, online, available http://knowledgeniru.blogspot.com/2010/06/china-plan-world's-biggest-dam-on.html (accessed on 29 March 2011).

14 See 'China Builds World's Highest Dam, India Fears Water Theft', online, available www.abovetopsecret.com/forumhread564740/pg1 (accessed on 10 January 2011).
15 *The Indian Express*, 22 April 2010.
16 For details see www.terradaily.com/reports/China_defends_Brahmaputra_dam_ project_amid_Indian_concern_999.html (accessed on 10 January 2011).
17 For details see www.rediff.com/news/column/killing-the-brahmaputra-in-installments/20110111.htm (accessed on 12 January 2011).
18 *The Hindu*, 16 November 2010.
19 'Pakistan Profile', Nuclear Threat Initiative, January 2009, online, available www.nti. org/e_research/profiles/Pakistan/index.html (accessed on 24 December 2010).
20 Z. Haider, 'Baluchis, Beijing, and Pakistan's Gwadar Port', *Politics and Diplomacy*, Winter/Spring 2005, pp. 96–97.
21 For details see M. Chakraborty, 'India and Pakistan in 2010: Re-viewing the State of Bilateral Relations', *World Focus*, New Delhi, annual number, November–December 2010, pp. 539–546.
22 A scholarly interpretation of China's changing positions on the Kashmir issue can be found in J.W. Garver, 'China's Kashmir Policies', *India Review*, 3:1, January 2004, pp. 1–24.
23 D.S. Rajan, 'India and China: Neither Rivals nor Partners', Paper No 2058 dated 10 December 2006, online, available www.saag.org/papers21/paper2058.html (accessed on 24 December 2010).
24 *The People's Daily*, 5 March 2007.
25 For details see D.S. Rajan, 'India and China: Neither Rivals nor Partners', *Dialogue* (New Delhi), January–March 2007, vol. 8, no. 3, online, available, www.asthabharati. org/Dia_Jan%2007/Raja.htm (accessed on 26 December 2010).
26 Prepared by the author from various tables and pages based on *Ministry of Commerce, Export–Import Data Bank*, Government of India, New Delhi, April–March 1996–97 to 2008–09.

Bibliography

Acharya, A., *China and India: Politics of Incremental Engagement*, New Delhi: Har-Anand Publishers, 2008.

Arpi, C., *Tibet: The Lost Frontier*, New Delhi: Lancer Publishers, 2008.

Bajpai, K.P. and S.P. Cohen, *South Asia after the Cold War: International Perspectives*, Boulder, Colorado: Westview Press, 1993.

Baru, S., *Strategic Consequences of India's Economic Performance*, New Delhi: Academic Foundation, 2006.

Bhasin, H., *The Big Three: The Emerging Relationship between the United States, India and China in the Changing World Order*, New Delhi: Academic Foundation, 2009.

Boquerat, G. and F. Grare, *India, China, Russia – Intricacies of an Asian Triangle*, New Delhi: Lancer Books, 2004.

Chakraborti, T., 'India's Southeast Asia Policy in the 21st Century: Perambulating the Horizon' in Y. Yagama Reddy (ed.), *Emerging India in Asia-Pacific*, New Delhi: New Century Publications, 2007, pp. 154–179.

Dutt, V.P., *India's Foreign Policy*, New Delhi: Vani Educational Books, 1985.

Frankel, F.R. and H. Harding (eds), *The India–China Relationship: What the United States Needs to Know*, New York: Columbia University Press, 2004.

Garver, J., *Protracted Contest: Sino-Indian Rivalry in the Twentieth Century*, Seattle, Washington: University of Washington Press, 2001.

Guruswamy, M. and Z.D. Singh, *India China Relations: The Border Issue and Beyond*, New Delhi: Viva Books Private Limited, 2009.

Jain, B.M., *India in the New South Asia: Strategic, Military and Economic Concerns in the Age of Nuclear Diplomacy*, London: I.B. Tauris & Co Ltd, 2010.

Kurlantzick, J., *Charm Offensive: How China's Soft Power is Transforming the World*, Melbourne: Melbourne University Press, 2007.

Nayak, A.K.J.R. and M.G. Jomon, *India in the Emerging Global Order*, New Delhi: Tata McGraw-Hill, 2008.

Pradhan, R.D., *Dragon Shadow over Arunachal: A Challenge to India's Polity*, New Delhi: Rupa & Co., 2009.

Ranganathan, C.V. and V.C. Khanna, *India and China: The Way Ahead*, New Delhi: Har-Anand Publications, 2004.

Sidhu, W.P.S. and J. Yuan, *China and India: Cooperation or Conflict?*, Boulder, Colorado: Lynne Rienner, 2003.

Singh, R. (ed.), *China and India in Asian Power Politics*, New Delhi: VIJ Books, 2011.

Singh, S., *China–Pakistan Strategic Cooperation: Indian Perspectives*, New Delhi: Lancer Books, 2007.

Smith Jr., W.W., *Tibetan Nation: A History of Tibetan Nationalism and Sino-Tibetan Relations*, New Delhi: Saujanya Books, 2009.

Wasim, M., *China–India Border Conflict: Recent Perspective*, New Delhi: Prashant Publishing House, 2010.

Yee, H. and I. Storey (eds), *The China Threat: Perceptions, Myths and Reality*, London: Routledge, 2004.

Internet sources

1 http://pmindia.nic.in/speeches.htm (accessed on 4 December 2010)

2 www.jamestown.org/single/%3Fno_cache% (accessed on 24 December 2010)

3 www.ipcs.org/article/india/chinas-dam-on-the-brahmaputra-cause-for-concern-3174.html (accessed on 10 January 2011)

4 www.saag.org/papers21/paper2058.html (accessed on 24 December 2010)

Part II

Identity, democracy and order

6 From inter-ethnic conflict to plural democracy in Sri Lanka

Martin Mulligan

Introduction

At 8 a.m. on a relatively crisp morning in April 2008, many thousands of young men had formed an enormous line outside the Bureau for Foreign Employment in Colombo for when the doors would be opened an hour later. Near the front of the line the faces were anxious because the weight of bodies was beginning to push on them; further back the atmosphere was more relaxed, even jovial, and still-hopeful young men, clutching essential documents in see-through folders, were joining the back of the line well over a kilometer from where it began. Word had got around that South Korea and Japan would issue a total of 3,000 work visas on this day for fit young men. The successful applicants would join an expatriate Sri Lankan workforce of more than 1.5 million, around 20 percent of the overall Sri Lankan workforce.[1] For a long time women made up the majority of such 'cyclical migrants,' often leaving their children at home to work as 'domestics' in countries ranging from Kuwait to Italy. Now there are growing opportunities for young men[2] and remittances from workers abroad have become one of Sri Lanka's leading industries. Sri Lanka has overtaken Bangladesh to have the highest percentage of GDP made up of inward remittances in South Asia.[3] Statistics cited by Judith Shaw[4] show that remittances make up nearly 10 percent of the nation's GDP and 34 percent of its export earnings.

Having lived among Sri Lankans in Australia for 25 years and having visited the country many times in that period, the author can vouch for the fact that Sri Lankans invariably have a deep affection for their homeland. Even poor people who lost their homes in the devastating tsunami of December 2004 often say that they could not imagine wanting to live in any other country.[5] Yet by 2005 the number of people leaving the country every year to work abroad had exceeded 230,000.[6] After nearly 30 years of civil war and the collapse, in 2006, of a fragile yet promising ceasefire agreement, it seemed that confidence in the future of Sri Lanka was at an all-time low. Of course, the tsunami – which killed over 30,000 people and left a further 100,000 homeless – did not help. Yet this natural disaster triggered a rare moment of unity in a nation divided, and current sagging national morale[7] is more clearly related to social tensions and conflicts that have never been adequately addressed. To understand why morale-sapping divisions have become so endemic in Sri Lanka, we need to begin by reviewing the process of nation formation that has followed independence from Britain in 1948. This paper will then aim to put the failings of nation-building into a broader historical and geopolitical context, because a 'new wave' of Sri Lankan scholars has been offering some fresh perspectives on Sri Lankan identity that could become circuit-breakers for the debilitating and self-perpetuating conflict. Of course, this is not just an exercise in rethinking history, because the identities that have been solidified in the period of 'independent' nation-building continue to be reproduced on a daily basis through social, cultural, and political processes, as Siri Hettige has demonstrated in his ground-breaking work on education, identity formation and citizenship in contemporary Sri Lanka.[8]

It may seem presumptuous for a non Sri Lankan to offer such suggestions regarding the nation's future, even if they are based primarily on the work of Sri Lankan scholars. However, it should be noted that the author has a long-standing and ongoing commitment to the country that provides half of his children's heritage. Furthermore, as the expatriate Sri Lankan writer Qadri Ismail has suggested,[9] there are many people living outside the country who are determined to 'abide by Sri Lanka,' and this includes expatriates and other committed friends. A broadly based dialogue is needed to break through the gridlock of narrow and divisive preoccupations, and there should be a role for interested and engaged 'outsiders' in such a dialogue.

Failings in post-independence nation-building

In sharp contrast to India, Sri Lanka had little trouble 'winning' its independence from Britain in 1948. As early as 1927 the British set up a commission, headed by English House of Lords member Lord Donoughmore, to draft a constitution capable of uniting the emerging nation, and over a period of two months it heard representations from around 140 individuals and delegations interested in protecting the identity and rights of different sectors of the population.[10] Historian Nira Wickramasinghe has said that the work of the commission stimulated new forms of political activity in Sri Lanka aimed at promoting diverse ethnic identities,[11] and the commission found that the rights of 'ethnic minorities' should be given constitutional status. Ironically, however, the 1931 constitution that was based on Donoughmore's recommendations led to a sharp decline in Tamil representation in the island's legislative council because the earlier system of 'communal representation' was replaced by elections based on universal suffrage.[12] The intention of the 1931 constitution was to establish the institutions of liberal democracy that could protect the rights of all 'citizens,' and yet it created new tensions between Tamil and Sinhalese political representatives.

A subsequent commission, headed by English Lord Soulbury and established in 1944, set up a bicameral parliament based on the Westminster model with executive power vested in a prime minister and cabinet, although the British Governor General retained the power to appoint the members of cabinet until independence in February 1948. Although the Soulbury Report stressed that Sri

Lanka should see itself as a 'unitary state,' it reaffirmed the importance of protecting the rights of ethnic and religious minorities. Critics of the constitution that was based on the Soulbury Report say that it introduced an adversarial political culture in place of a requirement to negotiate across ethnic and religious boundaries.[13] Certainly Lord Soulbury simply assumed that the principles of liberal democracy, as they had evolved in Europe, could be easily transposed to Sri Lanka without taking into account the long and complex history of identity formation referred to above. However, as we shall see below, it is surely an exaggeration to blame the Soulbury Constitution for the political culture that evolved after independence.

It is important to note that although the leader of the Tamil Congress, G.G. Ponambalam, agreed to join the independence government led by Prime Minister D.S. Senanayake, many Tamil leaders did not support the concept of the 'unitary state' and several of them formed the Federal Party in 1949 to push the establishment of semi-autonomous provinces across the island. In 1957 the Federal Party managed to convince the government led by Prime Minister Solomon Bandaranaike to set up Regional Councils, including separate Regional Councils in the Tamil-dominated northern province and in the eastern province where Tamil Hindus and Tamil-speaking Muslims make up the majority. Politically active Buddhist monks condemned the agreement reached between Bandaranaike and the leaders of the Federal Party, and rumors spread that the Tamils were preparing for an invasion of the ancient and sacred Sinhalese cities of Anuradhapura and Polonnaruwa. The false rumors sparked violent conflicts between Sinhalese and Tamil people in the border areas between the north and central provinces, which soon turned into anti-Tamil riots that spread across the island in 1958: an early sign of how easily the ethnic tensions could turn into violence. Under pressure from the political Buddhist monks, Bandaranaike revoked his agreement with the leaders of the Federal Party in 1958, and devolution of power was off the agenda for a while.

Solomon Bandaranaike is a pivotal figure in post-independence Sri Lankan politics because although he himself was born into a wealthy family in which English was the primary language, he subsequently adopted all the trappings of Sinhalese nationalism to win a base of support in the southern and western provinces.[14] Promoting himself as a devout Buddhist, Bandaranaike invoked the legacy of the man who is commonly seen as the father of an early 20th-century Buddhist revival movement, *Anagarika* Dharmapala,[15] and in the 1930s he formed the radical Buddhist organization called Sinhala Maha Sabha. Although he was elected to parliament as a member of the ruling United National Party, Bandaranaike formed a breakaway Sri Lanka Freedom Party in 1951 which, in turn, became the dominant partner in a coalition that almost annihilated the UNP in the 1956 elections. A supreme populist, Bandaranaike pitched his appeal at the religious piety of the rural Sinhalese masses, predominantly in the south and west, and he conflated the struggle for national independence with the Sinhalese Buddhist revival movement popularized by Dharmapala. One of his early acts as prime minister was to introduce a law to make Sinhala the official national language, and he worked to give Buddhism an equally privileged position. Ironically, Bandaranaike was assassinated in 1959 by a Buddhist priest who thought he had not gone far enough in making Sri Lanka a Buddhist nation. However, his widow Sirimavo Bandaranaike was subsequently elected prime minister, and in two terms (1960–65 and 1970–77) she continued with the policies that her husband had initiated.

Ironically, the promotion of Sinhalese nationalism did little to improve living standards for the Sinhalese masses, and in 1971 the rather charismatic Rohana Wijeweera – who drew inspiration from both Che Guevara and Mao Zedong – managed to convince thousands of young people to join in a revolt in which they attempted to take over 93 police stations and military posts with predominantly home-made weapons, resulting in the deaths of 63 police and military personnel.[16] Of course the insurrection failed – resulting in reprisals that killed well over 5,000 'insurrectionists'[17] – but the Janatha Vimukti Peramuna (JVP) that Wijeweera formed continued to promote a rather extreme form of Sinhalese nationalism, and in the mid-1980s they launched a more sustained armed uprising, especially in the south. In part the JVP uprisings reflected caste divisions in Sinhalese society,[18] and it is rather ironic that disaffected young people from the fishing caste (*Karavas*) in the south became such fervent Sinhalese nationalists. This is less surprising, however, when it is understood that their interpretation of national history inverted the relationship between *Karavas* and the more traditionally dominant *Goigama* caste.

The promotion of Sinhalese nationalism has triggered the emergence of a new form of Tamil nationalism in Sri Lanka. In both their origins and evolution, the Tamils centered on Jaffna in the north and those centered on Batticaloa in the east are quite different from each other,[19] and yet the idea of an independent Tamil state of Eelam in the north and east began to gain popular Tamil support in the 1970s. Almost mirroring the formation of the JVP in the south and west, the Tamil Students Federation that was formed in 1970 morphed into the Tamil New Tigers in 1972 and then into the Liberation Tigers of Tamil Eelam (LTTE) in 1975.[20] In a provocative gesture, the Tigers had chosen their animal emblem because it had been the emblem of the Chola kings of southern India who had invaded Sri Lanka in the eleventh century. Like the JVP, they promoted the path of armed insurrection, but they were far more effective in building an armed wing because they could raise funds in nearby Tamil Nadu and from the Sri Lankan Tamil diaspora spread across many countries. In an interesting interview conducted in 1981, LTTE leader Velupillai Prabakaran said that his heroes included Chola kings and Napoleon Bonaparte[21] and he is widely acknowledged as being an effective military leader. Under Prabakaran's leadership the LTTE set out to eliminate their Tamil political opponents – sometimes violently – and after a massive wave of anti-Tamil violence spread across Sri Lanka in July 1983 they began an armed struggle that has periodically 'liberated' parts of the north and east from rule by Colombo. The Tigers lost much of their support in India when they admitted responsibility for the assassination of Indian Prime Minister Rajiv Gandhi in 1997, but they were able to turn back repeated assaults by the

Sri Lankan armed forces until their final demise in May 2009, and it seems that they provided fairly effective local government during their period of domination. The Tigers promoted an extreme form of Tamil nationalism, and they effectively killed off a promising peace initiative when they called for a boycott of the presidential elections in 2005. However, their extremism can partly be seen as a response to equally extreme and divisive forms of Sinhalese nationalism. Such extremism on both sides has radically eroded the middle ground.

Failed gestures towards devolution

After many years of populist rule by the Bandaranaikes, the wealthy businessman J.R. Jayawardene came to power at the head of the United National Party in 1977, and under the guise of getting the country moving again he introduced a new constitution to create a Gaullist-style presidential system. Under this reform, adopted in 1978, the president, who would be elected by popular vote every six years, would become both head of state and head of the executive, with the power to appoint members of cabinet. Jayawardene served in that position from 1978 to 1988, and he was succeeded by Ranasinghe Premadasa, who made full use of his presidential powers until he was killed by an LTTE suicide bomber in 1994. Sri Lankans suggest that both President Premadasa and President Chandrika Kumaratunga – who came to power soon after Premadasa – were able to exercise political leadership on some important issues. However, it is equally certain that the centralization of political power has led to increased corruption, lack of transparency and open abuse of power. The populist president elected in 2005, Mahinda Rajapakse, has managed to shore up a majority for his party in parliament by appointing political opponents, as well as two of his own brothers, to positions in the cabinet. By 2008 Sri Lanka had a cabinet with over 100 members, which possibly makes it the biggest in the world!

With political power so firmly entrenched in Colombo it is hardly surprising that other developments have also centered on the capital and the surrounding district. For example, some 55 percent of the nation's GDP is generated in the western province surrounding Colombo, which accounts for only 28 percent of the population.[22] Even more dramatic is the fact that some 60 percent of the nation's medical practitioners operate in Colombo.[23] The migration from rural to urban areas is higher than at any time in Sri Lanka's history, and Colombo is growing at a faster rate than any other population center in the country.

There have, of course, been numerous efforts to end the war between the Sri Lankan armed forces and the forces of the LTTE. In order to neutralize support for the LTTE in Tamil Nadu, President Jayawardene sought the intervention of the Indian government; concerned with long-term unrest in a neighboring country, the Indian government led by Rajiv Gandhi agreed to intervene, provided that new action would be taken at a national level to restore the rights of the Tamil minority. In 1987 India sent in a massive 'peace-keeping force' to the Jaffna Peninsula, and President Jayawardene introduced the 'Thirteenth Amendment' to the Constitution, to restore both Tamil and English as 'official languages' and to set up Provincial Councils in nine different provinces across the island, based on the model of federalism operating in India. Not surprisingly, military intervention from India raised fears and concerns among the Sinhalese majority, who commonly invoke the eleventh-century invasions by Chola kings to suggest that India harbors a desire to annex the island. Furthermore, the Tamil Tigers put up unexpectedly fierce resistance to the presence of the Indian peace-keepers, and it soon became apparent that the latter had only served to inflame the situation. Although some efforts were made to officially acknowledge the use of Tamil and English as secondary languages, Sinhalese retained its domi-nance, and opposition to the Provincial Councils scheme, especially from the LTTE, meant that it was dropped.

Proposals for devolving power in Sri Lanka have cropped up repeatedly since the Donoughmore Constitution of 1931, which included proposals to set up a network of provincial councils to improve the efficiency of national government. However, many of these proposals have failed to reach the point of implementa-tion, and others have been rather token in their intent and impact. As already mentioned, the Federal Party was established by Tamil politicians in 1949 to promote devolution and it succeeded in reaching agreements, first in 1957 with the government led by Solomon Bandaranaike and again in 1967 within the gov-ernment led by Dudley Senanayake, aimed at establishing a system of provincial or district councils. However, both pacts were scuttled by the resistance put up by opposition political parties, and the Federal Party disappeared after a poor showing in the national elections of 1970.[24] President Jayawardene's 1978 pro-posal to set up District Development Councils (DDCs) also ran into stiff political resistance, and when these councils were eventually set up they had little author-ity and little impact. Jayawardene revived the idea of Provincial Councils in 1984, and he included them in the Thirteenth Amendment to the constitution that was driven by the Indo-Lanka Accord of 1987. Under this proposal the national president held the power to appoint the head of each Provincial Council and to dissolve them, and in an attempt to woo Tamil separatists, it was also proposed that formerly identified northern and eastern provinces would be amalgamated into one province with a clear Tamil majority. However, this scheme did not win over the LTTE and its growing base of support in the north and east, and once again resistance led by opposition political parties prevented its implementation.

The most ambitious plan for devolution to date was that put forward by the government led by President Chandrika Kumaratunga in 1995, which centered on the formation of Regional Councils and a new role for a regional governor appointed by the national president on the advice of the elected Regional Council Chief Minister. Under this proposal, Regional Councils would be given desig-nated powers that would be listed and defined as an amendment to the national constitution. Although this proposal attracted the support of moderate political parties and many Muslim leaders, it was again opposed by the LTTE and it was effectively scuttled by the intransigent attitude of United National Party leader Ranil Wickramasinghe, who described it as a threat to national unity. Ironically Wickramasinghe was elected as prime minister in 2001 while Kumaratunga was still in position as president, and he unexpectedly initiated peace talks with the LTTE, independently mediated by Norway. A ceasefire agreement was signed in February 2002 and this was followed by drawn-out negotiations between the government and the LTTE over conditions for peace that would once again include a devolution of power. By July 2003, proposals were on the negotiating table, for new Provincial Administrative Councils and an Interim Self-Governing Authority for the combined provinces of the north and east. Although President Kumaratunga had played an active role in getting the LTTE to the negotiating table, her Sri Lanka Freedom Party (SLFP) began to criticize the peace proposals, under pressure from Sinhalese nationalists in the south and east, and now it was Kumaratunga's turn to block Wickramasinghe's initiatives.

After the populist SLFP leader Mahinda Rajapakse succeeded Kumaratunga as president in 2005, the peace negotiations slowed to a halt and the ceasefire agreement steadily unraveled. Rajapakse sought to take advantage of a deep split in the LTTE, between the leaders in the northern and eastern provinces, by dissolving the merger of the two provinces and by announcing that elections would be held for a Provincial Council in the 'liberated' eastern province in May 2008. With support from the SLFP, the leader of the LTTE break-away party – the TMVP – was elected as chief minister of the province. However, this left Muslims, who form a majority in the southern half of the eastern province, unhappy, and their political leaders began demanding a separate Muslim 'unit' in the southeast.[25]

From this account it is clear that political gamesmanship – from various sides – has consistently undermined attempts to implement some form of devolution, which must surely be part of any meaningful political solution to nearly thirty years of divisive conflict. Any attempt to provide political leadership has been undermined by the populism of the 'moderate' political leaders, who are thus unable to build a consensus that lies somewhere between the extremes of Sinhalese nationalism and Tamil separatism. However, the failure of political leadership reflects a much longer failure – dating back to the early part of the 20th century –to build some kind of consensus about what Sri Lanka might look like as an independent but multicultural nation.

'Illiberal democracy'

An excellent analysis of the failings of nation-building offered by Sisira Edirippulige[26] points out that the path towards national independence that began with the Donoughmore Commission of 1927 meant that Sri Lanka has adopted the trappings of democracy but very little of its reality. He draws on the work of Fareed Zakaria in saying that an overt commitment to the principles of liberal democracy have masked the emergence of a very 'illiberal' form of democracy in Sri Lanka, as in many nations in the under-developed world.[27] Zakaria has suggested that 'illiberal democracy' has been a 'growth industry' in the modern world, especially in nations that won their independence in the period following World War II. Sri Lanka has been better than many of the 'new nations' in giving the appearance of democracy – and it can still boast of a relatively high commitment to freedom of expression. However, Edirippulige demonstrates that the term 'illiberal democracy' still fits the Sri Lankan model as it has evolved over the last 50 to 60 years.

Of course, liberal democracy was born of the European Enlightenment, and its principles do not always work well in Third World settings. Old traditions – e.g., caste divisions in India and Sri Lanka – cut across principles of representation and equal rights, and the very concept of the nation may be weak in societies with much older social institutions. Furthermore, as Gupta has pointed out, the state 'must play an interventionist role' in emerging nations with weakly developed national economies, and this can lead to 'the phenomenon of command politics.'[28] We have seen in Sri Lanka that 'command politics' and centralized economic development tend to go hand-in-hand and that this has undermined any meaningful attempts to devolve political power.

Eric Meyer has suggested that at the time of independence Sri Lanka was in a far better position than India to build a prosperous modern nation.[29] These advantages included higher levels of education and literacy, weaker influence of the divisive caste system, the use of English as a national 'link language' that also facilitated international communication, and long-established trading and cultural links with many other parts of the world (partly reflecting Sri Lanka's location on the planet). However, the failure to resolve the deadly conflict over a period of nearly three decades suggests that Sri Lankan democracy is built on rather flimsy foundations, and many of the advantages listed by Meyer have been forfeited.

As mentioned in the introduction, this paper is interested in drawing on the work of 'new wave' Sri Lankan scholars to identify proposals for deepening democracy and resolving entrenched conflicts in Sri Lanka. As also mentioned in the introduction, the attention focused on post-independence nation formation is not just a matter of correcting historical records, because this period has created deep divisions over questions of identity and belonging that continue to be reinforced in ongoing social, cultural and political practices. For example, Siri Hettige is continuing to warn that the conditions that led to the JVP-led youth rebellions of 1971 and the mid-1980s are being constantly reproduced in the way that the education system operates in Sri Lanka today,[30] and that there are other divisive consequences flowing from the fact that education is 'ethno-linguistically segregated.'[31] While the civil war has created simmering resentments that could erupt in new conflicts in the future, the defeat of the Tamil Tigers in May 2009 has at least provided a window of opportunity to break out of the cycle of violence and reprisal. A sustained outbreak of peace would lift sagging spirits inside the country and tap a wellspring of international goodwill. A national dialogue aimed at creating a new plural identity for Sri Lanka will attract strong international interest. However, before focussing on ways of stimulating a new dialogue about Sri Lankan identity, it will be useful to demonstrate that the difficulties facing the nation as a whole are also confronting complex local communities. The problems of Sri Lanka will not be sorted out by people sitting in Colombo alone but by a rethinking of the lessons of coexistence that are part of the heritage of many local communities across the island.

The Hambantota story

The community centered on the old township of Hambantota, on the southeast 'corner' of Sri Lanka, is interesting because it has an unusual 'ethnic mix' with a fairly even split between those who identify primarily as Muslim (a religious identity) and those who identify as Sinhalese (an 'ethnic' identity). There is evidence of human settlements in the area surrounding Hambantota dating back to the fifth century BCE, and Hambantota itself is renowned for its deep natural harbor.[32] The harbor has been a center of fishing activities for many centuries, and it is adjacent to a system of coastal lagoons that have yielded salt that has been traded across Sri Lanka and abroad for a similar span of centuries. Not far from Hambantota, at the mouth of a big river that flows out of the central highlands – the Welawe Ganga – European archeologists are continuing to work on a deeply layered dig site which has yielded evidence that trading ships had been coming here from different parts of the world for up to 2,000 years. No doubt the river was an important trading route stretching towards the interior, connecting local Sri Lankan communities to the world. Because of its position in the world it is now thought that Sri Lanka was on the 'Silk Route' that enabled trade to occur between the 'Far East,' the Middle East and Europe long before the Europeans were able to travel so far in their own ships.[33]

It seems that traders from the Far East, mainly from the Malay peninsula, arrived in flat-bottomed wooden boats called *sampans*, still used in Malaysia, Indonesia and Vietnam. Indeed, it is speculated that the name Hambantota comes from combining a corrupted version of *sampan* with the Sinhalese word *tota*, which means harbor, to create a name meaning 'sampan harbor.'[34] Sometimes the Muslims living in and around Hambantota are called 'Malay Muslims,' and some of them still speak a version of Malay, even though their primary language is now Tamil. Hambantota Muslims have also 'invented' a couple of sweets that are now popular right across Sri Lanka and that reflect both Middle Eastern and Far Eastern influences. So the Muslim community in Hambantota has ancient and dispersed global connections that are distinct from the origins and connections of some other Muslim communities in Sri Lanka. In other words, the community in and around Hambantota reflects some of the categories of identity that are defined nationally in Sri Lanka, and yet the local story is different and unique.

A little to the east of Hambantota is the ancient Buddhist center of Tissamaharama which was once a seat of power for the Ruhuna kingdom, dating back to the third century BCE, which played a significant role in the creation of Sinhalese identity.[35] Further to the north is the ancient temple complex of Kataragama, which is equally revered by Hindus and Buddhists, attracting religious pilgrims from right across Sri Lanka and from India. Clearly, Hambantota is located at the intersection of several powerful historical narratives that give it an unusual, multicultural identity. Many Hambantota residents have told the author that the local community has a proud history of religious and ethnic tolerance that ought to be seen as a model of coexistence by the rest of Sri Lanka.

Because of its location on the eastern side of Sri Lanka, Hambantota bore the brunt of the 2004 tsunami and around 3,000 people died; many of them were swept away from a weekly market held on a narrow isthmus of land, and deposited in the nearby lagoon. A densely packed village surrounding an ancient mosque – which was dominated by Muslim fishermen and their families – was completely destroyed, with heavy loss of life. A bigger mosque, on higher ground, and the main Buddhist temple, also on high ground, became the immediate refuge for people who managed to escape the clutches of the monster waves, and they soon became temporary morgues for the dead.[36] From there, the survivors were dispersed into safe refuges, often in Sinhalese villages away from the coast, and tsunami survivors in the area have repeatedly told the author that they were overwhelmed by the generosity of the district community, which showed no discrimination along ethnic or religious lines, in responding to the unprecedented disaster. The head of the Hambantota District Chamber of Commerce (HDCC), Azmi Thassim, told the author in an interview conducted one year after the tsunami that community leaders began to gather on a daily basis in the HDCC offices – largely because it had not been damaged and had retained electrical power – and that this rather ad hoc gathering turned itself into a committee that aimed to ensure that aid would be distributed according to need. Thassim said that there were numerous occasions when members of the committee were called on to lobby the district authorities or international aid agencies over grievances related to the distribution of aid or the relocation of victims and their families. After several weeks of daily activity, the committee moved to a weekly schedule of meetings, and several months later this changed to a monthly schedule. However, the committee that aimed to keep the multicultural community united in the face of disaster continued to meet and act for 18 months after the disaster struck.

At the time the tsunami struck, Mahinda Rajapakse was prime minister and already aspiring to become president at elections scheduled for November 2005. He came from an area close to Hambantota, and he 'enjoyed' a political rivalry with another local politician who was the son of former Sri Lanka President Ranasinghe Premadasa. Hambantota was also at the center of world attention for a period after the tsunami, with visits made by UN Secretary-General Kofi Annan and World Bank President James Wolfensen. This unusual and rather unexpected combination of circumstances prompted Rajapakse to single Hambantota out for special attention, and he promised to 'build back better' by acting on rather tentative plans to turn the old town into a much more significant regional center. A large area of rural land under government title – located several kilometers away from the sea – was set aside for building a 'new town' with just over 1,600 new homes for tsunami victims, funded by a range of international NGOs.[37] The Hambantota Urban Development Authority (UDA) was then charged with responsibility to draw up plans to integrate the 'new town' into a much bigger plan to create a new regional growth center that might be driven by a combination of increased tourism and the construction of a major new port facility.[38] An agreement was struck with the Chinese government whereby the Chinese would construct the new harbor by excavating a large lagoon on the western side of Hambantota and connecting it to the sea. Plans were also made to shift administrative and commercial offices from the old town to the new town, so that the old town could be turned into a tourism precinct. Construction of the new harbor began in early 2008, and by this time progress was also being made on the promise to improve the road link from Colombo all the way to Hambantota. However, promises to also complete the rail link from Colombo to Hambantota and to build Sri Lanka's second international airport nearby had not yet been firmed up.

Bold plans for Hambantota were based on the assumption that 'economic development' would create new job opportunities for a community that had depended heavily on fishing and the salt industry. However, the Chinese brought their own laborers with them to construct the new harbor, and it was unclear what job opportunities there might be in the harbor operation, which was intended to focus on the trans-shipment of containers from large carriers to smaller vessels. Plans for a major boost in tourism seemed hopeful at best, at a time when international tourism in Sri Lanka had virtually collapsed because of the resurgence of violent conflict. The ending of the war in May 2009 has meant a slow return of international tourism, but in July 2011 it was still not clear that Hambantota would attract enough tourists to make the plans for the town work. Indeed, there seemed a real danger that the old town could lose its past vitality. Construction of the harbor resulted in permanent closure of the old access road into Hambantota, meaning that through traffic now bypasses the old town completely.

Furthermore, hopes for a better future may be poor compensation for real hardship that the redevelopment has inflicted on those who were devastated by the tsunami. For a start, fishermen who were relocated to the 'new town' found it difficult or expensive to travel the distance to the fishing harbor, and this problem was exacerbated by the fact that rough, unsealed roads in the new town became virtually impassable after heavy rain. Those who had lived, sometimes for generations, in the village adjacent to the fishing harbor were told that they could not rebuild houses on the land they had occupied. They were initially told they could make use of the land to store boats and equipment, but when plans were unveiled to turn the area into a new harborside park for tourists, they learned that they would have no special access rights to the land at all.[39] Once the new harbor zone was proclaimed it became apparent that many houses would be demolished in a process that locals began to refer to as the 'harbor tsunami,' and the displaced residents would be relocated to the far-away new town. Furthermore, the cutting of the old highway through Hambantota meant that roadside traders – mainly Muslims who sold their famous sweets to tourists and Kataragama pilgrims – suddenly lost their trade on a promise that they would be given access to new stalls on the new highway, even further from where they lived.

Because the new developments in Hambantota impacted most heavily on Muslim fishermen, who had lived in the village near the old mosque, and Muslim traders operating on the old highway, there was a growing sentiment that Sinhalese politicians were discriminating against them and in favor of the Sinhalese community.[40] This threatened to damage long-standing traditions of peaceful coexistence, and things came to a head when threats were made to demolish the old mosque because it fell within the proposed park for tourists.[41] However, this was a step too far for the local community, and efforts to restore the tsunami-damaged mosque intensified, with the active support of the Sinhalese community.

The story of Hambantota suggests that it can be seen as a kind of microcosm of Sri Lankan society at large, because a history of coexistence at the local level can be undermined by national conflicts (for example, in the resultant demise of tourism) and national political agendas. Decisions made primarily in Colombo do not take into account local realities and sensitivities, nor do they value the proud history of coexistence that offers hope to more divided local communities, for example, in the nearby Ampara District. In the wake of the tsunami, Hambantota's 'civil society' acted resolutely to prevent new and damaging divisions, but a lack of attention by national and district authorities to the social impacts of proposed new developments could undermine their efforts in the longer term.

Rethinking hybrid identities

Demographic data is not collected very frequently or systematically in Sri Lanka and identities are defined by a rather inexact mix of linguistic, religious and cultural criteria. Broadly speaking we can say that the Sinhalese make up around 74 percent of the population, and that most people in this category identify as being Buddhist and use Sinhala as their primary language. The traditions and habits that came to prevail in the area ruled by the kings of Kandy came to be seen as the most 'authentic' expressions of Sinhalese culture because this was the last region to fall under the influence of European colonizers. Writers such as the historian Nira Wickramasinghe[42] have argued that this notion of authenticity masks a much more complex and interesting story of identity formation for the Sinhalese. Furthermore, Bruce Matthews[43] has pointed out that the 'united' Sinhalese identity is cross-cut by other identity formations related, primarily, to caste and religious affiliation, and any sense of unity largely stems from the Buddhist revival movement led by the priest Dharmapala in the early part of the twentieth century. Yet Sinhalese may be the least problematic category of 'ethnic' identity in Sri Lanka.

Tamil-speaking Hindus make up around 14 percent of today's population, and historians now agree that Tamils have been in Sri Lanka as long as those who now identify as Sinhalese. However, the Tamil Hindu communities centered on Jaffna and those centered on Batticaloa, for example, are quite distinct from each other in their origins and historical evolution[44] and Tamil society in Sri Lanka has taken different forms from Tamil society in southern India,[45] especially in regard to caste structures. To complicate matters even further, the British brought in different communities of 'low-caste' Tamil Hindus to work on the tea plantations of the central highlands, and so by the time British rule was coming to an end there was little basis for a common sense of Tamil identity across Sri Lanka. As Kandy became the center of 'authentic' Sinhalese culture, Jaffna set itself up as the center of 'authentic' Sri Lankan Tamil culture and, eventually, the heartland of Tamil Eelam. Any sense of a united Tamil identity in Sri Lanka has only arisen as a reaction to the hegemony of Sinhalese identity,[46] and the idea of a Tamil 'homeland' centered on Jaffna is a very recent phenomenon. Although Tamil-speaking Hindus have prevailed in the coastal communities stretching from Jaffna to Batticaloa for a very long time, a territorial segregation of Tamil and Sinhalese identities is really the product of the 'ethnic conflicts' that have escalated into prolonged violence since 1983. Before 1983, Tamils were more widely dispersed across the island.

The third major 'ethnic' identity in Sri Lanka is defined even less precisely as simply Muslim, and this category makes up around 7 percent of the population. The majority of Sri Lankan Muslims trace their origins back to India, and they use Tamil as their primary language. However, as already mentioned earlier, there are also Muslims who can trace their origins back in time to the Malay peninsula, and they include Malay as one of their languages. Sri Lankan 'Burghers' make no secret of their hybridity, because their surnames often reflect the fact that they have Dutch or Portuguese ancestors. The Dutch or Portuguese influence extended to the fact that most Burghers adopted Christianity as their religion. However there is no use of Dutch or Portuguese language, and most of the Burghers speak both Sinhala and English. To complicate matters a little further, many of the 'low-land Sinhalese' – i.e., those not connected to the Kandy kings – have Dutch or Portuguese ancestors as well, as demonstrated in the prevalence of surnames such as De Silva or Pereira.

Sinhalese nationalism has been based on a mythological claim that the Sinhalese people are north Indian – or Aryan – in origin and that they settled in Sri Lanka before the Tamils started to come. Crucial to the mythology surrounding Sinhalese identity is the story of how the Sinhalese king of Anuradhapura, King Devanampiyatissa, converted to Buddhism in the third century BCE, because it is suggested that a 'pure form' of Buddhism was thus preserved in Sri Lanka after it went into decline in India. The Rajarata kings of central Sri Lanka, it is suggested, subsequently faced a long and difficult struggle to preserve Sinhalese Buddhist identity against repeated incursions from southern India, particularly at the time of the Chola empire in the eleventh century CE. In view of this mythological account of identity formation, Nira Wickramasinghe points out that it is quite ironic that the traditions and customs adopted by the Kandy kings came to be seen as the most authentic expression of this identity, because they show very clear influences from southern India. The Kandy kings developed a close relationship with the Nayakkar empire centered on Madurai in Tamil Nadu, and commonly went to Madurai to find a wife. At one point a Nayakkar was even invited to take the throne in Kandy.[47] According to Wickramasinghe,[48] the irony is that a mix of Kandy and south Indian/Nayakkar influences is thought to produce a more 'authentic' form of Sinhalese identity than the mix of 'low-country traditions' and European influences that prevailed in the south and west of the country. As Wickramasinghe points out,[49] this irony is made even more complete by the fact that the British played a key role in selecting Kandy as the heartland of the most 'unspoiled' form of Sinhalese culture, because this then encouraged Sinhalese nationalists of the twentieth century to do the same in campaigning for their independence from Britain.

While the Sinhala language appears to be more closely related to northern Indian languages than to Tamil, the kinship structures of Sinhalese society are much more clearly south Indian in origin.[50] There is little doubt that the Sinhalese identity emerged in Sri Lanka through a mixing of influences brought from several parts of India and that influences from Tamil Nadu and Kerala are clear.[51] A seminal article written by Leslie Gunawardana in 1990[52] suggests that the term Sinhalese probably referred first to a particular ruling house or dynasty and only subsequently came to refer to all the people in that kingdom. As already mentioned, an injection of southern Indian cultural influences continued within Sinhalese culture right through to the time of the Kandy kingdoms in the nineteenth century. In other words, Sinhalese identity is clearly hybrid in its origin and evolution, and it is also clear that Sri Lankan Tamil identities have taken different forms from what is found in Tamil Nadu through a process of cultural evolution and interaction with emerging Sinhalese cultural formations. This history of hybridity and interaction undermines many of the myths used to promote rival forms of Sinhalese and Tamil nationalism in Sri Lanka and this, in turn, makes possible a new and much more dynamic way of thinking about the nation's complex and multilayered identity. This, then, is a crucial starting point for promoting a new national dialogue that can unlock the current gridlock.

Sri Lankan scholars who are promoting the concept of hybridity as a way of breaking the deadlock over competing nationalisms[53] are drawing on the work of leading international cultural theorists such as Homi Bhabha and Robert Young.[54] They are also suggesting that Sri Lankan anthropologist Gananath Obeyesekere was a pioneer in this way of thinking, as revealed in work published in the 1970s and 1980s.[55] There are also other scholars of Sri Lankan identities who have made a significant contribution in this area; Bruce Matthews and Dagmar Hellmann-Rajanayagam are prominent among them. They include people who have shown a determination to 'abide by Sri Lanka' in its troubled times.

Of course, it is important not to discount the role of mythology in creating a robust sense of identity, and Bruce Kapferer[56] has rightly stressed that it would be impossible to unravel the mix of history and mythology – passed through many generations – that underpins current Sri Lankan identities, even if that were deemed desirable. Indeed, any attempt to discredit mythology per se in Sri Lanka is likely to make it even more influential, as Kapferer has suggested. However, the recent history of violent conflict might be enough to demonstrate the importance of drawing a clear distinction between history and mythology

and the valuable roles that each can play. Mythology can produce rich and evoc-
ative stories of self-identification, but it becomes dangerous if used to deny the
validity of other forms of identity formation, largely because it is not interested
in dialogue. More contestable accounts of history, on the other hand, can
promote dialogue and increase respect for cultural diversity.

Deepening democracy

A fundamental rethinking of complex and layered identify formation in Sri
Lanka is critical for breaking the deadlock between sharply competing forms of
nationalism that have escalated in the period since independence in 1948. The
breaking of this deadlock could, in turn, end a period of intense introspection
(caused by the intractable internal conflict) and allow Sri Lanka to rethink its
opportunities for global connectedness, which Eric Meyer identified as the
opportunity born of the country's unique history and its location in the world.[57]
A durable peace agreement would lift the sagging spirits of people living in Sri
Lanka, lead to the return of many emigrants, and help to revive the flagging
economy. After 25 years of violence it should be clear that a military 'solution'
to the conflict will not bring about enduring peace and that a political solution is
essential. So what are the key ingredients of a political solution?

As already suggested above, it must involve a serious commitment to a devolution of political power that has non-partisan political support in Colombo. The
old emphasis on the need for a 'unitary state' to prevent the fragmentation of Sri
Lanka should be abandoned, because the conflict of nearly 30 years has created
very strong momentum *towards* fragmentation and entrenched division, rather
than the reverse. Internationally, there are many models of national constitutions
that are based on the principles of federation that have helped to prevent, rather
than cause, internal conflicts. It is surely time to go beyond gestures towards the
establishment of semi-autonomous provinces into something real and sustained.

Increasing centralization of government in Colombo has also weakened the
capacity of local government in Sri Lanka, and this weakness hampered
the efforts to respond to the devastating impacts of the tsunami.[58] For example,
the national announcement (which came within days of the tsunami) that a 100-
meter building-free buffer zone would be created around the entire coast of Sri
Lanka caused enormous difficulties for local authorities, to the extent that the
inflexible national policy was eventually abandoned. Similar difficulties arose
over the role of the central government in allocating land for new settlements for
tsunami victims and in setting building standards for the new constructions.[59]
Perhaps the preoccupation with ethnic conflict means that little serious attention
has been given to increasing the capacity of local government in Sri Lanka; the
post-tsunami experience should be enough to make this a higher priority.[60]

As already mentioned, years of conflict and centralization of political power
have not destroyed 'civil society' in Sri Lanka. There are many effective non-
government organizations that remain independent of government, there is still a
relatively free national media (despite some incidents of intimidation), and the

work of critical scholars can still be published in Sri Lanka[61] with their books freely available inside the country. Many critical scholars write regularly for Sri Lankan newspapers, especially those published in English, and many of them argue that there is a critical need to deepen democracy in the country.[62] Sri Lankans, it might also be noted, retain a robust sense of humor that often makes fun of their political leaders. However, an emphasis on identifying the key ingredients for a healthy 'civil society' may not pick up more subtle shifts in the moods of public discussion or perceived constraints on what can and should be discussed. It is not hard to detect a growing politicization of public discussion over the last 30 years, and this tends to undercut dialogue and the expression of dissident ideas.

There is, of course, widespread pessimism about Sri Lanka's future that also tends to suppress debate and discussion. While civil society has not been dismantled, the 'space' for public discussion has been eroded. There was a notable exception to this in the period immediately following the tsunami, when a perceived need to put aside old divisions was discussed very widely and with considerable enthusiasm.[63] This change of mood, it can be argued, led to a change in the rhetoric of political leaders on both sides of the Sinhalese/Tamil divide. However, when the politicians began to revert to the 'blame game' the mood shifted to greater pessimism and an opportunity was lost.[64] As Margo Kleinfeld has noted,[65] it is impossible to keep a 'humanitarian space' separate from 'political space,' at least for any length of time, and so the failure to build on the post-tsunami spirit of unity was a failure of political leadership, rather than a failing of civil society. In hierarchically organized states it is all too easy for political leaders to close or radically confine the space in which civil society can operate.

In order to reconceptualize civil society as a 'space' in which the discussion of ideas can thrive it is useful to refer to Jeffrey Alexander's recent work on what he has called the 'civil sphere.'[66] Taking his lead from French sociologist Emile Durkheim, Alexander is interested in exploring the conditions in which 'feeling for others' – or solidarity – can override self-interest in order to create a society in which coexistence and respect for others become the norm. For Alexander, it is not enough to simply note the existence of civil society or the existence of a 'public sphere' in which ideas can be freely debated but rather to promote the norm of solidarity as a 'common secular faith.' He wants to enrich Jurgen Habermas' conception of the 'public sphere' with the normative conception of solidarity to create what he has called the 'civil sphere.' This broader and more normative conception of the space in which civil society can operate seems to capture something of the essence that is currently missing from public debate in Sri Lanka. When religious and ethnic identities have become so divisive it might be useful indeed to promote a 'common secular faith' that values coexistence and respect for diversity. Alexander devotes a considerable portion of his massive book to the idea of 'civil repair' as a response to deep social division, and Sri Lanka can be seen as a society in which civil repair is urgently needed.

Despite the complexities of cross-cutting, hybrid identities, it is clearly important in Sri Lanka to create more inclusive communities at all levels from the local to the national. The 'civil sphere' can also be seen as the space in which inclusive expressions of community can be shared and contested without losing a shared commitment to the norm of peaceful coexistence.

Habermas' notion of the 'public sphere' has been used to promote a conception of democracy – most commonly called 'deliberative democracy' – in which ideas about good governance would be more openly and more transparently debated before being turned into policy and law. The Australian scholar John Dryzek, for example, has promoted the idea that policy formation needs to reflect on competing discourses that represent a broad array of interests and concerns that are often ignored by elected politicians who see themselves as the representatives of society.[67] It is dangerous, Dryzek warns, to allow any single discourse – e.g., the discourse of neoliberalism – to become hegemonic, and so competing discourses, each following a different logic, need to be considered by policymakers. In his recent work,[68] Dryzek has argued that processes of deliberation are particularly important in societies that have become deeply divided by a failure to respect a diversity of views, and this certainly reflects the experience of Sri Lanka.

Advocates of 'deliberative' or 'radical' democracy[69] want to flush out the powerful influence of largely hidden and cashed-up lobby groups who have inordinate influence on politicians, and they argue that much greater transparency in policy debates will radically reduce all forms of political 'corruption' (from the subtle and legal to the extreme and criminal). The concentration of political power in the office of the presidency in Sri Lanka has made it difficult to properly pursue allegations of corruption made against leading members of government over the last 20 years or more, and so steps to increase transparency and to reduce the influence of cashed-up lobby groups would be valuable. A combination of devolution and transparency is needed to reverse the dangerous trends towards centralization of political power that were discussed earlier in this chapter.

Very large Sri Lankan diasporas have played a problematic role in Sri Lankan politics over the last 20 to 30 years. It is widely acknowledged,[70] for example, that the Tamil diaspora – spread across Asia, Europe, North America and Australia – has played a crucial role in supporting armed struggle by the LTTE, and that part of the Sinhalese diaspora located in Western countries supported rebellions by the JVP in the 1980s. It is probably even easier for people who are no longer living in the country to engage in ideological 'warfare' because they are remote from the consequences of violent conflict, and because their conception of Sri Lankan identity might be based more on distorted, even romanticized, memories rather than the realities of daily life in difficult circumstances. At the same time, the loyalty of expatriate Sri Lankans for their 'homeland' can also be seen as an 'asset' that has not been used wisely by Sri Lankan governments focused on internal problems. As noted earlier, there has been a rapid growth in the numbers of people who leave Sri Lanka temporarily to support their families through remittances, and most of these people retain their Sri Lankan citizenship, even if they live abroad for years at a time. Like it or not, the large and growing Sri Lankan diaspora will continue to have a big influence on the country's future, and Sri Lankan identity has already taken on some transnational characteristics. As Eric Meyer noted[71] Sri Lanka has always been more open than neighboring India to cultural influences from abroad, and this gives Sri Lankan society a more cosmopolitan flavor.

By dint of necessity and opportunity, then, it seems important for Sri Lanka to think about ways to engage more actively with its diasporas. Such an engagement will not be productive, however, if the internal civil conflict remains dead-locked, and the opportunity to 're-engage' the diasporas in a productive way may only come when a meaningful peace process is initiated. At the same time, a meaningful engagement of the diasporas in the peace process could give that process greater momentum and revive international enthusiasm for the future of the country. As Mark Whitaker has pointed out,[72] the high profile developed by the independent Tamil news and discussion website, tamilnet.com, shows how internet technology can facilitate discussion across transnational diasporas.

The idea of engaging diasporas in the internal politics of the 'homeland' is very new, and recent initiatives in this regard, e.g., by Italy, need to be carefully assessed. However, the idea of extending democracy to a transnational constituency may also become a way of deepening democracy in the homelands. As John Dryzek has suggested,[73] the challenge for democracy in an increasingly insecure and divided world is to become more transnational, and Sri Lanka could potentially lead the way in this regard.

Returning to Hambantota

This paper has traveled a long way in time and space; from early origins of identity formations in Sri Lanka to the entrenched 'ethnic conflicts' of recent decades, and from a particular local community to far-flung Sri Lankan diasporas. Let us end by returning to Hambantota where a local community with a very proud history of cross-cultural tolerance is now threatened with new kinds of division. A multitude of stories suggest that, despite very heavy losses, this community responded quite magnificently to immediate crisis caused by the tsunami, and yet a failure to properly take into account the local social impacts of post-tsunami redevelopment has created new and dangerous social tensions. This reflects the weaknesses of Sri Lanka's highly centralized political system and its failure to adequately develop local government capacity. Through the formation of the 'Rebuild Hambantota' committee, civil society did its best to ensure that diverse social needs were considered, but it was not given space in which to operate by a largely remote polity focused on its own conception of national development. However, the norm of 'solidarity' – which Alexander focused on[74] – is currently at a low ebb in Sri Lanka and this tends to undermine the work of civil society. Furthermore, the post-tsunami construction of a new container harbor by the Chinese government means that Hambantota has suddenly become more globally integrated without having much idea of what the consequences of that might be. Hambantota's unique history and its legacy of peaceful coexistence might well be seen as a national treasure in a country mired in entrenched ethnic conflict, and yet this is not being valued as much as the area's potential for intensified economic development. A narrow conception of economic assets is outweighing due consideration of unique cultural assets, even though it has become abundantly clear that the nation's economy will continue to suffer as long as the failure to respect cultural diversity continues to promote violent conflict.

Local, national and transnational issues have become deeply intertwined in Sri Lanka in a kind of Gordian knot that needs to be cut through so that a more constructive way of weaving the threads together can be undertaken. This requires courage, a willingness to admit that things have become hopelessly stuck, and a genuine desire to learn from the mistakes of the past. However, a fresh beginning for Sri Lanka would attract enormous international interest and goodwill.

Notes

1 Statistics cited here were included in a presentation by Colombo University Professor Siri Hettige at RMIT University, Melbourne, on 14 March 2008.
2 According to statistics cited J. Shaw, *Migrant Remittances and Low-income Households in Sri Lanka*, 2008, the percentage of women in this expatriate workforce has shrunk from 73 percent in 1995 to 59 percent in 2006.
3 Hettige, see note 2.
4 Shaw, 2008.
5 As was demonstrated in a survey of tsunami victims conducted by researchers from the Globalism Research Centre at RMIT University in Melbourne in late 2007.
6 According to statistics cited by Shaw, 2008.
7 As reflected in discussions the author has had with a very wide range of people in Sri Lanka between 2005 and 2008.
8 S. Hettige, 'Education, Identity Formation and Citizenship', 2009.
9 Q. Ismail, *Abiding by Sri Lanka*, 2005.
10 N. Wickramasinghe, *Sri Lanka in the Modern Age*, 2006, p. 102.
11 Ibid.
12 S. Edirippulige, *Sri Lanka's Twisted Path to Peace*, 2004, pp. 40–43.
13 See, for example, K. Godage, 'Will the "Donoughmore" System Bring a Cure', *Daily Mirror*, Colombo, 15 July 2008, p. A15.
14 E. Meyer, *Sri Lanka: Biography of an Island*, 2003, pp. 130–131.
15 The term *angarika* refers to a status in Buddhism that is between that of a priest and a lay person.
16 Wickramasinghe, *Sri Lanka in the Modern Age*, p. 237.
17 Ibid.
18 See, for example, B. Matthews, 'Tightening Social Cohesion and Excluding "Others" among the Sinhalese', 2004, pp. 89–91.
19 See K. Indrapala, *The Evolution of an Ethnic Identity*, 2007.
20 Wickramasinghe, *Sri Lanka in the Modern Age*, p. 282.
21 Ibid.
22 Statistics cited in this section were included in a presentation given by Colombo University Professor Siri Hettige at RMIT University, Melbourne, March 2008.
23 Ibid.
24 Wickramasinghe, *Sri Lanka in the Modern Age*, p. 278.

25 As reported widely in Sri Lankan media in the aftermath of the provincial council elections in May 2008.

26 Edirippulige, *Sri Lanka's Twisted Path to Peace*.

27 Work of Zakaria is cited in Edirippulige, ibid., p. 17.

28 As cited in Edirippulige, op. cit., ibid., p. 160.

29 Meyer, *Sri Lanka*.

30 S. Hettige, *Unrest or Revolt*, 1996.

31 Hettige, 'Education, Identity Formation', 2009.

32 H.A.P. Abeyawardana, *Heritage of Ruhuna*, 2001, p. 2.

33 R.C. Jirasinghe, *Rhythm of the Sea*, 2007, p. 23.

34 Ibid.

35 Abeyawardana, *Heritage of Ruhuna*, pp. 2–3.

36 Jirasinghe, *Rhythm of the Sea*, 2007, pp. 15–19.

37 Ibid., pp. 62–67.

38 The author was able to view the plans for Hambantota during a visit to the UDA in October 2007.

39 The experiences of people in this area is based on interviews conducted by the author in 2007.

40 A sentiment the author heard expressed during a visit to Hambantota in April 2008.

41 Ibid.

42 N. Wickramasinghe, 'From Hybridity to Authenticity', 2004.

43 Matthews, 'Tightening Social Cohesion', 2004.

44 See Indrapala, *Evolution of an Ethnic Identity*.

45 See D. Hellmann-Rajanayagam, 'From Difference to Ethnic Solidarity among the Tamils', 2004.

46 Ibid.

47 A. Guneratne, 'What's in a Name?', 2002, p. 26.

48 Wickramasinghe, 'From Hybridity to Authenticity.'

49 Ibid.

50 See Guneratne, 'What's in a Name?.'

51 Ibid.

52 The article by Gunawardana, titled 'The People of the Lion: The Sinhala Identity and Ideology in History and Historiography', is cited in Guneratne, "What's in a Name?', pp. 35–36.

53 See, for example, N. Silva (ed.), *The Hybrid Island*, 2002.

54 According to Silva, ibid., pp. i–iv.

55 According to Silva, ibid.

56 B. Kapferer, *Legends of People, Myths of State*, 1988.

57 Meyer, *Sri Lanka*.

58 The difficulties encountered in post-tsunami recovery have been identified in research conducted by the author since 2004.

59 Ibid.

60 This view has been expressed strongly by Colombo University Professor Siri Hettige in a presentation at RMIT University, Melbourne, on 14 March 2008.

61 See, for example, S.H. Hasbullah and B.M. Morrison (eds), *Sri Lankan Society in an Era of Globalization*, Colombo: Vijitha Yapa Publications, 2004.

62 For example, in an article in the *Daily Mirror* in July 2008 (see Note 13), K. Godage wrote that democracy in Sri Lanka is 'a mere shell of the real thing; the kernel has been removed by our politicians.'

63 This observation is based on the author's monitoring of media debates and discussions in the month following the tsunami.

64 This is based on the observations of the author during trips to Sri Lanka in 2005 and 2006.

65 M. Kleinfeld, 'Misreading the Post-tsunami Political Landscape in Sri Lanka', 2007.

66 J.C. Alexander, *The Civil Sphere*, 2006.
67 See, for example .S. Dryzek, *Deliberative Democracy and Beyond*, 2000.
68 J.S. Dryzek, 'Transnational Democracy in an Insecure World', 2006.
69 The term 'radical democracy' was coined by Ernesto Laclau and Chantalle Mouffe in their work in the 1980s.
70 See S. Pinnawala, 'Damming the Flood of Violence', 2004.
71 Meyer, *Sri Lanka*.
72 M.P. Whitaker, 'Tamilnet.com', 2004.
73 Dryzek, 'Transitional Democracy.'
74 Alexander, *The Civil Sphere*.

Bibliography

Abeyawardana, H.A.P., *Heritage of Ruhuna: Major Natural, Cultural and Historic Sites*, Matara: Ruhuna Development Bank, 2001.

Alexander, Jeffrey C., *The Civil Sphere*, Oxford: Oxford University Press, 2006.

Dryzek, John S., *Deliberative Democracy and Beyond: Liberals, Critics, Contestants*, Oxford: Oxford University Press, 2000.

Dryzek, John S., *Deliberative Global Politics: Discourse and Democracy in a Divided World*, Cambridge: Polity Press, 2006.

Dryzek, John S., 'Transnational Democracy in an Insecure World', *International Political Science Review*, 27, 2006, pp. 101–119.

Edirippulige, Sisira, *Sri Lanka's Twisted Path to Peace: Some Domestic and International Obstacles to the Peace Process*, Pilimathalawa: Resource Management Foundation, Sri Lanka, 2004.

Guneratne, Arjun 'What's in a Name? Aryans and Dravidians in the Making of Sri Lankan Identities' in Neluka Silva (ed.), *The Hybrid Island: Culture Crossing and the Invention of Identity in Sri Lanka*, London: Zed Press, 2002.

Hellmann-Rajanayagam, Dagmar, 'From Difference to Ethnic Solidarity among the Tamils' in S.H. Hasbullah and Barrie M. Morrison (eds), *Sri Lankan Society in an Era of Globalization: Struggling to Create a New Social Order*, Colombo: Vijitha Yapa Publications, 2004.

Hettige, Siri (ed.), *Unrest or Revolt: Some Aspects of Youth Unrest in Sri Lanka*, Colombo: Goethe Institut Colombo and American Studies Association, Sri Lanka, University of Colombo, 1996 (second edition).

Hettige, Siri, 'Economic Policy, Changing Opportunities for Youth, and the Ethnic Conflict in Sri Lanka', in D. Winslow and M.D. Woost (eds), *Economy, Culture and Civil War in Sri Lanka*, Bloomington, IU Press, 2004.

Indrapala, K., *The Evolution of an Ethnic Identity: The Tamils in Sri Lanka 300 BCE to 1200 CE*, Colombo: Vijitha Yapa Publications, 2007 (second edition).

Ismail, Qadri, *Abiding by Sri Lanka: On Peace, Place and Postcoloniality*, Minneapolis: University of Minnesota Press, 2005.

Jirasinghe, Ramya Chamalie, *Rhythm of the Sea*, Hambantota: Hambantota District Chamber of Commerce, 2007.

Kapferer, Bruce, *Legends of People, Myths of State: Violence, Intolerance and Political Culture in Sri Lanka and Australia*, Washington, DC: Smithsonian Institute Press, 1988.

Kleinfeld, Margo, 'Misreading the Post-tsunami Political Landscape in Sri Lanka: The Myth of Humanitarian Space', *Space and Polity* 11:2, 2007, pp. 169–184.

Matthews, Bruce, 'Tightening Social Cohesion and Excluding "Others" among the Sinhalese' in S.H. Hasbullah and Barrie M. Morrison (eds), *Sri Lankan Society in an Era of Globalization: Struggling to Create a New Social Order*, Colombo: Vijitha Yapa Publications, 2004.

Meyer, Eric, *Sri Lanka: Biography of an Island: Between Local and Global*, Colombo: Viator Publications, 2003.

Pinnawala, Sisira, 'Damming the Flood of Violence and Shoring Up Civil Society in an Era of Globalization' in S.H. Hasbullah and Barrie M. Morrison (eds), *Sri Lankan Society in an Era of Globalization: Struggling to Create a New Social Order*, Colombo: Vijitha Yapa Publications, 2004.

Shaw, J. *Migrant Remittances and Low-income Households in Sri Lanka: Development Policy Issues*, Melbourne: Monash Asia Institute, Monash University, 2008.

Silva, Neluka (ed.), *The Hybrid Island: Culture Crossing and the Invention of Identity in Sri Lanka*, London: Zed Press, 2002.

Silva, Neluka, 'Introduction' in Neluka Silva (ed.), *The Hybrid Island: Culture Crossing and the Invention of Identity in Sri Lanka*, London: Zed Press, 2002, pp. i–iv.

Whitaker, Mark P., 'Tamilnet.com: Some Reflections on Popular Anthropology, Nationalism and the Internet', *Anthropological Quarterly* 77:3, 2004, pp. 464–498.

Wickramasinghe, Nira, 'From Hybridity to Authenticity: The Biography of a few Kandyan Things' in S.H. Hasbullah and Barrie M. Morrison (eds), *Sri Lankan Society in an Era of Globalization: Struggling to Create a New Social Order*, Colombo: Vijitha Yapa Publication, 2004.

Wickramasinghe, Nira, *Sri Lanka in the Modern Age: A History of Contested Identities*, London: Hurst and Company, 2006.

7 Ethno-nationalism in Pakistan

Challenges for the state – an overview

Alok Bansal

Pakistan is going through tumultuous times. The process of Talibanization is eroding the already weakened state institutions, the economy continues to be in a precarious state, and the menaces of regionalism and sectarianism have grown further in recent times. Since the February 2008 elections, the regional aspirations of various ethnic groups, namely the Punjabis, Pakhtoons, Baloch, Sindhis, Mohajirs and Seraikis, and their efforts to assert their sub-national identities have started resurfacing. Pakistan, from the very beginning, had illogical boundaries, which cut across sub-national groups with stronger identities than that of the state itself. In the recent past, many scholars have predicted that Pakistan could well be the next Yugoslavia.[1] It has failed to build a national identity, and consequently, with the exception of Punjabis, all the other groups perceive themselves as Pakhtoons, Baloch, Sindhis Mohajirs or Seraikis first and Pakistanis next. All these groups also suffer from a persecution complex and feel that they are being discriminated against by the Punjabi elite. Contentious issues like the Kalabagh Dam, division of federal revenues, distribution of Indus water and frequent dismissal of elected state governments have fueled this feeling of alienation. The problem has been aggravated by the fact that the state has failed to build any credible institutions.

The Pakistani elites in their pursuit for national unity have attempted to quash any aspirations for regional autonomy expressed by the ethnic minorities, perceiving federalism as a prelude to separatism. The primary challenge to Pakistan's efforts to establish a unitary structure emerged from a strong sense of ethnicity among various groups residing there. Pakistan's political elite, therefore, were against providing encouragement to these nascent sub-national identities, whether symbolically, by recognizing their socio-cultural and linguistic identity, or politically, by accommodating them in the state structure on the basis of ethnicity.[2] Right from its inception, the Pakistani federal government had problems accommodating provincial aspirations and usurped the legitimate powers of the provincial governments.[3] The problem was further aggravated by the fact that the Muslim League, which created Pakistan, had very little support in the areas that came to constitute Pakistan. To counter the ethno-national aspirations of the populace, the Pakistani state right from the beginning promoted an all-inclusive Islamic identity to subsume various ethnic identities. The

process was fairly successful but in due course gave rise to a bigger Frankenstein, that of radical Islam. As the menace of Talibanization, a manifestation of
radical Islam, threatens the very existence of Pakistan, an attempt is being made
to de-emphasize this Islamic identity. This is giving a further fillip to ethno-
nationalism and has revived ethnic fires in regions that had hitherto remained
quiet.

Today the nationalist parties in Balochistan and Khyber Pakhtoonkhwa (KP),[4]
including the ruling Awami National Party (ANP) have been at the forefront of
the struggle for autonomy. They have also been supported in their quest by the
Muttahida Quaumi Movement (MQM)[5] and Sindhi nationalist parties. Sindhi
nationalists have, however, not been able to garner the requisite support, as the
ruling Pakistan Peoples' Party (PPP) is perceived to be dominated by Sindhis.
The recent floods, and the perception that the towns and villages in Sindh were
flooded to save farms in Punjab, have further alienated the Sindhi masses, and if
Zardari is forced out of power, it could boost the simmering Sindhi nationalism.
During the last few years there has been a growth of the Seraiki movement,
which has been demanding a separate province for the Seraiki-speaking population. The movement of Internally Displaced Persons (IDPs) during the military
operations in Swat and South Waziristan and consequent political and ethnic
dissent have further exposed the cleavages between various provinces.[6] This
chapter discusses the genesis and the current state of various ethno-national
movements in Pakistan, their likely trajectory, and the causes that have created a
sense of alienation among ethnic minorities.

Genesis of the problem

Pakistan's political and administrative profile was shaped during the first decade
of its existence. The ethnic fault-lines were entrenched during this decade and an
opportunity to bridge the gap by creating an inclusive federal structure was irre-
trievably lost by the short-sightedness of its leaders. The new state structure that
emerged from the chaos and turbulence of Partition, and the tumultuous early
years, ensured the dominance of the center and its bureaucratic-military arm over
political institutions and processes. Consequently, Pakistan emerged as an over-
centralized polity, which stifled the growth of democratic institutions and found
it extremely difficult to accommodate the demands for equity from a diversified
population belonging to different regions.[7] This centralized polity and its
entrenched bureaucracy, backed by a strong military apparatus, prevented Pakistan from collapsing in its infancy. However, this diverted attention from the
task of creating viable political institutions and processes, which were urgently
needed to inculcate a sense of participation in the population and to give endur-
ance and vitality to the process of nation-building. Two constituent assemblies
(1947–54, 1955–56) spent eight years trying to make decisions regarding the
distribution of powers between the center and the provinces, representation in
the federal legislature, the electoral system, the national language and the relationship between the legislature and the executive. The delay in formulating a

constitution created much uncertainty, so that by the time the constitution was adopted in 1956 it did not have general support across the ethnic spectrum.[8]

The dismissal of Dr Khan Sahib's government in North West Frontier Province (NWFP), despite its majority in the legislature within the first week of Pakistan's creation, marked the beginning of a process whereby provincial aspirations as well as constitutionalism were brushed aside by an autocratic federal government. Other actions in the initial years, like separating Karachi from Sindh and announcing in Dhaka that Urdu alone would be the national language of Pakistan, indicated that even Jinnah paid scant regard to provincial aspirations.[9] The leaders of the Muslim League, by and large, hailed from the provinces of India and did not have adequate support in Pakistan. As a result, they were more comfortable with the bureaucrats, who came from Muslim minority provinces in India, than with the leaders hailing from Pakistani provinces, who were considered parochial and lacking sufficient commitment to the party. As a result they were not in favor of holding early elections. The party leadership was fearful of a revolt by the provincial leaders, and kept a firm hold over the party by assigning the key offices to the migrants or to those provincial leaders who had been co-opted into the system. Criticism within the party was discouraged. Any opposition to the Muslim League from within the party or outside was equated with criticism of the state. This strategy did not help the faltering fortunes of the Muslim League. The provincial leadership created personal cliques and their interaction with the national leadership was shaped mainly by their factional considerations. The national leadership did not hesitate to play one faction off against another to make its writ effective in the provinces, rather than working towards making the party a coherent and effective political machine.[10]

Mohammed Ali Jinnah wanted to build a strong state relying on the threefold principle 'One Nation, One Culture, One Language.' As Pakistan was intended to be the homeland of the Muslims of British India, its language could only be Urdu, which was associated with Indian Muslims. Jinnah may have had an ideology but missed the social and geographical realities. Pakistan as conceived had many languages and cultures within its boundaries. Only a minority population used Urdu in most regions of Pakistan.[11] Similarly, there was no single culture that had deep roots in Pakistan. Forcing an alien language and culture on the population went against the task of nation-building.

In Pakistan, as in many states which have numerous sub-national groups, there has been an imbalance in the distribution of power among those groups. Some 'sub-nations,' because of their early industrialization, monopolize economic and political power and become dominant. In the case of Pakistan, the Punjabis and the migrants from India dominated the military and bureaucracy. This group rapidly became the economic, political and military power center of Pakistan. According to veteran Pakistani journalist Khaled Ahmed, 'Leadership in Pakistan will always be supplied by Punjab because it controls two-thirds of the seats in the National Assembly. Smaller provinces may produce intellectually superior leaders but they will not be able to assert themselves nationally.'[12] This has caused resentment in other ethnic groups like the Sindhis, Baloch and

Pakhtoons, who felt that the Punjabis and Mohajirs were dominating the power structure like the Hindus and Sikhs before Partition.

The Pakistani nation-state project has its historical roots in the two-nation theory, the *raison d'être* of the state.[13] In the post-independence period the inability of various elite factions to agree on constitutional democracy paved the way for a more authoritarian and theocratic type of state ideology, where the strength or power of the state over society was based on its punitive capabilities rather than persuasive ones. As a result, separatist movements have arisen seeking to break away from the state. The Islamic factor was used to counter them by directly appealing to religious affiliations and was successful in the initial years in some regions. However, over a period of six decades, almost all ethnic groups have started asserting their ethnic identity. The regional aspirations of the main ethnic groups in Pakistan are discussed in the following pages.

Pakhtoons

In 1947, the biggest challenge to the Pakistani state came from the aspirations of its ethnic population, especially those in NWFP, who strongly espoused the cause of Pakhtoon nationalism. In the 1946 elections, held under the British, the Pakhtoon majority in NWFP had rejected the Muslim League and its two-nation theory and had instead elected a Congress government under Dr Khan Sahib, elder brother of Khan Abdul Ghaffar Khan (Frontier Gandhi). It was only in a referendum held in mid-1947, when it was clear that the creation of Pakistan was inevitable, that the people of NWFP voted for it. At that time Khan Abdul Ghaffar Khan pressed for a third option, the creation of an independent Pakhtoonistan, but the British rejected it outright. The referendum was boycotted by Khan Abdul Ghaffar Khan and his followers. Of the total population of 3.5 million, only 572,799 were entitled to vote, and of these only 289,244 voted to join Pakistan. Most others boycotted the polls at the behest of Khan Abdul Ghaffar Khan.[14] In 1947, Afghanistan formally staked its claim to all Pakhtoon-inhabited territories up to the Indus.[15] However, when the British refused the Afghan claims, the Afghan government went on to oppose Pakistan's entry into the United Nations.

To stem the threat of Pakhtoon nationalism, within one week of Pakistan's creation, the democratically elected government of Dr Khan Sahib was dismissed despite enjoying clear majority in the legislative assembly. The Pakistani government also attempted to crush the supporters of the Khan brothers with brute force; a number of them were imprisoned and many others were brutally massacred at Babrra Sharif in 1948. To counter the secular appeal of Pakhtoon nationalism as propounded by Khan Abdul Gaffar Khan, radical Islamic thought was encouraged in the region. The Pakistani establishment encouraged religious political parties like Jamaat-e-Islami and Jamiat Ulema-e-Islam (JUI) to spread their influence among the Pakhtoons. At the same time, to prevent the consolidation of the Pakhtoons, the Federally Administered Tribal Areas (FATA) were not merged with NWFP, although the British policy of maintaining substantive military presence in the region to control the restive tribesmen was dispensed with. Subsequently, after the Bangladesh War, when the ANP government in Balochistan passed a resolution to merge Pakhtoon-dominated Northern Balochistan with NWFP, it was not agreed to by the federal government, primarily with the intent of keeping the Pakhtoons fragmented in different provinces, so as to dilute the Pakhtoon identity of NWFP. Similarly, the attempts to rename the province as Pakhtoonwa, despite finding support in the provincial assembly, were rejected repeatedly by the government of Pakistan, on the pretext that the province had a fairly large percentage of Hindkowans and other ethnic minorities. However, the main reason was the Pakistani perception that naming the province as Pakhtoonkhwa or Pakhtoonistan would provide legitimacy to Pakhtoon sub-nationalism. The name was eventually changed on 15 April 2010, more than two years after the ANP came to power in the province, and that too after it agreed to prefix Khyber to Pakhtoonkhwa, even though Khyber is not even part of the province.

Pakhtoon nationalism and the idea of Pakhtoonistan did get a fillip in the early 1970s when the Pakistani Army intervened in Balochistan and NWFP. The overthrow of the Afghan monarchy by pro-Pakhtoonistan elements, led by Sardar Daud Khan, gave much-needed impetus to this movement. The Afghan government under Daud Khan actively raised the Pakhtoonistan issue in international forums, including the United Nations. It also provided support and aid to exiled Pakhtoon leaders like Khan Abdul Ghaffar Khan, Ayub Khan Achakzai and Ajmal Khattak. The Afghan support to Pakhtoon nationalism is based on the old territorial conflicts between Afghanistan and the British colonialists, which ended in the Gandamak Treaty of 1878, and the Durand Agreement of 1893, which divided the Pakhtoons between two states. Afghans consider these treaties to have been signed under duress.[16] The ethnic proximity of Afghan Pakhtoons, who are a dominant group in Afghanistan, always keeps the Pakistan government on tenterhooks. This explains Pakistan's quest for a weak and pliable government in Kabul. There is another school of thought, which believes that the Durand line has become defunct after 100 years as per the Durand Agreement, signed in 1893. This leaves Pakistan without a well-defined western boundary.

However, notwithstanding the strong moorings of Pakhtoon national identity, the Pakistani state has succeeded in diffusing Pakhtoon nationalism. Besides, Islamization, the fragmentation of Pakhtoons in three separate political entities and the large-scale presence of Pakhtoons in the Armed Forces have also contributed to this. As Pakistan has been under the direct or indirect control of the Army for most of its existence, the Pakhtoons derived a disproportionately higher share of benefits from the federal kitty. The large presence of Pakhtoons in the Armed Forces ensured that their concerns were generally taken into account while making decisions on state policy. The fact that the Kalabagh Dam, which will inundate large areas of Khyber Pakhtoonkwa (KP) to provide large-scale irrigation facilities to Punjab, has not come into being despite its apparent benefits is primarily because it has been opposed by the KP provincial government; otherwise the Punjabi elite would have ensured its construction despite the opposition of Sindh and Balochistan.

Pakhtoon nationalism received a severe jolt during the Saur Revolution in Afghanistan. The ongoing Pakistani agenda of the Islamization of the Pakhtoon population received enormous support from the US and Saudi Arabia. Mujahids were replaced by Talibs and the extreme radicalization of youth along Islamist ideology led to Talibanization. The large-scale influx of refugees from Afghanistan, which was largely welcomed in NWFP and FATA, provided impetus to the process of Talibanization of Pakhtoon society, as a large number of pro-Taliban elements infiltrated the social fabric of this province. The success of Muttahida Majlis-e-Amal (MMA) in the province in the 2002 elections was a manifestation of this process. However, in the aftermath of the US operations against the Taliban in Afghanistan and the rise of Tehrik-e-Taliban Pakistan (TTP), when all the attempts of the West and the Pakistani state failed to put the genie of Taliban back into the bottle, an attempt was made to prop up the ANP in the run-up to the 2008 elections; it was felt that an ANP victory would check the growing strength of Islamic militants in the province as well as in other Pakhtoon regions, since the party had strong grass-root-level support. The party in the run-up to the elections revived its age-old ideology of Pakhtoon nationalism with the tacit understanding of the West as well as the Pakistani establishment, hoping that it would be able to draw Pakhtoon youths away from the Islamic extremists. The Taliban also realized that the success of the left-leaning secular ANP could cause a major dent in their influence in their main recruiting base, and accordingly launched major attacks on ANP cadres. Despite its electoral victory in the 2008 elections, the ANP has not been able to sell Pakhtoon nationalism as an alternative to Islamic radicalism. Although it has succeeded in renaming the province, getting a larger share from the federal coffers and stalling the Kalabagh Dam, Pakhtoon nationalism despite its relative growth has not really caught the fancy of the Pakhtoon youth. The ANP, being a component of the federal government in Islamabad, lacks the credibility to espouse a strong nationalistic line, and the Pakhtoon political community remains divided in KP, FATA and Balochistan. Meanwhile the Taliban continues to espouse an alternative ideology in the region and to grow. Perhaps consolidation of the Pakhtoon areas in a single political entity could change that. As of now, however, Pakhtoon nationalism does not pose any significant threat to the Pakistani state.

Sindhis

The authoritarian and strongly centrist policies of the state have been largely responsible for the alienation of the subordinate provinces of Pakistan. Nowhere is the contrast so starkly manifest than in Sindh. Sindhi Muslims opted for Pakistan at Partition, but their problems began thereafter. Sindh, second only to Punjab in population and wealth at the time of Partition, had enormous untapped agricultural potential. Sindh's unexploited soil was still in the process of being 'colonized' by farmers from outside the province, who were immigrants from Punjab or retired army officers. With India's Partition, Sindh was forced to accommodate another set of immigrants, the Mohajirs: Muslims from areas that remained in India, but opted for Pakistan. Unlike the Sindhi Muslims, who were mainly illiterate peasants at the time of Partition, the largely Urdu- and Gujarati-speaking Mohajirs were mainly from the educated and elite Muslim bureaucratic and business communities of India. They cornered most of the government jobs and private business in Sindh on the basis of merit and hard work. The continued absence of Sindhis in state employment, and their not getting a reasonable share of the wealth produced by its cities, was sufficient ground for their frustration and grievances. In 1948, Sindhis were also deprived of their capital city Karachi, which was separated from Sindh, despite strong opposition from its chief minister Ayub Khuhro, to become the Federal Capital area under the central government. This was viewed as an attempt to dismember Sindh and to change the ethnic composition of Karachi by colonizing it with refugees from India.[17]

Sindh has been a feudal society, and although various political dispensations in Islamabad tried to change it, they have never succeeded in breaking the hold of the tribal and feudal chiefs in Sindh. The feudal lords from Sindh have always resented the fact that right from its inception, the Pakistani government and more importantly its military have been dominated by the Punjabis. Despite Sindh being the bread-basket of Pakistan and having a strategic location, only two percent of Pakistan's armed forces and five percent of federal civil servants are Sindhis. Of around 2,000 industrial units operating in Sindh only a quarter are controlled by them. Even in the overall population of the province, they are the minority, only 45 percent, the rest being Punjabis, Pakhtoons, Baloch, or Mohajirs who had migrated from India. The percentage of Sindhis in their capital, Karachi, is even less.[18]

Sindhis have always had a strong socio-cultural identity, and Sindhi language has a rich literature and a distinct script of its own. However, the Urdu-speaking migrants to West Pakistan sought to impose Urdu as the official language of the new state, and received support from Jinnah himself. As Urdu had united the Indian Muslims before Partition it was presumed that it would also unite them in building a strong Pakistani nation-transcending provincial and ethnic loyalties. Efforts to impose Urdu in Sindh have infuriated the Sindhis immensely and have been perceived as attempts to marginalize their rich culture. As a nation with a multilingual society, it was politically naive for Pakistan to officially choose Urdu as the national language, as it was spoken by only 7.5 percent of its population. The fact that the feudal-bureaucratic structure, entrenched mainly in Punjab, that had initially succeeded the colonial masters had adopted Urdu as its language of literacy contributed to its imposition as the national language. The subsequent entrants into the power structure, the military leadership and the capitalists, came either from the ethnic groups whose language of literacy was Urdu, or from very small ethnic groups who did not have the wherewithal to assert themselves culturally.[19] The requirement to learn in Urdu made it the language of the elite. Punjabi, Pashto and Balochi did not have well-defined scripts and as a result people from Punjab, KP and Balochistan could not impart education in the native language. On the other hand, Sindhi had been a language with a written script long before the arrival of Arabs. The province, even during British rule had used Sindhi language as the medium of instruction and partially as an official language. The province with such a well-defined linguistic nationality obviously resisted the imposition of an alien language. However, the Sindhi language was suppressed by the Pakistani state and the Sindhis were thereby turned into second-class citizens in their own homeland, in a manner that many Sindhis described as a fascist attempt at cultural genocide.[20] In 1957 the University of Karachi disallowed students from answering questions in Sindhi, triggering an acute sense of resentment in Sindhis.[21] It was only in July 1972 that the Sindh Assembly passed a resolution declaring Sindhi to be official language of the province.

The settlement of refugees who migrated from India (Mohajirs) to the urban centers of Sindh, to spaces vacated by Hindu Sindhis who were forced to leave for India, turned these cities into Mohajir citadels. According to Shaukat Hyat Khan, Liaqat Ali Khan, the first prime minister of Pakistan, wanted to create a seat for himself and thereby facilitated the settlement in Karachi of refugees from Uttar Pradesh, by allowing them into Pakistan though Khokhrapar. These refugees got most of the jobs in the cities and deprived locals of their rightful share. This eventually led to the Sindhis' hatred of Mohajirs, which exists to this day.[22] Sindhis not only became a minority in their own state, they were virtually driven out of the main cities of Karachi and Hyderabad. The 'sons of the soil' see themselves dispossessed by the Mohajirs, and the migration of large numbers of Pakhtoons and Punjabis to Sindhi cities in recent years has further compounded the problem. There has been a large scale influx of Pakhtoons into Karachi from FATA and Malkand division of KP, where security forces have launched operations against the Taliban. The three main cities of Sindh – Karachi, Hyderabad and Sukkur – are now totally dominated by Mohajirs, and the fertile land of Northern Sindh is almost totally under the control of Punjabis, which include many former members of the Armed Forces. The Sindhis are scattered in the barren and desolate Sindh countryside. Most Hindu businessmen, who were controlling business in Sindh as in most of Pakistan, migrated to India after Partition, and the businesses in the urban centers of Sindh passed on to non-Sindhis, who came in to fill the void.

In 1983, the province erupted in a violent demonstration against Zia's rule. Thousands of Sindhi nationalists defied the army in the interiors of Sindh to fight for the elusive 'Sindhudesh.'[23] The movement petered out with the passage of time. Reduction in Sindh's share of Indus water due to various barrages and dams constructed upstream has notionally reduced the land under irrigation in Sindh. The proposed construction of the Kalabagh Dam evokes strong emotions in Sindh, as it is perceived that the availability of water to Sindh would be further reduced. There are reports that salinity levels have been rising in the lower reaches of Sindh, thereby turning fertile lands into barren tracts.

The intriguing aspect of Sindhi nationalism has been that notwithstanding genuine grievances, the Sindhi nationalists have not been able to generate a lasting mass movement. A plausible explanation could be that factionalism and hierarchy pervade Sindhi society, and sectional interests tend to prevail over

Sindhi nationalism. The external environment has also not been conducive to the secessionists. In the absence of a large and prosperous overseas community, superpower backing or effective help from India, the secessionist bid stood no reasonable chance against the organized might of the Pakistani state. The Sindhi nationality question raised by the Jiye Sindh Movement (JSM) has subsided, but a permanent solution, which will bring Sindhis to the national mainstream, is still elusive. The irrationality and arrogance that led to the conflict in 1983 may reappear if the situation deteriorates again.[24] Meanwhile most of the Sindhi nationalist leaders have been co-opted by the Pakistani state. Internal dissent within their ranks has further weakened the cause of Sindhi nationalism and has splintered the JSM into numerous factions.[25] Although Sindhi nationalists at present are too weak to threaten the Pakistani state, they have not given up their struggle and continue to express their simmering resentment. In 1999, at an international Sindh Conference in Washington, nationalist leaders like Mumtaz Bhutto and G.M. Syed's son Imdad Shah termed the 'ideology of Pakistan' to be a 'concoction of ill conceived interpretations of Islam and socio-economic constructs to support a heavily militarised fascist state.'[26]

During the 2008 elections, there was a resurgence of Sindhi nationalism after the assassination of Benazir Bhutto, and many anti-Pakistan slogans were raised. However, the emergence of the PPP government led by President Asif Ali Zardari, a Sindhi, at Islamabad has kept Sindhi nationalism in check. With the position of Zardari weakening, Sindhi nationalism has started raising its head, even though the attempts to unite various factions of the Sindhi independence movement Jeay Sindh Quaumi Mahaz (JSQM) have failed. Many of them believe that the problems of Sindh cannot be resolved within the framework of parliamentary democracy.[27] In the aftermath of military operations in Swat, when large number of IDPs from the region moved to Sindh, the nationalists organized large-scale protests demanding a ban on their movement to Sindh. There were some violent actions also against Pakhtoons and their establishments.[28] Sindhis assert that when operations were launched against Bugtis and Marris in Balochistan, many of them moved to adjoining districts in Sindh and took over most of the lower-end jobs. They feel that similar phenomena will repeat with the Pakhtoon IDPs, who have migrated as a result of the operations in FATA and Swat valley. Some members of the JSQM openly stated, 'We don't want autonomy. We want independence from Pakistan.'[29]

The unprecedented floods faced by Sindh in 2010 and the large-scale devastation caused has further infuriated the Sindhis. It is widely believed that Sindh was flooded to minimize the losses in Punjab. Sindhis believe that they had not only suffered from manipulations of the water courses upstream in order to benefit the province of Punjab, but that the general attitude of the upstream leaders towards Sindh had also prevented mutual solidarity at a time when eight to nine million Sindhis were affected. They have demanded that flood aid be distributed among the provinces in accordance with the losses suffered, and not on the basis of their population, as is being proposed by the federal government.[30]

There is also a perception that the federal government has not done enough for the Sindhis affected by the floods. A proposal to impose a Sindh-specific tax to meet the losses has given an impression that the federal government wants to palm off the burden of flood relief on the people of Sindh. President Zardari has of late started playing the Sindh card deftly, and his removal could inflame the simmering embers in Sindh. Some PPP leaders have started asserting that Zardari is being targeted only because he is a Sindhi. They claim that Pakistan will break up if he is removed.[31] As the percentage of Sindhis in the Armed Forces, especially in the officer corps, is miniscule, the military regimes are generally perceived as anti-Sindh. There is a large-scale antipathy towards the army in general in Sindh. Many believe that Sindhi villages and farm lands were flooded by breaches made on the banks of the River Indus to save the military cantonments in Sindh.[32] The Army is therefore trying to create another Sindhi leader, who could be installed at the national level, to counter the Sindhis' sense of deprivation. The attempts to unite various factions of the Pakistan Muslim League (PML) under Pir Pagaro appear to be a step in this direction. However, with or without Pagaro, the removal of Zardari from the presidency by the security establishment, if attempted, will provide a fillip to Sindhi nationalism.

Mohajirs

Mohajirs, or the refugees from India, consider themselves to be the creators of Pakistan – its ideologues. Being in the forefront of the struggle for Pakistan, they were naturally in a dominant position and were ardent supporters of Pakistani nationalism, as opposed to the regional identities professed by the Sindhis, Pakhtoons and Punjabis. It is ironical that more than six decades after Pakistan's creation, they should still be called Mohajirs, or refugees. They were not only in the forefront of the struggle for Pakistan but also formed the core of the Muslim League. The Mohajir elite and intelligentsia opted for a Pakistan where the ghost of Mughal glory could be resurrected under their leadership. The people from India, mainly from Uttar Pradesh, who went to live in Pakistan were politically more enlightened and culturally more refined than those among whom they chose to go and live.

The first generation of Mohajirs came to Pakistan in 1947 looking for the 'foot of the rainbow,' both culturally and economically. Religion had motivated them to migrate to the 'land of the pure.' The euphoria generated by the creation of a new Islamic country for the Urdu-speaking Muslims of South Asia took them to Pakistan in their thousands. Though most of the migrants (the majority being Punjabis) settled in Punjab, more than 20 percent settled in Karachi and other urban centers in Sindh. The distinctive social habits and cultural outlook of the Sindhis drew boundaries between the two (ethnic) communities and kept 'these outsiders' in specified areas in cribbed isolation on ethnic grounds.[33] The genesis of the ethnic conflict that erupted in Karachi and other parts of urban Sindh lies in the concentration of Mohajirs within Sindh, where a common religion is too weak to bind the locals with other groups who were brought into the

area after Partition. A common language and culture could facilitate the assimilation of refugees from East Punjab into West Punjab. However, migrants from
other parts of India did not find areas of cultural or linguistic similarity and
moved to Karachi, which was the seat of power and hence the avenue for
employment opportunities. They subsequently moved to other urban centers of
Sindh, such as Hyderabad, Sukkur and Khairpur. These Urdu speaking migrants
were better educated and had a distinctive set of cultural and social values quite
different from the feudal and largely uneducated Sindhis. In the absence of
restrictions imposed by a predominantly feudal society, these migrants were
more amenable to modern education and ideas.[34]

The Mohajirs were better educated and substantially benefited from the
migration of Hindu and Sikh elites. Their status rose steadily and they dominated
government jobs and professional assignments. The Mohajir elite took full
control of the bureaucracy and established its hold over the most developed areas
of Sindh – Karachi, Hyderabad and other urban centers. However, subsequent
political developments, like Jinnah's death, the assassination of Liaqat Ali Khan,
and the creation of One Unit, contributed to the diminishing Mohajir dominance
in the Pakistani polity.[35] The ascent of the Army in the national polity enabled
the much larger nationalities of Punjabis and Pakhtoons to move up and expand,
while the Mohajirs' hold began to shrink. After the 1965 war the Mohajirs were
accused of spying for India to destabilize Pakistan. The Punjabi bureaucratic-
military clique gradually eroded Mohajir dominance in Pakistan's politics, and
with the shift of the capital from Karachi to Islamabad, federal power irrevocably shifted to Punjab. As Yahya Khan undid the 'One Unit' and returned Karachi
to Sindh, the Mohajirs' sense of insecurity began to grow. The first ever free and
fair elections organized in Pakistan (by Yahya Khan) made the Mohajirs conscious of their 'numerical inferiority.'[36]

After the creation of Bangladesh, Pakistan witnessed the ascendance of
Zulfiqar Ali Bhutto, a Sindhi, to the highest office of power. This resulted in
Sindhi assertiveness, and the provincial government introduced the Sindhi language in education and passed a Sindh Language Bill in 1972, which made the
knowledge of Sindhi language essential for provincial jobs. The government also
reserved 60 percent of government jobs and educational places for Sindhis living
in rural areas, primarily with the intent to keep Mohajirs, who were living in
urban Sindh, out. This brought the Mohajir protestors out on the streets. Subsequently, during the 1973–75 phase, the Mohajirs along with other political
opponents were condemned as anti-nationals by Bhutto and persecuted.[37] Meanwhile, Soviet intervention in Afghanistan brought a new set of immigrants to
Karachi – Pakhtoons, who were soon running Karachi's transport and dealing in
arms and narcotics. Pakhtoons, unlike Sindhis, were neither docile nor willing to
accept the Mohajir supremacy in the metropolis. This resulted in the first violent
ethnic clashes betweens Mohajirs and Pakhtoons in 1985.[38] Several bouts of
ethnic violence occurred after 1985, when Altaf Hussain (leader of the MQM)
first gave the call for a movement against the Punjabi dominated state. They
faced increased discrimination under Zia-ul-Haq and were slaughtered in large

numbers, especially in rural Sindh during President Ghulam Ishaq Khan's 'Operation Clean-up' in 1992.[39]

It was during the tumultuous eighties that the Mohajirs organized themselves into the Mohajir Quaumi Movement, which subsequently morphed into the Muttahida Quaumi Movement (MQM). The movement, which represented and championed the cause of the Urdu-speaking migrants living in the urban centers of Sindh, rose from nowhere to the center stage of the Pakistani political scene during this tumultuous period. Mohajirs constitute the majority of Karachi's skilled work force. The rise of the MQM and the ensuing struggle for Mohajir rights led to a number of violent clashes in Karachi. During the past two-and-a-half decades, thousands of Mohajirs have been killed, but the movement has grown in strength and has spread to Hyderabad, Sukkur, Liaqatabad, Nizamabad, and other urban centers. The government tried to break up the movement by creating and then supporting a rival 'Haqiqi' faction, but the writ of the MQM continues to run unabated in the urban centers of Sindh.[40] Under the regime of General Musharraf, a Mohajir, MQM initially seemed to have lost some steam, but it soon succeeded in extracting its pound of flesh from Musharraf in return for its support. It used its proximity to power to eliminate the Haqiqi faction from its last remaining bastions in Karachi, and gerrymandered the parliamentary constituencies in Karachi and Hyderabad to increase its political clout. Despite change of government, it has retained its leverage on power and still retains the capability to cripple life in Karachi – the economic hub of Pakistan.

The MQM represents, therefore, a type of ethno-nationalism which has surfaced in the modern world: settler groups who employ all means to take control of a territory to which they are recent arrivals. This is patently manifest from the way the MQM intends to bring about demographic change in its favor. Thus, while it shares with the Sindhi nationalists and secessionists an interest in opposing further influx into Sindh from Punjab and other Pakistani provinces, it favors the repatriation to Pakistan of the 250,000 Biharis stranded in Bangladesh since 1971, with the right to settle in Sindh. The Biharis, being Urdu speakers, are likely to prefer settling in Karachi or Hyderabad, thereby strengthening the Urdu-speaking component of the Sindh population.

At one stage the MQM propounded the idea of separating Karachi and Hyderabad from the rest of Sindh and creating a new province; however, after realizing that they had no support for it either within Pakistan or outside, it has started casting itself as urban Sindhis. It has tried to strike some sort of an alliance with the Sindhi nationalist parties and has made common cause with them. It successfully forced Musharraf to shelve the Kalabagh Dam. The MQM also made attempts to include other ethnic groups and emerge as a political party of the entire middle class. For a while it even espoused the cause of Baloch nationalists and took up cudgels on their behalf, but the Baloch did not find its subsequent withdrawal on the issue endearing. It even fielded a large number of candidates who were not Mohajirs in the elections, but did not really succeed. Its attempts to forge a common alliance with other smaller ethnic groups against the Punjabi domination have not succeeded, as its interests in Karachi clash with theirs. The Mohajirs have also retained their Indian links at socio-cultural levels. The MQM's agitations against Punjabi domination have often prompted the Pakistan government to dub the MQM as Indian agents.[41]

The MQM has been at the forefront in opposing the increasing influx of Pakhtoons into Karachi after the operations in KP and FATA, as Mohajirs have traditionally had a hostile relationship with Pakhtoons in Karachi, who, unlike Sindhis, are willing to take up arms against Mohajirs. Continued influx of Pakhtoons into urban Sindh in general and Karachi in particular might tilt the ethnic balance against the Mohajirs.[42] In the last elections the ANP secured two seats in the provincial assembly from Karachi; MQM has since then been opposing the Pakhtoon influx, projecting it as growing Talibanization of the city. In January 2010, 24 people were killed in Karachi during just four days of clashes between MQM and ANP. Again in October 2010 over 70 people, mostly Mohajirs, were killed in increasing violence in Karachi.[43] The growing challenge to Mohajir supremacy in Karachi will result in frequent violence and an increased assertion by the Mohajirs of their ethnic identity.

The Baloch

The Baloch have rebelled four times since Pakistan's creation, demanding greater autonomy, or even an independent state, which would reunite the five million Baloch in Pakistan, Iran, and Afghanistan under one flag.[44] Of various strands of sub-nationalism threatening Pakistan's nationhood, Baloch nationalism poses the strongest challenge. Unlike Pakhtoon nationalism, which withered with time, Baloch nationalism has only grown in strength over the decades. In over six decades of Pakistan's existence, the Baloch have always been outside of the mainstream, and this is the reason that while Pakhtoons assimilated in Pakistani society, the Baloch moved away. Linguistically, the Baloch are not a homogenous group; they speak Balochi, a language of Persian origin, and Brahui, a Dravidian language akin to Gondi in Central India. Despite Balochi and Brahui being as different as chalk and cheese, the Baloch have been united by a common narrative of history and a sense of perceived persecution by the Pakistani state. Baloch nationalism has created separatist and nationalist sentiments within a culturally distinct ethnic group that had its own autonomous history and did not change much under British rule. In the pre-colonial period, Balochistan was a loose tribal confederacy, which enjoyed virtual independence, even though at different times they accepted the suzerainty of the Persian emperor or the Afghan kings.[45]

The Baloch inhabit almost half of Pakistan's area but comprise only five percent of Pakistan's population. The Baloch territory has immense natural resources and most of Pakistan's energy resources. The Baloch joined Pakistan quite reluctantly. The predominant Baloch ruler, the Khan of Kalat, was forced to sign the merger document. The use of the Pakistani security forces to pressurize the Khan to sign the instrument of accession triggered the first armed insurgency led by Prince Karim, brother of the Khan, in 1948.[46] After the initial rebellion, the Baloch have risen in revolt thrice and have faced the security forces in 1958, 1963–69 and 1973–77. Though the insurgencies in the past have been crushed with a heavy hand, they have left scars which are yet to heal. Each insurgency has been more intense than the previous one, and the organizational capabilities and the popular support for the insurgents have increased with each insurgency. At the height of the insurgency in 1973, 55,000 insurgents faced 80,000 Pakistani troops supported by the Pakistan Air Force as well as the Iranian Air Force. More than 5,000 insurgents and over 3,300 soldiers were killed in the insurgency, which lingered on until 1977.[47]

The current phase of insurgency started in 2004, but gained force after a female doctor, Shazia Khalid, was allegedly raped by an army officer in Sui in January 2005.[48] Unlike the previous insurgencies, the current insurgency is supported by all the major tribes and is spread across the entire Baloch territory. The movement is being propelled by educated Baloch youth, including women from Balochistan and Karachi, which is home to around 2.5 million Baloch.[49]

The Pakistani establishment has often tried to trivialize the current discontent in Balochistan by projecting it as a product of feudal leaders' apprehensions that the mega-developmental projects in Balochistan will expose their subjects to the outside world and weaken their hold on them. However, a careful analysis of the events shows that ethnicity intertwined with a sense of political isolation and relative economic deprivation continues to be a potent force in promoting Baloch mobilization. The absence of genuine federalism and the lack of any real decision-making powers with the provincial government have increased the alienation of the population. Even the Chief Minister claims that he has no say on the deployment of security forces within the province.[50] As for other smaller ethnic groups, perceived Punjabi hegemony is the single most important factor for Baloch alienation, and it is much more pronounced among them than among other ethnic groups for historical and economic reasons.

One of the contributing factors has been their relative absence from various organs of the government. There are scarcely any Baloch in the Pakistani Army, civil service, or diplomatic corps. Balochistan continues to be grossly underrepresented in all the organs of the Pakistani state; even most of the provincial jobs are held by outsiders. As a result people find it difficult to identify themselves with the government. The government and its organs are therefore perceived as aliens lording over Baloch territory.[51]

There is also the case of perceived economic exploitation by Islamabad. The Baloch feel that their natural assets are being exploited without giving them anything in return. A case in point is Sui Gas, which was being supplied to almost all the households and industries across Pakistan except in Balochistan. Even today only 6 percent of Balochistan's population has a gas connection. Ironically, these connections came a decade after gas had been supplied all over Pakistan. In fact, had the Zia regime not decided to set up an Army corps headquarters in Quetta, there would still be no gas there. Within Pakistan, the maximum poverty and unemployment rates are in Balochistan.[52] Balochistan has the poorest social indicators within Pakistan; its literacy rate at 29.81 percent is much lower than the national average of 39.68 percent. It has a high infant mortality rate of 158 children dying out of every 1,000, only 38 percent of the population has access to clean drinking water, and only 25 percent of the rural population has access to electricity.[53]

The Baloch also fear that they are being marginalized in their own province by the rising influx of Pakhtoon and other Pakistanis. The influx of a large number of Afghan refugees of Pakhtoon origin has created an imbalance in the numerical strength of the two communities. Already the Northern Districts are overwhelmingly dominated by Pakhtoons. This feeling of being reduced to a minority has also led them to oppose the mega-infrastructural projects being undertaken in Balochistan. They perceive that these will not result in greater economic opportunities for them but will only be used by outsiders to colonize their land and reduce them to a minority. The project that has caused maximum distress is Gwadar Port, with the Pakistani establishment predicting that it will be another Karachi. But the Baloch fear that they will be reduced to an insignificant minority within their own province. In addition, Gwadar has been connected to Karachi, but has not been connected to Quetta through the Baloch hinterland; as a result, the rest of the province will not derive any benefit from these projects. This has made the people restive, as they feel that they are being converted into a landlocked province despite having the longest coastline in the country.[54]

With the return of democratic governance in Pakistan, it was hoped that the situation in Balochistan would improve. However, the elections in 2008 were largely boycotted by the nationalists, and consequently the provincial government hardly represents the people. The popular perception is that decisions regarding Balochistan are taken by the federal security establishment without taking the provincial establishment into confidence. Many Baloch nationalists have disappeared or have been killed 'allegedly' by the security forces. The alienation from Islamabad is at an all-time high, and besides security personnel, hundreds of Punjabi settlers have been eliminated by various Baloch groups. Consequently thousands of Punjabi settlers, including government officials, are migrating out of Balochistan.[55] The nationalists are also ensuring that the educational institutions in Balochistan neither hoist the Pakistani flag nor sing the Pakistani anthem.[56]

Balochistan has an extremely inaccessible terrain with a long coastline, and borders Iran and Afghanistan. The population has never really been reconciled to the concept of Pakistan and a large portion of the territory was virtually independent during British rule. Any insurgency in the region is always difficult to quell. Successive governments in the past had selectively co-opted Baloch leaders in order to keep the Baloch uprisings under control. However, this has not worked, and today the Baloch disenchantment with Pakistan appears complete.

Seraikis

The people in the Seraiki belt of Southern Punjab speak the Seraiki dialect and consider themselves to be a separate linguistic and ethnic group as distinct from the Punjabis. The heartland of Seraiki culture is the former Princely State of Bahawalpur in Southern Punjab. At the time of Pakistan's independence, it was one of the wealthiest Princely States on the subcontinent. The vast majority of the people of Bahawalpur speak Seraiki. There are also Seraiki speakers in neighboring parts of Sindh, Balochistan and NWFP. They have been clamoring for a separate state since the 1960s. Like the Sindhis and the Baloch, the Seraikis argue that their cultural rights are being suppressed and that they are being economically exploited by Punjab. Many Punjabis, however, refuse to accept that the Seraikis are a distinct cultural, let alone national group, and dismiss their language as nothing more than a dialect of Punjabi.[57]

At first the Seraikis restricted themselves to a demand for language rights. Seraiki and Punjabi are to a large extent mutually intelligible, but the Seraikis insisted that they had a separate linguistic tradition. By the 1970s their demands were becoming increasingly political, and activists even produced maps of Seraikistan.[58] This area included not only the Bahawalpur Princely State but also the whole of the Southern half of Punjab and the district of Dera Ismail Khan in NWFP. Although their leadership has always been highly fragmented, the decision to limit the extent of Seraiki claims has attracted broad support among Seraiki speakers.[59]

The Seraikis' primary demands are: recognition as a separate nationality; official documents to be written in Seraiki; more Seraiki language programs on radio and television; increased employment quotas for Seraikis; and the formation of a Seraiki regiment in the army. Seraiki areas are highly fertile and provide a substantial proportion of the two main crops of Pakistan, cotton and wheat, but no industrial investment has been made in the region. The Indus Water Treaty has further deprived them of the waters of Sutluj and Beas, which used to flow through the region. The Seraikis as a result see the rest of Pakistan as exploitative.

The central government has never made any serious efforts to address Seraikis' demands. As the Seraikis live in Punjab, their campaign has always faced the implacable opposition of not only the Army but also the Pakistani establishment dominated by Punjabis. The Seraikis argue that this reflects their under-representation in the Pakistani bureaucracy: the Army's tendency to recruit in Northern Punjab means the Seraikis have never been a force to reckon with within the Army.[60] The people from other smaller states of Pakistan, i.e., Sindh, Balochistan and NWFP, are keener on the creation of this new state, as it would reduce the pre-eminence of Punjab in the body politic of Pakistan. The movement received a fillip after the 2008 elections. Many Seraiki intellectuals merely want the restoration of defunct Bahawalpur State, which was dissolved in 1955, while others want the province to be created out of Seraiki-speaking districts in Punjab and KP. They claim that the disparity between the Seraiki region and other parts of Punjab had made creation of the province inevitable.[61]

In July 2009, some district councils passed resolutions for the creation of a Seraiki province, whilst some others passed resolutions for the revival of the Bahawalpur State. The proposal for a Bahawalpur State has, for the first time, received support from the Punjabi-speaking populace of the region as well. Over 16 MNAs and 32 MPAs (Members of the National/Provincial Assemblies), cutting across party lines, were believed to be supporting this cause.[62] However, with the district councils having been dissolved, the movement has lost its momentum. Some of the political groups fighting for the creation of a separate Seraiki state have joined the Pakistan Oppressed Nations Movement (PONM). Though dormant, the issue has the potential of becoming an irritant for Pakistan.

Conclusion

There are other smaller ethnic minorities who voice their grievances from time to time. After the renaming of NWFP as KP, there was a strong movement for the creation of a Hazara province by the Hindko-speaking populace of the province, which is concentrated in Hazara Division. Although Hindko speakers are in a majority in Hazara, it also has a fair share of people speaking Pashto, Gojri and Kohistani. The demand appears to be politically motivated, as it is supported by the defeated politicians of PML(Q), the Quaid-e-Azam faction of the PML, who are opposed to the ANP and also want to settle a score with PML(N) leader Nawaz Sharif. The demand is strongest in Abbottabad, Haripur and Mansehra districts, whereas the Pashto-speaking majority in Battagram district is quite wary of the proposal.[63] The Pakhtoons' contempt for people from Hazara, who overwhelmingly voted for Pakistan in 1947, is the root cause of the demand for a new province.[64] The movement appears to be petering out. Although the ANP government has opposed the separation of the region, the creation of a separate Hazara province, while merging Pakhtoon territories from FATA and Balochistan into KP, would meet the ethnic aspirations of both Pakhtoons and Hindkowans.

Pakistan today is at a crucial juncture, and ethnic identities will become more pronounced as the state de-emphasizes its Islamic identity. It would be more appropriate to accommodate these aspirations in a genuinely federal structure rather than react to them defensively and feel threatened by them. The use of force to crush the ethnic aspirations of the people only increases the alienation of various ethnic groups. The accommodation of provincial aspirations through genuine political decentralization will reduce the growing support for separatist ethnic movements. However, bonding the four provinces in an acceptable and workable federal structure will demand a great deal of attitudinal readjustment by the Punjabi-dominated federal leadership. As time passes the challenge to Punjabi domination is only going to get more strident.

Notes

1 M.A. Weaver, *Pakistan in the Shadow of Jihad and Afghanistan*, 2002, p. 7.
2 S.S. Pattanaik, 'Pakistan's North West Frontier', 1998, pp. 761–762.

3 I.A. Rehman, 'The Rise and Fall of Democracy', 1997, p. 32.
4 Earlier known as North West Frontier Province (NWFP).
5 It was set up as Mohajir Quaumi Movement, a party to espouse Mohajirs' cause, and although the name was changed to give it a broader acceptance, it continues to be a Mohajir party.
6 G.B. Ahmed, 'No IDPs, Please', 2009, p. 35.
7 H.A. Rizvi, *Military, State and Society in Pakistan*, 2000, p. 57.
8 Ibid., p. 68.
9 A. Siddiqui, 'The Great Leap Backwards', 1997, pp. 37–38.
10 Rizvi, *Military, State and Society*, pp. 69–70.
11 C. Jaffrelot, *Pakistan Nationalism Without a Nation*, 2002, p. 8.
12 K. Ahmed, 'Leadership for the New Millennium', 2004, p. 302.
13 F. Ahmed, *Ethnicity and Politics in Pakistan*, 1998, p. 282.
14 Khan Abdul Wali Khan in *Facts are Facts*, 1987, as cited in 'NWFP Referendum 1947' on http://pakteahouse.wordpress.com/2008/07/10/history-is-not-a-farce-the-nwfp-referendum/ (accessed on 6 September 2010)
15 O. Caroe, *The Pathans: 550 B.C.-A.D. 1957*, Karachi: Oxford University Press, 1976, p. 436.
16 F. Ahmed, *Ethnicity and Politics*, p. 185.
17 O.B. Jones, *Pakistan: Eye of the Storm*, 2002, p. 114.
18 Weaver, *Pakistan in the Shadow*, p. 73.
19 F. Ahmed, *Ethnicity and Politics*, p. 50.
20 Ibid., p. 56.
21 Jones, *Pakistan*, p. 115.
22 S.H. Khan, *The Nation that Lost its Soul*, 1995, p. 178.
23 Weaver, *Pakistan in the Shadow*, pp. 73–74.
24 F. Ahmed, *Ethnicity and Politics*, p. 43.
25 IDSA, *Whither Pakistan? Growing Instability and Implications for India*, New Delhi: Institute for Defence Studies and Analyses (IDSA), 2010, p. 39.
26 Jones, *Pakistan*, p. 130.
27 'Sarki Admits Failure in Uniting JSQM Factions', *Dawn*, 27 March 2009.
28 A. Pathan, 'Complete strike in interior Sindh against IDPs' influx', *The News*, 26 May 2009, also see 'ANP holds protest rally in Hyderabad', *The News*, 28 March 2009, 'Killing of JSQM man sparks protests', *Dawn*, 25 July 2009 and 'Attack on JSQM rally: Six vehicles set on fire, many damaged in violent protests' *Dawn*, 25 July 2009.
29 G.B. Ahmed 'No IDPs', p. 34.
30 'Sindh sovereignty linked to peace in region: WSC', *The News*, 14 October 2010, p. 2.
31 B.N. Malik, 'Ethnically Federal', *The News*, Internet Edition, 9 January 2010.
32 'Sindh sovereignty linked to peace in region: WSC', *The News*, 14 October 2010, p. 2.
33 M.G. Chitkara, *Mohajir's Pakistan*, 1996, p. 43.
34 Backgrounder from www.satp.org/satporgtp/countries/pakistan/backgrounders/index.html (accessed on 10 November 2010)
35 Jones, *Pakistan*, pp. 114–115.
36 Ibid., pp. 116–117.
37 Ibid., pp. 117–119.
38 Ibid., pp. 121–122.
39 Ibid., p. 127.
40 Chitkara, *Mohajir's Pakistan*, p. 45.
41 J.N. Dixit, 'Pakistan's India Policies', 1995, p. 236.
42 G.B. Ahmed 'No IDPs', p. 34.
43 'Karachi violence threat to govt: Economist', *The News*, 24 October 2010, pp. 9, 12.
44 Weaver, *Pakistan in the Shadow*, p. 93.

45 Ibid., p. 93.
46 Y. Babbar, 'Separate Ways', 2009, p. 46.
47 P. Sahadevan, 2000, pp. 16–17.
48 Babbar, 'Separate Ways', p. 47.
49 S. Dharejo, 'The Young also Rise', 2009, pp. 57–58.
50 M. Ahmed, 'Meri Marzi Ho To Security Forces', 2009, p. 63.
51 A. Bansal, *Balochistan in Turmoil*, 2010, pp. 227–231.
52 Ibid., 231–234.
53 A. Wahab, 'A Province in Peril', 2009, pp. 49–51.
54 Bansal, *Balochistan in Turmoil*, pp. 224–227.
55 S.T. Hussain, 'Regime of Fear', 2010, p. 43.
56 Babbar, 'Separate Ways', p. 45.
57 Jones, *Pakistan*, p. 140.
58 T. Rahman, *Language and Politics in Pakistan*, 1990, p. 178.
59 Jones, *Pakistan*, p. 140.
60 Ibid., p. 141.
61 S. Ahmad, 'Borders of "Seraiki province" ', *Dawn*, 10 April 2009.
62 R. Klasra, 'Is Bahawalpur Province a Pipe Dream after all?', 2009.
63 Y. Rahimullah, 'From Protests to Movement', 2010.
64 K. Jahangiri, 'The real Hazara problem', 2010.

Bibliography

Ahmed, F., *Ethnicity and Politics in Pakistan*, Karachi: Oxford University Press, 1998.
Ahmed, G.B., 'No IDPs, Please', *Newsline* (Karachi), June 2009.
Ahmed, K., 'Leadership for the New Millennium: Medievalism on the Eve of 2000 AD' in K.A. Ahmed, *Pakistan: Behind the Ideological Mask*, Lahore: Vanguard Books Pvt. Ltd., 2004.
Ahmed, M., 'Meri Marzi Ho To Security Forces Ko Pooray Balochistan Say Nikal Doon', *The Herald* (Karachi), July 2009.
Babbar, Y., 'Separate Ways', *Newsline* (Karachi), June 2009.
Bansal, A., *Balochistan in Turmoil: Pakistan at Crossroads*, New Delhi: Manas Publications, 2010.
Chitkara, M.G., *Mohajir's Pakistan*, New Delhi: APH Publishing Corporation, 1996.
Dharejo, S., 'The Young also Rise', *Newsline* (Karachi), June 2009.
Dixit, J.N., 'Pakistan's India Policies: Role of Domestic Political Factors', *International Studies*, July–September 1995.
Hussain, S.T., 'Regime of fear', *Newsline* (Karachi), April 2010.
Jaffrelot, C., *Pakistan Nationalism Without a Nation*, New Delhi: Manohar Publishers and Distributors, 2002.
Jahangiri, K., 'The Real Hazara Problem', *The News* (Karachi), 6 May 2010.
Jones, O.B., *Pakistan: Eye of the Storm*, New Delhi: Penguin Books India, 2002.
Khan, S.H., *The Nation that Lost its Soul: Memoirs of a Freedom Fighter*, Lahore: Jang Publishers, 1995.
Klasra, R., 'Is Bahawalpur Province a Pipe Dream after all?', *The News* (Karachi), 14 July, 2009.
Pattanaik, S.S., 'Pakistan's North West Frontier: Under a New Name', *Strategic Analysis*, 22:5, August 1998.
Rahimullah, Y., 'From Protests to Movement', *The News* (Karachi), 4 May 2010.
Rahman, T., *Language and Politics in Pakistan*, Karachi: Oxford University Press, 1990.

Rehman, I.A., 'The Rise and Fall of Democracy', *Newsline* (Karachi), August 1997.

Rizvi, H.A., *Military, State and Society in Pakistan*, London: Macmillan Press Ltd, 2000.

Sahadevan, P., *Coping with Disorder – Strategies to End Internal Wars in South Asia*, Colombo: Regional Centre for Strategic Studies, 2000.

Siddiqui, A., 'The Great Leap Backwards', *Newsline* (Karachi), August 1997.

Wahab, A., 'A Province in Peril', *Newsline* (Karachi), June 2009.

Weaver, M.A., *Pakistan in the Shadow of Jihad and Afghanistan*, New York: Farrar, Straus and Giroux, 2002.

8　Islamism and its varied dimensions in South-Central Asia

Kunal Mukherjee

Islam has been used as a political instrument by Muslim rulers over the centuries. The Arab, Ottoman, Persian and Mughal empires were created in the name of Islam, and yet they cannot be referred to as Islamic, as the dominating factor was the king and not the Quran.[1] Many of these rulers did not fight for Islam but for their own interests. Islamic resurgence in Muslim-majority countries has included both a greater emphasis on personal piety and the reassertion of Islam in national politics.[2] The use of Islamic vocabulary in political discussion in contemporary Pakistan is not unusual in light of the country's history.[3] Both governments and opposition movements have appealed to Islam when their power base has lacked political legitimacy. Pakistan was founded in the name of Islam, but it had little else in the way of common national or cultural values around which to unite.[4] And although many Pakistani political leaders did not like it, faced with the gravity of the situation few could resist the temptation of appealing to Islam.[5] It was the only course open for leaders who discouraged mass politics, failed to adopt meaningful political platforms, and avoided elections, and in the words of an observer, an Islamic State became a political motto to be used by the Muslims to continue indefinitely their predominant position in Pakistani politics.[6] Although many of the political figures of Pakistan were statists and the key concern was survival, they had to look into the needs of the more Islamist sections of the population in case they lost their support. Although Islamism is multidimensional, much of Islamism in Muslim-majority contexts like Pakistan is closely related to power politics and is a highly politicized affair; but the degree of politicization of the religion differs from one period to another depending on the ruler. Forays into the domain of the *ulama* (Islamic theologians) and the Islamic groups by politicians, and the resultant sacralization of the political discourse, could sometimes also generate uncontrollable and undesirable outcomes.[7]

Islamism is the term given to the extreme politicized version of Islam that argues that Islam is in a state of conflict with the West, with non-Muslims, and with other Muslims who are seen as insufficiently pious by revivalists. Islamism has been compared with other 'isms' of the previous century. Following fascism, Marxist Leninism and Nazism comes Islamism, a twentieth-century belief system or political ideology: ordering power and wealth; trying to create a 'just' society, with the imposition of *sharia* law, by regimenting people according to a perceived plan; but this time with an Islamic orientation. Ordinarily, the beginnings of Islamism are traced back to the Muslim Brotherhood in Egypt in the first half of the 20th century, but one could go back to the times of Muhammad Abdul Wahab in the mid eighteenth century. Along with Ibn Taymiyya, Mawdudi and Qutb are considered to be the main pillars of present-day 'Islamic fundamentalism.' It is the aim of this chapter to look at the various dimensions of Islamism in South-Central Asia. The situation in relation to Islamism in the region is very complex and multidimensional, and thus to get a comprehensive and all-embracing picture of this complex problem, one needs to look at both external influences and internal influences on Islamism in the region. Although currently there is a lot of literature available on Islamism in the region, the situation needs to be continuously revisited because the problem of Islamism still persists.

Sixty years after its founding as a homeland for India's Muslims, Pakistan straddles the fault line between moderate and militant Islam.[8] The northwest parts of Pakistan, especially Waziristan, are also where the two conflicting forms of Islam meet: the relatively relaxed and tolerant Islam of India versus the rigid Islamism of the Afghan frontier. The clash between moderates and extremists in Pakistan today reflects this rift and can be seen as a microcosm for a larger struggle among Muslims everywhere.[9] A decade after 9/11, the forces of Islamic radicalism are gaining strength and challenging Pakistan's moderate majority. Islamic militants have turned the borderlands between Pakistan and Afghanistan into a new base for Al-Qaeda.[10] Because of the infiltration of Islamists from Afghanistan and other parts of Central Asia into the North West Frontier Provinces of Pakistan, one needs to have a clear understanding of Islamism in the Central Asian context which has spilled over into South Asia. This process of Islamist infiltration from Central Asia to Pakistan is often termed the 'Talibanisation of the northwest frontiers of Pakistan.' The spillover or ripple effects from Afghanistan and other parts of Central Asia into Pakistan may be seen as external factors that are contributing to the growth and rise of Islamism in Pakistan. However, there are also internal factors which will be discussed later in the chapter.

External factors contributing to Islamism in Pakistan

Spill over effects from Central Asia and Afghanistan

The green banner of Islam was brought to Central Asia by Arab crusaders about 1,400 years ago, but it was not until the nineteenth century that Islam established itself as the dominant religion of the regional population. Central Asian Muslims received their first introduction to the wider Muslim community or *ummah* through the Afghan *jihad* against the then Soviet Union in the 1980s. The Afghan *mujahideen*, backed by the US and Pakistan, were to play a major role in clandestinely reopening the borders between Central Asia and Afghanistan and South Asia that Stalin had closed in the 1920s. Hundreds of Uzbek, Tajik and other Central Asian Muslims came clandestinely to fight alongside the *muja-hideen* and to study in Pakistani *madrasas* (religious seminaries). The one-way trickle became an extensive two-way flood after the breakup of the Soviet Union, when Saudi, Afghan and Pakistani missionaries traveled in Central Asia preaching radical Islamism and funding the construction of mosques and *madrasas.* After the Soviet Army withdrew from Afghanistan, Pakistan was left with thousands of battle-hardened *mujahideen* who had no homes or families to return to.[11] Many settled in refugee camps in Peshawar and Quetta. Some were encouraged to take the holy war to Kashmir.

The dismantling of the Soviet Union almost immediately paved the way for an ideological vacuum, and many at the time thought that the religious ideology of Islam would fill in this space. It is believed that between 1982 and 1992, approximately 35,000 Islamic radicals from 53 Muslim countries passed their baptism of fire with the Afghan *mujahideen.*[12] Thousands of Muslim radicals and students from Central Asia came to study in the new *madrasas* that the Zia government began to fund both in Pakistan and along the Afghan border.[13] In Afghanistan, Western arms and funds have played a crucial role in bolstering the Afghan fundamentalist camp in its war against the Marxist camp in Kabul.[14] The Islamic faith as part of the traditional lifestyle and culture of Central Asians was used by the newly-born states as an important attribute of national self-identification. A construction boom of mosques reached every distant corner of Central Asia. The strength of Islamic militancy in Central Asia, however, is not the same throughout the region. For instance, the Ferghana valley region and Afghanistan have a much stronger presence of Islamists than parts of Kazakhstan. This could be because in Kazakhstan, which has a long border with Russia, the Russian presence has possibly diluted the Islamist presence in the country.

The Central Asian Islamic ideology sprang from an extreme form of Deobandism, a branch of Sunni Hanafi Islam, which was preached by Pakistani Islamic parties in Afghan refugee camps in Pakistan. The Deobandi movement grew out of the seminary of Deoband (*Dar-ul-Ulum*) founded in India in 1867, which aimed to give its pupils intellectual resources to strengthen their assertion of their Islamic identity.[15] The founders of Deobandism, Mohammed Qasim Nanautawi and Rashid Ahmad Gangohi, were conscious of the extent to which power had shifted away from the Muslims to a new British and Christian elite in South Asia, and their aim was, above all, to preserve and promote an Islamic identity in this changing world. Although both were classically trained religious scholars or *alim* (theologians), they were dissatisfied with the quality of Islamic education then available.[16] The Deoband seminary in South Asia not only re-emphasized traditional standards, through the study of the *Hanafi* School of jurisprudence, but also sought to use Islamic law as a bulwark against the inroads of non-Islamic influences. Its curriculum firmly excluded English or Western subjects.[17] The rejectionist stance towards non-Islamic knowledge is clearly seen in the comment by the luminary and rector of Deoband, Ashraf Ali Thanawi (d. 1943) that 'to like and appreciate the customs of infidels is a grave sin.' The seminary also promoted a distinctive ethos which de-emphasized purely local ties in favor of the separate unity and identity of the group of Deobandis, whatever their geographic origin, fostering a style of Islam that preferred universal practices and beliefs to local cults and customs, and emphasizing the diffusion of scripturalist practices and the cultivation of an inner spiritual life.[18]

The Deobandis took a restrictive view of the role of women, opposed all forms of hierarchy in the Muslim community, and rejected Shias, but the Taliban were to take these beliefs to an extreme which the original Deobandis would probably have never recognized. While the Taliban hardly strikes one as modernist, their appetite for theocracy, desire to remake the world, and creative approach to scriptural interpretation all have fundamentalist overtones.[19] The Taliban followed Deobandist practices, which included the virtual enslavement of women and the crushing of all opposition to the Taliban's rigorous Sunni Islam, laws and protocols of conduct. Transgressors suffered the harshest punishment: there were beatings or floggings for violation of dress code for men and women, amputations of hands and feet for theft, stoning to death for adultery, and burial alive for sodomy.[20]

A common feature of all Islamist groups is the division of the world between 'insiders' and 'outsiders,' 'the saved' and 'the sinners,' and the belief in the binary of *dar-ul-Islam* (land of the faithful) and *dar-ul-harb* (land of the infidel). Islamism confers identity on the individual by granting him or her a group membership card, an entrée into the club of born-agains who identify themselves and each other by outward symbols of social conduct. Islamic law stipulates that it is a Muslim's duty to wage war not only against those who attack Muslim territory, but also against apostates, polytheists and people of the book, at first restricted to Jews and Christians but later extended to other faiths who refuse Islamic rule. There are some Quranic verses, referred to as the 'sword verses,' which are quoted selectively to legitimize unconditional warfare against non-believers and were used by jurists to justify their expansion.[21]

Islamism is above all a socio-cultural movement, embodying the protest and frustration of a generation of youth that has not been integrated socially or politically.[22] The growing economic and political crises in Pakistan, Afghanistan and Southern Central Asia is thus helping to fuel Islamist tendencies as a new generation of younger, unemployed youth become attracted to this violent form of religiosity. The collapse of the Soviet Union and its economy left Central Asia in a very precarious position. If Uzbekistan and other Central Asian countries have not been very successful in promoting development strategies, it is largely because of a lack of business expertise and the difficulties the region has had in maintaining access and links to the large markets in the Middle East and Europe. This difficulty is to some extent because of Central Asia's landlocked geographical position and the mountainous terrain of the region, which have made access to the outside world increasingly difficult. Unless the Central Asian states are able to generate economic growth and development by building the oil and gas pipelines and the road and railway links for their exports to the outside world, they will continue to face economic crises that will in turn fuel Islamic radicalism. The collapse of the Soviet commercial infrastructure had two immediate results in Uzbekistan. It deprived the Uzbeks of markets for Uzbekistan's goods, and it cut the country off from traditional suppliers. At the same time, the longer the Central Asian governments delay in allowing opposition parties to coexist within more democratic and tolerant state structures, the more they are likely to drive the Islamist challenge underground.[23] This will in turn legitimize terrorism as an alternative way of dealing with the government. In Uzbekistan, for instance, President Karimov's use of force whilst dealing with the rising tide of Islamism has threatened to lead Uzbek society to a further escalation of civil, religious and political turmoil. This in turn could also have spillover or ripple effects in South Asia. Karimov's government acted energetically to exclude competing political groups from gaining influence. For instance, the Birlik was allowed to exist, but its efforts met with much more official opposition than any other informal movements elsewhere in the region. The government used legislative means and media to counter the growth of the 'informals.'[24] It could thus be argued, to some extent, that economic crises and political high-handedness have paved the way or at least given rise to Islamism in Central Asia, which has spilled over into Pakistan because of the long border the latter shares with Afghanistan.

The Taliban and Afghanistan's influence on neighboring Pakistan

The Taliban embraced an extreme interpretation of *sharia* or Islamic law that took the rest of the Muslim world by surprise. They closed down all girls' schools. and women were rarely permitted to venture out of their homes even for shopping.[25] The Taliban banned every conceivable kind of entertainment including music, television, videos, cards, kite-flying, and most sports and games.[26] The Taliban's brand of Islamism was so extreme that it appeared to denigrate Islam's message of peace and tolerance and its capacity to live with other religious and ethnic groups. They were to inspire a new extremist form of Islamism across Pakistan and Central Asia, which refused to compromise with traditional Islamic values, social structures or existing state systems. One of the concepts which the Taliban held was that women should be neither seen nor heard because they drove men away from the prescribed Islamic path and into 'wild temptation.' Although many Muslim countries have supported the anti-Taliban Northern Alliance to halt the further advancement of the Taliban, countries including Pakistan and Saudi Arabia have backed the Taliban. In the post-cold war period, this has caused unprecedented polarization across the region.[27] The Taliban represented no-one but themselves and they recognized no other Islam other than their own. They had an anti-Shia stance as well as an anti-minority-community approach. Their ideological base was an extreme form of Deobandism which was being preached by Pakistani Islamic parties in Afghan refugee camps in Pakistan. It is believed that the Taliban's interpretation of Deobandism has no parallel in the Muslim world. Pakistani Deobandi groups and the Taliban have strong links because of their vehement opposition to Shi'ism and Iran. The Taliban's new model for a purist Islamic revolution has created immense repercussions in Pakistan, and to a more limited extent in Central Asia. Pakistan, an already fragile state beset by an identity crisis, an economic meltdown, ethnic and sectarian divisions, and a rapacious ruling elite that has been unable to provide good governance, now faces the spectre of a new Islamic wave led by neo-Taliban groups. Border regions are in constant flux and are of utmost importance. Borders between Afghanistan and the Central Asian republics are particularly volatile.[28] By 1998, Pakistani Taliban groups had banned television and videos in towns along the Pashtun belt, imposing *sharia* punishments such as stoning and amputation in defiance of the legal system, killing Pakistani Shia, and forcing people, particularly women, to adapt to the Taliban dress code and way of life. The Taliban also clamped down on homosexuality. Kandahar's Pashtuns were known for their affairs with young boys and the rape of young boys by warlords, and the punishments introduced were inhuman. Two soldiers caught indulging in homosexuality in Kabul, in April 1998, were beaten mercilessly and then tied up and driven around Kabul with their faces blackened with engine oil.[29] Men accused of sodomy faced the previously unheard-of 'Islamic' punishment of having a wall toppled over them. It could be argued that Pakistan's support for the Taliban is thus coming back to haunt the country itself, even as Pakistani leaders appear to be oblivious of the challenge.

As an illustration of Afghani Islamist forces infiltrating Pakistan, mention may be made of the Lashkar-e-Taiba (LeT), which although it was founded in the Kunar province of Afghanistan has been the most prominent Ahle Hadith group operating in Pakistan and Kashmir in recent times.[30] The LeT is the militant wing of a large religious organization, Markaz Dawa ul Irshad, which was formed in the mid- to late 1980s by Hafiz Muhammad Saeed, Zafar Iqbal and Abdullah Azzam. The Pakistani government formally banned the group and froze its assets during the crackdown in January 2002. The Markaz runs a large self-sufficient complex at its headquarters near Lahore. While it receives much of its funding and resources from Pakistani patrons, it casts its ideological net much wider. Besides fighting to bring Kashmir into the fold of pristine Ahle Hadith Islam, LeT also wants to unite the entire Muslim community of South Asia and beyond. The extent of LeT assets is not fully known, but the group receives donations from the Pakistani diaspora in the UK and the Gulf region, and also receives financial support from Muslim NGOs and business people from Pakistan and Kashmir.[31]

After the fall of the Taliban in 2001, when Al-Qaeda and the Taliban were regrouping in Waziristan, their bids to establish training camps and bases were of a very basic nature, being based mainly in mud-house compounds and offering only rudimentary training such as in the use of AK-47s and grenades, ambush techniques, explosive materials, and basic explosive techniques.[32] They also received some indoctrination in global *jihad*. Various Al-Qaeda commanders started training sessions in South Waziristan, but the whole process was abandoned in 2003, when the Pakistan Army started its operations.[33] However, from 2004 onwards, the main training bases were shifted to North Waziristan, in the town of Mir Ali. With the help of Abdul Khaliq Haqqani and Moulvi Sadiq Noor, prominent Arab scholars Sheikh Essa and Abu Yayha Al Libbi placed increasing emphasis on the struggle for the creation of an Islamic Emirates in the region. They believed once an Islamic Emirates was established, *jihad* would have official status and any person opposing *jihad* or the cause of *jihad*, like the Pakistan Army, would be declared *zindiq* (heretic).[34] This new perspective bred the concept of suicide bombing and the acceptance of killing *zindiq* Muslims. Thus some of the training programs were refocused around the preparation of suicide jackets, their detonation, and techniques to enhance the effectiveness of suicide attacks.[35]

The Tehrik-I-Taliban Pakistan (students' movement of Pakistan) is an umbrella group of various Taliban factions operating mainly in south Waziristan. With the main aim of removing foreign, mainly Western non-Muslim forces from Pakistani soil, the TTP calls for the establishing of a *sharia*-based home-land.[36] Many of the Islamists recruited by the TTP, as with Islamism generally in Pakistan, were originally trained and indoctrinated by the CIA, to fight the former Soviet Union in Afghanistan. The TTP arose out of the residue of the *mujahideen* left redundant after the withdrawal of the Soviet Union from Afghanistan. Such fighters, trained and eager for *jihad*, established numerous militant groups in Afghanistan, Kashmir and Pakistan, groups which in turn influenced the emergence of later factions including the TTP.[37] The TTP has been blamed for several attacks in Pakistan, including the assassination of Prime Minister Benazir Bhutto in December 2007. Based on the Sunni Deobandi tradi-tion, the TTP shares an anti-Western approach with other Islamist groups. Although Western culture per se is regarded as *jahili* or ignorant and corrupt, particular animosity is felt against the US. The TTP condemns US air strikes on Pakistani soil and US involvement in neighboring Afghanistan. The Pakistan government, particularly that of Musharraf and his successor Zardari, has been criticized by the TTP and other Islamists as being puppets and cronies of the US, and also for being responsible for supporting America's 'dirty war.' The TTP believes that many of Pakistan's leaders work for the US government, and regards the ISI (Pakistan's intelligence agency) as an extension of the CIA.[38] Adopting the *takfiri* doctrine of the medieval jurist, Ibn Taymiyyah, revived by Mawdudi and Qutb, the TTP justify their stance of fighting other Muslims; under this doctrine, the Pakistani government, due to its allegiance to Western *kufr* (heretic) states, is regarded as *ridda* or apostate, *fasidah* or corrupt ruler, cor-rupted by the enchantment of Western ideas. Therefore the TTP wages what it terms defensive *jihad* against the Pakistan Army. The Pakistan Army was seen by the Islamists not as a Muslim army but a mercenary army on the payroll of the US. The TTP has destroyed numerous schools which catered for the educa-tion of girls, restricted women's employment and visibility in public spaces, killed those opposed to their version of Islam, banned the shaving of beards, and prevented people from availing themselves of the Benazir income-support agree-ment, a government project to provide financial aid to women. It is alleged that the TTP threatened doctors of public-sector hospitals in Peshawar who wore

Western suits and not the traditional 'shalwar kameez.' Similarly, female doctors were directed to observe *purdah* and cover their faces from male colleagues. The implementation of *sharia*, and its treatment of *kufr* as second-class citizens, has also led to the persecution of minority groups.

The Iranian revolution and its global impact

Some scholars like John Esposito have analyzed the extent to which major events like the Iranian Revolution of 1979 and the ideas of Khomeini have influenced Islamism in South-Central Asia and other parts of the Muslim world.[39] Iran's interest in Central Asia was based initially on its ties with the Persian-speaking Tajiks, and Tehran sought to establish a sphere of influence in a region of great importance and competition. Its ambitions were further fueled by a desire to export its own brand of politically active Islam.[40] Although Central Asia has no tradition of such Shiite Islamic fundamentalism, the Iranian creed might well exert a strong appeal in a time and place of socio-economic deprivation.[41] The Iranian revolution provided Central Asians who had access to short-wave transmissions with a contemporary model of an Islamic society.[42] Similarly, although Afghanistan has had its own Islamic revival, its Islamism has to some extent been influenced by the events in Iran.[43] The Iranian revolution, which brought an Islamic government into power, catapulted revolutionary Islam as a potent ideology on to the international scene, and impacted on Islamist movements and Islamist ideology throughout the Muslim world. Khomeini, the chief ideologue of the Iranian revolution, argues that the *ulama* (theologians) should commit themselves to ousting corrupt officials and repressive governments, which should be replaced by Islamic jurists. He argues for the subordination of political power to Islamic precepts, and calls on the *ulama* to bring about an Islamic state and to participate in its legislative, executive and judicial affairs; he also offers a program of action to establish an Islamic state. An Islamic state requires an Islamic ruler who should know the *sharia* thoroughly and must be absolutely just in its application. The Shias believed that the *imams* were the ones who possessed these qualifications, but in the absence of an *imam*, Muslims must find an alternative in order to avoid living in anarchy or under alien rule.[44] Though lacking the infallibility and personal superiority of an *imam*, a just *faqi* or jurist is qualified to lead an Islamic state. Such jurisprudents are also to oversee the actions of the legislative and executive branches. At its simplest, the *vilayat-i-faqi* is the rule of the divine law as interpreted and applied by the just *faqi*. In the next section, we will see the repercussions that the Iranian revolution may have had on Pakistan and the process of Islamization in Pakistan.

Internal factors that have strengthened Islamism in Pakistan

The program of Islamization and General Zia

Because of Pakistan's commitment to Islam, the authorities in Pakistan promised that the law of the country would be in accordance with the tenets of Islam.

From the very beginning, it was the plan of the *ulama* or theologians that Islamic law would be the law of Pakistan. This is the reason why all three constitutions of Pakistan have contained clauses to the effect that the laws of Pakistan would be in accordance with the Quran and the Sunnah. But no concrete steps were taken in this direction in the first 30 years of Pakistan's history.[45] The period of Islamic revivalism, popularly known as Islamization, started in 1977, most of it carried out by one man, General Zia ul Haque. The various players in the program also had specific agendas. From President Zia's standpoint, a central aim of Islamization was to provide legitimacy for his protracted military dictatorship.[46] Having overthrown the elected government of Zulfikar Ali Bhutto in 1977, Zia badly needed a justification for his repeated rebuffs to popular demands for a return to democracy. Zia, a devout Sunni whose personal piety was respected even by his foes, found in the Islamization campaign an ideal pretext for retaining power.[47] Via Islamization, Zia forged alliances with Sunni clerics. Islamization included steps like compulsory prayers in government offices during working hours, the review of textbooks to make them conform to Islamic teachings, emphasizing Pakistan's national Islamic ideology, making Urdu the official language and the medium of instruction, and the compulsory wearing of national dress at government functions and feasts.[48] Under a presidential order, the month of fasting was legally enforced by prescribing punishment, if violated publicly; radio and television were made to change their programs to conform with Islamic teachings; in order to encourage the observance of Islamic standards, measures were taken to eliminate obscenity and vulgarity from audio-visual media, art galleries, newspapers, journals, magazines and films.[49] Also Islamic penal laws were introduced, and *sharia* courts were given the authority to determine whether or not the laws of the country were in accordance with Islam. To solve the country's economic problems, Zia promised to implement a true 'Islamic economy,' and consequently the *zakat* and *ushr* ordinance, 1980 (mandating charitable donations and Islamic taxes), was promulgated.

Pakistan has been in the grip of a raging debate on the issue of the *hudud* laws ever since they were introduced in 1979. This year also coincided with the Iranian Revolution, thus the two could possibly be linked. There are some who ask for complete repeal of these laws, others who insist on keeping them as they are, and a third group calling for amending and reforming these laws to make them more responsive to human and social conditions.[50] The *hudud* are the penalties that the Quran and the Sunnah of the prophet have prescribed for certain crimes. Theft, robbery, *zina* (fornication, adultery, rape), false accusation and drinking are crimes for which *hudud* have been prescribed.[51] The model society that Islam seeks to establish is an ideal that requires continuous struggle toward its realization. Laws are made and enforced to curb evil and to move society closer to the ideal. Much hue and cry has been raised against the harshness of the *hudud* punishments. In considering whether to commit a crime, one is lured by a temptation but deterred by the prospect of punishment. If, in one's reckoning, the pleasure of the crime exceeds the punishment, one might commit it; but if the deterrence is greater than the urge, one would be more likely to refrain. *Sharia* has prescribed punishments keeping in view this law of the human psyche and nature. The more heinous the crime, the harsher the punishment, so that society is purged of its wicked and depraved elements.[52]

Some envision Islamization as changing the nature of Pakistani society, seeing it as the means of putting all women in *purdah*, promulgating religious modes of education, and strictly enforcing *sharia* law. For others, Islamization means expanding gender-role equality, pursuing scientific knowledge and applying traditional moral principles to contemporary circumstances.[53] Regarding Islamization in the rural parts of Pakistan there are two alternative views. Some see villagers as unsophisticated savages who are prone to customs of the Hindu religion. Others associate villagers with religious simplicity, and their religious behavior is seen as pure and wholesome. Therefore, some believe that true Islamization would happen if village simplicity were brought to the urban centers whereas others think true Islamization would happen if the city, along with the theologians, mullahs and Islamic publications, are brought to the countryside.[54] However, it should be noted that villagers do not see themselves as participants in the government's Islamization effort, primarily because they do not identify with government efforts in general; the government has always been viewed by them from a distance with considerable suspicion.

Zia's Islamization was vigorously denounced by Pakistanis representing all parts of the political spectrum, who saw it as a fresh pretext for resisting demands for the restoration of democracy and for undermining the constitution. The Islamization decree seems to have been prompted by Zia's fears of upcoming elections, and he may have planned to exploit 'Islamic' criteria to disqualify Benazir Bhutto, Zia's most formidable opponent, on the grounds that women serving in high political office contravened *sharia*.[55] The question may arise, how successful was the process of Islamization? While Zia was alive, Pakistan's Islamists, though not able to achieve all their goals, had reason to be pleased with the general direction developments had been taking. However, Zia's Islamization program may have better served his interests than it did the cause of Islamism. For Zia, Islamization offered a pretext for perpetuating his military rule and refusing to allow freely contested elections on a party basis, in which Benazir Bhutto's Pakistan People's Party would have been sure to emerge victorious.[56]

The role of religious educational institutions in Pakistan

When Pakistan became an ally of the US in its war against terrorism in the aftermath of the events of 9/11, it became the focus of world attention. Its *madrasas/ madaris* (religious educational institutions or seminaries) and their perceived role in harboring terrorists and nurturing terrorism have generated heated debate. From one side of the aisle, the seminaries have been accused of spreading fanaticism and exporting terrorism, while the other side vehemently protests this contention.[57] The West is wary of these seminaries because they are alleged to be breeding and nourishing Islamist terrorists. The media, government, policy-making institutions, the 9/11 Commission, and the US Congress are all appre-hensive of these seminaries. Numerous reports have highlighted their syllabi, curricula, content and function and have strongly recommended that steps be taken to rescue the world from their 'evil designs.'[58] Hasty policy decisions have been made and large funds released to reform them as quickly as possible. So far, no credible information or authentic data about their nature, their role in Pakistani society and contribution to Islamism, their financial setup, or their acceptance in society in comparison with other institutions of learning have come to the fore. In the absence of reliable information, the situation has only worsened and the task of differentiating truth from rumor has become difficult.[59] It thus becomes increasingly important to distinguish between what a *madrasa* is and what it is not and what type of education is being imparted in them.

Since the creation of Pakistan, the educational system has been divided into two main categories. On the one hand there were the government-run British schools, colleges and universities, whose syllabi were prepared under the supervi-sion of the British with an eye to providing a workforce for the colonial govern-ment according to the priorities of the British government; on the other hand there were Muslim educational institutions called *madaris*, which were established with the objective of preserving and promoting Islamic sciences and the arts. First, there are the *maktab*, which are devoted to reading, reciting and learning the Quran by heart, with a view to enabling the common man to perform daily or regular religious duties. Second, there are the *madrasas*, which are regular educa-tional institutions where education in the Islamic sciences – Quran, Hadith, Fiqh, theology, Arabic language etc. is imparted at various levels. The multiplication of *madrasas* continued with the passage of time, owing to differences of interpreta-tion of the teachings of the Quran and the Hadith, and also taking into account teachers' diverse backgrounds and interests.[60] Pakistan's seminaries belong to four schools of Islamic jurisprudence and are affiliated with five religious educa-tional boards. Of these boards, Wifaq-ul-Madaris al Arabiya is the largest with respect to the number and strength of its affiliated institutions. This board links itself with India's Dar-ul-Ulum in Deoband, which was founded by Muhammad Qasim Nanatawi and Rashid Ahmed Gangohi in 1866. These two ideologues clearly had a very anti-Western approach while setting up the seminary in 19th-century India. The whole purpose was to create an impregnable barrier between the British and the South Asian Muslim community and to prevent Western life-styles and ideas from creeping in. They attempted to set up a school where Islamic learning would be promoted and which would help Muslims to preserve a distinct Islamic identity through learning and not be polluted by the influences of British rule. The second biggest is the Tanzim-il-Madaris. These institutions are called Barelvi after the *madrasa* that Maulana Ahmad Raza Khan (1856–1921) established in Bareilly in India's Uttar Pradesh province. The third is the Wifaq-ul-Madaris al Salfiya, which belong to the Ahle-e-Hadith school of Sunni Islam. The fourth is Rabita al Madaris, run by the *ulama* associated with the Jamat-i-Islami. Though they tend to rise above sectarian differences, their majority follows the Deobandi school of jurisprudence. The fifth and last are the Wifaq-ul-Madaris al Shia, which represents the Shia branch of Islam.[61]

Now of course the question maybe asked, to what extent are these seminaries harboring Islamist terrorism in Pakistan? It could be safely argued that, while it is difficult to say to what extent these institutions are harboring terrorism directly, some of them, especially those associated with Deobandism, are definitely encouraging and contributing to Islamist tendencies in Pakistan. The Deobandi seminary, which was established to resist the cultural influences of British colonial rule has similar aims today as Islamist ideologues try to resist the cultural influences of McDonaldization or Americanization, and thus both have an anti-Western approach in common. We can safely conclude that there is a coexistence of Islam (the religion itself) and Islamism (political ideology) in these seminaries. The *madrasa* system in Pakistan has continued to grow and provides religious education, free board and lodging to poor children who would otherwise receive no education at all. Religious seminaries provide an alternative to a deficient schooling system in the public sector.[62] Unfortunately the government has been unable to enforce *madrasa* registration, order full disclosure of all sources of funding, or monitor the type of Islam being taught, e.g., Salafi, Deobandi, etc. Nor is there any credible monitoring of the qualifications and the radical views of the teachers, many of whom have strong links with seminaries in Afghanistan.[63]

The Jamat-i-Islami in Pakistan

Mawdudi, the founder of the Jamat-i-Islami in Pakistan, is without doubt the most influential of contemporary Islamic revivalist thinkers, and his views have influenced Islamic revivalism from Morocco to Malaysia, leaving their mark on thinkers such as Sayid Qutb (Egypt) and on events such as the Iranian Revolution of 1979.[64] His contribution to the development and strengthening of Islamism is so important that we will not be able to get a balanced picture of Islamism and the contributions he made to Islamism unless and until we have some understanding of his life and thought. His ideas emerged at a time of flux in the history of the Muslim community in South Asia, during the first half of the twentieth century. Mawdudi was writing at a time when South Asia was in a situation of political turmoil, when the Indian subcontinent was going through a transitional phase progressing towards independence from British colonial rule, and therefore Mawdudi's ideas were inextricably linked with communal politics. His views were informed by the acute despair that gripped the South Asian Muslim community, and were therefore directed at finding solutions to this predicament. The Indian Muslim community during the first half of the 20th century was highly fragmented along ethnic and linguistic lines, and therefore Mawdudi's aim was to arrest this process of Islamic decline. To realize this objective, he sought to underscore Muslim identity and to foster unity and accord so that the needs of Muslims could be addressed at the national level.[65] Once that was accomplished, the community could then establish viable political structures rooted in the cultural symbols of Islam that would be able to sustain a broadly-based movement in a modern political context.[66]

The first step was to assert Indian Muslim identity in the face of a departing colonial order and the political aspirations of the Hindu majority. Islam could survive in the subcontinent only if Muslims were on top of the political system, as they had been for centuries in South Asia, throughout the Middle Ages, from the days of the Turkish sultans or Slave dynasty right up until the last Mughal emperor. Mawdudi was driven by the vision that stressed the dichotomy between Muslims and non-Muslims and that wanted Muslims to be ruled by Islamic law alone. As a political activist, he understood the power of Islam as a symbol in galvanizing the Muslim community and legitimizing political action. As his ideas developed, his emphasis shifted from widely-shared Indo-Muslim traditions to narrowly-interpreted Islamic doctrines.[67] He put forth a view of Islam with an invigorated, pristine and uncompromising outlook intended to galvanize Muslims into an ideologically uniform and hence politically indivisible community, one that would assert its demands and remain unyielding before the overtures of the Hindu majority.[68] Mawdudi's aim was to scrape away centuries of Hindu cultural influence by replacing assimilation with expurgation, accommodation with reassertion, diversity with unity, and submission with defiance.[69] By confirming the distinctive qualities, cultural identity, and social values and mores of Muslims, Mawdudi would erect around the Muslim community an impregnable communalist wall that would exclude outside influences.[70] In cultural seclusion, Mawdudi hoped the dejected South Asian Muslim community would once again be emboldened and the Islamic identity in South Asia would be saved. Therefore, at the heart of Mawdudi's stance was the belief that religious authenticity was the solution to the problems faced by Muslims, and this led him to attempt to cleanse Muslims of Western influence and centuries of Hindu cultural accretions by emphasizing Islamic dogma. The erection of communal boundaries and the search for identity in Mawdudi's works increasingly cast the world in terms of good and evil, converting history into an arena for an apocalyptic battle between the two.[71] In political terms, this meant the rejection of British rule in India and also the rejection of its replacement with any form of Hindu rule. In intellectual terms, the necessity of a reign of virtue, an Islamic Order, set Mawdudi on a search for the means to reorganize Muslim society and imagine it anew.[72] This finally led to the creation of the Jamat-i-Islami.

The Jamat-i-Islami was headed by Mawdudi for 31 years (1941–1972).[73] The Jamat is one of the oldest and most influential of the Islamic revivalist movements and the first of its kind to develop an Islamic ideology, a modern revolutionary reading of Islam and an agenda for social action to realize its vision.[74] The Jamat's ideology and activism have been important in Pakistani politics and to Islamism more generally across the Muslim world. It has helped to create a distinctly Islamic voting bloc; it has institutionalized religio-political action and sacralized national political discourse; and it has contributed to the Islamization of Pakistan.[75] It mounted pressure on the ruling elite to mould Pakistan's political system and constitutional apparatus in accordance with Islamic political doctrines as laid down by the Quran and the Sunnah.[76] Leaders like Jinnah, Ayub Khan and Bhutto faced a stiff challenge from the conservative Jamat when they suggested building Pakistan along secular lines. Mawdudi's religio-political awareness had first been aroused in Hyderabad in the Deccan, when the Nizam's authority had begun to wane and where political activism had shifted the time-honored balance of power to the Hindus.[77] Hindu hostility towards Muslims in South Asia strengthened when Hindu revivalist movements like the mahasabha and the Arya Samaj launched aggressive anti-Muslim public campaigns. Hindu hostility also included the Shuddi campaign, whose mission was to reconvert unwilling low-caste converts to Islam back to Hinduism, and this obviously challenged the place of Islam in South Asia. Mawdudi's discourse, although motivated by the Hindu challenge, was also directed at the West. He premised his reading of religion and society on a dialectic view of history, in which the struggle between Islam and *kufr* or disbelief was supposed to culminate in a revolutionary struggle; the Jamat was supposed to be the vanguard of that struggle. Mawdudi adopted modern ideas and values, mechanisms, procedures and idioms, weaving them into an Islamic fabric and thus producing a hybrid ideological perspective. The terms 'revolution,' 'vanguard,' 'ideology,' 'democratic caliphate,' 'theodemocracy,' cropped up over and over again in his polemic, and these were used to define the Jamat's agenda. The Jamat demanded a government inspired by and obedient to the writ of the *sharia*, which would promise a utopian order that gave direction to Islamic social action. For the Jamat, that state would be erected according to the rules and procedures stipulated by Mawdudi.[78] The Islamic Revolution, according to Mawdudi, was to be a top-down process in which the revolution would be spearheaded by society's Islamic leaders or *ulama* (theologians), similar to the Iranian *faqi* (Islamic jurists). He summed up the Jamat's plan of action in the following terms: First, it would bring intellectual change in the minds of the people. Second, it would organize them in order to make them suitable for a movement. Third, it would reform society through social and humanitarian work. Finally it would endeavor to change the leadership. Once the Jamat had taken over in terms of political power, society would gradually be Islamized and all socio-economic maladies would be cured.

Throughout its history in Pakistan, the Jamat added to the national political discourse concerns for Islamic ideals, but the party's success in intellectual and ideological domains found no reflection in politics.[79] It has influenced politics but failed to control politics. The Jamat proved capable of forming socio-political alliances predicated upon an Islamic political program, but not of entering into the fundamental political debates of the country, and hence it found no means to secure power for the party. In Pakistan, on some occasions, the government sought to contend with Islamic revivalism by eliminating the Jamat, as was the case during Liaqat Ali Khan's time and the early period of Ayub Khan's rule, and then by challenging its religious position, a tactic that not only failed, but emboldened Islamic revivalism.[80] In 1958 and 1977 the Jamat's drive for power was checked by decisive state action, but after 1977 the state sought to control Islamic revivalism by involving it in the political process more directly. As the Jamat's case proves, protracted involvement in the political process also creates barriers to the growth of revivalism and immunizes the political process to its challenge. It requires replacing a purely ideological orientation with an accommodation of pragmatic politics, and this leads to compromise, which transforms revivalist movements into political institutions tied to the system.[81]

The Jamat politicized Islam in Pakistan, but failed to reap any benefits from it. The Jamat proved the efficacy of Islam as a political force, but it had no means to prevent others from exploiting religion for political gain.[82] The Jamat was initially conceived as a 'holy community' in which high standards and ideological commitment limited membership, but with the passage of time it got involved in the political processes of South Asia, and no other revivalist movement has matched its political influence.[83] However, it has failed to mobilize the masses for collective action for any sustained period of time under an Islamic banner. Pakistani politics is changing and so is the Jamat. The political fortunes of the party may improve, although operating in the political process, especially in a democracy, will require it to embark upon changes that will inevitably diminish its commitment to its original ideology if it is to succeed and deal with pragmatic politics. Following an uncertain start and periodic confrontations with the government, it utilized its campaign for an Islamic constitution to allow it to replace its original ideological orientation with greater pragmatism, so as to articulate a political program and generally to move along the path of becoming a full-fledged political party.[84] It found a clear-cut political platform by amending its Islamic vision to include a commitment to democracy and constitutional rights. In the process it infused the political discourse with religious references and ideas whose language and symbols have left an indelible mark on Pakistani politics.[85] The Islamist groups in Pakistan came to constitute a very clear interest group making specific demands on the state. Although these religious parties, the Jamat most notably among them, continued to fight the state, the synthesis between religion and the state was nevertheless strengthened.

Concluding remarks

Thus from the above discussion we can clearly see that Islamism is a multidimensional phenomenon, and that to understand the complexities associated with Islamism in Pakistan, one needs to look carefully at both internal and external factors that have given rise to Islamism and strengthened it. It was important to go into a detailed discussion of the factors causing Islamism because only after analyzing the causes can one come up with possible solutions. Clearly, Islamism does not happen because of this cause or that cause, but because of a complex combination of factors and multiplicity of events. Factors may also be long-term ones and some may act as triggers. Although this chapter has been primarily divided into external factors and internal factors contributing to the rise of Islamism in Pakistan, one should not view the two categories as water-tight compartments, since there may also be grey areas. For instance, the discussion on

Pakistani seminaries comes primarily under the heading of 'internal factors,' but many of these seminaries in Pakistan actually have strong links with other seminaries in Afghanistan and other parts of Central Asia.

The chapter started by analyzing some of the external factors that may have contributed to the growth of Islamism in Pakistan, and laid special emphasis on the spillover effects or ripple effects of events happening in Central and other parts of Asia. In this connection, we looked at the spillover effects from the current situation in Afghanistan regarding Islamic militancy, and also the impact of major events like the Iranian Revolution, which might have also had a knock-on effect on the strengthening of Islamist forces in Pakistan. It was important to look at the situation in Central Asia, especially at Afghanistan and the Taliban, because of the infiltration of militants from across the border, and the Talibani-zation of the north-west frontiers of Pakistan, especially Waziristan. This was crucial because Pakistan shares a long border with Afghanistan. Also, we noted the economic crisis and political turmoil in parts of Central Asia, especially Uzbekistan and Afghanistan which have proven to be breeding grounds for Islamic radicalism. Central Asian Islamism could possibly be seen as a response to the incomplete economic modernization process introduced by the Soviets in the region, and the distorted economic and political institutions that were intro-duced to serve Soviet needs; this in turn had a knock-on effect on parts of Paki-stan. The communist legacy of the Soviets has expressed itself through Central Asian presidents like Karimov who had been communist officials in the past. Their tight grip on politics, inability to deal with the deteriorating economic crisis, and general policy of high-handedness and repression towards Islam had not only exacerbated the situation but had actually added fuel to the fire of Islamism, forcing many Islamist groups to go underground or spread to parts of Afghanistan and Pakistan.

The chapter then moved on to some of the internal factors that strengthened the forces of Islamism in Pakistan. In this connection, the chapter looked at the program of Islamization and the roles played by General Zia, by religious educa-tional institutions and by the Jamat-i-Islami in Pakistani politics. The interaction between the Jamat and other Sunni Islamist elements and politicians has most cer-tainly sacralized the national political discourse, and thus we see the fusion between religion and politics. Politicians like Zia have used Islamist groups to further their own interests, especially when their power base has lacked political legitimacy, but Islamist groups have also used politicians to enhance their position in Pakistani politics. Regarding the seminaries, although it is difficult to say whether or not these are the new recruiting grounds of Islamism, one could safely argue that the institutions associated with the Jamat and the Deobandi tradition most certainly make use of a very black-and-white, uncompromising approach, which may not advocate terrorism directly but definitely encourages Islamist and anti-Western tendencies. Thus, it becomes increasingly important to note the coex-istence of Islam/religion and Islamism/political ideology in these seminaries.

The situation in South Central Asia in relation to Islamism is thus very complex but not irreparable. The problem of Islamism could be solved to some degree by the introduction of political pluralism and economic reform in places like Uzbekistan and Afghanistan. As we know that poverty and political conservatism are inextricably linked with the rise of Islamism, more political and economic openness could possibly solve the problem. Clearing up the situation in Central Asia would relieve Pakistan to some degree because some of the Islamists from Central Asia are infiltrating Pakistan and causing mayhem. It will be difficult to patrol the NWFP border because of the long border that Pakistan shares with Central Asia, especially Afghanistan; therefore, it would be best to introduce both political and economic reform in Central Asia. The introduction of reform is thus the long-term answer to the problem. Introduction of such reforms would solve Islamism in Central Asia to some extent since Islamists would be able to operate freely in political arenas and would not feel the need to flee the country and move to places like Pakistan, or for that matter be forced underground. The need of the hour is thus both political and economic reform. Introduction of any kind of reform is of course a long-drawn, protracted and arduous process, so it is doubtful whether the international community, spearheaded by the US and regional governments, are likely to get their hands dirty and get involved in the reform process in South Central Asia. The situation within Pakistan could also be solved to some extent by introducing political reform, because much of Pakistani politics is intrinsically tied up with religious groups; the problem of Islamism could be solved to some extent by making the government more accountable to the people, by responding to demands coming from below and the need for stronger democratizing tendencies. This could take the form of competitive village elections, the reform of the civil service and bureaucracy, changes in the recruitment processes to the political parties, decentralization of power to local governments, gradual spread of the rule of law, and also through the invigoration of the provincial legislatures and the national parliament.

Notes

1 A. Hussain, *Islamic Movements in Egypt, Pakistan and Iran*, 1983.
2 A.M. Weiss (ed.), *Islamic Reassertion in Pakistan*, 1986.
3 B. Metcalfe, *Islamic Contestations*, 2004, p. 236.
4 S. Nasr, *The Vanguard of the Islamic Revolution*, 1994, p. 117.
5 Ibid., p. 117.
6 Ibid.
7 Ibid., p. 138.
8 D. Belt, 'Struggle for the Soul of Pakistan', 2007, p. 32.
9 Ibid., p. 40.
10 A. Baker, 'The Truth about Talibanisation', 2007, p. 18.
11 S. Beg, 'Pakistan's Tribal Areas: A Battle for Jihad' in R. Durward and L. Marsden (eds), *Religion, Conflict and Military Intervention*, 2009, p. 151.
12 R. Sagdeev and S. Eisenhower (eds), *Islam and Central Asia*, 2000, p. 215.
13 Ibid., p. 215.
14 D. Hiro, *Islamic Fundamentalism*, 1988, p. 1.
15 G. Kepel, *Allah in the West*, 1997, p. 90.
16 P. Lewis, *Islamic Britain*, 1994, p. 36.

17 Ibid.
18 Ibid., p. 36.
19 W. Maley, *Fundamentalism Reborn?*, 1998, pp. 18–19.
20 M. Ruthven, *A Fury for God*, 2002, p. 171.
21 J. Esposito, *Unholy War*, 2002, p. 35.
22 O. Roy, *The Failure of Political Islam*, 1994, p. 194.
23 Sagdeev and Eisenhower (eds), *Islam and Central Asia*, p. 235.
24 G. Gleason, 'Uzbekistan: From Statehood to Nationhood' in I. Bremmer and R. Taras (eds), *Nation and Politics in the Soviet Successor States*, 1993, p. 352.
25 A. Rashid, *Taliban*, 2000, p. 2.
26 Ibid., p. 2.
27 Ibid.
28 Ibid., p. 93.
29 Ibid., p. 115.
30 N. Howenstein, 'The Jihadi Terrain in Pakistan', 2008.
31 Ibid.
32 S.S. Shahzad, 'The Gathering Strength of Taliban and Tribal Militants in Pakistan', 2007.
33 Ibid.
34 Ibid.
35 Ibid.
36 S.R. Valentine, 'The Tehrik-i-Taliban Pakistan', 2009.
37 Ibid.
38 Ibid.
39 J. Esposito, *The Iranian Revolution*, 1990.
40 B. Rumer, 'The Gathering Storm in Central Asia', 1993, pp. 89–90.
41 Ibid.
42 M.B. Olcott, 'Soviet Central Asia: Does Moscow fear Iranian Influence?' in Esposito (ed.), *The Iranian Revolution*, 1990, p. 205.
43 Ibid.
44 D. Hiro, *Islamic Fundamentalism*, 1989, pp. 160–163.
45 R. Mehdi, *The Islamization of the Law in Pakistan*, 1994, pp. 24–25.
46 M. Marty and R.S. Appleby (eds), *Fundamentalisms and the State*, 1993, p. 123.
47 Ibid., p. 124.
48 Mehdi, *The Islamization of the Law in Pakistan*, pp. 25–26.
49 Ibid., pp. 25–26.
50 M.T. Usmani, 'The Islamization of Laws in Pakistan', 2006, p. 287.
51 Ibid.
52 Ibid.
53 R. Kurin, 'Islamization: A View from the Countryside' in Weiss (ed.), *Islamic Reassertion in Pakistan*, pp. 115–116.
54 Ibid., pp. 116–117.
55 Marty and Appleby (eds), *Fundamentalisms and the State*, p. 126.
56 Ibid., p. 128.
57 K. Rahman and S.R. Bukhari, 'Pakistan: Religious Educational Institutions', 2006, p. 323.
58 Ibid., p. 324.
59 Ibid., p. 324.
60 Ibid., p. 326.
61 Ibid.
62 Beg, 'Pakistan's Tribal Areas', 2009, p. 151.
63 Ibid., p. 151.
64 S. Nasr, *Mawdudi and the Making of Islamic Revivalism*, 1996, pp. 3–4.
65 Ibid.
66 Ibid.

67 Ibid., pp. 5–6.
68 Ibid.
69 Ibid.
70 Ibid.
71 Ibid., p. 51.
72 Ibid.
73 Nasr, *The Vanguard of the Islamic Revolution*, 1994.
74 Ibid.
75 Ibid.
76 P. Joshi, *The Jamat-i-Islami*, 2003.
77 Nasr, *The Vanguard of the Islamic Revolution*, p. 4.
78 Ibid.
79 Ibid., p. 219.
80 Ibid.
81 Ibid., p. 220.
82 Ibid.
83 Ibid., p. 221.
84 Ibid., p. 146.
85 Ibid.

Bibliography

Baker, A., 'The Truth about Talibanisation', *Time*, April 2007.
Belt, D., 'Struggle for the Soul of Pakistan', *National Geographic*, September 2007.
Bremmer, I. and R. Taras (eds), *Nation and Politics in the Soviet Successor States*, Cambridge: Cambridge University Press, 1993.
Durward, R. and L. Marsden, *Religion, Conflict and Military Intervention*, Farnham: Ashgate, 2009.
Esposito, J. (ed.), *The Iranian Revolution: Its Global Impact*, Miami: Florida University Press, 1990.
Esposito, J., *Unholy War: Terror in the Name of God*, Oxford: Oxford University Press, 2002.
Hiro, D., *Islamic Fundamentalism*, London: Paladin, 1989.
Howenstein, N., 'The Jihadi Terrain in Pakistan: An Introduction to the Sunni Jihadi Groups in Pakistan and Kashmir', Bradford: Pakistan Security Research Unit, Briefing no. 1, 2008.
Hussein, A., *Islamic Movements in Egypt, Pakistan and Iran*, London: Mansell, 1983.
Joshi, P., *The Jamat-i-Islami: The Catalyst of Islamization in Pakistan*, New Delhi: Kalinga, 2003.
Kepel, G., *Allah in the West*, Cambridge: Polity Press, 1997.
Lewis, P., *Islamic Britain*, London: I.B. Tauris, 1994.
Maley, W., *Fundamentalism Reborn: Afghanistan and the Taliban*, London: Hurst, 1998.
Marty, M. and R.S. Appleby (eds), *Fundamentalisms and the State: Remaking Politics, Economics and Militance*, vol. 3, Chicago: Chicago University Press, 1993.
Mehdi, R., *The Islamization of Law in Pakistan*, Richmond: Curzon Press, 1994.
Metcalfe, B., *Islamic Contestations*, Oxford: Oxford University Press, 2004.
Nasr, S., *The Vanguard of the Islamic Revolution: The Jamat-i-Islami*, Berkeley: California University Press, 1994.
Nasr, S., *Mawdudi and the Making of Islamic Revivalism*, Oxford: Oxford University Press, 1996.

Rahman, K. and S.R. Bukhari, 'Pakistan: Religious Educational Institutions', *Muslim World*, 96, April 2006.

Rashid, A., *Taliban: Islam, Oil and the New Great Game in Central Asia*, London: I.B. Tauris, 2002.

Roy, O., *The Failure of Political Islam*, Cambridge: Harvard University Press, 1994.

Rumer, B., 'The Gathering Storm in Central Asia', *Orbis*, Winter 1993.

Ruthven, M., *A Fury for God*, London: Granta, 2002.

Sagdeev, R. and S. Eisenhower (eds), *Islam and Central Asia: An Enduring Legacy or an Evolving Threat?*, Washington, DC: Center for Political and Strategic Studies, 2000.

Shahzad, S.S., 'The Gathering Strength of the Taliban and Tribal Militants in Pakistan', Bradford: Pakistan Security Research Unit, Briefing no. 24, 2007.

Usmani, M.T., 'The Islamization of Laws in Pakistan: The Case of the Hudud Ordinances', *Muslim World*, 96, April 2006.

Valentine, S.R., 'The Tehrik-i-Taliban Pakistan: Ideology and Beliefs', Bradford: Pakistan Security Research Unit, Briefing no. 49, 2009.

Weiss, A.M. (ed.), *Islamic Reassertion in Pakistan*, New York: Syracuse University Press, 1986.

9 Maoists in power

Emergence of a new Nepal

B.C. Upreti

> Revolutionary movements, history suggests, typically coalesce in opposition to closed or exclusionary, as well as organizationally weak (or suddenly weakened), authoritarian regimes.
>
> (Theda Skocpol, 1995)

The Nepalese state and political system entered a new phase of transformation after the successful completion of the elections to the Constituent Assembly in April 2008. This new phase has been characterized as the beginning of a new Nepal. The declaration that henceforth Nepal would be a republican state, after more than two centuries of monarchic rule, is a turning point in its history. Federalism, secularism and an inclusive form of democracy are the salient features of this new Nepal.

Nepal has just embarked on the process of state-building. But it is not only a question of political transformation; the issues of social and economic transformation are equally significant. The objective of building a new Nepal cannot be realized unless socio-economic transformation takes place in the country, so as to build a viable socio-economic base for the successful working of political democracy. Therefore, Nepal still has a long way to travel to attain the objectives of the new Nepal. The issues of inclusive democracy, federalism and so on still need to be resolved fully. There is no doubt that a new beginning has taken place and so there are vast opportunities for bringing about change, but there are several challenges as well. The political parties, including the Maoists, and the civil society of Nepal have to deal with these challenges and seize the opportunities. Much will depend on how the hopes and aspirations of a new Nepal and the Nepalese people are incorporated in the new constitution of Nepal. This chapter is an attempt to analyze the democratization of Nepali politics and the challenges that lie ahead.

Historical context

Nepal has a population of around 28 million and lies between India and China. It is one of the poorest countries in the world, with a GNI per capita of $1,201 (ppp 2008), and Human Development Index value of 0.428, according to the UNDP's Human Development Report 2010. Its HDI rank is 138 (out of 169 countries), although the Human Development Report 2010 also states that some poor nations, including Nepal, are making 'faster development gains' and ranks Nepal in third position in the non-income HDI category. In the lap of the Himalayan mountain range, Nepal is popular with mountaineers and tourists and known for its scenic beauty and mountains, including Mount Everest (the highest mountain in the world). Its proximity to Tibet and its ethnic diversity have influenced its geopolitics, while some of its ethnic groups, such as the Sherpas, have earned an international reputation for themselves. The Nepalese kingdom was consolidated in the eighteenth century under the Gurkha king Prithvi Narayan Shah. It lost some territory to British India and existed in its shadow until 1950, when it was able to emerge from the clinches of the hereditary Rana rule and embarked on the path of democracy.

The ethnic composition of Nepal's population and its cultural heritage have been deeply influenced by both India and Tibet. Migration from both of these countries has contributed to Nepal's ethnic diversity. Hinduism is the dominant religion, but some of the Mongoloid ethnic groups (and of Tibetan origin) such as the Sherpas and Tamangs follow Buddhism. Hinduism has always had a central place in Nepal's political system. The constitutions of 1959 and 1962 declared that Nepal is a Hindu monarchy, and stipulated that the ruler must be an adherent of Aryan culture and a follower of Hindu religion.

Nepal was ruled by the despotic Ranas for many years. However, influenced by the success of the nationalist movement in India, educated middle-class leaders started the anti-Rana movement and demanded the democratization of Nepal. The popular movement ended the autocratic rule of the Ranas and a new phase in Nepali politics began. Under King Tribhuvan, a coalition government consisting of the representatives of the Nepali Congress and members of the Rana family was formed in 1951. However, it soon disintegrated. The Nepali Congress was unable to provide leadership and became divided into various factions. A form of parliamentary government was introduced by the 1959 constitution, but the ministers and the parliament remained subordinate to the king, who remained the ultimate source of authority.

The first free elections to the parliament were held in February 1959. The Nepali Congress won an absolute majority of the seats (74/109) and its leader, B.P. Koirala, became Prime Minister and formed a cabinet. However, the following year the monarch, King Mahendra, dismissed the Koirala government, as he felt that Nepal was not ready for some of the changes proposed by it, especially land reforms. He did not want to alienate the powerful landowning classes. More importantly, King Mahendra did not want a constitutional monarchy and was opposed to Western political institutions. As a result, he opted for a three-tier *panchayat* (village assembly) system that was, he felt, in keeping with Nepal's culture and tradition but at the same time allowed popular association with the administration. This was formalized by the 1962 constitution. But it was not a progressive measure. Real power remained with the king and all political parties were banned.

Widespread demonstrations forced King Mahindra's successor, King Birendra, to call for a nationwide referendum in May 1979 to determine the future form of Nepal's government. The choice was between a partyless *panchayat* system and a multiparty (parliamentary) form of government. The results of this referendum, held in May 1980, were interesting and gave an indication of the direction in which the nation was moving. The vote went in favor of the *panchayat* system by a narrow margin, which allowed it to continue for many more years. However, a large proportion of the population wanted a parliamentary form of government. This necessitated constitutional reforms, and elections to the Rashtriya *panchayat* were held in May 1981.

The pro-democracy movement eventually forced the king to promulgate a new constitution in November 1990. It provided for a parliamentary system of government, fundamental rights for citizens and a system of multiparty democracy based on universal suffrage.

The movements of the 1990s

Political process in Nepal has been highly unstable and fragile during the last two decades. The people of Nepal have witnessed a number of political upheavals: the birth of the Maoist movement in 1996, the massacre of the royal family in 2001, the suspension of democratic processes, a royal coup, and the second democratic revolution of 2006 have engendered political instability and uncertainty. Yet it is through these uncertain situations that the country has stepped into a new phase of political transformation.

The 1990 movement for democracy (Janandolan) was a major landmark in the political history of Nepal. It hastened the demise of the authoritarian *panchayat* system and initiated a process of democratization. The 1990 movement was the collective effort of all sorts of political parties, associations, the masses and civil society. Therefore there were a lot of expectations regarding socio-economic and political transformation in the country. However, the working of the democratic governments in the subsequent years failed to realize these expectations. While the traditional political elite still remained a major center of power, the feudalistic orientation of the society and the economy continued to persist.[1] The democratic forces failed to provide a stable government and order in the country. Frequent changes of government, internal conflicts within the political parties, and leadership clashes made the political situation complex and untenable. The fulfillment of popular needs and aspirations and socio-economic transformation became secondary to political maneuvering and the politics of power.

These conditions took Nepal to a critical phase of revolutionary change towards the second half of the 1990s in the form of the Maoist insurgency. The insurgency (also called the 'People's war'), which gradually covered nearly two-thirds of the country, challenged the basic premises of the Nepalese society and state, and called for a protracted guerrilla war against the establishment and ultimately a new Nepal. Interestingly, the Maoists got widespread support from the rural areas, the Tarai region of the country, minority ethnic groups, *dalit* (the lowest castes), women and other such categories and groups of the society that had serious complaints against the authoritarian, hierarchical and exclusive nature of the Nepali state. The Maoist agenda included the establishment of a republican and federal state, and social transformation based on equality, equity, justice and freedom. Initially the government did not take the Maoist insurgency seriously and tried to deal with it as a law-and-order problem. The repressive measures of the government led to the expansion and militarization of the Maoist movement.[2]

The brutal murder of King Birendra and his family members in mid 2001 gave a new twist to Nepali politics. The new king, Gyanendra, a highly ambitious person, wanted to take all power in his own hands. A violent situation emerged due to the Maoist insurgency, the unstable political conditions, and fragmentation among the democratic forces. This encouraged King Gyanendra to gradually take power away from the representatives of the people. In October 2002 he suspended the elected government and the parliament, declared a state of emergency and formed a new government of his own choice. His quest for political supremacy reached a climax in the form of the 2005 royal coup and the imposition of his full control over the politics of the country. However, King Gyanendra's actions proved to be self-defeating and counter-productive, as they not only aroused the democratic sentiments of the people but also provided an opportunity to the political parties and the Maoists to come closer to each other. King Gyanendra also faced strong international pressure to restore democracy. However, the Maoists and the democratic forces realized that the monarchy was the main obstacle to democracy and stability in Nepal. The mobilization of the political parties and their understanding with the Maoists resulted in two significant developments: the unconditional cessation of insurgency by the Maoists, and the second democratic movement of April 2006, resulting in the restoration of democracy in the country.

The peace process in Nepal began in mid-2006 with the Maoists entering into the political mainstream. The Maoists tactfully succeeded in forging a broad consensus with the political parties regarding their agenda for restructuring the Nepali state: abolition of monarchy, declaration of a secular and republican state, federalism, and elections to the Constituent Assembly. The Maoists joined the interim government. The peace process was marked by the management of the armed forces, an interim constitution, etc. Despite political tangles, violence in Tarai, and delays, the interim government succeeded in holding elections to the Constituent Assembly in April 2008. With this, the first phase of the restructuring of the state was completed in Nepal.

Formation of the Constituent Assembly

Elections for 575 seats of the 601-member Constituent Assembly (CA) were held on 10 April 2008. Twenty-six members were nominated from the civil society. For the first time, a dual electoral system was adopted (for the elections): 240 seats were allocated by the First Past The Post system (FPTP) and 335 seats by a Proportional Representation system (PR). The basic objective behind adoption of the dual electoral system was to make the Constituent Assembly as representative as possible in terms of communities, regions and political parties. The importance of the Constituent Assembly elections was underlined by the fact that it was the cornerstone of the peace process and of the restructuring of the state in Nepal. The postponement of the CA elections twice in June and November 2007 had worried not only the Maoists, political parties, and people in Nepal, but also the international community. The Maoists were particularly worried because the furtherance of their political agenda depended on the formation of a CA.

Altogether 74 political parties registered with the Election Commission in order to participate in the CA elections. One significant aspect of this was the rise of ethnic-based and regional parties. All the political parties were required to nominate candidates for elections under FPTP and to submit a closed list of candidates for PR. The major political parties in terms of their nominations were Nepali Congress, CPN (Maoist), CPN (UML), Rashtriya Prajatantra Party, Rashtriya Prajatantra Party (Nepal), Jan Morcha Nepal, Rashtriya Janshakti Party, CPN-Unified, etc.

One significant feature of the CA elections was that all the political parties decided to contest separately (see Table 9.1). Thus the Seven-Party Alliance, a group of parties that had joined forces to spearhead the reform movement, became redundant in the elections. There was more or less consensus among the major political parties over the issues of abolition of the monarchy, a republican state, secularism, federalism, inclusive democracy, and equal relations with the neighbors.

It is interesting to note that only nine political parties out of 54 that had nominated their candidates in the elections could seek entry into the CA. The Communist Party of Nepal (Maoists) emerged as the largest party with 120 seats followed by Nepali Congress (37), CPN (UML) (33) and Madheshi Janadhikar Forum (30).

Under the PR system 26 political parties got representation on the basis of total votes secured by them. However, most of the political parties had a marginal representation. The CPN (Maoist) got 100 seats, NC 73, CPN (UML) 70, and MJF 22. Thus CPN (Maoist) secured a total of 220 seats. Though none of the political parties got a majority, the rise of the Maoists as the largest party was a significant development. An insurgent group that had been involved in violence and protracted war only two years back emerged as the main political force. It was unexpected for many. The NC and CPN (UML) were particularly in a fix over the outcome of the CA elections. They perhaps did not expect such a defeat, particularly the NC, which was considered to be the largest party in the country. The Constituent Assembly opened doors for the first time for *dalits* (7), ethnic groups (80), Madheshis (54) and women (30). It thus assumed the character of an inclusive body to a large extent.

The emergence of Maoists as the largest party in the CA underlined two basic factors: that the Maoists had emerged as a strong political force, thereby posing

Table 9.1 Party position in the Constituent Assembly

S.No.	Party	FPTP	PR	Total
1	CPN (Maoist)	120	100	220
2	Nepali Congress	37	73	110
3	CPN (UML)	33	70	103
4	MJF	30	22	52
5	TMLP	9	11	20
6	Sadbhawana Party	4	5	9
7	NMKP (Nepal Workers and Peasants Party)	2	2	4
8	Jan Morcha Nepal (People's Front)	2	5	7
9	Rashtriya Janmorcha	1	3	4
10	Rashtriya Janshakti Party		3	3
11	Rashtriya Prajatantra Party		8	8
12	CPN (ML)		8	8
13	CPN (Joint)		5	5
14	Rashtriya Prajatantra Party (Nepal)		4	4
15	Rashtriya Janmukti Party		2	2
16	CPN (Unified)		2	2
17	Nepal Sadbhawana Party (A)		2	2
18	Nepali Janata Dal		2	2
19	Sanghiya Loktantrik Rashtriya Manch		2	2
20	Samajbadi Prajantantra Janta Party, Nepal		1	1
21	Dalit Janajati Party		1	1
22	Nepal Pariwar Dal		1	1
23	Nepal Rashtriya Party		1	1
24	Nepal Loktantrik Samajbadi Dal		1	1
25	Chure Bhawar Rashtriya Ekta Party		1	1
26	Independents	2	0	2
	Total	**240**	**335**	**575**

an identity crisis for the NC and the UML; and that a tone had been set for the furtherance of the Maoist agenda of restructuring the state.

The Constituent Assembly in action: abolition of the monarchy

In its first meeting on 28 May 2008, the Constituent Assembly formally declared the abolition of the monarchy as a political institution and as a system of governance. It also formally declared Nepal a federal democratic republic. It was indeed a major decision and altered the course of political development in Nepal. It also realized the long-awaited demand of the Maoists. There was almost a consensus over this issue in the Constituent Assembly. With the abolition of monarchy, Nepal was declared a republican state. This clearly shows that a highly-placed political and religio-cultural institution had lost its credibility. The people of Nepal gave up their faith in, and respect and sympathy for, the institution of monarchy. The murder of King Birendra and then Gyanendra's attempts to hold on to power in fact marked the beginning of the decline of the monarchy.[3]

Gyanendra's lust for power, his anti-people measures and his steps to wield power brought him down in popular perception/estimation. After the 2005 royal coup the democratic forces, which earlier had always looked for a rapprochement with the king, also realized that the monarchy was the main adversary to democracy and stability in the country. Their changed perception towards the monarchy brought them closer to the Maoists and the monarchy became a common enemy of both the political parties and the Maoists. Both developed a consensus over the abolition of monarchy and declaring Nepal a republican state. Although monarchy still had a support base among the old nobilities/aristocracy, the armed forces and the business community, it was weak and fragmented. It was no longer possible for it to withstand strong anti-monarchy waves. Some alternatives like 'ceremonial monarchy,' 'baby monarchy,' etc. were suggested, but the Maoists had presented the issue of a republican state quite forcefully. The abolition of the 239-year-old monarchy cleared the way for the restructuring of the state and the society. King Gyanendra vacated the Narayanhity Royal Palace on 11 June 2008 rather quietly.

Formation of the government: failure of the consensual model

The verdict of the CA elections was accepted by all the political parties, despite the fact that some political parties were shocked by their performance in the elections. Equally surprising to some was the emergence of CPN (M) as the largest party in the Constituent Assembly. Roadblocks soon began to emerge to the formation of a government due to the unexpected verdict. Interestingly, before the elections the political parties had reached an understanding that irrespective of the electoral outcome they would work together on a consensual basis. In fact, it was in the post-April 2006 phase that the consensual model was adopted by the political parties. The Seven-Party Alliance itself was an example of a consensual approach. Later on, this approach was extended to the CPN (Maoists). Despite certain complexities, the consensual model worked quite well in promoting the peace process. In the interim constitution a provision was made that the politics of consensus should continue. The consensus approach was required even more after the CA elections, as a coalition government was the only alternative. However, on 13 July 2008 the Constitution Assembly passed an amendment to the interim constitution which stated that the government would be formed on a majority basis. It was a departure from the earlier understanding of consensus. Further, the amendment made a provision that the President, Vice President, CA Chairman, Deputy Chairman and Prime Minister would be chosen on the basis of a political understanding, and if such an understanding was not forthcoming they would be elected on the basis of a simple majority.[4]

The way the politics of government formation took place raised a number of questions. It indicated that even at a crucial stage of political transformation, the style and idioms of Nepali politics had not changed much. The process of government formation was delayed, as none of the political parties came forward to lend its support to others. G.P. Koirala, head of the interim government, declined to resign from the Prime Ministership till a new government was constituted. There was a lot of controversy over this issue. The CPN (M) leader Prachanda opined that:

> We do not want Koirala to step down or resign. Rather we want him to be the guardian of the new coalition and guide it at every step. Actually we want him to play a political role similar to Sonia Gandhi in the United Progressive Alliance government in India.[5]

The NC, MJF and CPN (UML) made an alliance to capture the positions of President, Vice President and CA Chairman, respectively. There was also an attempt to form a national government with the NC, MJF, CPN (UML) and CPN (M), but it ended in failure. The CPN (M) finally managed to make an alliance with MJF and CPN (UML). The CPN (M) nominated Prachanda as its candidate for the Prime Ministership, while the NC nominated Sher Bahadur Deuba as its candidate. Prachanda won with 464 votes, while Deuba got only 13 votes. Twenty-one political parties in the CA gave their support to CPN (M). The People's Front and Nepal Workers and Peasants Party however boycotted the voting. The NC decided to remain in opposition. Both the NC and the CPN (M) blamed each other for the difficulty in reaching a consensus over the issue of the formation of the government.

The election of the President and the Vice President also reflected sharp differences among the political parties. The Nepali Congress declared Ram Baran Yadav as its presidential candidate, and the CPN (M) nominated Ram Raja Prasad Singh. The required vote to win the election was 298 out of 594. Ram Raja Prasad Singh secured 270 and Ram Baran Yadav 283 votes, thus neither secured the required votes.[6] Ram Baran Yadav later won the election by a margin of 26 votes in the second round of voting, held on 21 July 2008.[7] The Rashtriya Prajatantra Party (Nepal), Nepal Workers and Peasants Party, and CPN (Unified) decided to boycott the election. Parmanand Jha of MJF won by 305 votes, against 243 votes secured by Shasta Shrestha, in the election of the Vice President. The Chairmanship of the CA went to CPN (UML). It is clear that the earlier understanding regarding governing on the basis of a consensus failed when the political parties were faced with the question of sharing power. This also indicated that the Maoist-led coalition government was to face a complex political situation.

Issues before the Maoist government

The working of the Maoist government was not smooth. It had to deal with a complex situation. The Nepali Congress party had already adopted a tough attitude towards the new government. It had blamed the government for failing to maintain peace, stability, and law and order in the country. In fact, the NC had adopted a tough stance against the Maoist government since the beginning.

Perhaps its own performance in the CA elections was reflected in its attitude towards the government. It was due to this unhelpful attitude of the opposition political parties that Prime Minister Prachanda threatened to quit the government.

A new constitution had to be drafted within two years of the formation of the CA. The politics of power-sharing took almost six months and the constitution drafting process finally started on 16 December 2008. The government and the political parties did not appear to be very serious about the time-frame and the urgency of the drafting of the constitution. Issues like federalism and inclusive democracy need to be debated and are time-consuming to implement. The drafting of the constitution could have been smooth and timely only if there had been a consensus among constituent political parties in the CA. In fact, constitution drafting seems to have become a secondary issue. The frequent boycotts of the CA meetings by the political parties created more problems. The CPN (M), CPN (UML) and NC, however, reached an understanding on 25 December 2008 that the peace process would be taken to a logical conclusion.

Two issues that had dominated Nepali politics for nearly a year were law and order, and the integration of the People's Liberation Army (PLA) with the Nepali army. The activities of the Young Communist League (YCL) were a major cause of concern as far as the problem of law and order was concerned.[8] The YCL had been substantially involved in murder, abduction, intimidation of opponents, extortion, forced seizures, etc. In order to counter the activities of the YCL, the CPN (UML) had created its own organization called Youth Force (YF). Clashes had occurred between YCL and YF quite frequently. Prime Minister Prachanda had promised to bring YCL within the purview of the law and to control their conduct, but YCL remained a challenge to the peace process in Nepal all through the tenure of the CPN (M). The government seemed to be hopeful of controlling the activities of the YCL, but nothing could be done. It had on the contrary tried to defend YCL at times, stating that it was a political organization.

About 19,600 Maoist combatants were living in UN-monitored camps at the time of writing (the UN mission in Nepal (UNMIN) was established on 23 January 2007 by UN Security Council resolution 1740). It is accepted by all that the ongoing peace process can only be completed with the integration of these combatants with the Nepalese army or their proper rehabilitation elsewhere. An Army Integration Special Committee (AISC) was constituted by the Prachanda government under the Chairmanship of Deputy PM and UML leader Bam Deo Gautam, with the provision for the inclusion of one member each from the NC, CPN (UML) and MJF, while the CPN (M) had two members. The NC did not join the committee, demanding that it should be given an equal number of seats with the Maoists. The demand was later conceded and the AISC then had two members each from the four political parties. However, it was unable to arrive at any acceptable formula for the rehabilitation of the Maoist combatants.[9]

Apart from the inclusion of the Maoist combatants, the democratization of the army has also been an important issue.[10] However, the settlement of the problem of the PLA is not that straightforward. Some political parties are still not very forthright over this issue. It is believed that the merger of PLA with the army would further consolidate the position of the CPN (M).

In the Maoist conclave held at Kharipati from 21 November to 26 November 2008 it was resolved that:

1. Of the three stages of the Maoist People's War, the Maoist revolution in Nepal has currently reached the stage of strategic offence with its own indigenous characteristics.
2. The PLA's main role is to serve as a force to complete the revolution and prevent counter-revolution. It has to prove itself as a force of creativity, firmness, offense, dynamism and invincibility.
3. The PLA will be prepared politically and ideologically for the offensive to complete the revolution.
4. The PLA will undergo ideological and political training on Prachandapath and MLM (Marxism, Leninism and Maoism). The Training will be at basic, intermediate and advanced levels.
5. There will be regular interactive meetings with the party committee in the army.
6. The integration of the PLA will be used in a manner that will further the cause of proletarianism and revolution. The issue of army integration should be used in this context.

This resolution created doubts regarding the political character of the army were it to merge with the PLA.

There were several other obstacles to the peace process, which remained unattained for political reasons. The attacks on the media, delays in the return of seized properties, and fresh incidents of seizure of properties and land grabbing were serious problems. The attacks on the Himal media and the Kantipur office at Biratnagar in December 2008 gave rise to concern regarding lawlessness in the country.

Challenges of peace in the Tarai

The situation has recently become much worse in the Tarai region. It was expected that peace would return in the Tarai after the Eight Point Agreement was signed on 28 February 2008. The Madheshi Janadhikar Forum (MJF), Nepal Sadbhawana Party – Rajender Mahato (NSP-RM) and Tarai Madheshi Democratic Party (TMDP) subsequently joined mainstream politics and participated in the elections to the CA. However, there are 14 armed groups continuing their armed struggle in the region.[11] They have been trying to use the Madheshi sentiments to further their political motives.

These groups have been involved in killings, bomb blasts, intimidation, threats to government officials, etc. The districts of Saptari, Siraha, Dhansusha, Mahottari, Sarlahi, Rauthat, Parsa and Bara have been the most affected. The government has been struggling to bring the groups into mainstream politics, initiating talks with some of the groups in October 2008. Madhesi Virus Killers and Samyukta Jantantrik Tarai Mukti Morcha agreed to the talks. The Jwala Singh faction of the Janatantrik Tarai Mukti Morcha (JTMM-J) laid down certain pre-conditions.[12] The Jai Krishna Goit faction of Janatantrik Tarai Mukti Morcha rejected the offer. There can be no doubt that peace and stability in Tarai is a major issue at present. The rights and aspirations of the people of Madhesh have to be dealt with amicably.

The first round of talks between the government and the JTMM-Rajan was held in Janakpur on 10 January 2009 and ended in a five point understanding. The Peace and Reconstruction Minister Janardan Sharma, who is also the Coordinator of the government negotiating team, and Rajib Jha, Chief Negotiator of the JTMM-Rajan, signed the agreement. It agreed to a cessation of hostilities and the government's pledge to treat the armed group as a political outfit. During the talks JTMM-R proposed the cantoning of its fighters like the Maoist combatants, to which the government did not agree.[13]

The Raman Singh led faction of the Madheshi Mukti Tigers had announced a four-member negotiating team which would participate in the dialogue with the government. The group however asked for security for its team and laid down pre-conditions for talks, such as release of its cadres from police custody and the withdrawal of cases against them. The government also had a dialogue with the Kirat Janbadi Workers Party on 18 January 2009, and agreed to provide security to it and to declare its cadres as political activists. These references clearly indicate that there has been a lot of political mobilization in Tarai. A number of politically motivated groups have been active in Tarai and they are looking for a political space. There is a lot of discontent and distrust in Tarai and how to contain it is a big issue.

On 21 February 2009 the government reached a five-point agreement with the Liberation Tigers of Tarai Ilam at a dialogue held in Birganj. The government agreed to ensure the security of the negotiating teams of the various organizations. This shows that the government was conscious of the problems in the Tarai and was trying to bring various groups to the negotiating table.

Problem of the identity of political parties

The political parties are no doubt the main vehicles of democratic consolidation. Most of the political parties are supportive of the idea of a New Nepal. The concept of a federal democratic republican state has already been accepted. But one has also to note that with this, the basic contours of Nepali politics are undergoing a drastic change. The feudal, monarchic nucleus of Nepali politics has been abolished. Most of the political parties and political leaders revolved around this nucleus, despite their democratic ethos and actions. The political parties have now to transform themselves to create their independent self-image and identity.[14] The political parties themselves cannot remain untouched by the emerging inclusive character of Nepali politics. Therefore, the political parties are bound to undergo a process of internal democratization. Ethnic, gender, *dalit* and regional issues will also affect the organizational, ideological and leadership characteristics of the parties. To what extent the present leadership of the major political parties is prepared to endorse these trends is a significant issue. The rise of CPN (M) as a strong political force in the emerging New Nepal has posed yet another problem for the political parties like the NC and the CPN (UML).

The political parties are also likely to confront fresh issues of ethnicity, regionalism, minorities, *dalits*, etc. that are likely to dominate Nepali politics in the years to come. There is also a need to recast and reshape the ideological and policy orientation of the political parties. The success or failure of the political parties in the new Nepali politics would depend on the extent to which they are able to shape a new identity in the context of the shifting paradigm of the new politics.

Federalism, inclusive democracy and the New Nepal

Federalism and inclusive democracy are the basic aspects of the New Nepal. There is already a consensus over the federal principle. However, a federal model is yet to be decided for the country. It is certain that in the present context of Nepalese politics a federal structure has become a necessity. There cannot be any denial of the fact that the Tarai region and the ethnic groups have been marginalized and discriminated against within the unitary state of Nepal. Both the people of Tarai and the ethnic groups have been politically mobilized during the last decade. The question of autonomy and inclusiveness has become significant in the context of the present political transformation. Thus federalism has become a major instrument of conflict resolution, peace and stability in Nepal, and it is inescapable. At the moment, the Maoist model of dividing Nepal into different autonomous units is the only formula available for a wider consideration.[15] It is not clear if there is a national consensus over this model or whether the Constituent Assembly is going to incorporate this model in the new constitution. It is also not clear if Nepal is going to draw from other models of federalism available in various parts of the world. So far generally two types of arguments have been made regarding federalism. One is ethnic federalism. There seems to be lot of support for ethnic federalism, particularly among the Mongolian communities. Some autonomous regions based on ethnic identity have already been outlined.[16] But there are problems relating to ethnically dominant and minority regions. Ethnic federalism is a sensitive issue as it is related to inter-community relations. It is full of challenges because it also opens doors for the politicization of ethnicities and identity politics, thereby creating space for the rise of ethnic conflicts. If the problem of smaller ethnic groups is not properly addressed, it may lead to identity politics.

Territorial or geographical federalism has been more popular in the context of Tarai. Tarai has strong claims, on the basis of geographic features, to become an autonomous region. The people of Tarai have been talking in terms of 'One Madhesh One Pradesh.' But there are distinct ethnic and linguistic identities within Tarai that have been aspiring for autonomy. Here the more important issue is whether or not the ruling elite of Nepal would accept Tarai as a single federal unit for historico-political reasons at large? There are also problems of development in the mountain region, but people in this region are not politically motivated compared to Tarai. It appears that in the Nepalese context there would be a need to take into consideration both ethnic and territorial federalism.

The problem of equitable distribution of resources is also important.[17] A proper balance has to be created between the communities and the regions. On the whole the issue of federalism is important and needs to be addressed, but it is challenging as well. It has to be dealt with in a long-term perspective. The sharing of natural resources, food security, and land reforms are important issues that need to be properly addressed in a federal structure. It also needs to be noted that federalism is not an end itself. It is only a mechanism and a process, and not in itself a remedy for all ills. One may also be reminded that federalism may resolve some problems but could generate more problems if not addressed properly.

The inclusive character of the Nepali democracy is gradually emerging. The CA elections are a sharp departure from the past in this regard. The ethnic, regional, gender and *dalit* groups are seeking political representation. All these groups are politically mobilized and have come forward to seek representation in the emerging political structures. The minority groups are also demanding proper political representation. There is no doubt that a lot of social and political mobilization has taken place among groups, communities and regions in Nepal in the post-2006 phase. The secularization of politics has further contributed to this mobilization.

The issue of economic transformation is also significant. In fact, the long-term sustainability of peace, stability and democracy would depend upon the realization of popular aspirations and needs. The ten long years of Maoist insurgency caused economic losses and hardships to the people of Nepal. The diversion of funds to defense and security blocked development projects. There is a need both to provide economic relief to the people and to create conditions for economic development, equity and justice. Nepal's urgent needs are infrastructural development, poverty alleviation, employment, land reforms and resource mobilization. It is also necessary to take care of issues relating to regional imbalances.

The role of the international community

The external support structure is equally important. It is a fact that the Maoist insurgency led to serious concerns among the international community. The Maoists were also declared as terrorists by the US. The US, the UK, India and other countries supported the Nepalese government in finding a military solution to the Maoist problem. The post-2006 developments have also attracted the international community's attention, and they look forward to democratic sustainability and peace.

It was difficult for countries like the US to accept a Maoist government in Nepal initially. However, the Americans are likely to change their attitude towards the upcoming political scenario in Nepal.[18] The Maoists too had viewed the US as an expansionist power. But looking to the needs of development, they would not be able to afford inimical postures towards the US and its Western allies.

The Maoists also adopted inimical postures towards India during the insurgency. They perceived India as an expansionist power. India provided armed assistance to the Nepalese government to fight against the insurgency. But there also existed several informal channels of interaction between political leaders, parties, groups and individuals in India and the Maoists of Nepal. The situation took a turn after the 2005 royal coup. There was a perceptional change among Maoists vis-à-vis India. Some of the Maoist leaders themselves played a role in softening the party's attitude towards India. India also played a significant role in the Maoist-SPA understanding and the initiation of the peace process.

With the formation of the Prachanda government there was a lot of speculation in India regarding the Maoist government. Prachanda had said that his party would like to develop friendly relations with both the neighbors. There has been a general impression that the government of the Maoists would have a leaning towards China. Prachanda's visit to China, although not a political visit, added to these impressions. The Indian media projected it as Prachanda's natural tilt towards China. It is true that China is a close neighbor of Nepal. It is also true that the Maoist government had an ideological affinity with China. But Nepal's relations with India are on a different level. History bears testimony to the fact that no other country can provide an alternative to Nepal's relations with India.

There has been an attitudinal change in both India and Nepal towards each other since the formation of the first new government, after the 2008 elections. The role India can play in rebuilding democracy and stability in Nepal is an important issue here. India as an immediate neighbor having various layers of mutual interactions can play a role in Nepal's efforts towards consolidation of peace.[19] The fact remains that an unstable and conflict-ridden Nepal has also been a problem for India. It is also a widely acknowledged fact that India can play and has been playing a significant role in the socio-economic reconstruction of Nepal.

The then Prime Minister Prachanda's first official visit to New Delhi in September 2008 was an indication that Nepal would seek India's larger co-operation. Any mature political leadership in Nepal would understand that the need of the hour is India's support in peace-building not a conflictual relationship with that country. There are certain important issues between India and Nepal, such as the 1950 Treaty of Peace and Friendship, mutual co-operation for water resources development, open borders, migration, Gurkha recruitment to Indian armed forces, etc. These are issues that can be taken up at a later stage. India should concede to Nepali demands if it serves the interest of Nepal. At the moment more important issues are Indian assistance for socio-economic reconstruction in Nepal, Indian investments, joint ventures, and mutual trade. India's approach should be to build confidence in the new government in Nepal. It seems to be equally important to consider what help India can give to Nepal in constitution-making, building a federal structure, etc. India has a plural society and it has gone a long way in dealing with ethno-cultural and regional sentiments and demands. Nepal can benefit from India's vast experience in dealing with its own issues and challenges.

The Maoists out of power: setback to peace process

In May 2009, the Prime Minister of the Maoist-led government, Prachanda, unexpectedly decided to resign from the government. The sudden downfall of the Maoist government gave a serious jolt to the peace process in Nepal. The resignation of Prime Minister Prachanda came after a conflict over the issue of the sacking of the army chief, General Katwal. The argument of the government was that the army chief had disobeyed the orders of the government and was in conflict with the ministry of defense. The bone of contention was the rehabilitation and absorption of the Maoist combatants in the army. The Seven-Party Alliance had agreed on the rehabilitation of the Maoist combatants and for the interim period they were put in cantonments and kept under the supervision of a team headed by the representative of the UNO. The army chief delayed the rehabilitation process, and this led to his removal by the government and the appointment of a new army chief. This decision did not come as a recommendation from the President. The government issued the orders, but the President did not agree with them, and reinstated Mr. Katwal as army chief. It appeared that the decisions of the government and the President respectively lacked coordination and were politically motivated. The fact is that the other political parties like the Nepali Congress and the UML had agreed with the Maoist formula of rehabilitation, but never liked it and did not show any interest, as they thought that the Maoist combatants were politically motivated.

But one has also to understand that it was due to a complex political situation that the resignation of the Maoists from the government took place. In fact the issue of the rehabilitation of the Maoist combatants had been delayed considerably, and there was strong internal pressure from the party organization over this issue. One may also add here that internal differences were surfacing within the party. It also appears that Prachanda took a rather hasty decision, not realizing what the consequences would be for his own party. Whatever may be the reasons, the fact remains that it derailed the peace process. Prachanda blamed foreign forces for his resignation.[20] It was a way of covering up serious inter- and intra-party feuds that were responsible more than anything else for his resignation.

The ruling coalition that emerged under the leadership of Madhav Nepal of UML was a weak government. The history of coalition governments in Nepal has demonstrated that they have a bleak future. It is also significant that the Maoists are the largest party in the Constituent Assembly. The peace process and the making of the constitution cannot progress without the active co-operation of the Maoists.

However the CPN (M) has been in an agitational mood since its ouster from the government. They did not support the UML government and continued street demonstrations and *bandhs* (strikes). The Maoists demanded the formation of a national government. The government was not prepared to listen to them, as the UML was not in a position to take any independent decision. In these circumstances Nepalese politics entered yet another complex phase. The situation of uncertainty and conflict delayed the process of constitution-making, and the issue of the rehabilitation of the Maoist combatants also remained unresolved. The UML government worked under pressure and constraints. Madhav Nepal had to resign from the government in August 2010 due to strong pressure from the Maoists against the continuation of the UML government. The time-frame for the finalization of the new constitution has also been increased by a year. However, the political situation in Nepal seems to have become more critical after the resignation of the UML government, as it has not been possible to elect a new Prime Minister by the Constituent Assembly even after six rounds of voting. According to the provisions of the constitution, this process will continue until a candidate gets a majority of the votes in the Constituent Assembly. This continuing political uncertainty at a critical stage of political transition clearly reflects the divided politics and lack of political consensus in Nepal.

Conclusion

To sum up the discussion it can be said that at a critical stage of political transformation, Nepal still lacks political unity and consensus among its various political actors. The delays in constitution-making and settling the contentious issues have created apprehensions about peace and political stability in the country.

There can be no doubt that the resolution of the Maoist insurgency, the Maoist entry into mainstream democratic politics, and the declaration of a republican state in Nepal are developments that no one could have visualized or anticipated even a few years ago. It has taken the country half-way towards realizing the vision of building a new democratic Nepal. But Nepal's problem since the beginning has been that of one step forward and two steps back. It is true that in the post-2006 phase there have been significant developments that have taken place towards building a democratic republican state. But the political elite of Nepal have not realized the significance of the social and political mobilization that has taken place in the country over the years. The ethnic upsurge, regional movements, the *dalit* awakening, gender issues and women's movements, and the mobilization of the minority communities are significant developments that may in fact decide the future course of Nepali politics. How the Nepali state is going to address these issues is unclear. The people of Nepal have already decided in favor of a federal state and inclusive democracy. But the delay in the finalization of a new constitution is a problem. It has given rise to a lot of speculations regarding the nature of federalism and so on.

The issues of socio-economic transformation are yet to be resolved properly, as the country has still not been able to make any decisions about the fundamental political superstructures. The people of Nepal have a lot of expectations from the New Nepal, but unfortunately the country is still struggling with leadership issues at the time of writing. These need to be resolved before the government can start devising a strong mechanism for delivering the goods to the people. On the whole the search for a New Nepal is still passing through a critical phase and many issues need to be resolved.

Notes

1 For details see Haftun *et al.*, *People, Politics and Ideology*, 1999; M. Hutt (ed.), *Nepal in the Nineties*, 1993; B.C. Upreti, *Nepal, democracy at cross roads*, 2007; M. Lawoti, *Towards a democratic Nepal*, 2005; K. Ogura, *Kathmandu Spring*, 2001.
2 For insights into the Maoist insurgency some references are D. Thapa, *A kingdom under Seige*, 2003; L.R. Baral (ed.), *Nepal: Facets of Maoist Insurgency*, 2006; B.R. Upreti, *Armed conflict and peace process in Nepal*, 2006; U.P. Pyakurel, *Maoist movement in Nepal*, 2007; B.C. Upreti, *Maoists in Nepal*, 2008.
3 See Upreti, *Maoists in Nepal*.
4 D. Kumar, 'Nepal future order in paradox', Akrosh, 2:40, July 2008, pp. 17–18.
5 *The Hindustan Times*, 4 June 2008.
6 *The Hindustan Times*, 20 July 2008.
7 *The Hindustan Times*, 22 July 2008.
8 In a meeting of the Central Secretariat of the CPN-Maoist held on 8 January 2009 it was concluded that anarchy had set in among some of its cadres, which needed to be corrected.
9 See http//satp.org/satporgtp/countries/Nepal/index.html
10 PM Prachanda said on 5 February 2009: 'YCL is only a political group [that] now works on development works [sic].'
11 L.R. Baral (ed.), *Nepal, New Frontiers of Restructuring of the State*, 2008, p. 5.
12 Some of these groups are: Janvadi Tarai Mukti Morcha-Rajan, Janvadi Mukti Morcha-Jwala, Janvadi Mukti Morcha-Goit, Madhesh Rastra Janatantrik Party – Revolutionary, Kirat Janvadi Workers Party, ATMM, Madhesh Mukti Tigers, Liberation Tigers of Tarai Ilam, Madheshi Virus Killers, etc.
13 Jwala Singh, president of JTMM-J, said on 14 January 2009 that his party would sit for talks with the government only if the latter met four pre-conditions: release of its detained activists, withdrawal of fake cases against its activists, declaration of a ceasefire, and guarantee of security of its leaders. Nepal Assessment 2009, available http//satp.org/Nepal/index.html
14 B.C. Upreti, 'Challenges in the post election scenario in Nepal', 2009, pp. 23–25.
15 Ibid.
16 See P. Sharma, *Unravelling the mosaic: Spatial aspects of ethnicity in Nepal*, Kathmandu: Himal Books, 2008, quoted in T.B.T. Magar, 'Ethnic federalism in Nepal', 2008.
17 Magar, 'Ethnic Federalism', pp. 22–23.
18 The visiting US Assistant Secretary for the Bureau of South and Central Asian Affairs, Richard Boucher, said on 12 February 2009 that 'The more they [Maoists] act within the political system and abandon the past practices of terrorism and violence, the easier it will be for us to finish the review.' See G. Sharma, 'No US timetable to remove Nepal Maoists terror tag', available:www.reliefweb.int/rw/rwb.nsf/db900SID/CJAL-7P7MR2?OpenDocument
19 See, 'Debate: Dealing with Maoists Nepal', *Indian Foreign Affairs Journal*, Vol. XIV, 2008.
20 *The Hindustan Times*, 11 May 2009; also see 'Drift in Nepal – Political parties yet to learn', *The Statesman* (Kolkata), 28 August 2010.

Bibliography

Baral, L.R. (ed.), *Nepal: Facets of Maoist insurgency*, New Delhi: Adroit, 2006.

Baral, L.R., *Nepal: New frontiers of restructuring of the state*, New Delhi: Adroit, 2008.

Baxter, C., Y.K. Malik, C.H. Kennedy and R.C. Oberst, *Government and politics in South Asia*, Oxford and Boulder, CO: Westview Press, 1998.

Chadda, M., *Building democracy in South Asia*, London and Boulder, CO: Lynne Riennar, 2000.

Hoftun, M., W. Raeper and J. Whel, *People, politics and ideology: Democracy and social change in Nepal*, Kathmandu: Mandala Book Point, 1999.

Hutt, M. (ed.), *Nepal in the nineties: Versions of the past, visions of the future*, New Delhi: Oxford University Press, 1993.

Lawoti, M., *Towards a democratic Nepal*, New Delhi: Sage, 2005.

Lawoti, M. and A.K. Pahar, *The Maoist insurgency in Nepal: Revolutions in the 21st century*, London: Routledge, 2010.

Magar, T.B.T., 'Ethnic federalism in Nepal: Challenges and opportunities', *Nepali Journal of Contemporary Studies*, 3:1, September 2008.

Pyakurel, U.P., *Maoist movement in Nepal: A sociological perspective*, New Delhi: Adroit, 2007.

Ogura, K., *Kathmandu Spring: The people's movement of 1990*, Kathmandu: Himal Books, 2001.

Skocpol, T., *Social revolutions in the modern world*, Cambridge: Cambridge University Press, 1995.

Thapa, D., *A kingdom under siege: Nepal's Maoist insurgency 1996 to 2003*, Kathmandu: The Printhouse, 2003.

Upreti, B.C., *Nepal, democracy at cross roads: post 1990 dynamics, issues and challenges*, New Delhi: Kanishka Publishers, 2007.

Upreti, B.C., *Maoists in Nepal: From insurgency to political mainstream*, New Delhi: Kalpaz Publications, 2008.

Upreti, B.C., 'Challenges in the post election scenario in Nepal', *Economic and Political Weekly*, 24:11, 14 March 2009, pp. 23–25.

Upreti, B.R., *Armed conflict and peace process in Nepal*, New Delhi: Adroit, 2006.

10 Making sense of insurgencies in North-East India

An overview

Namrata Goswami

Today the peace and security of the country is being challenged by threats emanating from cross-border terrorism, insurgency in the north-eastern areas and the emergence of left wing extremism in certain parts of the country.

(Pranab Mukherjee, Finance Minister, December 2010)

The North East of India is one of the most picturesque and unique regions of the Indian subcontinent. Home to more than 220 major tribes and various other subtribes, the region has witnessed the mass migration of people from South East and East Asia since time immemorial. One of the most important migrations occurred in 1228 when the Ahoms, led by Sukapha (belonging to the Tai race), crossed over the Patkai ranges from Burma and reached Assam.[1] The Ahoms reigned over Assam for more than 600 years and were successful in forging tributary relations with various other tribes like the Dimasas and the Nagas. However, with the Treaty of Yandaboo in 1826 and the beginning of British colonial rule in the North East Frontier Agency (NEFA), the policy of 'divide and rule' was adopted, wherein the hills of Assam were clearly demarcated from the plains with the Inner Line Regulation Act of 1873 and the Excluded Areas Act of 1880. This initiated a process of gradually destroying centuries-old relationships between the hills and the plains, the consequences of which resulted in separate states for the Nagas in 1963 and the 1972 reorganization of states in the North East, creating further territorial and political divisions of an otherwise historically homogeneous space under the Ahom kingdom. Even today, the borders of many of the North Eastern states are questioned by some of the tribes inhabiting these highly volatile and insecure spaces. The North East is also strategically important to India, located as it is among four countries neighboring India, namely, Bangladesh, Bhutan, China and Myanmar. As a result, India's 'Look East' policy is dependent on the North East for an optimal opening to the countries of South East Asia via Myanmar.

This chapter attempts to make sense of some of the recent major insurgencies in Assam, Manipur and Nagaland, such as the United Liberation Front of Asom (ULFA) and the Dima Halam Daogah (DHD, both Nunisa and Garlosa factions) in Assam; the United National Liberation Front (UNLF) in Manipur; and the

National Socialist Council of Nagalim led by Thuingaleng Muivah and Isak Chisi Swu (NSCN-IM) in Nagaland.

Insurgencies in the North East

Insurgencies in the North East started with the Nagas, whose movement can be traced back to 1918 with the formation of the Naga Club. In 1946, the Naga National Council (NNC) was formed, and it declared Naga independence on 14 August 1947, a day before India declared its own independence. The Naga movement turned violent in the 1950s and is still active under the aegis of the NSCN (IM). Manipur has also been grossly disturbed by armed violence on the part of the UNLF, formed on 24 November 1964. Another significant Manipuri separatist armed group known as the Revolutionary People's Front (RPF) and its armed wing, the People's Liberation Army (PLA), have been engaging in armed struggle since 1976. The RPF and the PLA were supposedly trained by the Chinese in the 1960s and 1970s in Maoist guerrilla warfare, and both outfits aim at violent revolutionary change to bring about a classless society in Manipur. Neighboring Assam, the most dominant state in the North East in terms of demography and resources, has also been plagued by insurgent violence since 1979 with the formation of the ULFA. The hills districts of Assam, North Cachar Hills and Karbi Anglong also witnessed the rise of armed groups in the 1990s like the DHD and the United Peoples' Democratic Solidarity (UPDS). Most of these insurgent groups have thrived primarily due to strong external influences. Countries like China in the 1960s and the 1970s, as well as Pakistan and later on Bangladesh, have supported most of these outfits in their fight against India by making available arms, training and most importantly base areas for under-ground camps. The UNLF, ULFA and NSCN (IM) procure small arms through Bangladesh's Cox Bazar area. Indian intelligence sources indicate that the ULFA has benefited the most, with camps in Halughat (near the Bangladesh-Meghalaya border), Dhaka, etc. The outfit runs around ten bases in the Mymensingh region with four bases, run by the UNLF.[2]

Causes of the insurgencies

Though it is not easy to discern the internal causes of the insurgencies, the stated political objective of most of the major insurgent groups is independence from India. Only the DHD demands a separate ethnically-slanted state within India comprising the Dimasa population. At first glance, the stated position of 'independent statehood' appears non-negotiable, yet when one delves into the underlying interests and needs of the actors, there is the possibility of reconciliation. Most conflict analysts emphasize the importance of identifying basic needs, which lie at the root of any conflict. For example, John Burton writes that 'there are certain human needs concerned with development, as well as survival, which are ontological and universal… Their frustration is a sufficient explanation of political and social instabilities. Policies of intervention and attempts at resolving conflicts fail unless this is taken into account.'[3] Therefore, if basic needs like security, identity and livelihood are resolved, conflicts do get transformed, as has happened in the case of Mizoram in India.[4] In the North East, however, added to issues of identity, ethnicity, social and cultural assertions, political empowerment and land, the colonial residue of being treated as 'excluded, partially excluded' areas based on the Inner Line Regulation of 1873 continues to be a dominant reality. Due to the lack of a pre-colonial and colonial integrative policy with the rest of India, the hill people resist and also resent the post-colonial Indian state's expansion march into the hill interiors.

The major violent insurgent movements

ULFA

The radical turn in Assamese nationalism may be traced back to the influx of illegal migrants from East Pakistan after the Partition of India in 1947, and from Bangladesh since 1971. This massive migrant flow created an unstable situation among the Assamese middle classes and the rural masses, who resented the rapidly changing demographic profile of the state and the loss of land to the Bengali migrants. Also, violent protests erupted upon the Union government's decision to transport crude oil from Assam to a refinery at Barauni, Bihar, as it was viewed as exploitative of Assam's natural resources. Along with the exploitation of oil, the revenue earnings of which mostly went to the central government, the revenues from Assam's other famous product – tea – was also going to the head offices located in West Bengal. Mass agitations against Delhi's exploitation of Assam's resources thereby ensued. The most proximate cause of the Assam Agitation (1979–1985) was, however, malpractices in the electoral procedure of 1979, when in the Mangaldoi Assembly elections, 45,000 illegal migrants' names were found on the voter list. The first strike against this was kick-started on 8 June 1979. The All Assam Students' Union (AASU)-led agitation demanded that the 1951 National Register for Citizens be utilized to determine the citizenship of all those living in Assam. Subsequently, the 1983 state elections, with many illegal migrants on the voter list, and the state's heavy-handed response to non-violent dissent, aroused the embers of one of the most persistent violent ethnic movements in Assam – the ULFA. The ULFA was formed on 7 April 1979 at Ranghar, in Sivasagar, a site of historical significance since the time of Ahom rule. Most of the recruits of the ULFA were drawn from the Asom Jatiyabadi Parishad (AJYCP), which professed Marxism and advocated the Assamese right to dual citizenship and self-determination. The outfit advocated scientific socialism, Assamese nationalism and self-determination, or Swadhin Asom (Independent Assam), and from 1992 onwards widened its support base by stating that theirs was a movement for all Asombashis (people who resided in Assam). ULFA sought to revert Assam's status to the Ahom-ruled, pre-1826 Assam, as before the treaty of Yandaboo between the British and the Burmese.[5]

ULFA's Vice Chairman, Pradip Gogoi, states that his organization's political objective is 'Sovereign, Socialist Assam' in which 'All indigenous people must stay, all others must leave.'[6]

DHD (Nunisa and Garlosa factions)

The DHD was formed in 1995 after most of the cadres of the erstwhile Dimasa National Security Force (DNSF) surrendered with the exception of its commander Jewel Garlosa.[7] It was under his leadership that the DHD was organized into a violent force. The stated demand of the then unified DHD (it subsequently broke into two factions in 2003) was a unified Dimaraji state comprised of Dimasa-inhabited areas of North Cachar Hills district, Karbi Anglong district, Cachar district, parts of Nagaon district in Assam, and Dimapur- and Dimasa-inhabited areas in Dhansiripar in Nagaland. Interestingly, the demands of the NSCN (IM) for a unified *Nagalim* (Greater Nagaland), the UPDS for a Karbi state, the DHD for a Dimasa state, and the Kuki Revolutionary Army for a Kuki Regional Council consist of conflicting claims to overlapping territorial space. Indeed, the emergence of multifarious ethnic violent groups with claims over the same territory has further complicated the situation in these remote areas of Assam. The DHD (Nunisa faction), led by Dilip Nunisa and Pranab Nunisa, has a cadre base of about 800, mostly drawn from the villages in Karbi Anglong and North Cachar Hills districts. On the other hand, the Black Widow (associated with the Jewel Garlosa faction) is a very reclusive group mostly based in the thickly forested areas of Langting, Darangibra, Mupa, Maibang subdivision, Mahur, Laisong, Harangajao, Boro-Haflong and Haflong. Its cadre strength is about 200 to 250 heavily armed youths, mostly belonging to the above mentioned areas.[8]

UNLF

The UNLF, founded by Arambam Samaranda Singh, draws its credence from the historical argument that Manipur was forcefully inducted into India in 1949. The outfit is based on a leftist ideology vis-à-vis the economic and social alienation of the people of Manipur. The outfit's support base is mostly from Meiteis[9] inhabiting the Imphal valley in Manipur, as well as the North Cachar Hills of Assam. Samaranda was killed by suspected Kanglei Yawol Kanna Lup (KYKL)[10] militants on 10 June 2001, and the current leader and Chairman is Raj Kumar Meghen.[11] The UNLF has a rather strong following in Meitei areas of Manipur. There exists a strong belief among its cadre base and sympathizers that it is important to have armed, ethnically aligned groups, as the Meiteis genuinely fear the NSCN (IM)'s agenda of Nagalim (Greater Nagaland).[12] The Nagalim map includes all Naga-inhabited areas in Nagaland, Manipur, Assam and Arunachal Pradesh. Manipur had erupted into violence in 2001 when the Union government extended the cease-fire with the NSCN (IM) to Naga-inhabited areas in Manipur. The resistance turned so violent that the Union government had to revoke the move. The situation, in fact, reflects the classic 'security dilemma' faced by states at the systemic level. When one state arms itself, it leads to insecurity in neighboring states, as the latter are uncertain about the former's intention. Consequently, the best way to protect a state is to increase its armament. This situation is also reflected in situations when two or more ethnic groups occupy the same space. When one ethnic group arms itself, other ethnic groups also arm themselves, creating a vicious cycle of 'violence' versus 'counter-violence.'[13]

The Naga insurgency

The Naga ethnic conflict has a long historical trajectory tracing back its roots to 1918, with the formation of the Naga Club by 20 members of the Naga French Labour Corps, who had served in World War I. The wartime knowledge motivated the few who had come in contact with the European battlefields to politically organize themselves as a distinct ethnic political identity. The Club submitted a memorandum to the Simon Commission in 1929, in which it stated that the people of Naga areas and that of mainland India had nothing in common between them. Therefore, it would benefit both to stay separate and form their own political entities as and when the British left India. In 1946, the Club was further reinforced with the formation of the Naga National Council (NNC) under the leadership of A.Z. Phizo, a charismatic leader belonging to the Angami tribe. Phizo had been trained by the British during World War II on the Burma Front against Japanese forces, and he utilized that knowledge to impart training in guerrilla warfare to the NNC members.[14] Significantly, a Nine Point Agreement known as the Akbar Hydari Agreement was signed between the moderates in the NNC, like T. Sakhrie and Imkonglba Ao, and the Governor of Assam, Sir Akbar Hydari, on 29 June 1947. The Agreement gave the Nagas rights over their land as well as executive and legislative powers, but the Agreement was rejected by Phizo. On 14 August 1947 the NNC, led by Phizo, declared independence, a day before India attained its own independence. The 1950s, 1960s and 1970s were tumultuous periods in Naga history, with militancy on the rise, coupled with the state's military response propelled by acts like the Armed Forces (Special Powers) Act, 1958, amended in 1972. The crossfire between the state forces and the NNC resulted in many non-combatant deaths as well as human rights violations. There were numerous efforts at peace by the Union Government, which resulted in the grant of statehood to Nagaland in 1963 and the establishment of a peace mission in 1964. However, it was the loss of bases in East Pakistan after the emergence of a new state – Bangladesh – as well as the constant pressure from Indian security forces, that motivated the NNC under Z. Huire to sign the Shillong Accord of 1975. The Shillong Accord, however, repeated the tragic story of the Nine Point Agreement in that it split the Naga rebel movement. The Shillong Accord was the proximate cause for the foundation of the original unified National Socialist Council of Nagaland (NSCN). Replicating Phizo's aversion to the Hydari Agreement, Thuingaleng Muivah, Isak Chisi Swu and

S.S. Khaplang condemned the Shillong Accord as a sellout to the Union government, and formed the NSCN in Myanmar in 1980. Subsequently, due to intense differences between Khaplang, Muivah and Swu, the NSCN split, with Muivah and Swu forming the NSCN (IM) while Khaplang formed the National Socialist Council of Nagaland, NSCN (K), in 1988. Incidentally, both the NSCN (IM) and the NSCN (K) came under cease-fire with the Union government in 1997 and 2001 respectively.

Making sense of the use of violence

Since most of the conflicts in North East India are of an asymmetric variety, the logic of interest that drives conflicts of the inter-state variety does not apply to it. However, though a state is always the stronger party, the tactics and strategy of guerrilla warfare by the weaker armed groups provide them with the wherewithal for a protracted conflict, aimed at wearing down the will of the stronger party to the conflict. Significantly, the NSCN (IM), ULFA, UNLF and the DHD have a declared strategy of protracted armed conflict. Interestingly, cease-fires are seen as a phase when an outfit can regroup, recruit, finance and re-arm itself. This has happened in most cases. The ULFA and the NSCN (IM) most decidedly re-armed and regrouped themselves during the cease-fire phase. The Governor of Assam, Lieutenant General (Retd) Ajai Singh, in his address on 26 January 2006 on the occasion of Republic Day, stated that the ULFA has 'regrouped and consolidated its weak positions' by taking advantage of the cease-fire during the period of indirect talks through the People's Consultative Group (PCG).[15] (The PCG was the 11-member civilian group formed by ULFA in September 2005 to talk to the central government on its behalf.) His views were also echoed by the Assam Chief Minister, Tarun Gogoi, who stated that 'in retrospect, I admit that the judgment may be a little wrong when we offered a ceasefire to the ULFA.'[16] Military operations against the outfit were suspended by the government from 13 August to 24 September 2006. During this period, the ULFA reorganized its units in the traditional strongholds of Dibrugarh, Sivasagar and Tinsukia, formed new battalions like the 27th battalion and moved into new areas like Karbi Anglong.[17] Similarly, the NSCN (IM) has also increased its cadre-base from 1,000 in 1997 to 5,000 in 2009. It has also increased its hold in Mokokchung, Tuensang, Mon and Dimapur in Nagaland, Ukhrul and Tamenglong in Manipur, and across the border in the North Cachar Hills district of Assam.[18]

The UNLF started its overt violent movement in 1990 with the formation of its armed wing, the Manipur Peoples' Army (MPA). In December 1991, the MPA attacked Central Reserve Police Force (CRPF) personnel at the Loktak Hydel Power Project, 30 km from Imphal, resulting in the death of five CRPF personnel. Interestingly, such violence is not condemned outright by the public, as the reform agenda of the outfit has a wide-ranging appeal in a society reeling under the influence of violence, drugs coming across the border from Myanmar, and AIDS. Myanmar is a part of the 'golden triangle' with Laos and Thailand, and transports huge amounts of drugs and disease into India's North East.

According to the UN Office on Drugs and Crime (UNODC), poppy cultivation is on the rise in Myanmar, with an estimated production of 460 metric tonnes by 163,000 households spread over 27,700 hectares in 2007 alone.[19] Drug addiction and injected heroin use are rampant among North Eastern youths, due to the easy availability of drugs from Myanmar, through the drug routes along Moreh, Mokokchung and Champai, the three border districts in Manipur, Nagaland and Mizoram respectively.[20] That aside, if a common pattern of UNLF violence is to be gauged, the outfit is primarily focused on attacking Indian security forces and is rather careful not to engage in indiscriminate violence. In fact, the UNLF denied any hand in the killings of Bihari migrants in Manipur in 2008, arguing that their fight is not against any civilians. Rather, their protracted struggle is against the Indian state.

The violence of the DHD (N) is characterized by its protracted nature. It has not disarmed despite signing a cease-fire with the Union government. A recent video of a DHD (N) training camp situated deep in the jungles of Cachar district revealed that the outfit is training young boys and girls, aged 12 to 18, to handle sophisticated weapons. Phaizan Dimasa, Assistant Commandant at the DHD Harangajao Camp, admitted that there were nearly 500 child or teenage insurgents in his outfit.[21]

Increase in violence

Despite cease-fires between the Union government and the insurgent outfits, the cult of violence continues to dominate the social fabric in North East India. In fact, cease-fires appear to have benefited the security forces rather than society at large. In this context, the ULFA has increasingly attacked Hindi-speaking people, especially from the year 2005 onwards. In January 2006, it killed nearly 55 Hindi-speaking people across Dibrugarh, Sivasagar, Tinsukia and Dhemaji districts.[22] In 2007, it changed its area of operation and struck in the Karbi Anglong district of Assam on 11 August killing 14 Hindi speakers. The violence was speculated to be the handiwork of the 27th battalion of ULFA in collaboration with the Karbi Longri Liberation Front (KNLF).[23] The worrisome issue in the recent ULFA-related violence of 2008–2009 is the diabolical link between the ULFA, Harkat-ul-Jihad-al-Islami Bangladesh (HuJI-B)[24] and Pakistan's Inter-Services Intelligence (ISI), which has to be broken if one hopes to bring down the killings. Significantly, it must be stated that ULFA's killings of innocent Bihari migrants might be influenced by its Bangladesh linkage; the Bihari migrants are a competitor to the illegal Bangladeshi migrants in Assam's cheap labor market. Therefore, Bangladeshi pressure groups could have, as a *quid pro quo*, demanded that the ULFA take violent action to deter more migration from Bihar, so as to benefit their own people migrating to Assam for a livelihood.

On the other hand, the NSCN (IM)'s fratricidal killings against the NSCN (K) are vitiating the atmosphere in Naga areas in recent years. In 2008 alone, 40 or more combatants on both sides lost their lives in factional clashes. Phek district was one of the most affected, with NSCN (IM) and NSCN (K) caught in open crossfire throughout 2008. Ironically, a year earlier, on 25 July 2007, a day after the Joint Forum Working Committee (JFWC) of Nagaland Gaon Burahs (village headmen) Federation and Nagaland Doabasi (elders) Association made the formal declaration of cease-fire among the Naga underground factions in Dimapur, the NSCN (IM) and NSCN (K) clashed in the heart of Phek town. Around 400 to 500 rounds were fired, gripping the townspeople with fear for their lives. These factional clashes have not abated, even after pressure from civil society groups to give up violence.[25] The split in the NSCN (IM) in November 2007 and the formation of a new faction from within its fold, the National Socialist Council of Nagaland (Unification), also increased violence levels.

The UNLF broke up into two factions, one led by Meghen and the other led by Namoijam Oken, in 1990, resulting in a bloody factional clash that left more than 100 people dead. The Oken group subsequently merged with other groups like PREPAK and formed the KYKL. The UNLF, through the MPA, has accelerated its violent activities against the security forces. In 2008 alone, it killed more than ten security personnel. On 15 March 2008 the UNLF claimed that it had killed more than five Assam Rifles personnel in Minnou village near the Myanmar international border, under Moreh police station in the Chandel district. UNLF spokesman Tombi Singh stated that its 293rd battalion had carried out the attack on the Assam Rifles outpost.[26] Similarly, on 21 February 2008, the outfit claimed that it had killed five security force personnel at Muolvaikhup village under Kamjong subdivision in the Ukhrul district. The spate of such violence and the counter-violence by the state forces has increased the death toll on both sides substantially.[27]

With regard to the DHD (N), the recent spate of violence in the North Cachar Hills should be viewed as a consequence of power battles with factional fights mainly aimed at dominating the allocation of resources and territory. Given the fact that both groups are heavily dependent on the extortion networks run in common areas, the violence is mostly about who dominates what, where and how. The local politicians are also involved in the turf-battle, as they appease the militants through bribes or other clandestine rewards so as to ensure support from pockets of the population dominated by either group. Such a linkage is however fraught with high risks to personal security. A specific episode will illustrate this argument. The North Cachar Hills District Council was scheduled to hold elections on 12 June 2007. In order to garner votes, three Congress District Council Members tapped the Black Widow faction of the DHD. The end result of this particular outreach was tragic for the local Dimasa political community. On 4 June 2007, in a gory act of violence, the then Chief Executive Member of the District Council, Purnendu Langthasa, along with Executive Member Nindu Langthasa, both belonging to the Congress party, were shot dead at point-blank range by the Black Widow at a location near Umrangshu police station area.[28] The Black Widow, while claiming responsibility for the deaths, accused both leaders of electoral malpractices.[29] A few days latter, Ajit Bodo, another Congress leader and member of the District Council, who had been kidnapped by the Black Widow, was found dead near Maibong subdivision. By killing high-profile local politicians in cold blood, the Black Widow was assert-ing its own power and influence in these remote areas of Assam. Police intelli-gence indicates that the outfit has been constantly helped by the NSCN (IM) in its combat operations and as a result, despite its meagre cadre base – 150 to 200 cadres – the outfit has been successful in creating an atmosphere of extreme fear.

External support: the regional dimension of the insurgency

Insurgencies in the North East might not have thrived as they do today, had there been no external support. The North Eastern states share a 4,500 km, highly porous border with China in the north, Myanmar in the east, Bangladesh in the southwest and Bhutan, whereas it precariously clings to the rest of India by a 22-km narrow strip of land in Bengal known as the 'Chicken's Neck.' Both the ULFA and the NSCN (IM) have training camps in Myanmar and Bangladesh. Significantly, the unified National Socialist Council of Nagaland (NSCN) was formed in Myanmar on 31 January 1980.[30] In 1986, ULFA established linkages with the unified NSCN. Both the rebel groups have strong connections with the Kachin Independence Organization (KIO) in Myanmar.[31] A year earlier, ULFA had set up camps in Bangladesh. Southern Bhutan also offered a safe haven for bases, as it was densely forested, and the Royal Bhutan Army (RBA) did not possess the wherewithal to fight these armed groups in the 1980s and 1990s. However, on 15 December 2003 the RBA and the Royal Body Guards (RBG), employing 6,000 military personnel, forcefully expelled 3,000 armed rebel/ insurgent groups like ULFA and KIO from Bhutan and destroyed nearly 30 training camps. Many top ULFA functionaries were also arrested. ULFA has since then regrouped around the India-Bangladesh border near Meghalaya, as well as in Kachin state in Myanmar, Arunachal Pradesh, and Assam's major dis-tricts like Tinsukia and Sivasagar.

ULFA leader Arabinda Rajkhowa and Commander-in-Chief Paresh Barua operated from Bangladesh until Rajkhowa's arrest in December 2009. Barua now operates from Myanmar-China border areas. In 2004, New Delhi gave a detailed list of 194 insurgent camps in Bangladesh to Bangladeshi authorities.[32] The ISI and the Bangladesh Directorate of Field Intelligence (DGFI) have also been supporting ULFA's subversive activities. Reports indicate that several ULFA cadres received training from the ISI in camps in Pakistan, Bhutan and Bangladesh as recently as 2005–2006.[33] In December 2006, the arrested ULFA militant Prabal Saikia revealed that ULFA is seeking to use Shillong–Cherra-punji–Pynursla routes for shipment of arms from Bangladesh.[34] ULFA had also supposedly received training from the Kachin Independence Organization (KIO) in Myanmar. The Kachin National Army (KNA) had taken INR100,000 per head to train ULFA cadres in Myanmar during the 1980s and 1990s. The state's counter-response to ULFA's violent dissent were massive counter-insurgency operations, namely Operation Bajrang (1990), Rhino I (September 1991) and Rhino II (March 1992). These operations succeeded in denting ULFA's strength and destroyed many of the camps in upper Assam. Yet ULFA leaders managed to shift base to Bangladesh, Bhutan and Myanmar. From 1995 onwards, India has conducted counter-insurgency operations along with the Myanmar's army known as the Tatmadaw. These operations have not been very successful.

The NSCN (IM) takes the help of the Karen National Union (KNU), which has been fighting the Myanmar junta since 1947. The outfit has also ventured into the Chinese black market in Yunnan province. Small arms are shipped through the Chittagong port in Bangladesh. It has also had a procurement officer in the Philippines named Anthony Shimray, who has deep connections with the South East Asian small arms network.[35] In order to get a deeper sense of these external linkages, it is important to understand that the Nagas and the Meiteis had played a crucial role in the Burma Front (1942–1945) against the Japanese assault during World War II. Formed in 1942, the famous Chindit guerrilla force was led by the legendary British Lieutenant Colonel, later Major General Wingate, who had vast experience in unconventional warfare in Sudan and Ethiopia against Italian forces during World War II and in the Middle East against Arab forces. The Chindits comprised English forces, mostly from the north of England, Burmese forces made up of the Kachins and the Karens, and Naga, Manipuri and Mizo forces, who provided local intelligence. Units that comprising up to 300 individuals made up an overall force of 20,000 men led by Wingate.[36] This joint training, experiences in the Burma jungle, and successes in thwarting the Japanese, immensely influenced the Nagas, Mizos and Manipuris. Phizo himself fought alongside the British in the Naga areas and in Burma; so did Laldenga, the leader of the Mizo National Front.

China also began to aggressively support revolutionary movements across the world after the Communist takeover in 1949. Thereafter, it provided strong political, economic and logistical support to various revolutionary groups in North East India, ostensibly motivated by the goal of countering Western imperialism and Soviet revisionism in Asia. In return for this support, most of these insurgent groups supported the 'One China policy' with regard to Taiwan. China's experience in guerrilla warfare became a great attraction to the North Eastern insurgent groups. The Nagas were greatly inspired by the Chinese ideas of 'Peoples' War' and 'protracted struggle.' The NNC was financed, trained and mentored by China. The relationship grew intense during the Chinese Cultural Revolution (1966–1968). In 1966, Muivah, then a member of the NNC, led a 130-strong Naga guerrilla force in a three-month trek to Yunnan province in China, mostly helped by the Kachins. He later moved on to Beijing to get political training, thus becoming the first Naga to visit China, he was followed by Isak Chisi Swu and Moure Angami in 1968. China's help to the Mizos is also well documented. These were subsequently followed by help to outfits like the UNLF. ULFA was also in contact with China in the 1990s. However, Deng Xiaoping's 'good neighbor policy' stopped Chinese aid to these outfits, except for the flow of illegal Chinese arms through the black market via Cox Bazar near the Bangladesh-Myanmar border.

Interestingly, the 1961 Kachin insurgency's sophistication in jungle warfare (largely grown out of their World War II experience) skills spread rapidly.

Subsequently, the KIO became one of the most ardent trainers of groups like the NNC, NSCN, ULFA and MNF. Pakistan's hand is also well known in supporting these insurgencies. Bangladesh has also been accused by the Indian security agencies of harboring ULFA insurgents, though the former has always denied it. As recently as 12 April 2008, Bangladesh Rifles' Director General, Major General Shakil Ahmed, stated in a joint press conference with Border Security Force Director General K. Mitra that ULFA Commander-in-Chief Paresh Barua was 'no longer staying in Bangladesh.' This was of course an implicit admission that he had earlier been in Bangladesh territory; Indian intelligence, however, believed that Barua was still in Bangladesh territory. The BDR chief also denied the presence of any Indian insurgent camps in its territory.[37]

Conclusion

In conclusion, it must be stated that many political, social and security analysts have argued that the ULFA, UNLF, DHD and the NSCN (IM) only pretend to espouse people's causes. The ambitions of the people to improve their region's socio-economic condition, in conjunction with historical sub-national narratives, demanding acceptance of a unique identity and culture, have been used by rebel/insurgent leaders to justify their violent tactics of engagement.[38] Such arguments are valid and worth engaging with, but they fail to capture a distinct reality. These rebel/insurgent groups are rooted in local civil societies. Young cadres might be misguided, impoverished and illiterate, yet they are deeply aware of the rebel outfits' version of political and social history. These youths believe that the present conditions of poverty and tribal melancholy can be redressed by an independent status. The Indian state's failure to deal directly with these radical ideologies has only aggravated the situation.[39] Also, the cycle of armed conflicts in the North East, along with the military counter-response of the Indian state and other approaches such as negotiations, cease-fires, bribes to entice surrender, and the engineering of splits in insurgent groups, have resulted in the militarization of society and the region, perpetuating the insidious practice of the establishment of 'safe havens' by armed groups across the border in neighboring countries and human rights violations by both state forces and insurgents. Hence, what is perhaps the need of the hour is to bring about security in the life of the common man, by establishing the state's law enforcement agencies on a war footing. Also, the state must effectively monopolize the use of violence.[40] Otherwise, if the pattern of weak state structures continues, insurgent violence will be the order of the day, for the foreseeable future, in states like Assam, Manipur and Nagaland.

Notes

1 Y. Saikia, 'The Tai-Ahom connection', *Seminar*, online, available at www.india-seminar.com/2005/550/550%20yasmin%20saikia.htm (accessed on 11 April 2009).
2 S. Bhaumik, *Insurgencies in India's North East*, 2007.
3 J.W. Burton, *Global conflict*, 1986. Sanjoy Hazarika, a member of the first National

Security Advisory Board (1998–1999) and former member of the Committee to Review the Armed Forces Special Powers Act, says that 'in the north-east, one of the critical problems is that of governance. Basic needs are not met, basic services are not delivered, so naturally people get alienated.' See 'Seeking solutions in India's north-east', *OneWorld South Asia*, 10 December 2010. Similarly, Gogoi writes that New Delhi has initiated development programs in Assam and created a new ministry for the development of the North East. However, the government has not fully succeeded in its efforts, primarily because development funds do not reach the targeted population due to corruption and lack of vigilance. See D. Gogoi, 'Resurrection of a sunset dream', 2007.

4 The Mizo conflict was resolved with the grant of statehood in 1987, which fulfilled the basic needs of the insurgency for political power-sharing and cultural and social rights. For more details see N. Goswami, 'Building on the Naga peace process', 2008.

5 S. Baruah 'The state and separatist militancy in Assam', 1994.

6 S. Hussein, 'Exclusive interview, Pradip Gogoi, jailed ULFA vice chairman', *The Week News Magazine*, 20 July 2003, online, available at http//www.the-week.com/23jul20/events/9.html (accessed on 5 January 2007).

7 Interview with Pranob Nunisa, self-styled Commander in Chief and President of DHD, Haflong, 19 July 2007.

8 Data gathered by the author during field trip to Dhansiripar, Karbi Anglong, 11–13 February 2009.

9 Meiteis are the inhabitants of plains in and around Imphal Valley. They are the largest ethnic group in Manipur and are generally Hindu Vaishnavites in religious orientation.

10 Kanglei Yawol Kanna Lup (KYKL), meaning 'the organization to save the revolutionary movement in Manipur,' is a Meitei insurgent group formed in January 1994 following the merger of the Oken faction of the United National Liberation Front (UNLF), the Meiraba faction of the People's Revolutionary Party of Kangleipak (PREPAK) and the Ibo Pishak faction of the Kangleipak Communist Party (KCP).

11 See B. Sarangthem, 'United Liberation National Front (UNLF)', online, available at www.eastarmy.nic.in/combating-militancy/unlf-01.html (accessed on 23 March 2008). Also data compiled after conducting interviews with Manipuri researchers based in Delhi, February 2008. Names not mentioned in order to maintain secrecy of source.

12 See N. Goswami, 'The naga narrative of conflict', 2007.

13 See C.A. Hartzell, 'Structuring the peace', 2006.

14 See 'Chindits Special Force Burma 1942–44', online, available at www.chindits.info/ (accessed on 22 April 2008).

15 'Assam Timeline 2007', online, available at www.satp.org/satporgtp/countries/india/states/assam/timelines/index.html (accessed on 5 March 2007).

16 *The Sentinel* and *The Assam Tribune*, 16 January 2007.

17 '8 ULFA ultras arrested, Karbi Anglong bandh tomorrow', 17 November 2006, online, available at www.zeenews.com/znnew/articles.asp?rep=2&aid=336232&sid=REG (accessed on 11 December 2006).

18 Field visit by author to Nagaland, July–August 2007.

19 Field visit by author to Manipur-Myanmar border in August 2008. Also see UN Office on Drugs and Crime (UNODC) fact sheet, 'Opium Poppy Cultivation in South East Asia 2007', online, available at www.unodc.org/pdf/research/icmp/fact_sheet_SEA_2007.pdf (accessed on 11 January 2007).

20 UN Office on Drugs and Crime (UNODC), 'Drug use in the northeastern states of India', online, available at www.unodc.org/india/drug_use_in_ne.html (accessed on 15 February 2008).

21 See R. Bhattacharya, 'Assam's teenage guerrillas', online, available at http://times-now.tv/NewsDtls.aspx?NewsID=5960# (accessed on 18 February 2008).

22 See 'Dealing with ULFA's terror', online, available at www.idsa.in/publications/ stratcomments/InternalSecurityCluster220107.htm (accessed on 17 January 2006).

23 'Karbi Anglong massacre toll goes up to 14', *The Assam Tribune*, 13 August 2007, p. 1.

24 The Harkat-ul-Jihad-al Islami Bangladesh (HuJI-B), the Bangladesh chapter of HuJI, a radical Islamic outfit, was established in 1992, reportedly with assistance from Osama bin Laden's International Islamic Front (IIF).

25 See 'Phek admn, public cautions faction', *Nagaland Post*, 15 April 2008, online, available at www.nagalandpost.com/Statedesc.asp?sectionid=58545 (accessed on 16 April 2008).

26 See S. Bhaumik, 'Rebels kill six Indian soldiers', 2008.

27 See 'United National Liberation Front', online, available at www.satp.org/satporgtp/ countries/india/states/manipur/terrorist_outfits/unlf.htm (accessed on 13 March 2008).

28 See N. Thakuria, 'Counter-productive for Congress in NC Hills', online, available at www.indigenousherald.com/innerpages/commentaries9.html (accessed on 9 August 2007). Interview with Alan Jeme, Judge, NC Hills District Council, Haflong, Assam, 20 July 2007.

29 See S.G. Kashyap, 'Militant groups admits to killings accuses Congress of using them', *The Indian Express*, 6 June 2007, online, available at www.indianexpress.com/ story/32845.html (accessed on 7 June 2007).

30 See 'Nagalim', online, available at www.unpo.org/member_profile.php?id=41n (accessed on 21 February 2007).

31 S. Tucker, *Among insurgents*, 2000, pp. 82–85.

32 'No insurgent camps: Dhaka assures Delhi', *The Tribune*, 4 March 2007, online available at www.tribuneindia.com/2007/20070304/nation.htm#1 (accessed on 23 March 2007).

33 See S.K. Ghosh, *Pakistan's ISI*, 2000.

34 *The Assam Tribune*, 5 December 2006.

35 R. Egratau, *Instability at the gate*, 2006, p. 78.

36 See BBC documentary, 'Gladiators of World War II: Fighting units of World War II – The *Chindits*', Nugus/Martin Production, 1943.

37 V. Mohan, 'ULFA chief not in Bangladesh', 2008, p. 21.

38 S. Baruah, *Durable disorder*, 2005, pp. 99–106.

39 N.G. Mahanta, 'Accommodating the third voice in conflict zones', 2008.

40 It is interesting to note that that is precisely what the Indian authorities are doing. According to newspaper reports, in August 2010, security forces in Assam and Arunachal Pradesh launched a joint counter-insurgency operation to evict militants of the Isak-Muivah faction of the National Socialist Council of Nagaland (NSCN-IM) that were allegedly involved in raiding border villages, leading to a volatile situation in the region. See 'Operation against Naga rebels in Assam, Arunachal', *The Statesman* (Kolkata), 23 August 2010.

Bibliography

Baruah, S., 'The state and separatist militancy in Assam: Winning a battle and losing the war?', *Asian Survey*, 34:10, October 1994, pp. 863–897.

Baruah, S., *Durable disorder: Understanding the politics of northeast India*, Oxford: Oxford University Press, 2005.

Bhaumik, S., *Insurgencies in India's North East; Conflict, co-option and change*, Working Papers, Washington, DC: East West Center, 10 July 2007.

Bhaumik, S., 'Rebels kill six Indian soldiers', BBC News, 16 March 2008, online, available at http://news.bbc.co.uk/2/hi/south_asia/7299156.stm (accessed on 18 March 2008).

Burton, J.W., *Global conflict*, Brighton: Wheatsheaf Books Ltd., 1986.

Egratau, R., *Instability at the gate: India's troubled Northeast and its external connections*, New Delhi: Centre de Sciences Humaines, 2006.

Ghosh, S.K., *Pakistan's ISI: Network of terror in India*, New Delhi: APH Publishing House, 2000.

Gogoi, D., 'Resurrection of a sunset dream: ULFA and the role of the state' in J. Saikia (ed.), *Frontier in flames: North East India in Turmoil*, New Delhi: Penguin-Viking, 2007.

Goswami, N., 'The Naga narrative of conflict: Envisioning a resolution roadmap', *Strategic Analysis*, 31:2, March 2007, pp. 287–313.

Goswami, N., 'Building on the Naga peace process: Lessons from Mizoram', IDSA Fellow's Seminar, April 2008.

Hartzell, C.A., 'Structuring the peace: Negotiated settlements and the construction of conflict management institutions' in T.D. Mason and J.D. Meernik (eds), *Conflict prevention and peacebuilding in post-war societies*, London: Routledge, 2006, pp. 31–52.

Mahanta, N.G., 'Accommodating the third voice in conflict zones' in P.D. Das and N. Goswami, *India's North East: New vistas for peace*, New Delhi: Manas, 2008, pp. 95–107.

Mohan, V., 'ULFA chief not in Bangladesh: BDR', *Times of India*, 13 April 2008.

Tucker, S., *Among insurgents: Walking through Burma*, Delhi: Penguin, 2000.

Part III

The changing security agenda

11 Human security in South Asia and the role of the UN and its agencies

Sagarika Dutt

What is human security?

The concept of human security is people-centered and focuses on the security of the individual. It is 'a critical concept in so far as it raises questions about the focus and assumptions of realist security studies,'[1] especially its preoccupation with the state. The end of the cold war opened up space for new thinking in the field of international relations and development studies that influenced international agendas. Human security is associated with the post-cold war discourse about security and was first articulated in the 1994 UN Human Development Report.[2] The late Mahbub ul Haq made a major contribution to the development of this concept. In his own words, human security 'is a child who did not die, a disease that did not spread, an ethnic tension that did not explode in violence, a woman who was not raped, a poor person who did not starve'[3] and so on. It is not about (the possession of) weapons or about defense budgets, but about human well-being and dignity. Threats to human life and dignity range from war and conflict to hunger, disease and repression. In recent years terrorism and natural disasters have added to our concerns about our personal safety and well-being (although neither of them is a completely new phenomenon).

While human security is not synonymous with human rights, the violation of human rights does contribute to human insecurity. For example, where the rights of the child, as enshrined in international law – for example the Convention on the Rights of the Child – are violated, it leads to human insecurity for the children concerned. According to the International Labour Organization (ILO) there are millions of children around the world who are exposed to the worst forms of child labor such as work in hazardous environments, slavery or other forms of forced labor, illicit activities including drug trafficking and prostitution and involvement or participation in armed conflict. The ILO's standards on child labor are defined in the C182 Worst Forms of Child Labor Convention, 1999.[4] There is also a close relationship between human security and human development, and indeed economic development. Human development is measured by the Human Development Index (HDI), which has several aspects such as life expectancy at birth, adult literacy rate and income. Gender equality and female literacy rates also make a contribution to each country's HDI. While human security is about protecting individuals from threats in social, economic and political life as well as natural disasters, human development is about empowering people; 'together they can bring about a sustained improvement in human lives.'[5] Adding to the discourse, former UN Secretary-General Kofi Annan emphasizes that

> human security in its broadest sense embraces far more than the absence of violent conflict. It encompasses human rights, good governance, access to education and health care and ensuring that each individual has opportunities and choices to fulfil his or her own potential.

In the longer term it will reduce poverty, promote economic growth and prevent conflict. Nations need to realize that 'freedom from want, freedom from fear and the freedom of future generations to inherit a healthy natural environment' are the 'interrelated blocks of human and, therefore, national security.'[6] This chapter discusses some of the most important aspects of human (in)security in South Asia and argues that it is the duty of the state and the international community, represented by the United Nations and its agencies, to address them. This argument is supported by the recommendations of the International Commission on Intervention and State Sovereignty (ICISS).[7]

Development and security

While development has traditionally entailed the modernization of societies based on western models and (neo) liberal theories, security at both national and international levels has traditionally focused on the threat of external aggression, inter-state and more recently intra-state conflict and war (particularly post-World War II). However, critical development studies have addressed questions of global inequality and poverty.[8] According to critical Marxist literature on development, 'the underdevelopment of the south has gone hand in hand with the development of the north in a capitalist world economy.'[9] Andre Gunder Frank argues that the 'development of underdevelopment' occurs because the world capitalist system is characterized by a metropolis-satellite structure. The metropolis exploits the satellite, and as money is concentrated in the metropolis, the satellite is starved of potential investment funds and its growth is slowed down. 'At each point, the international, national and local capitalist system generates economic development for the few and underdevelopment for the many.'[10] Even political independence has not benefited former colonies in the developing world, as colonialism has been replaced by neo-colonialism. Dependency theorists have argued that political and economic relations between the North and the South 'reproduced a relationship of southern dependency and underdevelopment.' The South, in the main, remained a source of cheap labor and raw materials and 'the formal imperial relationship [was] replaced by less formal processes of exploitation.'[11] Also, integration with the global economy has only created a structure of core, periphery and semi-periphery states as posited by Wallerstein's

World Systems Theory. All these theories argue that the nature of North–South relations has been the cause of poverty in the South and may, therefore, be considered to be a form of structural violence. This in turn led to calls by the leaders of third-world states for a New International Economic Order (NIEO), to overcome their structural disadvantage.

However, Fierke argues that since the end of the cold war these critical discourses have been replaced by a neo-liberal agenda which promotes the free market. Meanwhile globalization has led to the production of a body of literature that has examined its impact, especially on developing countries.[12] 'In contrast to economic assumptions that globalisation is delivering economic growth for all, free market liberalisation since the 1980s had accelerated the gap between the rich and the poor' leading to 'a revolt from the margins.'[13] The power of international institutions has been highlighted by the issue of Structural Adjustment Programs imposed on third world countries that are in debt. Thus, 'liberal policies, imposed by international institutions have often had a detrimental effect on the populations of these societies, bringing greater hardship that has undermined the consolidation of democracy.'[14]

Scholars have argued that liberal discourses of development have focused on individual states and ignored the embeddedness of these states in historical relations that are global.[15] During the cold war, aid to developing countries suited the interests of the superpowers, but in the post-cold war era, the age of liberal triumphalism (à la Fukuyama), the emphasis was on the transformation of entire societies, also conceived as reconstruction of post-conflict societies along liberal lines. Besides, the large number of intra-state conflicts around the world led to the international community favoring humanitarian intervention. Both the theory and practice of humanitarian intervention have received adequate attention from the academic and scholarly community.[16] The acceptance of this concept gave both inter-governmental and international non-governmental organizations unprecedented access to regions of the world that had been far less accessible during the cold war, thus opening up borders. However, the developing world represented by the Non-aligned Movement refused to accept 'the right of humanitarian intervention,' demonstrating just how deeply divisive the issue was. In the end the UN's High-level Panel on Threats, Challenges and Change reaffirmed the importance of changing the terminology from the deeply divisive 'humanitarian intervention' to 'the responsibility to protect' if the international community was to forge a new consensus.[17] Critics also point out that where 'soft' intervention takes the form of foreign aid or international assistance the language of 'partnership and participation' is used, but there is no diffusion of real power. Furthermore, global security is often defined from a Western perspective and urges states to respond to the threat of global poverty travelling across international borders in the form of drugs, HIV/AIDS, climate change, illegal migration and terrorism.[18] Human security in the 21st century needs to be people-centered and not Western-centric. Nevertheless, state intervention is necessary in South Asia as there are demographic, social, economic and political structures in all the countries of South Asia, across the region, and indeed at the global level that are often the root causes of human insecurity in those countries. National efforts to address human security, therefore, need to address these structures. UN and World Bank funding is another way of channelling resources into development projects that they favor.[19] It is in this context that the issue of human security in South Asia is discussed in this chapter.

The state, the international community and human security

The state has a crucial role to play in promoting human security. This is under-lined by discourses on the state's responsibility towards its citizens, i.e., protect-ing its citizens (against all threats). Thus a distinction is made by the Human Development South Asia 2005 report (HDSA 2005) between human security and territorial security, which argues that 'without human security, territorial security becomes ineffective and ultimately, self-defeating.' But weak, failed and collapsed states may not be in a position to provide security to their citizens. Moreover, the state may be the cause of human insecurity. Reprimands by the international community may not produce any results, for example, the conflict in Darfur. Traditionally, inter-state conflict has been the cause of human insecu-rity; however, in the post-cold war world, intra-state conflict is a more common cause of human insecurity. Civilians are often the victims of conflict. This is illustrated well by the Rwandan genocide. It led to debates about the role of the international community, and 'shifting the terms of the debate away from the right to intervene towards the responsibility to protect.' Fierke writes that 'the latter rests on an interpretation of sovereignty that assumes the responsibility of a given state to protect its citizens. This perspective incorporates a concept of "human security" over more narrow definitions of national security.'[20] In 1999, a Canadian initiative put human security on the agenda of the Security Council in response to the 1994 genocide in Rwanda and the failure of the UN and the inter-national community to prevent it. By then the UN's peacekeeping operations worldwide had not only increased in number but had also become more complex (leading to second and third generation peacekeeping operations). The UN's function in any international crisis these days often has military, humanitarian, diplomatic, political, legal and economic dimensions. However, the UN cannot replace sovereign states, and the deployment of UN peacekeeping missions is not always the most effective way of dealing with conflict. The UN's calls for preventive diplomacy have often gone unheeded and need to be taken more seri-ously.[21] Moreover, the debate between communitarianism and cosmopolitanism indicates that the state cannot always be 'trusted' to protect its citizens and may need to be reminded about its responsibilities.[22] The UN Summit in 2005 emphasized that 'each individual state has the responsibility to protect its popu-lation from genocide, war crimes, ethnic cleansing and crimes against human-ity.' Unsuccessful attempts were made by countries like Egypt, Algeria, Pakistan, India, Russia, Cuba, Iran and Syria to block this agreement. It marked a turning-point for the UN, which had traditionally favored non-intervention in the internal affairs of member states.[23]

The responsibility of the state to provide security to its citizens may sometimes lead to a dilemma for the state, as illustrated by the conviction of Binayak Sen, human rights activist, for sedition because of his links with Maoists. He was sentenced to life imprisonment by a Chhattisgarh Court in India on 24 December 2010. Sen had spent much of his time trying to bring health care to people in impoverished tribal areas, and was awarded the Jonathan Mann award by the US-based Global Health Council. A group of 22 nobel laureates condemned his incarceration. The case of Binayak Sen has been compared with the case of jailed Chinese dissident Liu Xiaobo.[24] The state is tough on those who use violent methods to achieve their aims, as demonstrated by the Chhattisgarh Special Public Security Act and the Unlawful Activities (Prevention) Act. Waging a war against the state does not pay.[25] At the same time the underlying causes of the conflict need to be examined.

In improving human security in the developing world, states, international institutions (the United Nations, World Bank etc.), Western donors and International Non-Governmental Organizations (INGOs) all have a role to play. The UN's Millennium Development Goals (MDGs)[26] focus on some of the most pressing problems in the developing world and put pressure on governments to do something about them. UN agencies and INGOs have the potential to supplement the work of the state by providing funding and expertise for specific programs and projects and by providing humanitarian assistance during a crisis. Hampson and Penny argue that

> human security is now firmly entrenched in the language and policy of international affairs. That it is so is in no small measure due to the existence of the United Nations, which has played a key role in advancing and enforcing new international norms that place the individual – rather than the state – at the core of modern understandings of international security.[27]

Finally, as regards the responsibility of the international community to 'intervene' is concerned, Orford (cited in Fierke, p. 164) argues that it 'is already profoundly engaged in shaping the structure of political, social, economic and cultural life in many states, through the activities of, among others, international economic institutions.'

Human security in South Asia

The report on Human Development in South Asia 2005 produced by the Mahbub ul Haq Human Development Centre, Islamabad, focuses on the theme of human security. It points out that South Asia has a legacy of inter-state disputes, religious and ethnic divisions and resulting tensions, feudalism, militarization, and administrative, institutional and organizational structures inherited from the former colonial rulers. The conflict over the state of Jammu and Kashmir has not only resulted in the deaths, displacement and hardship of thousands of Kashmiris but has also cost India and Pakistan billions of dollars in terms of investments in armaments and related infrastructure, while slowing down the development of South Asian regional co-operation. The human costs of conflict are illustrated well by the Bangladesh war of independence (1971) and the civil war in Sri Lanka. All the conflicts in the region, including those in Afghanistan, have created large refugee populations whose protection has also become an important issue. The United Nations High Commissioner for Refugees (UNHCR) provides a legal framework for the protection of refugees (e.g., the 1951 Refugee Convention) and is also involved in providing humanitarian assistance to them. It is currently urging states to accede to the 1954 and 1961 statelessness conventions.[28] UNHCR's budget for Afghanistan and Pakistan in 2010 was US$104,751,062 and 176,687,665 respectively.[29] There are 1.7 million Afghan refugees currently living in Pakistan and over a million in Iran.[30] Since the end of the civil war in Sri Lanka in 2009, UNHCR has been involved in assisting thousands of internally displaced persons to return to their areas of origin. Its budget for Sri Lanka in 2010 was US$39,748,309.[31] The HDSA 2005 report makes a plea for de-militarization, arguing that 'increased militarisation threatens not only the internal stability of states but also regional security in South Asia.'[32] It also argues that there is a 'clear connection between material deprivation (poverty), issues of empowerment and identity formation;' inequality and lack of development breed discontent and can be a cause of political violence. Entire regions can become rebellious when they perceive themselves to be excluded from the process of development. This argument is broadly accepted by Indian ministers. During a visit to the Maoist-affected Gadchiroli district in December 2010 the home minister, P. Chidambaram, said that the Maoists can be contained with a combination of developmental activities and the deployment of security forces. The prime minister, Manmohan Singh, also referred to the spread of Naxalism in tribal areas, where the country's mineral wealth lies. He accepted that disaffection in these areas has been caused by social and economic factors and asserted that 'we have to handle this ... both as a law and order problem as also a development problem.'[33]

The HDSA 2005 report asserts that economic growth has created 'some oasis of affluence and security for a small group of people.' But the (human) deprivation of millions of people in the same region is creating social turmoil in many areas. Thus the issue of human security in South Asia needs to address the security of the masses in terms of their income, employment and livelihoods, food intake, health, education and the environment in which they live. However, the World Bank's regional brief for 2010 argues that there has been robust economic growth in South Asia, averaging 6 percent a year since 2000, and 'this strong growth has translated into declining poverty and impressive progress on human development.' The World Bank's strategy for South Asia rests on accelerating and sustaining growth, and economic growth is the key principle on which its assistance to South Asia is based.[34]

Economic security

Economic security is 'extremely important for ensuring human security.' South Asia has several striking characteristics in this regard: more than two-thirds of its population live below the international poverty line of two dollars a day,[35] it has high levels of income, wealth and asset inequality,[36] and extremely unequal access to and availability of quality healthcare, education and vocational training facilities. Needless to say it is the poorest people who are the most affected by economic insecurity. Furthermore, economic insecurity lies at the heart of many conflicts in the region. It also makes people more vulnerable and weakens their resilience when faced with other threats such as natural disasters, reducing their chances of survival in many cases. They simply cannot recover from a major crisis. For example, the worst floods in Pakistan's history occurred in 2010, affecting over 20 million people and submerging around 17 million acres of cropland. While millions of people are still homeless and need humanitarian assistance, experts feel that 'recovering from a natural disaster of this magnitude will take many years and billions of dollars.'[37] Moreover, in South Asia, the lack of social safety nets means that a person who loses his job or income, for whatever reason, cannot meet even his most basic needs. *Roti, kapra aur makan* or 'food, clothing and shelter' was the title of a film produced during India's socialist days. However, it is not just ideological; there are strong positive correlations between income levels and food intake, expenditure on health, education and other necessities. An uneven playing field is created in terms of opportunities for the poor, who are as a consequence denied the 'freedom to develop their potential,' an important aspect of human security.

A survey conducted by the authors of the HDSA 2005 report revealed that a high percentage of the respondents felt 'insecure in their employment,' while 35 percent of them feared that 'they would not be able to sustain even a subsistence standard of living without a job.' This fear is higher among the low-income earners, the less educated and the unskilled and self-employed. Research conducted by the present author in Kolkata, India in December 2010 revealed that the 'common man' (*aam aadmi*) looks to the government to help him to meet his basic needs, in terms of food and water, clothing, shelter, income and health care, and feels let down when that assistance is not forthcoming. People live on footpaths (pavements), do not have enough to eat or warm clothes to wear in the winter, and cannot afford medical treatment. In the rural areas they have to walk long distances to fetch water and often lose their land to the government.[38] Promises are made to them that factories will be opened on the land taken from them and that they will be given employment. But often this does not materialize and people have to fall back on casual work. Sometimes the industrial projects are abandoned and the land is returned to them, but it is no longer fit for agricultural use. Children from the poorest families often don't get an education, and some parents send children as young as five or six to work. Without a decent education there is no future for these children. There is a lot of human insecurity in ordinary people's lives.[39]

Finally, increasing integration with global markets as well as privatization has had an impact on the job security of the local labor force. The casualization of labor has been a cross-country phenomenon in South Asia. The low level of education and skill has prevented South Asian workers from benefiting from globalization. Also, World Trade Organization (WTO) processes and agreements have not led to any real gains for South Asia. The report of the Commission on Human Security (2003) argues that while the Bretton Woods institutions and the United Nations system set up after World War II 'have made major progress in strengthening market economies,' in the twenty-first century, 'corresponding energy must be devoted to cultivating "non-market" institutions to ensure human security within the market economy and to protect people during downturns and other crises.'[40]

Child labor

One of the consequences of economic insecurity and indeed poverty has been the use of child labor in both rural and urban areas. Although a distinction is often made between suitable and unsuitable types of work – an example of the former being light domestic work within the family, such as helping to prepare a family meal – the worst forms of child labor in South Asia include bonded labor, work in hazardous industries, child prostitution and child soldiers. Bonded labor is common India, Pakistan and Nepal, particularly among the lower castes, minorities and the poor. Some of them are born into bondage or become bonded labor to repay the loans of their parents. They are often used in agricultural work, brick kilns, the carpet industry, sports and textile industries, stone quarries and stone crushing, weaving, *bidi* rolling, plantations, and of course domestic work. According to the ILO there are over 200 million child laborers in the world, around half of whom are engaged in the worst forms of child labor.[41] The Convention on the Rights of the Child (1989) categorically states that 'states parties shall take all appropriate legislative, administrative, social and educational measures to protect the child from all forms of physical or mental violence, injury or abuse, neglect or negligent treatment, maltreatment or exploitation, including sexual abuse, while in the care of parent(s), legal guardian(s) or any other person who has the care of the child' (Art.19). In relation to child labor it states that 'States parties recognize the right of the child to be protected from economic exploitation and from performing any work that is likely to be hazardous or to interfere with the child's education, or to be harmful to the child's health or physical, mental, spiritual, moral or social development' (Art.32). The Convention defines a child as 'every human being below the age of eighteen years unless, under the law applicable to the child, majority is attained earlier.' States are also urged to provide for a minimum age or minimum ages for admission to employment; appropriate regulation of the hours and conditions of employment; and appropriate penalties or other sanctions to ensure the effective enforcement of the Convention. In both India and Pakistan the constitution prohibits the employment of children below the age of 14 in any factory, mine or any other hazardous occupation. Nepal too has laws prohibiting the employment of children under 14 and the employment of children between the ages of 14 and 18 in hazardous work. There are similar laws in Bangladesh and both Nepal and Bangladesh, have ratified ILO C138. However, there is laxity in the implementation of these laws, and the structural causes of child labor need to be addressed as well.

Health security

In the field of health, too, the poorest people are the most vulnerable. While overall life expectancy has improved and crude birth and death rates have come down, South Asia still has one of the highest infant and under-five mortality rates in the world. Also, HIV/AIDS emerged as a serious threat to South Asia a few years ago, with between two and 3.5 million people currently living with the disease in the region, according to the World Bank. The main factors responsible are sex work and injecting drug use, especially where these factors intersect. The government of India estimates that about 2.45 million Indians are living with HIV with an adult prevalence of 0.41 percent (2006). India's highly heterogeneous epidemic is largely concentrated in six states – in the industrialized south and west, and in the north-east. On average, HIV prevalence in those states is four to five times higher than in the other states. HIV prevalence is highest in the Mumbai–Karnataka corridor, the Nagpur area of Maharashtra, the Nammakkal district of Tamil Nadu, coastal Andhra Pradesh, and parts of Manipur and Nagaland. However, the epidemic appears to be stable or diminishing in some parts of the country. Other sources also acknowledge that India is an 'early achiever' on HIV prevalence, as regards its achievement of the Millennium Development Goals.[42]

Malaria has re-emerged as a result of it becoming resistant to conventional drugs, and so has tuberculosis. TB/HIV co-infection is a serious health threat to the poorest 20 percent of the population. Low levels of government expenditure on health have compounded the problem. Moreover, the focus has been on the curative rather than the preventive. The neglect of preventive and primary healthcare has resulted in the spread of several diseases that could be prevented by spending a smaller amount of money 'upstream' rather than 'downstream.' Another problem is that the health care system is inequitable and does not offer the same quality of service to all. Ironically, the most vulnerable sections of the population, the poor, rural populations especially in backward regions, the less educated, women and children, receive the poorest quality of service or none at all. Also, health care provided by the public sector is poor. On the other hand, private sector treatment is far too expensive for the poor and these days even for the middle classes. Hospitalization in some instances can cost as much as US$300 per day.[43] Private medical insurance may be the way forward but at present does not cover the entire middle class, let alone the poorest people in South Asian society.

However, it has always been the policy of the Indian government to keep the prices of essential drugs low. This is also a Millennium Development Goal.

While this benefits the poorest people in the country, as members of the WTO, India had to strengthen its patent laws in 2004. Seeking to allay fears that the new patent regime would result in an increase in drug prices, the Commerce and Industry minister, Mr. Kamal Nath, clarified that 97 percent of the drugs would be off patent, including some lifesaving and essential drugs. The Commission on Human Security notes that the WTO tried to strike a balance between the intellectual property rights of drug companies and the needs of developing countries. It concludes that a major objective will have to be 'to have intellectual property rights systems that advance human security through the efficient development of appropriate drugs and the facilitation of their extensive use.'

Food security

There is a close relationship between health security and food security because of the widespread prevalence of poverty in the region. More than 300 million people are undernourished, and although the average per capita availability of food improved in all the countries of South Asia between 1990 and 2002, severe inequality in land and income distribution prevents the poorest people from meeting their minimum daily nutritional requirements. Furthermore, the gender disparity in intra-household access to food exacerbates the food insecurity of women (and also girls and children). However, food insecurity in the region is mostly related to low access rather than low availability of food. The public food distribution system and other food distribution programs in South Asia have mostly been inefficient and poorly targeted. The growing population (even with reduced growth rates) and present demographic structures could lead to South Asia accounting for nearly half the developing world's under-five children suffering from malnutrition.[44]

Around one billion people go hungry every day, according to the World Food Programme (WFP). In recent years, high food prices have been another area of serious concern. The *New York Times* noted recently that 'world food prices continued to rise sharply in December [2010], bringing them close to the crisis levels that provoked shortages and riots in poor countries three years ago, according to newly released United Nations data.'[45] Economists recommended stockpiling key grains to prevent a serious crisis. In India annual food inflation stood at 14.44 percent in December 2010, 'on the back of skyrocketing prices of onions, fruits, vegetables, milk, eggs, meat and poultry.'[46] Food inflation had peaked in early 2010, touching 17.8 percent and making it necessary for the government to keep an eye on the situation. The finance minister admitted that the government was concerned about inflation and that it is one of the challenges facing the country.

Environmental security

While natural disasters such as the Gujarat earthquake (2001) which killed over 20,000 people, the Tsunami of 2004, the Pakistan earthquake (2005) which killed around 73,000 people and is the worst in the country's history, and finally, the Pakistan floods of 2010, have caused widespread devastation in certain parts of the region, environmental problems are not new in South Asia. To the extent that some of them are caused by human activity they can be linked to population growth, industrialization and even climate change. The authors of HDSA 2005 write that 'environmental degradation endangers the most fundamental aspect of human security by undermining the natural support systems on which all of human activity depends.'

In South Asia the size of the population, its rate of growth, and its density and distribution are important variables which impinge on environmental security. The total population for the region as a whole is between 1.4 and 1.5 billion. According to World Bank sources the population of each country is as follows: India: 1.123 billion; Pakistan: 162 million; Bangladesh: 159 million; Nepal: 28 million; Afghanistan: 22 million; Sri Lanka: 20 million; Bhutan: 0.66 million; and the Maldives: 0.3 million.[47] The population growth rate for the region is 1.5 percent. While India has a slightly lower growth rate of 1.4 percent, Pakistan, Afghanistan, Nepal and Bhutan have higher growth rates of 2.3 percent, 2.4 percent, 2 percent and 2.3 percent respectively. The urban population in all the countries constitutes less than 30 percent of the total population (but is gradually increasing). Bangladesh has the highest population density in the region (followed by the Maldives), and Bhutan has the lowest. The resource-to-population ratio is low and there is no new land to cultivate. In Pakistan the number of hectares per person declined from 0.45 in 1947 to 0.20 in 1982 due to population increases, and the agricultural sector's failure to keep up with population growth is reflected in shortfalls in food production.[48] Agricultural production in the region can be increased only by expanding irrigation facilities and using better quality seeds and fertilizers. However, India's much lauded 'green revolution' has not been repeated else where. In Nepal only about 20 percent of the total land area is arable, and this has led to mass migration to the Tarai region and to India. Population growth rates vary from state to state, and within each state from place to place. Family planning was introduced in India many years ago, and population control measures have produced some results. In South Asia fertility levels have fallen from 5.3 births per woman in 1980 to 3.2 births per woman in 2001.[49] However, fertility levels in some parts of the region are still considered to be too high, for example, in Nepal. Finally, land reforms have not always been successful in 'empowering' the landless or bringing about a redistribution of wealth.

In the rural areas where the bulk of South Asia's people live the main issues are land degradation, deforestation and loss in biodiversity, soil erosion and siltation, water scarcity, floods, droughts, and storms. Land degradation and (top) soil erosion in the region are largely a result of land use practices, high rates of deforestation, poor irrigation and drainage practices that lead to waterlogging, inadequate soil conservation, over-grazing, degradation of marine and coastal ecosystems, and salinity, mostly from the intrusion of sea water in low lying areas such as near the Bay of Bengal.[50] In Pakistan over 25 percent of the total irrigated area suffers from salinity. The demand for firewood and agricultural land, leading to forest clearing for cropping and grazing, has denuded South Asia's forests. Commercial and also illegal logging to satisfy burgeoning demands for timber has compounded the problem of deforestation. Social movements, such as the Chipko movement, have opposed unsustainable practices and commercial logging.

Floods are a threat to human security in some parts of South Asia, for example Bangladesh. The geographical location of Bangladesh is responsible for the severity of the floods that affect the country regularly. Several rivers flow through Bangladesh on their way to the Bay of Bengal, including the turbulent Brahmaputra. Severe flooding results when the peak flows in the Ganges, the Meghna and the Brahmaputra coincide. Flooding is exacerbated by the southwest monsoon winds that raise the mean tide levels in the Bay of Bengal.[51] The diversion of rivers can also cause flooding, as recently witnessed in Pakistan.

Flooding can cause a humanitarian crisis. In Pakistan, even six months after the floods of 2010 UNICEF was still responding to the urgent needs of flood affected people. It was providing clean water to an unprecedented 3.5 million people daily and sanitation facilities to more than 1.9 million people, according to UNICEF sources. The floods have revealed severe malnutrition among children in Sindh province, well above the WHO's 15 percent emergency threshold level, which triggers a humanitarian response. UNICEF's representative in Pakistan has said that UNICEF 'is extremely concerned about this finding and is working with the federal and provincial government authorities concerned to reach and treat these children.'[52]

On the other hand, the demand for water, especially in areas with insufficient rainfall, leads to excessive exploitation of groundwater resources, resulting in drought. This is particularly serious in Pakistan, where 60 percent of the land is semi-arid, and in western India, which is drought-prone. Water scarcity is a related issue. In India it is estimated that the per capita water availability declined from 6,000 cubic meters per annum in 1947 to about 1,898 cubic meters per annum in 1998 and is expected to decline further to 1,600 cubic meters by the year 2017.[53] Groundwater depletion has emerged as a major concern in India, Bangladesh and Sri Lanka, as it is estimated that as much as 70 to 80 percent of the agricultural production in some of these countries (e.g., India) depends on groundwater irrigation. The scarcity of water is accompanied by deterioration in water quality due to pollution and environmental degradation. Rapid and often unregulated industrialization and the dumping of hazardous industrial and toxic waste is one of the causes of water pollution. Untreated sewage and industrial effluents are a growing concern in the South Asian region. The rivers of South Asia, for example the Ganges, are some of the most polluted in the world, and the water is unfit for drinking and even bathing. Most of the waste-water of the developing world is discharged directly into streams, open drains, rivers, lakes and coastal waters without treatment. This results in water-borne diseases such as diarrhoea. Finally, serious arsenic contamination of groundwater resources has been detected in almost all the districts of Bangladesh. This can lead to skin ailments and cancers of the skin, lungs, urinary bladder and kidney, damage to internal organs and eventually death.[54]

Urban environmental problems

Urban environmental problems are often associated with poverty, but unplanned urbanization is equally responsible for the problems facing South Asian cities and towns today. Urban air pollution levels in the region are among the highest in the world and there is evidence that they have had an impact on human health, e.g., respiratory diseases. The main factors responsible are vehicle emissions, industrialization and use of thermal energy. The high urban population density is adding to the problem and also putting pressure on the provision of civic amenities. There is a scarcity of good quality and affordable housing, sanitation, clean and safe drinking water, and health services in most towns and cities. Poor solid-waste disposal also gives rise to an unhealthy environment and disease. Uncontrolled rural–urban migration and the 'natural' growth of urban populations is leading to the emergence of 'megacities' such as Mumbai and Kolkata that do not have the capacity to support their populations. According to a newspaper report published in late 2010 there are more than 5,000 small and big slums in Kolkata. For amelioration of the slums, the civic authorities have received funds from the UK-based Overseas Development Agency (ODA), the Asian Development Bank (ADB) and the World Bank. The slum improvement projects included setting up of toilets, construction of roads, installation of lamp-posts, and construction of children's playgrounds wherever space is available. The report notes that 'no steps have yet been taken to improve the living condition of the slum dwellers and the quality of life.'[55]

The Ministry of Housing and Urban Poverty Alleviation, Government of India, with the support of the United Nations Development Programme (UNDP), recently launched its first India–Urban Poverty Report (2009). It states that the country's urban population is increasing at a faster rate than its total population.[56] Although the pace of urbanization has been slower and lower than the average for Asia, the absolute number of people in urban cities and towns has gone up substantially. This has led to the urbanization of poverty. At the national level, rural poverty is higher than poverty in urban areas, but the gap between the two has decreased over the last couple of decades. GDP growth has not had an impact on urban poverty.[57] The slum population of India in cities and towns with a population of 50,000 or more was 42.6 million according to the 2001 census, which is 22.6 percent of the urban population of the states and union territories reporting slums. One of the MDGs is to 'achieve significant improvement in lives of at least 100 million slum dwellers by 2020.'[58] The most successful group of migrants is urban-to-urban migrants, who have better educational qualifications and skills. The report makes some recommendations including targeting vulnerable sections of the population and providing subsidized amenities to them, extending sewerage networks to slum areas, and use of solar, bio-gas and non-conventional energy for street lighting etc. But these are precisely the kind of policy recommendations that have been made umpteen times before.

Human rights, gender and human security

The close relationship between human rights and human security is illustrated well by the issues of discrimination and violence against women. The constitutions of most of the countries in the South Asian region recognize the rights of women enshrined in the Universal Declaration of Human Rights. The latter categorically states that 'all human beings are born free and equal in dignity and rights' (Art.1) and that 'everyone has the right to life, liberty and security of person' (Art.3). Building on the UN Charter that reaffirms faith in fundamental human rights and in 'the equal rights of men and women,' the Convention on the Elimination of Discrimination Against Women (CEDAW) recalls that

> discrimination against women violates the principles of equality of rights and respect for human dignity, is an obstacle to the participation of women on equal terms with men, in the political, social, economic and cultural life of their countries, hampers the growth of the prosperity of society and the family and makes more difficult the full development of the potentialities of women in the service of their countries and of humanity.

It commits states that have ratified or acceded to it 'to adopt appropriate legislative and other measures, including sanctions where appropriate, prohibiting all discrimination against women.' The document also states that the states parties to the convention are 'aware that a change in the traditional role of men as well as the role of women in society and in the family is needed to achieve full equality between men and women.' The issue of violence against women was also addressed by the Beijing women's conference (1995), and the Beijing Declaration reiterates that 'violence against women is an obstacle to the achievement of the objectives of equality, development and peace.'[59] Unfortunately, discrimination against women and girls is widespread in South Asia. It begins even before birth. The preference for a son can lead to female foeticide and female infanticide. In order to prevent foeticide, the sex of an unborn child is not revealed by the medical staff looking after a pregnant woman. UNICEF and other agencies are helping to immunize children (both male and female) against diseases such as polio and improve healthcare provision and nutritional levels.[60] The neglect of female infants and children leads to higher under-five mortality rates for girls, and partly explains why there are fewer women than men in South Asia

Women from the poorest sections of society do not have equal access to education and health care, and they do not have equal opportunity to participate fully in the economic and political life in their society. In some countries inheritance laws discriminate against women, making their economic position even weaker and leaving them open to exploitation. The combination of various factors such as patriarchal social structures, cultural norms, poverty, and lack of educational opportunities leads to the violation of women's rights and even violence against women. However, according to the UN Declaration on the elimination of violence against women (1993), some specific groups of women are more vulnerable than others. They include 'women belonging to minority groups, indigenous women, refugee women, migrant women, women living in rural or remote communities, destitute women, women in institutions or in detention, female children, women with disabilities, elderly women and women in situations of armed conflict.'[61] However, in South Asia domestic violence is the most common form of violence against women. The perpetrators of domestic violence are usually the husband and other male members of the family, but could include female members such as the mother-in-law. Among the countries of South Asia, the extent of domestic violence is the worst in Pakistan. Married women are, therefore, at higher risk than unmarried women. Another study notes that violence against women remains pervasive in Afghanistan. Over 87 percent of women are affected by domestic violence and 57 percent of girls are married before the age of 16; and 'there has been a documented rise in honour killings.'[62] Where domestic violence is culturally accepted and not recognized as a criminal offence by the state, it is difficult to bring about change. Furthermore, most of the time cases of domestic violence are not reported. Forms of domestic violence include dowry-related violence (including 'dowry deaths'), honor killings, and rape and sexual abuse. In India the state has adopted legislation to deal with the problem in the form of the Dowry Prohibition Act of 1961. According to a survey conducted in India in 2010, the recently notified Prevention of Domestic Violence Act, a landmark law safeguarding as well as providing legal counsel for women victims of domestic violence, has been well received and is helping to empower women.[63]

Another form of violence against women is the trafficking of girls and women.[64] According to HDSA 2005, every year 5,000 to 7,000 women and girls are trafficked for sex work from Nepal to brothels in India. Most of them are young rural girls as young as ten or 12. According to another report, the number of Nepali women and girls working in Indian brothels is above 70,000. The awareness-raising campaigns of women's rights activists and women's organizations have made a difference though. A study produced by CARE Nepal on the implementation of UN Security Council resolutions 1325 (adopted on 31 October 2000), on women and peace and security, and 1820 (adopted on 19 June 2008) on sexual violence against civilians in conflict zones, states that

> since 2006 the burgeoning Women's Movement has played a major role in successfully putting pressure on the [Government of Nepal] to amend discriminatory provisions relating to the ownership of property, the right of women to confer citizenship on their children, trafficking, marriage, sexual minorities, domestic violence, marital rape and abortion.[65]

Also, since the 2008 elections there is a record 33 percent representation of women in the Constituent Assembly. While the Maoist insurgency 'emancipated' some women within the Maoists ranks from the Hindu caste system and patriarchal structures in Nepalese society, it also led to many becoming widowed at an early age, making them prime targets for sexual exploitation. In a traditional and caste-dominated society, overcoming social exclusion needs to be a pillar of any poverty-reduction strategy. The CARE study found that in Nepal women, Dalits ('untouchables') and the 'tribal' indigenous ethnic groups, the Adivasi Janajatis or 'indigenous nationalities,' are confined to the margins of society. International pressure has been put on Nepal to bring about change. CARE, UNICEF, UNFPA, and UNIFEM, in collaboration with international aid agencies and many human rights and women's organizations, have lobbied for stronger measures to prevent and address gender-based violence and the high rate of trafficking. One of the problems noted by many researchers is the low level of awareness about women's rights and UN resolutions such as UNSC1325. In Nepal the main reason for this appears to be low levels of female literacy, especially in the Nepali language. In India too, many women are unaware of their constitutional rights, according to a survey carried out in the nation's capital by the Assocham Women's Development Foundation.[66] But apart from that women are often afraid of going to the police to report cases of rape or violence against them, sometimes because they fear being tried under customary law and accused of *zina* (sex outside marriage).[67] The HDSA2005 also notes that people in general are afraid of the police. The corruption of the law-enforcement agencies, police brutality, lack of representation, absence of the rule of law, and poor governance are all considered to be threats to human security in South Asia.[68] The issue of trafficking has been addressed at the regional level. All the countries in South Asia have signed the South Asian Association for Regional Co-operation (SAARC) Convention on preventing and combating trafficking in women and children for prostitution.[69]

Conclusion

The concept of human security has flourished under the UN umbrella. Both Mahbub ul Haq and Amartya Sen have made a major contribution to articulating the different aspects of human security and underlining its importance. The Commission on Human Security co-chaired by Sadako Ogata and Amartya Sen argues that 'the international community urgently needs a new paradigm of security.' The security debate has changed dramatically and focus has shifted from state security to the security of the people. However, as clarified by Frene Ginwala, human security does not replace the security of the state. The two aspects of security are mutually dependent. Security between states remains a necessary condition for the security of people, but national security is not sufficient to guarantee peoples' security. The state needs to protect its citizens against various kinds of threats, but they may sometimes require protection from the arbitrary power of the state, through the rule of law, the exercise of civil and political rights, and access to socio-economic opportunities.[70] This chapter has used a variety of sources, governmental, non-governmental and UN, to identify the main threats to human security in South Asia. It argues that the structural causes of human insecurity need to be addressed by the state, for example, controlling population growth, devising strategies for poverty reduction, generation of employment opportunities,[71] improving health care, promoting gender equality, and so on. The UN and its agencies, as well as INGOs, also have a role to play in two areas. The first area is that of standard-setting: for example, the Universal Declaration of Human Rights and conventions on the rights of children, discrimination against women, the protection of refugees and so on put pressure on states to protect their citizens and promote respect for their human rights. The second area is that of funding and helping states to achieve internationally agreed development goals, while at the same time encouraging them to come up with their own solutions to development challenges. For example, UNDP's programs in India cover critical areas such as poverty reduction, democratic governance, environment and energy, crisis prevention and recovery, and HIV and development. Its funding for its core programs was in the order of US$20,300,000 in 2009.[72] As a major donor agency, the World Bank spends a lot more in South Asia. In 2009 the Bank approved a total of 36 projects and IBRD/IDA loans worth more than US$5 billion, including US$272.6 million in grants. In recent years the World Bank has funded infrastructure projects in India such as the Rural Roads Project I and II, the Andhra Pradesh State Highways Project and the Powergrid-World Bank partnership. It has also funded human development and poverty alleviation projects such as the Pakistan Poverty Alleviation Fund and Rural Livelihoods projects.

Although this chapter was not about human development per se, nevertheless it is heartening to note that HDI rankings of South Asian countries have improved over the years. The UNDP's Human Development report for 2010 notes that the world's average HDI has increased 18 percent since 1990, reflecting large aggregate improvements in life expectancy, school enrolment, literacy and income. Only three countries in the world – the Democratic Republic of the Congo, Zambia and Zimbabwe – have a lower HDI today than in 1970.[73] There have been methodological innovations that have taken inequality within societies into account to produce an Inequality-adjusted Human Development Index, a Gender Inequality Index and a Multi-dimensional Poverty Index. The report also argues that while income and economic growth are vital for expanding people's freedoms, there is no significant correlation between economic growth and improvements in health and education, as innovations have allowed countries to improve health and education at very low cost.[74] Development thinking needs to be more flexible, and more thought needs to be given to designing suitable policies and strategies, as policies that work in certain contexts may not work in other contexts; there is always a danger of 'short-term success,' possibly due to dependence on aid or the desire to make political and electoral gains. The progress that has been made in the achievement of the MDGs needs to be sustained both globally and regionally, especially the reduction of poverty levels in different countries. In recent years, under the Delivering as One framework, several pilot countries have been exploring how UN agencies can best align efforts and support governments in achieving the MDGs and other internationally agreed development goals.[75] The focus on human security has taken development discourse to a new level. There is an urgency about it that compels states and organizations alike to respond to chronic threats such as hunger and disease as well as sudden acts of violence such as terrorism and natural disasters. In a region with a large population such as South Asia it has a lot of salience and requires a response that meets the aspirations of the people of the region. Finally, as MacFarlane and Khong write, 'in ethical terms, the security claims of other referents, including the state, draw whatever value they have from the claim that they address the needs and aspirations of the individuals who make them up.'[76]

Notes

1 K.M. Fierke, *Critical approaches to international security*, 2008, p. 149.
2 UNDP, *Human Development Report, 1994*. Chapter 2 of this report is entitled 'New dimensions of human security' and breaks human security down into the following categories: economic security, food security, health security, environmental security, personal security, community security and political security, but acknowledges that there can be other kinds of threats as well.
3 Mahbub ul Haq Human Development Centre, *Human development in South Asia 2005 – Human Security in South Asia*, 2006, p. 7.
4 The ILO website: www.ilo.org
5 Mahbub ul Haq Human Development Centre, *Human development*, p. 9.
6 Commission on Human Security, *Human Security Now*, New York, 2003, p. 4.
7 The recommendations of the ICISS were adopted by the UN General Assembly at the 2005 world summit. They stress that the 'responsibility to protect' resides first and foremost with the state whose people are directly affected. But a residual responsibility also lies with the broader community of states. See M. Barnett, 'Duties beyond borders', 2008, p. 200.
8 See, for example, M.A. Seligson and J.T. Passé-Smith (eds), *Development and Underdevelopment*, 2008.
9 Fierke, *Critical approaches*, p. 151.
10 A. Brewer, *Marxist theories of imperialism*, *Critical approaches*, 1986, pp. 161–62.
11 Fierke, *Critical approaches*, p. 151.
12 See for example R. Kiely and P. Marfleet (eds), *Globalisation and the third world*, 1998; R.M. Kelly, J.H. Bayes, M.E. Hawkesworth and B. Young (eds), *Gender, globalization and democratization*, Oxford: Rowman and Littlefield Publishers, 2001; L. Beneria, *Gender, development and globalization*, London: Routledge, 2003; S. Dutt, *India in a globalized world*, 2006; A. McGrew and N.K. Poku (eds), *Globalization, development and human security*, Cambridge: Polity, 2007; J.N. Pieterse, *Globalization and emerging societies: development and inequality*, Basingstoke: Macmillan, Palgrave 2009.
13 Fierke, *Critical approaches*, p. 152.
14 Ibid.
15 Fierke, *Critical approaches* and M. Duffield, *Global governance and the new wars*, 2001.
16 A. Schnabel and R. Thakur (eds), *Kosovo and the challenge of humanitarian intervention*, 2000; P. Alston and E. Macdonald (eds), *Human rights, intervention and the use of force*, Oxford: Oxford University Press, 2008; J.L. Holzgrafe and R.O. Keohane, *Human intervention: Ethical, legal and political dilemmas*, Cambridge: Cambridge University Press, 2003; T.G. Weiss and C. Collins, *Humanitarian challenges and intervention*, Oxford and Boulder: Westview Press, 2000.
17 R. Thakur, 'Humanitarian intervention', 2008, pp. 396–398.

18 UNDP, *Human Development Report, 1994*, p. 24.

19 See for example United Nations, *To unite our strength*, 2005. According to UNICEF sources in India, only 0.08 percent of India's gross national income is provided by donor agencies. Other South Asian countries get more donor assistance, but the issue is not just about money but adopting appropriate policies, devising strategies, and capacity building and utilization (interview with UNICEF in Kolkata on 1 September 2010).

20 Fierke, *Critical approaches*, p. 147.

21 The UN publication *An agenda for peace* stresses that 'the most desirable and efficient employment of diplomacy is to erase tensions before they result in conflict – or, if conflict breaks out, to act swiftly to contain it and resolve its underlying causes' (see Boutros Boutros-Ghali, *An agenda for peace*, New York: United Nations, 1992; also see B.G. Ramcharan, *Preventive diplomacy at the UN*, Bloomington: Indiana University Press, 2008).

22 M. Cochran, 'Cosmopolitanism and communitarianism in a post-cold war world', 1995.

23 In 2009 an attempt was made by a coalition of governments and skeptics at the UN to sabotage R2P despite Ban Ki-moon's presentation of the concept 'in the most cautious and reassuring of tones.' The skeptics included individuals on America's political right that were against the idea of costly pledges to wage wars in the name of protecting people in other countries. ('An idea whose time has come – and gone?', *The Economist*, 23 July 2009, online, available at www.economist.com/node/14087788/print)

24 'Binayak Sen convicted of sedition, given life sentence', *The Statesman* (Kolkata), 25 December 2010, p. 1; R. Puri, 'Will India win Nobel Prize?', *The Statesman* (Kolkata), 27 December 2010, p. 1.

25 'Cobra unit jawan killed in Maoist blast', *The Statesman* (Kolkata), 26 December 2010, p. 2; 'Maoists suffered losses in battle against forces', *The Stateman* (Kolkata), 13 December 2010, p. 5. The CPI (Maoist) politburo has apparently admitted that so far 10,000 revolutionaries have been killed by state forces.

26 The main MDGs are as follows: eradicate extreme poverty and hunger; achieve universal primary education; promote gender equality and empower women; reduce child mortality; improve maternal health; combat HIV/AIDS, malaria and other diseases; ensure environmental sustainability; develop a global partnership for development. The deadline for achieving these goals is 2015. Information available at www.un.orgmillenniumgoals/

27 F.O. Hampson and C.K. Penny, 'Human Security', 2008, p. 539.

28 Interview conducted with the UNHCR office in London, 17 November 2010. Also see A. Guterres 'Current trends in forced displacement and humanitarian action', 2010.

29 UNHCR, *Global Appeal 2010–2011*, 2010, p. 93.

30 UNHCR, *UNHCR and the European Union*, 2010.

31 UNHCR, *Global Appeal 2010–2011*, pp. 90–93.

32 Mahbub ul Haq Human Development Centre, *Human development*, p. 25; interview with the United Nations Military Observer Group for India and Pakistan (UNMOGIP), New Delhi, December 2007.

33 'Chidambaram claims drop in Naxal activity, lauds police role in Gadchiroli', online, available at www.dnaindia.com/print710.php?cid=1487356; 'PC visits Gadchiroli, reviews anti-Maoist operations', *The Statesman* (Kolkata), 29 December 2010; 'PM warns against twin dangers of Maoists, terrorism', *The Statesman* (Kolkata), 25 December 2010, p. 2.

34 World Bank, *South Asia Regional Brief 2010*, online, available at www.worldbank.org

35 However, the millennium development goal is to 'reduce by half the proportion of people living on less than a dollar a day.' Also, each country has its own national

poverty line, and according to UNDP sources the percentage of the population living below the national income poverty line is 27.5 for India and 22.59 for Pakistan. See UNDP website, available at www.undp.org, accessed on 22 February 2011.

36 However, according to the GINI index, inequalities of income in India are much less than in other countries.

37 Information available at www.criticalthreats.org/pakistan/floods. Contributions to Pakistan Flood Relief have been made by the US, Saudi Arabia, the UK, the EU Commission, private individuals and UN agencies, in that order.

38 Translated from Bengali, a carer's reflections on human security, notes written in December 2010.

39 It is interesting to note that Rahul Gandhi recently stated that the *aam aadmi*, defined as one 'who is not connected to the system' regardless of his economic status, religion, caste or education, 'builds his country everyday of his life and yet our system crushes him at every step ... we will never build a nation until we start recognising and respecting the common man.' See 'Rahul champions cause of *aam aadmi*', *The Statesman* (Kolkata), 20 December 2010, p. 2.

40 Commission on Human Security, *Human security now*, p. 78.

41 See ILO website for more information www.ilo.org

42 'HIV and AIDS in South Asia', World Bank website: www.worldbank.org; Raj Kumar, United Nations Economic and Social Commission for Asia and the Pacific (ESCAP), 'Progress of South Asia in MDG achievement compared to that of other regions: Key areas of concern', 4 November 2009, Kathmandu.

43 Research conducted in Kolkata, India in March 2007.

44 Mahbub ul Haq Human Development Centre, *Human development*, pp. 3 and 54.

45 'U.N. data notes sharp rise in world food prices', *New York Times*, 5 January 2011; also Channel Four News, UK, 3 February; 'World food prices reach new historic peak', Food and Agriculture Organization (FAO) website, available at www.fao.org, accessed on 4 February 2011.

46 R.C. Rajamani, 'Scams, food inflation take away from growth success', *The Statesman* (Kolkata), 1 January 2011; 'Tomato, garlic join price spiral – onions push inflation up', *The Statesman* (Kolkata), 24 December 2010.

47 World Bank website, available at www.worldbank.org, accessed on 22 February 2011. However, according to the 2007 World Population Data Sheet, the population (in millions) of each one of these countries in mid-2007 was as follows: Afghanistan: 31.9; Bangladesh: 149; Bhutan: 0.9; India: 1.1 billion; Maldives: 0.3; Nepal: 27.8; Pakistan: 169.3; Sri Lanka; 20.1. See Population Reference Bureau (USAID), *2007 World Population Data Sheet*, Washington, DC: Population Reference Bureau.

48 S. Hassan, *Environmental issues and security in South Asia*, Adelphi Papers 262, Autumn 1991, p. 9.

49 World Bank, *Mini atlas of global development*, 2004.

50 See G. Vasudeva, 'Environmental security.'

51 Hassan, *Environmental issues*, p. 18.

52 UNICEF, 'Pakistan floods uncover dire nutrition situation', available at www.unicef.org/media/media_57556.html?q=printme; Interview with David Bull, UNICEF, 29 January 2011, BBC News.

53 Vasudeva, Environmental security.

54 Mahbub ul Haq Human Development Centre, *Human development*, p. 94.

55 'Welcome to the city of slums: 5,000 and counting', Kolkata Plus, *The Statesman* (Kolkata), 30 December 2010. The present author finds these comments disappointing as she has conducted research on Kolkata from time to time and is aware of the efforts that have gone into projects such as CEMSAP; see S. Dutt, 'Megacities of joy', 2000.

56 The UNFPA notes that the population of the world is approaching 7 billion (up from 2.5 billion in 1950), with almost all the growth expected to occur in the cities of the

less developed countries, with profound implications for the development process. See UNFPA website: www.unfpa.org/public/home/about
57 See India: Urban Poverty Report 2009 – Factsheet, available at http://data.undp.org.in/poverty-reduction/Factsheet
58 See www.un.org/millenniumgoals/, accessed on 21 October 2003.
59 *The Beijing declaration* and *The platform for action*, Fourth World Conference on Women, Beijing, China, September 1995, New York: United Nations Department of Public Information, 1996, p. 73.
60 See for example UNICEF, *Country programme action plan 2008–2012*, 2008.
61 See UN General Assembly resolution A/RES/48/104, 20 December 1993. The resolution welcomes the role that women's movements are playing in drawing increasing attention to the nature, severity and magnitude of the problem of violence against women.
62 Gender Action for Peace and Security (GAPS), UK, *Global Monitoring Checklist*, 2010. This report provides a summary of the progress made to date on global implementation of UNSCR1325.
63 '70 per cent women ignorant of their legal rights: Study', *The Statesman* (Kolkata), 26 December 2010.
64 Mahbub ul Haq Human Development Centre, *Human development*, p. 123; UNFPA and AFPPD, *Violence against women in South Asia*, 2004.
65 L. Abdela, *Case Study – Nepal*, 2010, pp. 5–6.
66 '70 per cent women ignorant of their legal rights: Study', *The Statesman* (Kolkata), 26 December 2010.
67 GAPS, UK, *Global monitoring checklist*, p. 32.
68 In December 2010 at the Congress plenary in New Delhi, Sonia Gandhi said that 'both as a party and as a government we must confront corruption head-on' and that a new system of fast-tracking all cases that concern corruption by public servants including politicians, in a defined timeframe, was needed: *The Statesman* (Kolkata), 20 December 2010, p. 1. According to newspaper reports, Transparency International India has written to the prime minister demanding strengthening of the criminal justice system that includes police reforms and the enactment of the judicial accountability act, among other measures for tackling corruption; see 'Transparency International India writes to Singh – PM urged to tackle corruption head on', *The Statesman* (Kolkata), 2 January 2011.
69 UNFPA and AFPPD, *Violence against women*, p. 19.
70 Commission on Human Security, *Human security now*, pp. 2–3.
71 The Human Development Report 2010 flags up India's National Rural Employment Guarantee Act 2005. It commits the government to providing 100 days of employment to rural households on local public works at minimum wage. Laborers who are not given work are entitled to unemployment benefit. See UNDP, *Human Development Report 2010*, p. 106.
72 See UNDP's website, available at www.undp.org/; UNDP, *UNDP in India*, 2007.
73 UNDP, *Human Development Report 2010*, p. 3.
74 Ibid., pp. 1–5.
75 UNICEF, *Annual Report 2009*.
76 S.N. MacFarlane and Y-F. Khong, *Human Security and the UN*, 2006, p. 2.

Bibliography

Abdela, L., *Case study – Nepal, United Nations Security Council Resolution 1325 – Women's meaningful participation in peacebuilding and governance*, Vienna and Kathmandu: CARE International, 2010.
Barnett, M., 'Duties beyond borders' in S. Smith, A. Hadfield and T. Dunne (eds),

Foreign Policy – Theories – Actors – Cases, Oxford: Oxford University Press, 2008, pp. 190–203.

Brewer, A., *Marxist theories of imperialism: A critical survey*, London and New York: Routledge and Kegan Paul, 1986.

Cochran, M., 'Cosmopolitanism and communitarianism in a post-cold war world' in J. Macmillan and A. Linklater (eds), *Boundaries in question*, London and New York: Pinter, 1995.

Commission on Human Security, *Human security now*, New York, 2003.

Duffield, M., *Global governance and the new wars: The merging of development and security*, London: Zed Books, 2001.

Dutt, S., 'Megacities of joy: The environmental problems of Calcutta in the age of globalization', *Australian Journal of International Affairs*, 54:3, 2000.

Dutt, S., *India in a globalized world*, Manchester: Manchester University Press, 2006.

Fierke, K.M., *Critical approaches to international security*, Cambridge: Polity Press, 2008.

Gender Action for Peace and Security (GAPS), UK, *Global monitoring checklist on women, peace and security*, 2010.

Government of India, *Economic Survey 2009–10*, New Delhi: Oxford University Press, 2010.

Guterres, A., 'Current trends in forced displacement and humanitarian action: Challenges and opportunities confronting UNHCR', lecture delivered on 13 October 2010 at Refugee Studies Centre, University of Oxford.

Hampson, F.O. and C.K. Penny, 'Human security' in T.G. Weiss and S. Daws (eds), *The Oxford handbook on the United Nations*, Oxford: Oxford University Press, 2008.

Hassan, S., *Environmental issues and security in South Asia*, Adelphi Papers 262, Autumn 1991.

Kiely, R. and P. Marfleet (eds), *Globalisation and the third world*, London and New York: Routledge, 1998.

MacFarlane, S.N. and Y.-F. Khong, *Human security and the UN: A critical history*, Bloomington: Indiana University Press, 2006.

Mahbub ul Haq Human Development Centre, *Human development in South Asia 2005 – Human security in South Asia*, Oxford: Oxford University Press, 2006.

Orford, A., *Reading humanitarian intervention: Human rights and the use of force in international relations*, Cambridge: Cambridge University Press, 2003.

Schnabel, A. and R. Thakur (eds), *Kosovo and the challenge of humanitarian intervention*, Tokyo, New York, Paris: United Nations University Press, 2000.

Seligson, M.A. and J.T. Passé-Smith (eds), *Development and underdevelopment: The political economy of global inequality*, Boulder: Lynne Rienner, 2008.

Sen, A., *Development as freedom*, New Delhi: Oxford University Press, 2000.

Thakur, R., 'Humanitarian intervention' in T.G. Weiss and S. Daws (eds), *The Oxford handbook on the United Nations*, Oxford: Oxford University Press, 2008.

UNDP, *Human Development Report, 1994*, New York and Oxford: Oxford University Press, 1994.

UNDP, *UNDP in India*, New Delhi: UNDP, July 2007.

UNDP, *Human Development Report, 2010, The real wealth of nations: Pathways to human development*, New York: UNDP, 2010.

UNFPA and AFPPD, *Violence against women in South Asia: A regional analysis*, 2004.

UNHCR, *Global Appeal 2010–2011: Real people, real needs*, Geneva: UNHCR, 2010.

UNHCR, *Trees only move in the wind: A study of unaccompanied Afghan children in Europe*, UNHCR: Geneva, 2010.

UNHCR, *UNHCR and the European Union*, Brussels: UNHCR, 2010.

UNHCR, *With You: News of the all-round help that together we're bringing to refugees*, Autumn 2010.

UNICEF, *Country programme action plan 2008–2012, Government of India and the United Nations Children's Fund*, New Delhi: UNICEF, July 2008.

UNICEF, *The state of the world's children* (special edition), New York: UNICEF, 2009.

UNICEF, *Annual Report 2009*, New York: UNICEF, June 2010.

United Nations, *Platform for action* and *The Beijing declaration*, New York: United Nations Department of Public Information, 1996.

United Nations, *To unite our strength: 60 ways, six decades of the United Nations in India 1945–2005*, New Delhi: United Nations.

Vasudeva, G., 'Environmental security: A South Asian perspective', Arlington: TATA Energy and Resources Institute, no date.

World Bank, *Mini atlas of global development*, Washington, DC: World Bank, 2004.

World Bank, *World Bank annual report 2007*, Washington, DC: World Bank, 2007.

World Bank, *The World Bank in India 2007, India country overview*, New Delhi: World Bank, 2007.

World Bank, 'Newly built roads open up opportunities in rural India', *The World Bank in India*, 6:4, January 2008.

World Bank 'A partnership beyond expectations: The story of powergrid', *The World Bank in India*, 6:6, May 2008.

World Bank, *Andhra Pradesh state highway project*, New Delhi: World Bank, no date.

World Bank, *The World Bank group, working for a world free of poverty*, Washington, DC: World Bank, no date.

12 The impact of climate change in South Asia

Alok Bansal and Sreeradha Datta

The threat of climate change has been one of the primary concerns of the global community, ever since its disastrous impacts were brought to the notice of the public at large. The growing public concerns over the issue have clearly divided the international community and the cleavages between the developed and developing world have grown deeper in the last two decades. Statistics have pointed out that the developed nations were responsible for over 70 percent of the carbon emissions to date, although they were home to less than one-fifth of the world's population.[1] However, having caused the problem, the developed world expected the less developed states to sacrifice their growth to mitigate the ill effects of their actions. Clearly the principal producers of global emissions expected others to pay for sustaining the developed world's life style. At the 1992 Rio Earth Summit, the contrasting positions were clearly defined by both sides. The developed industrialized states refused to comply with the emissions cuts expected from them unless those nations that had just embarked on economic growth did the same. Similarly the smaller nations refused to adopt voluntary curbs that would affect their industrial growth, especially when the developed states had refused to implement the greater cuts and were not even willing to compensate the other group of nations for their efforts. The developed nations also wanted fast-growing economies like that of India and China to be subject to international scrutiny to ensure their commitments to carbon emission cuts. These cleavages became apparent during the negotiation of the Kyoto Protocol (KP) and subsequent developments. The United Nations eventually passed the Kyoto Protocol in 1997 asking for specific emission cuts by 2012. It recognized the principle that the industrialized developed countries need to make the maximum reductions. Although by 2009 the protocol had been signed by 187 countries, the US and Australia have refused to sign the protocol and consequently made the whole process ineffective.[2]

It has become increasingly clear in the last few years that targets for emission cuts have directly impacted 'existing power structures' both at the national and the international level. Indeed, attempts to steer the world towards a low-carbon economic development trajectory have thrown up challenges to the structures of power in the world economy – the production, knowledge, finance and security power structures.[3] Ironically, while less developed nations have lower levels of greenhouse emission they are more vulnerable to climate change. For instance, India's greenhouse emission is 15 percent lower than that of the USA; its per capita emission of 1.1 tonnes is significantly lower than the US per capita of 20 tonnes and an average of about 10 tonnes for several developed countries.[4] South Asia is comprised entirely of developing countries, which are at different stages of economic development. The per capita emission of South Asian countries is quite low as compared to the developed countries, but the adverse impact of climate change is likely to be much more disastrous for the region than for most other parts of the globe.

South Asia is a water-starved region. In fact more than 90 percent of the rain-water that South Asia receives is consumed. India, which has 16.8 percent of the global population, has only 4 percent of global freshwater reserves.[5] While, on the one hand, the region's capacity to support large populations is affected by the shortage of fresh water, on the other hand, rising sea levels due to global warming affect the very existence of some states within the region. Two of the countries most likely to be affected by global warming are in South Asia. According to reports sourced by the present authors, most of the islands in the Maldives will be either inundated or rendered unsuitable for habitation within a few years,[6] while the bulk of Bangladesh would probably be swept by tidal waves. Similarly the Himalayan glaciers are melting and retreating, and most of the new dams that are coming up on the Indus basin and the Ganges basin are actually banking on the glacial melting. However, this glacial melting is not going to continue indefinitely, and there may be no glaciers in a few decades. Irregular rain patterns and consequent overexploitation of ground waters have resulted in growing salinity in deltaic regions, especially in the Indus Delta. On the other hand the region has been afflicted by floods: in 2010 massive floods in Pakistan rendered millions homeless.

This chapter deals with the impact of climate change on the South Asian region and how the countries of the region, individually as well as collectively, are dealing with it. The first section of this chapter gives a broad overview of the issue of climate change and how it is impacting the South Asian region and their national action plans. The final section will review the progress of the South Asian states in dealing with the problem from a common platform, namely the South Asian Association for Regional Co-operation (SAARC); it will explore whether the states are moving towards a regional initiative to combat and adapt to climate change.

The problem of climate change in the South Asian context

The problem of climate change does not affect all the states in similar ways or in a linear fashion. In fact some states will face the adverse effects of climate change much more than others. The patterns of the last few years show that the states with the lowest carbon footprints are those which have faced the worst brunt of environmental degradation. South Asia, Africa and South East Asia are among the most vulnerable regions of the world, which will face the brunt of climate change.[7] Climate change is likely to increase global inequity, as some countries and areas within countries are able to adapt better while others have limited or no capacities to do so. Despite the criticality of the problem of climate change the states have yet to formulate clear short- and long-term policies to deal with disaster-like situations brought on by climate, energy, food and water crises.[8]

All problems relating to climate change affect the South Asian states. South Asia comprises 3.3 percent of the global landmass but is host to one-fifth of the world's population. It is among the most densely populated regions of the world and two of its countries face the prospect of extinction by rising sea levels on account of global warming.[9] It is one of the poorest regions in the world and has extremely low per capita energy consumption. Even the Maldives, which has the highest per capita consumption within the region, consumes less than half the world's average per capita consumption of energy. As a result, its direct contribution to climate change and environmental degradation is relatively small as compared to other regions. However, a variety of factors, including the melting of the Himalayan glaciers, rising sea levels, increased flooding, and tropical storms, as well as the impacts of population growth and pollution levels, have put additional pressures on natural resources and pose a serious challenge to the ecological, environmental and consequentially social landscape of all the states within South Asia. With the region's population poised to rise by another 800 million people by 2050, several of these problems will be compounded with the passage of time.

According to the fourth report of the Intergovernmental Panel on Climate Change published in 2007, climate change would pose the following challenges to South Asia:

- Melting of glaciers in the Himalayas would increase flooding, and this in turn would affect long-term water resources and their availability in South Asia.
- Climate change would compound pressures on natural resources and the environment, owing to rapid urbanization, industrialization and economic development.
- Crop yields in South Asia are likely to decrease up to 30 percent by the middle of the twenty-first century.
- Periodic floods and droughts would impact the health of the population.
- Rising sea levels would exacerbate inundation, storm surges, soil erosion and other coastal hazards.

Climate change could lead to epidemics and a wide range of other health-related problems with serious socio-economic consequences. The increased pressure on land due to large-scale inundation of islands and low-lying deltas could lead to massive migration of populations, both within the state and outside, leading to possible conflicts.[10]

Effects on South Asian natural resources

South Asian states are largely agrarian and heavily dependent on water. They also share common water resources and have similar water usage patterns, but over the years there has been a noticeable depletion of fresh water supply. Nearly 70 percent of the Himalayan glaciers are receding, which will eventually lead to severe water shortages in the region. Environmental changes have caused the river basins to dry and groundwater supply has decreased in several parts of South Asia.[11] This has been a major source of concern for many of the governments which have in the past years been confronted with this problem. National water policies have been formulated by some of the states like Bangladesh, Bhutan, and India. But intra- as well inter-state disputes along with multiple stakeholders within the domestic domain have led to poor implementations of the policies. Indeed, turf battles within states have not led to optimum utilization of these policies.[12] Lack of implementation of water policies directly impacts on agricultural output. Water scarcity adversely affects food supplies. Food scarcity has led to large-scale migrations. A growing population enhanced by migration puts additional pressure on already shrinking food grain production. The corresponding poverty in turn impedes effective methods of managing climate change. Poor societies are less equipped to handle climate change and environmental degradation.

Glaciers are an important storage place for fresh water. They accumulate mass during the monsoon and winter seasons at higher altitudes, and provide water at lower elevations during off seasons. The Himalayan region in Nepal has 3,252 glaciers covering 5,323 sq km, with an estimated ice reserve of 481 sq km. The International Centre for Integrated Mountain Development reports that some of these glaciers were found to have retreated by 30 to 60 meters. Tradekarding glacier has retreated over the last decade by 100 meters.[13] The rapid melting of glaciers would, through floods and various other ill effects, dramatically impact Nepalese biodiversity, the lives of people and their livelihoods, besides affecting the supply of fresh water. The retreating glaciers would also directly affect the entire sub-Himalayan region, especially the lower riparian states of Bangladesh, Bhutan, India and Pakistan, causing floods, drought, and shortage of fresh water.

Bhutan

According to a Chinese scientific survey undertaken in 2007, the Himalayan glaciers are receding faster than any other glaciers, and by 2050 the glacial cover could be reduced by a third, if the present rate of global warming continues. The glacial cover is expected to halve by 2090.[14] Mount Everest itself is retreating and glaciers are melting, leading to the creation of swelling lakes that could one day burst and cause massive flooding. Problems associated with this phenomenon affect several South Asian states, but Nepal and Bhutan, nestled in the foothills, will be affected most. The increased temperature has already led to a reduction in glacial cover in Bhutan. Receding glaciers have led to the formation of supraglacial lakes. Breaches in these lakes would result in frequent inundation and landslides in the valleys, where the population is generally concentrated. In coming decades the country will become increasingly prone to floods, cyclones, landslides and drought.[15] Furthermore, Bhutan's rivers are the backbone of the economy, with exports of hydropower-generated electricity accounting for more than 40 percent of national revenue, while 70 percent of the population lives in rural areas and depends heavily on irrigated agriculture. Climate change threatens to have a serious impact on river flows. The changing patterns of rain and snowfall, flash floods exacerbated by melting glaciers, and acute droughts in the dry season have all influenced the river flows.[16]

According to a World Bank (WB) report released in conjunction with the UN's Climate Change Conference in Copenhagen, Bhutan will see an increase in winter temperature of 1.5°C to 4.0°C by the 2050s. The report, entitled, 'Shared views on development and climate change,' states that there are no long-term climate data available on Bhutan, but available data during the 1990–2002 period point to an increase in rainfall inconsistency across the country. According to meteorology data, the average temperature in the Himalayan kingdom has increased by two degrees centigrade during the past five years. This has resulted in the late arrival of monsoons, adversely affecting paddy production. The records maintained by the Hydro-met Services Division indicate distinct and unprecedented changes in the pattern of rainfall. Besides agriculture, such rapid shifts affect the working of hydropower plants. Hydropower is a major export commodity of Bhutan.[17]

Bhutan, although one of the lowest emitters of greenhouse gases, is ironically exposed to higher risks of climate change. Indeed, the rapidly melting glaciers in the higher Himalayas have been likened to a 'silent tsunami in the Himalayas' and could lead to drying up of Bhutan's water sources. This could bring down crop production and also affect hydropower potential in the long run. The *Bhutan Environmental Outlook* for 2008 warns that the Himalayan glaciers have been retreating by 20 to 30 meters a year. Such rapid shrinking would not only cause widespread flooding but also Glacial Lake Outburst Flooding (GLOF). Bhutan has witnessed such GLOFs in 1957, 1960, 1968 and 1994 – that of 1994 being the worst – causing enormous loss of lives and property in the lower valleys of the country.[18]

The Asian Development Bank and Japan are both supporting projects in Bhutan to counter the harmful impacts of climate change on its rivers. The Japan Special Fund, financed by the Government of Japan and administered by ADB, is providing a $700,000 grant for building up the capacity of Bhutan's National Environment Commission. This organization is the nodal agency and designated national authority for climate change issues. It handles projects that are eligible to avail of carbon credits under the Kyoto Protocol. However, it has been hampered in its functioning because of a lack of experts and other capacity for developing mitigation and adaptation measures that can counter climate change. Bhutan has, however, committed to absorbing more carbon than it emits and to maintaining Bhutan's status as a net sink for greenhouse gases.[19]

Nepal

Nepal is one of the world's poorest nations, with 31 percent of its 28 million population living below the national poverty line. However, the population is overwhelmingly rural, with only 12 percent based in urban locations, thus resulting in a rural density of nearly 700 people per square kilometer. Nepal has one of the lowest emissions records in the world – just 0.025 percent of total global greenhouse gas emissions. Despite its low contribution to climate change, Nepal and its poor population suffer disproportionately higher impacts of climate change.[20] Large-scale glacial melting has resulted in frequent GLOFs causing large-scale destruction of arable land and property. Besides the GLOFs and the variability of river runoff (both of which pose severe challenges not only to hydropower, but also to rural livelihoods and agriculture), increasingly erratic patterns of rainfall are having devastating effects on Nepal's agrarian economy. Crop yields have lessened over the years. The loss of the Namche hydropower plant in 1985 revealed the high risks involved in the construction of such hydropower projects.[21]

In addition to the problems of GLOF and erratic monsoons, many of Nepal's rivers, which feed the irrigation systems, power grain mills and electricity plants, and supply drinking water for villages, are running dry. If prominent rivers like the Kosi, Gandak, and Karnali run dry, it would reduce the electricity generated by existing plants. This runoff decrease will also affect Nepal's economically feasible hydropower potential. The criticality of the situation led the Nepalese government to hold a cabinet meeting near Everest Base Camp at a height of 17,000 feet. The cabinet meeting, where some ministers were wearing oxygen masks, passed a resolution on climate change to highlight the danger global warming poses to the mountains and glaciers.[22]

Nepal has a few projects on the anvil but needs several more to address the problem more comprehensively. To buttress its efforts, Nepal also set up a 23-member climate-change network comprising a vast array of expertise involving experts from all walks of life. Nepal meanwhile also adopted the Adaptation Programme of Action in 2007. The idea of micro and small hydro projects is being examined. Also, Nepal has one of the most successful programs to derive fuel gas from cow dung. Electric vehicles using hydropower are another clean energy option that Nepal has chosen. Kathmandu has approximately 600 zero-emission electric vehicles, with the potential for a lot more.[23]

Other than these two Himalayan nations, the coastal South Asian states have their share of woes arising out of risks due to sea level rise and greater intensity and frequency of storms. Coastal countries such as Bangladesh, Maldives and Sri Lanka are exposed to problems of rising sea levels. The growing coastal populations in all these states, more specifically Bangladesh, are threatened with a rising tide of environmental refugees either permanently or seasonally as millions more are displaced due to an increased intensity and frequency of storms. Coastal states are facing increased erosion and loss of coastal protection from natural ecosystems such as coral reefs and wetlands.

Maldives

The Maldives is a group of over 1,000 scattered low-lying islands, which is extremely vulnerable to climate change and its associated impacts, especially the predicted rise of sea levels due to global warming. Ninety percent of the territory of this archipelagic nation of 90,000 sq km is under water. Only 202 islands are inhabited, while 87 others have been developed as exclusive tourist resorts. Although the Maldives contributes minimally to global greenhouse gas emissions, it faces an existential threat due to a deteriorating environment. The island nation lives under the continuous threat of environmental catastrophe and fears being engulfed by the rising waters of the Indian Ocean. Maldives, being coral islands, is surrounded by reefs and lagoons, and any threat to either of them poses a grave threat to the islands. On average, the islands are just two to three meters above the mean sea level. A two-meter rise in sea level would submerge virtually all the coral islands, scattered across 850 km from the Equator, and force their 360,000 citizens to evacuate. Consequently, a number of environmental issues impact on the very survival of the island nation.[24]

Reefs and corals are extremely vulnerable and can be destroyed by increasing pollution, which in turn makes the islands unstable. There have been occasions in the past when parts of some of the islands in the Maldives collapsed, posing a grave danger to the population residing there. In many cases, coral reefs have been dredged for construction activities. Extreme pressure on land has accentuated this problem. Large-scale construction and reclamation have taken their toll on the reefs and lagoons and have led to unusually high tidal waves. In 1987, a large wave caused widespread damage and destruction in the capital Male, including washing away large tracts of reclaimed land.[25]

The extent of the devastation that can be caused by huge tidal waves can be gauged from the tsunami that hit Maldives and parts of South and South East Asia in December 2004. One-third of the total population was severely affected. Around 53 of the 199 inhabited islands suffered severe damage. It is estimated that 20 islands were completely destroyed and 14 islands were evacuated. About 11,500 people were displaced. Over one-fifth of all tourist resorts suffered extensive damage. A large number of fishing boats and nets were also destroyed.[26] Fishing and tourism being the two major components of the Maldivian economy, the fastest growing economy in South Asia contracted in the aftermath of the tsunami and registered a negative growth.

According to a recent report by the International Panel on Climate Change (IPCC), the Antarctic and Greenland ice sheets are melting faster than anticipated; as a result the sea level is expected to rise between 20 cm and 60 cm by 2100. This could lead to catastrophic flooding of countries like the Maldives.[27] Besides, the Maldives is also facing acute problems of coastal erosion, growing salinity, spreading of tropical diseases like malaria, and loss of the coral ecosystem that supports the country's fishing industry. As a result, one of the first steps initiated by President Nasheed after his election victory was to create a sovereign wealth fund to be financed by tourism, to buy a new homeland for the inhabitants of Maldives in India, Sri Lanka or even Australia.[28] Changes in the environment caused by global warming have given way to rising sea levels. Already, over 97 percent of all inhabited islands and 45 percent of tourist resorts face varying degrees of beach erosion.[29]

The Maldives held the world's first underwater cabinet meeting in 2009 in a symbolic gesture to draw global attention to the perils of global warming. Maldives has also announced an ambitious program to become the first country in the world to attain carbon neutrality by 2020. According to the plan, fossil fuels could be virtually eliminated from the country. It also includes generation of electricity through renewable means and a transmission infrastructure that would include 155 large wind turbines, solar panels extending to half a square kilometer, and a biomass plant using coconut husks. Battery banks would be set up to provide back up when neither wind nor solar energy is available. The project not only covers homes and businesses, but even cars and boats, where diesel engines are being replaced by electrical engines run by batteries.[30]

Sri Lanka

Sri Lanka, an island nation of 65,000 sq km, has a coastline extending over 1,585 km. Around 32 percent of Sri Lanka's population live in the fragile coastal zone, comprising 24 percent of its area, which contributes 65 percent of its industrial output. The country is therefore extremely vulnerable to rising sea levels, which have been consistently eroding half of its coast line.[31] Water intrusion into coastal lagoons and estuary systems is taking place. Simultaneously the increase in temperature and relatively low levels of rainfall for over two decades has led to a decrease in ground water levels. Sri Lanka's paddy farmers have already adjusted the timing of the planting cycle in response to changing monsoon patterns, and are experimenting with rice varieties that can cope with less water and higher levels of salinity. Serious flooding destroyed 2.5 percent of harvests in early 2008 and again, later in the same year, forced major displacement in the troubled northern region.[32] The tea industry, Sri Lanka's main net foreign exchange earner, is badly affected by weather and drought conditions. A 10 percent annual increase in the length of dry and wet seasons in the main plantation area would enormously damage the soil and affect the tea crop. At the same time extreme, heavy rains tend to erode top soil and wash away fertilizers and other chemicals. It is widely believed that large parts of Northern Province including Jaffna peninsula, parts of Eastern Province, and Matara in Southern Province are in danger of being submerged due to rising sea levels caused by global warming. In the recent past this region's vulnerability was evident when the North and East bore the brunt of the December 2004 Asian tsunami.

Sri Lanka, with a per capita carbon emission level of 660 kg, is well below the IPCC's environmentally permissible carbon per capita level of 2,170 kg for 2009. According to former foreign minister of Sri Lanka, Rohitha Bogollagama, Sri Lanka is pushing for additional financial and technological incentives for developing countries to do their bit in dealing with climate change 'without compromising the legitimate development aspirations of developing countries.'[33] In 2002, Sri Lanka carried out research on the impacts of climate change in Sri Lanka, under the Climate Change Enabling Activity Project. Several studies related to agriculture, plantation, etc. were conducted under two research programs. Rainfall and temperature scenarios, impact on water quality, social impacts and impacts on upper watersheds were also studied. These exercises resulted in the identification of various adaptation and mitigation options in these areas.[34] The Government of Sri Lanka has also established the Centre for Climate Change Studies under the Department of Meteorology to conduct research related to climate change and related impacts. The Ministry of Environment and Natural Resources is now taking steps to prepare the Second National Communication on Climate Change. It has appointed a National Advisory Committee on Climate Change (NACCC), to advise the government on climate change and related issues.

Bangladesh

Bangladesh's geography makes it one of the most vulnerable countries to climate change. It faces the threat of increased flooding and storms due to its location in the delta of three large rivers – the Ganges, Brahmaputra and Meghna – as well as facing the Bay of Bengal. It is dominated by flood plains, with most of the land less than 12 meters above sea level. Bangladesh is also affected by two very different ecosystems (the Himalayas to the North and the Bay of Bengal to the South). The overall result is that it has too much water during the monsoon season and too little in the winter. In an average year, approximately one-quarter of the country is inundated. The climate change vulnerability of Bangladesh's poor is well recognized, with 70 million people likely to be affected by floods annually by 2050.[35]

Although Bangladesh's share of carbon gas emissions is negligible, it is one of the worst affected by climate change. Increased frequency and ferocity of floods, cyclones, droughts and other natural disasters triggered by climate change are already shrinking the inhabitable areas, forcing people to migrate to cities, and straining the limited urban civic infrastructure. A one metre rise of sea level would inundate a quarter of Bangladesh's territory and directly affect 11 percent of its population.[36] It is estimated that by 2050, at the present level of population growth and global warming, Bangladesh will have 300 million people living in an area of about 120,000 sq km, thereby increasing the country's population density to 2,500 or more per sq km.[37]

In an average year, 40 percent of Bangladesh's total land area is flooded, and river erosion washes away 1 percent of arable land. Bangladeshi scientists estimate that up to 20 percent of the country's land may be lost to flooding by 2030, spawning as many as 20 million 'climate refugees.'[38] Around one million people have been rendered homeless due to river erosion in Bangladesh over the last three decades as the mighty river Brahmaputra–Jamuna continues to widen. A study carried out under the BDCLIM (Bangladesh Climate) indicates that by the year 2050, the average annual runoff in the Brahmaputra basin would decline by 14 percent on account of climate change. The problem has been compounded because the flow of the rivers during the dry season has fallen, offering less resistance to the increasing power of the sea. This has created a vicious cycle. With salt water penetrating further inland and deeper into the groundwater, climate change – the root cause of the problems – is gradually destroying rice cultivation and livelihoods.[39]

At a macro level, Bangladesh is attempting to introduce changes brought about by socio-economic adjustments aimed at accelerating economic growth and human development. The other kind of intervention encompasses hazard adjustments aimed at reducing the impacts of, and controlling wherever feasible, disastrous natural events, such as floods, river bank erosion, cyclones and drought. Many traditional coping measures and government policies and programs have evolved, aimed at both controlling and reducing the impact of natural hazards.

The Government of Bangladesh has undertaken significant work in terms of disaster management by investing in flood protection and drainage schemes, coastal embankment projects, cyclone shelters and coastal 'greenbelt' projects. However, climate change is likely to increase the frequency and intensity of natural disasters in Bangladesh. The prospects of success of these and other measures will remain seriously constrained due to resource limitation and the limited ability of people and society to implement and maintain them effectively.

Bangladesh's National Adaptation Programme of Action (NAPA) highlights the main adverse effects of climate change and identifies adaptation needs. It contains US$77.4 million worth of climate-change adaptation projects; however, this is a 'wish-list,' and it remains to be seen which of the projects will come to fruition. The Bangladesh government in 2008 established a National Climate Change Fund (which will focus mainly on adaptation) with an initial capital of $45 million, and a Multi-Donor Trust Fund of $132 million with the support of the United Kingdom.[40] Under this plan, Bangladesh will establish a Centre for Research and Knowledge Management on Climate Change to ensure it has access to the latest ideas and technologies from around the world. In March 2010 in Dhaka, the donors were briefed about the Bangladesh government's stance on facing the changing climate, hearing that Bangladesh had already taken different types of measures to mitigate the adverse impact of climate change. But it is now apparent that the donors were not providing assistance to the projects requiring large-scale investments. They are giving funds for technical studies and planning only.[41]

Pakistan

The vulnerability of Pakistan to climate change was clearly demonstrated by the massive floods that affected the country in 2010; the floods submerged almost one-fifth of the country and affected 20 million people. According to the United

Nations Disaster Coordination Agency, the floods caused damage worth over 9.5 billion dollars and killed 1,985 people. However, a recent report from the Woodrow Wilson Center entitled 'Running on empty' has warned that Pakistan could face widespread water shortages within 25 years and that its water situation was 'extremely precarious.'[42]

Pakistan has a diverse landscape with sea shores in the south, ice peaks and temperate forests in the north and arid areas lying between fertile plains. Given its vast diversity, Pakistan experiences 11 climatic zones. This diversity adds to its vulnerability to natural hazards, which is further aggravated by low levels of development and weak systems of governance.[43] Climate change increases the susceptibility of agricultural zones to episodic natural catastrophes such as storms, floods and droughts, in turn exposing countries to the threat of socio-economic losses. According to the Water and Power Development Authority (WAPDA), per capita surface water availability plunged from 5,260 cubic meters per year in 1951 to just 1,100 cubic meters in 2006, and is expected to decrease further under the dual impacts of rising temperatures and increasing demand.[44] Pakistan, which is also a low emitter of greenhouse gases, is affected disproportionately by climate change and other global environmental problems. The former environment minister Mukhdoom Syed Faisal Hayat described the conditions aptly: 'Agricultural productivity in Pakistan was affected by the changes in land and water regimes. Dry land areas in arid and semi-arid regions were most vulnerable and affected agriculture productivity, putting the country's food security at risk.'[45]

In 2008 Pakistan set up a task-force to examine the effects of climate change on various sectors including agriculture. Pakistan also indicated its intention to develop efficient water management systems, create mass awareness campaigns and change cropping patterns. But it has not been able to come up with a National Action Plan on Climate Change, although in Pakistan's National Environment Policy of 2005, climate change was one of the issues under review.[46] The aim was to:

- implement a Clean Developmental Mechanism Authority;
- develop and implement policy and operational framework for effective management of CDM processes;
- promote the use of ozone-friendly technologies;
- phase out the use of ozone-depleting substances in line with provisions of the Montreal Protocol.

Despite the above, there has 'been an exponential growth in Pakistan's GHG emissions,' but it has low national capacities to tackle climatic challenges. Low levels of enforceability of environmental laws were also identified by public sector stakeholders, and blamed largely on absence of resources and political will.[47]

Despite suffering massive floods in 2010, the government of Pakistan has not come up with a policy on climate change. The Planning Commission constituted the Task Force on Climate Change with the stated objective of mainstreaming climate change into national and sectoral policies, but this and other Planning Commission Task Forces have not been active.

India

India is the world's fourth largest economy and fifth largest greenhouse gas (GHG) emitter, accounting for about five percent of global emissions. However, India's per capita emissions are low compared to those of other major economies. India has accounted for only 2 percent of cumulative energy-related emissions since 1850 on a per capita basis. India's per capita emissions are among the lowest in the world. In contrast to America's average emission of 20 tonnes of carbon dioxide, India produces only one tonne. But given India's billion-plus population, the absolute amount of GHG emissions from India make it one of the world's leading emitters. Nonetheless, India believes that not only can it meet its pledge of reducing carbon intensity by 20 to 25 percent by 2020 over 2005 levels, but could even improve upon it.

Several studies suggest that India is likely to be 'water stressed' by 2025 and 'water scarce' by 2050. The studies also warn of temperature rises between 3.5° and 5.5°C by the end of this century. Along with changes in monsoon patterns, India stands vulnerable to intensive cyclones, flash floods and related disasters. India's 7,500 km coastline will face the brunt of global warming and rising sea levels. Floods and droughts are the two contrasting situations that different states of India grapple with. Since the great famine of 1866, 2001 was the first time that drought of such a magnitude hit Orissa. It affected 25 of the state's 30 districts. The monsoon-driven floods in August 2000 affected the southern state of Andhra Pradesh. Variations of just 1° to 2°C temperature would adversely affect agricultural productivity. Low outputs of both wheat and rice would cause revenue loss of between 9 to 25 percent and could lead to food scarcity. All these visible changes have been brought on by global warming.

The annual per capita water availability in India has gone below 1,000 cubic meter – the situation would be described by experts as scarcity. Himalayan rivers are the largest sources of water for India. As a result of global climate change, there may be significant changes in the water endowment pattern.[48] The water statistics for India are a matter of concern. The World Bank in its 1999 report indicated that the overall water demand will increase from 552 BCM (Billion Cubic Meters) to 1,050 BCM by 2025, which will require the use of all available water resources in the country. The report also lists six of India's 20 major river basins below the water scarcity threshold of 1,000 cubic meters per year. The *Mckinsey Report* (2009) suggests that by 2030, water demand in India will grow to almost 1.5 trillion cubic meters, principally driven by population growth and the domestic need for rice, wheat and sugar.

India is pursuing a national action plan on climate change aimed at reducing dependence on fossil fuels, adapting to the changing climate and mitigating its harmful effects, but has made it clear that such a plan is different from accepting binding international commitments. China and India are among the developing countries under pressure to agree to emission reduction targets amid mounting evidence that GHG-driven global warming and its consequences threaten vulnerable populations.[49] India has refused to be browbeaten into accepting agendas and deadlines that developed economies have been imposing upon the less developed world. It has pledged to limit its per capita emissions so as not to exceed those of developed states and has been expanding its solar power – and not fossil fuels. In its search to supplement the present reserve of energy, India has initiated a serious program to shift to renewable sources of energy. Prime Minister Manmohan Singh has stated that India must take the lead in the development of science and technology related to mitigation of the effects and adaptation to climate change. India needs to increase its solar and nuclear supplies 'considerably.'[50]

However, the alternative path does come with a cost. The cost of switching away from fossil fuels in the next 20 years is now estimated at $10 trillion and will rise by $500 billion for each year of delay, says the International Energy Agency. The use of more energy-efficient technology will save about $8.6 trillion in that timeframe.[51] India has also announced the Jawaharlal Nehru National Solar Mission in 2010 to tap the potential of solar energy and also establish itself as the leaders in the use of solar energy.

Regional solutions: the way ahead?

The Asian Development Bank (ADB) and the UK government are financing a US$1.2 million study to help South Asia analyze the costs and benefits of climate change adaptation actions. The South Asia Cooperative Environment Programme (SACEP) is one of the principal programs aimed at developing a shared understanding of the effects of environmental degradation on the region. Formed in 1982, it aims at building national capacity to manage environmental issues. SACEP works on a whole spectrum of programs which are focused on capacity building; institutional strengthening for conservation and sustainable use of biodiversity; environmental information and assessment; and education and awareness. Working in conjunction with UNEP, its efforts are directed towards improvement of the legal and institutional framework. It is currently working on projects in Bangladesh, Maldives and Sri Lanka. The work of SACEP needs to be endorsed and supported by the different national governments in the region to bolster co-operation on the projects and on work related to adaptation of communities to the changing climate.[52]

Along with SACEP, SAARC has also started to include the environment in its mandate. The 16th SAARC Summit was held soon after the disappointing Copenhagen Summit, where the schism between the developed and less developed nations came in the way of charting a common path to fight the problems of climate change. The SAARC leaders accordingly adopted climate change as the theme for the summit and reaffirmed their commitment to address this challenge.[53] Members had hoped that the Copenhagen Summit would arrive at some sort of commitment on the peaking of emissions. Thus an Inter-governmental Expert Group on Climate Change to develop a clear policy direction and guidance for regional co-operation is envisaged in the SAARC Plan of Action on Climate Change. This group will meet at least twice a year to periodically monitor, review and make recommendations on the implementation of the decisions taken at the Summit meeting.

The final declarations at the Summit reflected the SAARC leaders' consensus that the global climate change negotiations should be guided by the principles of equity. Based on the principle of 'common but differentiated responsibilities according to respective capabilities,' enunciated at the UN Framework Convention on Climate Change (UNFCCC), SAARC leaders recommended a separate financing scheme for adaptation and mitigation, as well as technology transfer.[54] The optimism about the common position was obvious in the words of the chairman of the Inter-Governmental Panel on Climate Change: 'this is the first time you have a SAARC summit where the leaders of countries in the region are getting together on a very specific subject and I am optimistic.'[55]

Despite the optimism, it is important to note that within the framework of SAARC, except for the initial statements, there has not been any significant action to evolve an understanding of the issue. No attempt has been made to bolster the abilities of the countries in the region to adapt to and mitigate the effects of climate change. Most efforts are limited to the national action plans of countries in the region. The adverse impacts of climate change are already being witnessed in the region, particularly on biodiversity, agriculture, water resources, rainfall patterns, seasons, coastal inhabitations, and high altitude communities. Against this background, the efforts for finding solutions to the problem across a wide spectrum need to be intensified. Research and development, with a view to developing adaptation strategies for the vulnerable regions that fall within different national borders, need to be given importance. Within the debate about globalization, there is an emerging discourse on 'global governance,' to manage issues within the framework of trans-sovereign global politics.

Its unique geographical features along with its demographic setup will make South Asia a region which will face disproportionate consequences of climate change. It is imperative that the countries evolve and work towards collaborative arrangements to mitigate the adverse impacts of climate change and to develop sustainably. As discussed through this chapter, the common problems that confront the countries of the region are shortage of availability of fresh water resources, decline in crop yield, glacial melt leading to sea-level rise, and so on. The vulnerabilities of communities will be further exacerbated if no action is taken. Projects and programs with a view to developing sustainably and equitably need to be undertaken, such as rain water harvesting, management of different ecosystems, etc. Lastly, at international negotiations, South Asia as a region should work together to mobilize the necessary resources and finances to be able to move towards a 'low-carbon path' along with adaptation measures to protect its vulnerable population.

Climate change embodies a unique opportunity and challenge to the region. On the one hand, South Asia as a region is facing considerable challenges to its growth and development; non-linear and unpredictable effects of climate change have the potential to act as a 'threat-multiplier' which will further exacerbate the problems and issues of conflicts in the region. On the other hand, it presents an opportunity for the countries of the region to encourage greater co-operation in areas of common interest. In times to come, climate change will affect the region quite adversely and the leaders of the region need to make concerted efforts to deal with this challenge.

Notes

1 B.C. Parks and J. Timmons Roberts, 'Inequality and the global climate regime', 2008, pp. 623–624.
2 N. Sadeque, 'The carbon scam', 2010, pp. 54–55.
3 B. Lee, 'Managing the interlocking climate and resource challenges', 2009, p. 1110.
4 'Tough climate signal to West', *The Telegraph*, 1 March 2009, online, available at www.telegraphindia.com/1090301/jsp/nation/story_10608007.jsp
5 S. Prabhu, 'Special address', 2008, p. 6.
6 M. Henderson, 'Maldives president Mohammed Nasheed demands action on climate change', 2009.
7 M.Z.H. Jappa, 'Climate change monster', online (accessed on 31 August 2010).
8 B. Lee, 'Managing the interlocking', p. 1102.
9 B. Chellaney, 'Climate change and security in Southern Asia', 2007, p. 62.
10 C. Dasgupta, 'Energy, climate and security', 2008, pp. 54–55.
11 A. Jaitly, 'South Asian Perspectives on Climate Change and Water Policy', 2009, p. 17.
12 Ibid., p. 18.
13 D.B. Kattel, 'Scientists warn of Himalaya warming', online, available at http://english.ohmynews.com/articleview/article_view.asp?menu=c10400&no=362269&rel_no=1 (accessed on 6 September 2010).
14 Chellaney, 'Climate change and security', p. 65.
15 The World Bank report on *South Asia: Shared views on development and climate change*, Washington, DC, 2009, p. 190.
16 'Japan, ADB help Bhutan strengthen resilience to climate change', ADB News release, 25 January 2010, available at www.adb.org/media/Articles/2010/13144-bhutanese-climate-change-initiatives/
17 The World Bank report on *South Asia*, 2009, pp. 190–192.
18 Royal Government of Bhutan National Environment Commission, *Bhutan environment outlook 2008*, p. 36.
19 'Bhutan pledged to carbon neutrality', online, available at www.bridgetobhutan.bt/blog/?tag=climate-change (accessed on 27 December 2009)
20 Statement by Bhim Bahadur Rawal, Nepal Minister of Home Affairs, at 65th session of the UN General Assembly, New York, 27 September 2010.
21 *Glacial lake outburst flood monitoring and early warning system*, UNEP Environment Issues, online, available at www.rrcap.unep.org/issues/glof/
22 'Nepal cabinet holds meeting on Mount Everest' online, available at http://news.bbc.co.uk/2/hi/8394452.stm (accessed on 10 December 2010).
23 See Asian Development Bank/ICIMOD report *Environmental assessment of Nepal: Emerging issues and challenges*, Kathmandu, 2006, pp. 87–89.
24 I.H. Zaki and R.M. Parakh, *Small state security dilemma*, 2008, pp. 45–48.
25 Ibid., p. 48.

26 Ibid., p. 56.
27 R. Mckie, 'Figures deliver stark warning of a flooded future', 2009.
28 F. Williams, 'Climate is rights issue, says Maldives minister', 2007.
29 'National adaptation to climate change' background paper prepared by the Government of Maldives, Ministry of Housing, Transport and Environment, for the Maldives Partnership Forum (MPF) held in Maldives on 23–24 March 2009, p. 4.
30 D. Clark, 'Maldives first to go carbon neutral', 2009, p. 14.
31 U.K. Sinha *et al.*, 'Impact on India's bilateral relations with neighbouring countries', 2009, p. 135.
32 'Climate change in Sri Lanka', January 2009 OneWorld Net, online, available at http://uk.oneworld.net/guides/srilanka/climate-change
33 R.J. Perera, 'Sri Lanka seeks financial and technological incentives', 2009.
34 A. Herath, 'Climate change and energy in Sri Lanka', Asian Development Bank, online, available at www.adb.org/documents/events/2009/Climate-Change-Energy-Workshop/SRI.pdf
35 P. Shyamsundar and N. Beresnev, 'Climate change economics in Bangladesh', 2009.
36 Address by Sheikh Hasina, Prime Minister of Bangladesh, at 65th session of the UN General Assembly New York on 26 September 2010.
37 H. Imam, 'The challenge is even bigger', 2008.
38 Ibid.
39 Sinha *et al.*, 'Impact on India's bilateral relations', p. 129.
40 N. Antony, 'Bangladesh steps up to tackle climate change', SciDev Net, 11 September 2008, online, available at www.scidev.net/en/news/bangladesh-steps-up-to-tackle-climate-change.html (accessed on 31 August 2010).
41 S. Khan, 'Promised fund for climate change adaptation', 2010.
42 'Pakistan sinking into water crisis', online, available at http://ipsnews.net/news.asp?idnews=54441 (accessed on 12 February 2011).
43 'Pakistan's options for climate change mitigation & adaptation', Lead scoping study report, Study carried out for the British High Commission, Islamabad, March 2008, p. 5.
44 Ibid., p. 7.
45 Jappa, 'Climate change monster.'
46 National Environment Policy 2005, Government of Pakistan, Ministry of Environment, online, available at www.environment.gov.pk/nep/policy.pdf
47 'Pakistan's options for climate change mitigation & adaptation', p. 8.
48 J. Bandyopadhyay, 'Everybody loves a disaster', *The Telegraph*, 23 September 2008, online, available at www.telegraphindia.com/1080923/jsp/opinion/story_9862320.jsp
49 'Tough climate signal to West', *The Telegraph*, 1 March 2009, online, available at www.telegraphindia.com/1090301/jsp/nation/story_10608007.jsp
50 J. Shankar, 'Nations made limited progress at Copenhagen summit, India says', 4 January 2010, www.bloomberg.com/apps/news?pid=20601091&sid=amkLngC9s.Oo (accessed 31 August 2010).
51 Ibid.
52 United Nations and ADB: *Joint report on State of the Environment in Asia and the Pacific 2000*, New York: United Nations, 2000, p. 349.
53 'Towards a green and happy South Asia', Sixteenth SAARC Summit, 28–29 April 2010, Thimphu Silver Jubilee Declaration, available at www.saarc-sec.org/userfiles/16thSummit-Declaration29April10.pdf
54 Ibid.
55 'Is climate change South Asia's deadliest threat?', online, available at http://news.bbc.co.uk/2/hi/8646289.stm (accessed 21 July 2010).

Bibliography

Chellaney, B., 'Climate change and security in Southern Asia: Understanding the national security implications', *The RUSI Journal*, 152:2, April 2007.

Clark, D., 'Maldives first to go carbon neutral', *Observer*, 15 March 2009.

Dasgupta, C., 'Energy, climate and security: New dimensions of geopolitics' in D. Sharma and L. Noronha (eds), *Energy, climate and security: The inter-linkages*, New Delhi: Konrad Adenauer Stiftung, 2008.

Henderson, M., 'Maldives president Mohammed Nasheed demands action on climate change', *The Times* (London), 6 July 2009.

Imam, H., 'The challenge is even bigger', *Daily Star*, 28 May 2008.

Jaitly, A., 'South Asian perspectives on climate change and water policy' in D. Michel and A. Pandya (eds), *Troubled waters: Climate change, hydropolitics and transboundary resources*, Washington, DC: The Henry L. Stimson Center, 2009.

Jappa, M.Z.H., 'Climate change monster: Calamitous situation in South Asia demands urgent action', online, available at http://cmsdata.iucn.org/downloads/climate_change_monster.pdf (accessed on 31 August 2010).

Khan, S., 'Promised fund for climate change adaptation, mitigation', *The Financial Express* (Dhaka), 7 March 2010.

Lee, B., 'Managing the interlocking climate and resource challenges', *International Affairs*, 85:6, 2009.

McKie, R., 'Figures deliver stark warning of a flooded future', *New Zealand Herald*, 9 March 2009.

Parks, B.C. and J. Timmons Roberts, 'Inequality and the global climate regime: Breaking the north–south impasse', *Cambridge Review of International Affairs*, 21:4, December 2008.

Perera, R.J., 'Sri Lanka seeks financial and technological incentives at climate change summit', Sri Lanka News Network, 8 December 2009, online, available at www.srilankanewsnetwork.com/?p=810

Prabhu, S., 'Special address' in D. Sharma and L. Noronha (eds), *Energy, climate and security: The inter-linkages*, New Delhi: Konrad Adenauer Stiftung, 2008.

Sadeque, N., 'The carbon scam', *Newsline*, February 2010.

Shyamsunder, P. and N. Beresnev, 'Climate change economics in Bangladesh: A policy note', November 2009, online, available at www.unpei.org/PDF/bangladesh-workshop-oct09policy-note.pdf

Sinha, U.K., S. Datta, S. Chauhan and P.K. Gautam, 'Impact on India's bilateral relations with neighbouring countries' in *Security implications of climate change for India*, Report of the IDSA Working Group, New Delhi: Academic Foundation, 2009.

Williams, F., 'Climate is rights issue, says Maldives minister', *The Financial Times* (London), 4 March 2007.

Zaki, I.H. and R.M. Parakh, *Small state security dilemma: A Maldivian perception*, New Delhi: Lancer Books, 2008.

13 The politics of energy pipelines in South Asia

Shebonti Ray Dadwal

This chapter argues that continued economic growth in the South Asian region will, to a large extent, be determined by the region's access to adequate, secure and affordable supplies of energy resources, given that the regional demand for energy is growing at a rate of 6.6 percent per annum, and is set to double over the next two decades. Many of the countries can no longer meet their energy requirements from domestic resources and have to import increasingly large quantities of energy. Furthermore, modern forms of energy are inaccessible for more than half the population. As a result, they continue to be dependent on traditional fuels such as firewood, agri-waste and animal waste. This not only affects the quality of life of the people, but it also contributes to environmental degradation and pollution. Moreover, as concerns over climate change and global warming become stronger, the South Asian countries, particularly the larger energy-consuming ones, are being subjected to increasing international pressure to cut their emissions. Though there is a concerted move to raise the share of renewable energy such as solar, biomass and wind in their energy mix, the commercial viability of these resources is still questionable. As a result, fossil fuels continue to dominate the primary energy basket. However, given that natural gas is the cleanest fossil fuel available, more and more countries are turning to natural gas, particularly for the power and industrial sectors. The problem is that given the demand projections for the foreseeable future, there are not enough natural gas reserves in the region to satisfy demand. For India alone, which is also the largest market in the region, projections indicate that notwithstanding recent discoveries of substantial reserves, India will require increasingly large amounts of gas imports to meet its requirements.[1]

A similar situation exists for the second largest economy in the region, namely Pakistan. According to Pakistani energy specialists, the shortfall in gas supplies would be around 293 million cubic meters per day (mmcmd) by 2025, up from 5.4 mmcmd in 2009, due to the depletion in the existing resource base, and with no new discoveries coming on line. On the other hand, the demand for gas would increase due to increase in its usage, increase in population and expansion in gas utility connections to other parts of the country.[2]

One of the factors that have impeded trade in natural gas is the fact that most natural gas reserves are located at considerable distances from their markets.

Moreover, unlike oil, the very nature of natural gas makes transportation difficult, as gas has to be transported through dedicated pipelines to their contracted
markets. As a result, the countries that are the largest users of natural gas are
those that are comparatively close to their sources. Hence, the majority of the
world's gas trade is confined to Europe and North America, due to the existence
of large and growing markets and proximity to large sources of gas such as
Russia, Algeria and potentially Central Asia in the case of Europe, and Canada
in the case of the US.

While this problem can be resolved by converting natural gas into a liquefied
form (LNG) and shipping it to its destined market, LNG trade requires complex
and expensive infrastructure, such as liquefaction and re-gasification plants, and
storage terminals. It is only when trade entails transporting gas over distances of
over 3,000 kilometers that LNG becomes more cost-effective compared to piped
natural gas. However, the piped-gas trade is often faced with technical, economic, and more importantly political problems. The increased distance between
the gas reserves and large markets creates physical, technical and economic
difficulties for constructing pipelines, while the need to transit through a number
of countries and borders, some of which have unstable political environments,
requires protracted and complicated right-of-way negotiations.[3] Recently gas
supplies to Ukraine were disrupted by Moscow, thereby creating problems in
Europe, as the pipelines supplying Russian gas to Europe transit through
Ukraine.[4] This issue has clearly highlighted the role of politics in energy trade.

In the case of South Asia, the region is surrounded by countries that have
abundant natural gas reserves, such as Iran, Qatar and the Central Asian Republics in the west, and Myanmar in the east. While India is already importing substantial quantities of LNG from Qatar, it is also looking at options of importing
gas, both piped as well as liquefied, from other gas-exporting centers to meet its
increasing shortfall. These include Iran and Central Asian countries in the west,
and Southeast Asian countries and Bangladesh in the east. Since the mid-1990s,
India has made significant attempts to explore the feasibility of importing natural
gas from Iran and Turkmenistan in the west and Bangladesh and Myanmar in the
east. However, after decades of protracted negotiations, none of the projects are
even close to becoming operational. Several factors – political, financial and
technical – are responsible for this state of affairs. This chapter looks at three
projects, namely the Iran–Pakistan–India (IPI) project, the Turkmenistan–
Afghanistan–Pakistan–India (TAPI) project and the Israel–Turkey–India project,
which successive Indian governments were interested in, and explains why none
of them have got off the ground so far.

The IPI project

The IPI project had its genesis in a proposal made in 1989 by Abbas Maleki,
head of the Tehran-based International Institute for Caspian Studies. The 'Asian
Gas Pipeline,' as it was then called, was to involve the construction of a pipeline
with a capacity of 36 billion cubic meters per year from Bandar Abbas in Iran to

Calcutta. It was envisaged at the time that 10 percent of this gas would be consumed in the Iranian provinces, 20 percent in Pakistan, and the balance in India.

Subsequently, in 1993, the Australian firm Broken Hill Petroleum Corporation (BHP) proposed a pipeline to export Iran's gas to the west coast of India. Also, Crescent Petroleum, Trans Canadian Pipeline Ltd. and Brown and Roote Inc. proposed a gas pipeline transmission system from the Persian Gulf to South Asia; this was followed by another proposal in the mid-90s by a consortium of Shell, British Gas, Gas de France and Petronas for a major gas pipeline from Assaluyeh in the Persian Gulf to Sui in Pakistan and eventually to India. However, none of these projects ever went beyond desk studies for various technical, financial and political reasons. One of the main obstacles was the Indian government's concern regarding the safety of the supplies, given that the pipeline would need to traverse Pakistani territory. In fact, New Delhi had even proposed some alternative options. These included onshore and offshore pipelines from Iran and along the Pakistani coast to India; onshore from the Iranian gas fields terminal at Assaluyeh to the Pakistani border and through Pakistan to India; and shipping of LNG from Iran to India by tankers.

According to Abbas Maleki, India's first preference was the deep sea option in order to bypass Pakistani territory. Alternatively, India said that it would prefer a pipeline route going offshore from Iran and along the shallow sea route to India. However, he said that the first option would face major technical difficulties, such as laying and maintaining a pipeline 3,000 meters under the sea on the mountainous seabed, which would lead to additional costs and technical risks.[5] The second (shallow offshore) option too, he said, had its own problems. If the pipeline were to pass through the shallow territorial waters of Pakistan, the security concerns of India would not be eliminated. Some Indian analysts have argued that a gas pipeline passing through Pakistan's mainland with all the international and regional security guarantees would be less insecure than a pipeline going through the territorial waters of Pakistan. Also, according to Mr Maleki, the preliminary findings of a feasibility study showed that there was a major technical obstacle when the pipeline reaches the area where the Indus River pours into the Arabian Sea.[6]

However, in 2005, following an improvement in relations between India and Pakistan, the project received a new lease of life, for which many would give the credit to former Petroleum Minister Mani Shankar Aiyar.[7] Soon after, a Joint Working Group (JWG) between India and Pakistan was set up. Both countries also agreed to continue on the parallel track of bilateral negotiations, and also trilateral talks which would eventually converge into trilateral negotiations (with Iran), which were expected to begin by the end of the year, once the bilateral issues between the three participating countries had been resolved. Both sides expressed the view that negotiations to iron out the legal, commercial, financial and technical issues would take a couple of years, and the project was expected to be commissioned by 2009–10.[8]

The US steps in

But even as prospects appeared to be improving for the project, it faced severe road blocks behind the scene. Washington had, for some time, been expressing its concerns on Iran's clandestine nuclear weapons program and had, on several occasions, threatened to take action against Tehran on the grounds that Iran was only years away from acquiring a nuclear weapon.

For years, successive US administrations had been trying to isolate Iran by imposing sanctions under ILSA (Iran–Libya Sanctions Act) according to which any company, US or non-US, which invested more than $20 million in Iran would be liable to US sanctions. Washington's concern was that the Iran–India project would not only give a boost to the Iranian energy sector, but would also open up new possibilities for the export of oil and gas from the wider Caspian region. Therefore, when the Iran–India pipeline project was proposed, it came up with an alternative project – TAPI, or TAP as it was originally called, prior to India acceding to the project.[9]

During an official visit to India in March 2005, the then US Secretary of State Condoleezza Rice, while expressing her government's opposition to the IPI project, told India that it should refrain from signing the deal with Iran. At the same time, in an interview to a TV channel, she said, 'We will certainly want to discuss the energy needs of India. I understand that this is a growing, in fact burgeoning economy, and like the United States, we are all concerned about how we will meet our energy supply over the next decades and do that in a way that is clean for the environment.' She added that under the Next Steps in Strategic Partnership (NSSP) dialogue between the two countries, the US was prepared to discuss all issues, including the sale of civilian reactors to India, which it had hitherto been reluctant to sell due to proliferation concerns.[10]

This was followed by an offer from President George Bush in July 2005, during Prime Minister Manmohan Singh's visit to the US. Bush promised to get the Nuclear Suppliers Group (NSG) to relax its rules, so as to make a special exemption for India to enable her to acquire nuclear technology and fuel, thereby providing the requisite push to the moribund Indian nuclear energy program. Meanwhile Dr Singh made an announcement on 21 July 2005 in Washington expressing his reservations about the project. He remarked 'I don't know if any international consortium of bankers would underwrite this.'[11] This indicated that there was a new 'understanding' between the US and India vis-à-vis Iran.

Meanwhile, the US kept up the pressure on India. US ambassador to India David Mulford conveyed his administration's reservations about the Iran-India energy deal to the Manmohan Singh government during a meeting with Indian officials. This was corroborated subsequently in 2011 by WikiLeaks revelations, which also alleged that Mr Aiyar had been shifted from the petroleum ministry because of his support for the project.[12]

Although many in the Indian establishment were upset with Washington's stance, India took the difficult decision of voting with the US and the EU-3 in the IAEA against Iran. Following the resolution, Tehran lashed out against all the countries which had voted against it, including India, even threatening to review economic ties with these countries.[13] One of the casualties of India's vote was the $20 billion LNG agreement between India and Iran negotiated in 2005, according to which Iran was to supply India with five million metric tonnes of LNG. However, Iran has not ratified the deal to this day. In the meantime, according to a report in Tehran Times, Iran and Pakistan seem inclined to go ahead with the project without India's participation.[14]

Though the pipeline's fate continues to hang in the balance, Iran and Pakistan have stated that they would be going ahead with the project, with Tehran even claiming that 90 percent of the work on the pipeline was complete within its territory and that it was open for trade arrangements with any country in the energy sector, including India.[15] However, it seems unlikely that India will be part of the project, ostensibly due to differences over gas pricing. Recently, Tehran rejected New Delhi's pre-conditions for joining the project and even indicated that the volume reserved for India could be diverted to the Persian Gulf.

Tehran also would not promise secured gas delivery up to the Indian border, saying that the 'subject of gas transfer depended on India, as it did with Pakistan.' India, on the other hand, wants to pay for the gas only after delivery at the India–Pakistan border, to ensure safe passage of the supply through Pakistan. Tehran wants to hand the gas over at the said border under a trilateral pact, so that it would receive payment even if supplies were disrupted en route.[16]

Israel–Turkey–India gas project

Even as the IPI and TAPI projects were being negotiated, some new proposals were also being looked at, which sought to avoid the troublesome routes via Afghanistan and Pakistan. One of the plans was part of the ambitious Turkish-Israeli multi-million-dollar Medstream energy and water project, first envisaged in 2004, to transport water, electricity, natural gas and oil by pipelines to Israel from the Caspian region via Turkey.[17] In late 2008, Turkish Prime Minister Recep Tayyip Erdogan, during a meeting with Indian business leaders in Bangalore, placed the proposal on the table. The proposed pipeline would transport Caspian crude to Ceyhan port on Turkey's Mediterranean coast; it would thence be taken through a sub-sea pipeline to Israel from where it would be connected to the Eilat port on the Red Sea. From Eilat, India could ship the crude, thereby avoiding the choke points of Suez Canal. The project could be viable given that Indian Oil Corporation is already associated with the first leg of the pipeline project, with a 12.5 percent stake in the $2 billion Ceyhan Samsung pipeline, the other partners being Eni SpA of Italy and Calik Enerji A.S. of Turkey.[18] Officials from the three countries were expected to meet in April 2009 to discuss the project.

The second proposal was to revive a previous pipeline project between India and Oman that was proposed in the mid-1990s but which had to be shelved due to technical and sourcing problems. The current $6 billion (Rs.15,150 crore), 2,000 km pipeline proposal envisages a pipeline that will be laid from Oman to either Gujarat or Maharashtra, but transporting gas sourced from either Qatar or Iran, or both. The proposal was made by South Asia Gas Enterprise Pvt. Ltd (SAGE), a special project vehicle set up as an equal joint venture between the Siddhomal group, an Indian firm, and UK-based Deep Water Technology Co. The project was expected to take five years to be completed and would have a capacity of 31.1 mmcmd. The expected transportation tariff from the project was set at around $1.80 per mmBtu. Though this project has the potential to find a solution to sourcing gas from Iran despite the technical and economic challenges that are involved,[19] following the departure of Mani Shankar Aiyar from the petroleum ministry, this as well as the Medstream project have seen no further movement.

The TAPI project

This is not the first time that a trans-Afghan energy pipeline bringing Central Asian energy resources to South Asia has been attempted. A previous attempt was made soon after the fall of the Soviet Union by an Argentinian oil company Bridas, which became the first company to exploit Turkmenistan's energy resources and proposed to construct a pipeline through Afghanistan. Bridas was awarded exploration contracts by Turkmenistan for the Keimar and Yashlar blocks, near the Afghan border, and by March 1995 had signed accords with Turkmenistan and Pakistan to construct a pipeline into Afghanistan, which however was riven by civil war. In 1996, Bridas also succeeded in signing an agreement with the then Rabbani regime to build and operate a gas pipeline across the country. He then approached other companies, including Unocal, to form a consortium. However, Unocal, which had several former American defense and intelligence officials on its payroll, decided to go it alone, and formed its own US-backed consortium, CentGas, which included Saudi Arabia's Delta Oil, Gazprom and Turkmenrozgas. It negotiated with Turkmenistan for its own gas pipeline project, which essentially followed the same route as Bridas,' as well as with the Taliban, which had wrested control of much of Afghanistan from the Rabbani government. Thus followed years of wrestling between the two consortiums for the rights over a trans-Afghan pipeline.[20] Eventually, events in Afghanistan and the continuing strife in that country prevented either of the two consortiums from constructing the pipeline.

However, the project was revived in 2002. Following a meeting between the heads of government of Afghanistan, Pakistan and Turkmenistan in Islamabad on 29–30 May 2002, it was agreed that a gas pipeline traversing about 1,700 kilometers, which would transport up to 20 bcm of gas annually from Turkmenistan's Daulatabad fields in southeast Turkmenistan to consumers in Afghanistan, Pakistan and possibly India, would be constructed.[21] Five issues were identified as crucial to the project. These included:

- a confirmed market for the gas in Pakistan and India;
- ensuring that the Daulatabad gas reserves are sufficient to supply production over a period of 25–30 years;

- addressing Pakistan's and India's concerns with regard to possible disruption of supplies through the pipeline;
- techno-economic feasibility of the project; and
- mobilization of international oil and gas companies to take the lead role in the consortium for timely and cost-efficient construction of the pipeline, and operation and maintenance of the same in accordance with international standards.[22]

At the end of 2007, there were reports that New Delhi too would formally join the TAPI project, which was to be sponsored by the Asian Development Bank (ADB). The project also had the support of the US, for whom a trans-Afghan pipeline from Central Asia to South Asia was not only an opportunity to prevent economic and political advantages to Iran, but also part of a bigger geo-strategic agenda to wrest control of the former Soviet Union republics from Moscow. Controlling the region's vast energy resources as well as their transport network transiting the region was a key objective of Washington throughout the 1990s.

In December 2010, the participating countries signed the framework agreement and the Gas Pipeline Transmission Agreement in the Turkmen capital, Ashgabat, for the TAPI project to supply Afghanistan, Pakistan and India with 33 bcm of gas annually from Turkmenistan's Daulatabad gas field through Herat and Kandahar in Afghanistan, Quetta and Multan in Pakistan, to Fazilka on the India–Pakistan border. The pipeline's construction is scheduled to begin in 2012 and to be completed by 2014.

However, several issues pertaining to the project need to be sorted out by and among the parties involved before the project can come to fruition:

- Originally, the cost of the project was around $2 billion, but it has since escalated to around $7–10 billion. Moreover, few of the issues mentioned above have been resolved. Though Gaffney, Cline & Associates, a British consulting firm, announced in October 2008 that the first results of its audit of Turkmenistan's proven gas reserves stood between 4–14 trillion cubic meters (tcm) and that after the studies were completed, Turkmenistan was likely to have reserves of 38.4 tcm, that is, just 20 percent lower than those of Russia's, doubts persist with regard to the country's ability to deliver on its TAPI commitment. Turkmenistan has already contracted to supply Russia with around 50 bcm per year (bcm/y), China with 60 bcm/y (the two countries recently signed an agreement whereby Turkmenistan would supply an additional 20 bcm/y to China as against the earlier 40 bcm/y[23]) and Iran with 8 bcm/y.[24]
- Gas from the TAPI project would reportedly be far more expensive than that from the IPI project. According to some reports, Turkmenistan is demanding three times more than what India was negotiating with Iran. After adding transportation and transit fees to Afghanistan and Pakistan, India would get gas at the price of $18 per mmBtu (million British thermal units). However, according to media reports, in response to India's

counter-proposal of $200–$230 per thousand cubic meters, Turkmenistan has threatened that in case of non-materialization of the deal, the gas would be sold to Russia and China.[25]

• Funding for the TAPI project can commence only when the pipeline's route is secured. With tensions continuing in Afghanistan between the government and the Taliban, many analysts believe that security considerations may ensure that TAPI may never see the light of day.

One of the (US) objectives behind TAPI was to ensure that no country engages with or does business with Iran. Not only has the US employed pressure on India to abandon the IPI project, it is also discouraging Pakistan from pursuing the project. There are some reports of Washington offering Pakistan financial assistance to build an LNG re-gasification terminal in order to import LNG from suppliers such as Qatar instead of importing directly piped gas from Iran, as well as offers to assist Islamabad to import electricity from Tajikistan via Afghanistan. However, while the US strategy appears to have succeeded in the case of India, Pakistan has thus far appeared not to have succumbed to such pressure. Of course, in India's case, the discovery of substantial gas reserves in its own territory has placed it in a position where imports are no longer critical, at least in the short term, whereas in Pakistan's case, the need for energy has grown with no major indigenous discoveries taking place. However, given India's long-term need for large gas imports, concerns have been raised in India about the wisdom of withdrawing from IPI.[26]

Conclusion

There is no doubt that South Asia is energy deficient and needs access to extra-regional energy resources to feed its growing economies. Yet numerous projects to construct pipelines to import gas from its energy-rich neighborhood have failed due to concerns over security of supplies, disagreement over pricing and more importantly, a lack of trust between India and its neighbors.

In the case of the IPI pipeline, though officially the implementation of the project has been held up due to differences over financing between Iran, on the one hand, and India and Pakistan on the other, as well as differences over transport and transit fees between India and Pakistan, New Delhi's overriding concern has been the security of the pipeline section transiting Pakistan, and concerns over supply disruptions en route, be it due to political differences with Islamabad or due to the activities of non-state actors. Moreover, extra-regional issues, such as relations between Iran and the US, have also impinged on the project, with Washington pressuring both India and Pakistan against initiating commercial relations with Tehran. Also, as Prime Minister Manmohan Singh stated candidly during his visit to Washington in 2005, it would be difficult to find international financiers to underwrite the project. Pakistan has been stating that the IPI and TAPI projects could be successfully implemented even without India's participation. It has even announced that China would step in if India backed out of the projects. However, few, if any, statements have come out of Beijing on the IPI. Moreover, without the huge and growing Indian market, few investors would be willing to go ahead with a costly and politically sensitive project in the region.

In the case of the TAPI pipeline, despite the fact that both the US and the ADB are promoting the project, the unending turmoil in Afghanistan as well as the deteriorating political situation in Pakistan are the main concerns regarding the successful implementation of the project. Also, given that the pipeline will necessitate transit through Pakistani territory, New Delhi has the same concerns with regard to the security of supplies as is the case with the IPI pipeline. Moreover, other factors such as the pricing of the gas, technical difficulties in laying of the pipeline over hostile terrain, and whether Turkmenistan has sufficient reserves to dedicate to the project after having committed large amounts of gas to its contracts with Russia, China and Iran, make this project appear the least feasible among the proposed projects in the region.

In the eastern sector too, following the deal between Yangon and Beijing, which saw India's share of Myanmar's gas being sold to China, the Myanmar-India pipeline project is now shelved, with India and Myanmar now agreeing to develop their energy co-operation in other areas, such as hydroelectricity and the power sector. However, Bangladesh now appears to be keen to revive its energy co-operation with India, including the construction of a tri-nation gas pipeline, which could eventually see the development of a sub-regional energy grid. Nonetheless, as far as India's energy pipeline strategy goes, it would appear that for the time being at least, India's pipeline plans will continue to remain pipe dreams.

Notes

1 'Energy Requirements', *Integrated Energy Policy: Report of the Expert Committee*, New Delhi: Government of India, Planning Commission, August 2006, p. 26.
2 'Country to confront 0.507bcfd gas shortfall in 2010', *Daily Times* (Lahore), 5 February 2009, online, available www.dailytimes.com.pk/default.asp?page=2009%5C02%5C05%5Cstory_5-2-2009_pg5_1
3 Sylvie Cornot-Gandolphe, Olivier Appert, Ralf Dickel, Marie-Françoise Chabrelie and Alexandre Rojey, 'The Challenges of Further Cost Reductions for New Supply Options', 22nd World Gas Conference, 1–5 June 2003, Tokyo, Japan, online, available www.lngpedia.com/wp-content/uploads/lng_gas_pipeline/The%20Challenge%20of%20Further%20Cost%20Reduction%20for%20New%20Gas%20Supply%20Options%20-%20Cedigaz.pdf
4 Most Western countries believe that Russia is using its position as a major gas supplier to Europe and its pipeline network as a political tool to assert its influence in the former Soviet Union states and deter them from moving closer to NATO and Western powers.
5 Abbas Maleki's lecture on 'India's Energy Security: The Oil and Gas Dimensions', delivered on 10–11 April 2001 in New Delhi. The lecture was published by the International Institute for Caspian Studies.
6 Ibid.
7 Hooman Peimani, 'Piecing a Pipeline Together', online, available www.worldpipelines.com/Pipelines/Assets/Iran.pdf
8 'India and Pakistan Set Contours for Gas Pipeline Negotiations', Alexander's Oil &

Gas Connections, 13 July 2005, online, available www.gasandoil.com/goc/news/nts53384.htm

9 Siddharth Varadarajan, 'Rice Brings Reality Check on Indo-US Ties', *The Hindu*, 17 March 2005.

10 'Rice Woos India with Nuke Offer', *Washington Times*, 17 March 2005, online, available, http://washingtontimes.com/upi-breaking/20050316–052019–1831r.htm

11 PTI News, 22 July 2005.

12 'UPA's "Pro-U.S. Shift" Shameful: Opposition', *The Hindu*, 15 March 2011, online, available www.thehindu.com/news/national/article1540051.ece

13 'Iran says Nuclear Decisions Depend on IAEA, EU Behavior', *Tehran Times*, 28 September 2005.

14 'Peace Pipeline Without India?', *Tehran Times*, 11 April 2009, vol. 10563, online, available www.tehrantimes.com/index_View.asp?code=191917

15 '90% Work on IPI Pipeline Complete within Iran: Envoy', *The Economic Times*, 8 Feb 2011, online, available www.articles.economictimes.com.indiatimes.com/2011–02–08/news

16 Ibid.

17 Etgar Lefkovits, 'Israel and Turkey Plan Energy Pipeline', *Jerusalem Post*, 11 May 2006, online, available www.jpost.com/servlet/Satellite?cid=1145961328841&pagename=JPost%2FJPArticle%2FShowFull

18 Utpal Bhaskar, 'India to Attend Meeting on Turkish Pipeline Project', *Mint*, 25 November 2008, online, available, http://www.livemint.com/2008/11/25005838/India-ti-attent-meeting-on-Tur.html

19 Utpal Bhaskar, 'India to Revive West Asia Pipeline Plan', *Mint*, 9 April 2009, online, available www.livemint.com/2009/04/08233701/India-to-revive-West-Asia-pipe.html

20 Larry Chin, 'Players on a Rigged Grand Chessboard: Bridas, Unocal and the Afghanistan Pipeline', *Online Journal*, 6 March 2002, online, available, www.onlinejournal.com/archive/03–06–02_Chin.pdf

21 'Technical Assistance for the Feasibility Studies of the Turkmenistan–Afghanistan–Pakistan Natural Gas Pipeline Project', Asian Development Bank, TAR: STU 36488, December 2002, online, available www.adb.org/Documents/TARs/REG/tar_stu36488.pdf

22 Ibid.

23 'Turkmenistan Agrees to raise Natural Gas Supply to China', 2 March 2011, online, available http://news.xinhuanet.com/english2010/china/2011–03/02/c_13758150.htm

24 'TAPI Gas Price For India Higher Than IPI's', Indiaserver.com, 9 May 2008, www.india-server.com/news/tapi-gas-price-for-india-higher-than-3529.html

25 Ibid.

26 Hooman Peimani, 'Politicking Over Central Asia's Pipelines', *Journal of Energy Security*, 15 March 2011, online, available www.ensec.org/index.php?option=com_content&view-article&id=282:politicking-ver-central-asias-pipelines&catid=114:content0211&Itemid=374

14 The nuclear non-proliferation regime and the future of India– US nuclear energy co-operation

Sagarika Dutt

International co-operation in the field of nuclear energy is, and has always been, inextricably linked with the development of the nuclear non-proliferation regime. The US government has played a leading role in determining the main institutions, arrangements and understandings that form the foundations of this regime. The US Atomic Energy Act of 1954 liberalized nuclear trade but required recipients of American nuclear materials and technology to pledge to use them only for peaceful purposes. An international safeguards system was also established; the International Atomic Energy Agency (IAEA) was created in 1957, its main purpose being to promote 'practical application of atomic energy for peaceful uses throughout the world' and to apply safeguards at the request of the parties to any bilateral or multilateral arrangement, or at the request of a state (Statute of the IAEA). In May 1974 India conducted its first nuclear test, which was considered by the West to be an act of defiance and led to a major review of US nuclear policy. The US, Canada and other nuclear suppliers instituted stricter export guidelines to discourage other countries from following the Indian example. The Nuclear Exporters Committee (NEC) and Nuclear Suppliers Group (NSG) published a list of sensitive nuclear items, and the International Nuclear Fuel Cycle Evaluation was convened. Meanwhile the Nuclear Non-Proliferation Act was approved by the US Congress. It placed further restrictions on countries that depended on US nuclear aid, technology and materials. The Western states clearly wanted to ensure that competition for a greater share of the growing nuclear market did not lead to proliferation through indiscretion in transfers of sensitive items.[1] This chapter argues that the nuclear non-proliferation regime has not collapsed partly because the sponsors of this regime have superior political, economic and technological power on which the rest of the world depends.

On 10 October 2008, India and the US signed the 123 Agreement for co-operation between the two countries in the field of the peaceful uses of nuclear energy, a few days after Mr. Bush had signed the deal into law in the US.[2] This was the culmination of a process that began over three years earlier and gave rise to intense diplomatic and political debate. The agreement allows India access to nuclear reactors, fuel and technologies from the US after a gap of 34 years. Washington had terminated nuclear co-operation with India back in 1974 after New Delhi conducted a nuclear test in the Pokhran desert in Rajasthan. It makes

India the only country in the world able to pursue civil nuclear trade with other willing nations even though it has not signed the Nuclear Non-Proliferation Treaty (NPT) of 1968. This chapter explains how this 'deal' has affected domestic politics in India and, after analyzing the available evidence, concludes that the issue is not just about promoting strategic co-operation between the US and India, as many Indians believe, but is also about strengthening the nuclear non-proliferation regime.

India has not signed the NPT and the Comprehensive Test Ban Treaty (CTBT) but has declared a voluntary moratorium on nuclear testing. India's nuclear program began with the passage of the Atomic Energy Act on 15 April 1948, leading to the establishment of the Indian Atomic Energy Commission (IAEC). On 3 January 1954 the IAEC decided to set up a new facility – the Atomic Energy Establishment, Trombay (AEET). On 3 August 1954 the Department of Atomic Energy (DAE) was created, with Dr. Homi Bhabha as Secretary. This department answered directly to the Prime Minister and has continued to do so up to the present day.[3] India's nuclear program grew swiftly and it conducted nuclear tests in 1974 and 1998, which prompted Western countries, including the US, to impose sanctions on India. Due to its 'pariah' status for not signing the NPT and other international treaties, India's nuclear power program has developed largely without fuel or technological assistance from other countries. India's nuclear energy self-sufficiency extended from uranium exploration and mining through fuel fabrication, heavy water production, reactor design and construction, to reprocessing and waste management. Nuclear power supplied around 3 percent of India's electricity in 2007–08, and it is envisaged that this will increase to 25 percent by 2050 as imported uranium becomes available and new plants come on line. India is also developing technology to utilize its abundant reserves of thorium. It is estimated that India has 290,000 tonnes of thorium reserves, which is about one-quarter of the world's total reserves.[4]

A joint statement

Co-operation between the US and India in the field of civilian nuclear energy has been a controversial issue right from the start. Building on the Next Steps in Strategic Partnership (NSSP), a process started by the BJP government, India's Prime Minister Manmohan Singh and US President George Bush released a joint statement dated 18 July 2005. They asserted that 'as leaders of nations committed to the values of human freedom, democracy and the rule of law, the new relationship between India and the United States will promote stability, democracy, prosperity and peace throughout the world.' This sweeping statement is followed by a further emphasis on their 'common values and interests' which will form the basis of efforts 'to create an international environment conducive to [the] promotion of democratic values' and 'to combat terrorism relentlessly.' The statement then gives a list of fields in which the two countries will co-operate. They are the economy; energy and the environment; democracy and development; non-proliferation and security; and high technology and space.[5]

A key action point is to 'support and accelerate economic growth in both countries through greater trade, investment and technolog[ical] collaboration.' In the field of energy and the environment the statement made it clear that the US–India Energy Dialogue would address issues such as energy security and sustainable development. The two leaders agreed on the need 'to promote the imperatives of development and safeguarding the environment' and 'commit to developing and deploying cleaner, more efficient, affordable and diversified energy technologies.' Discussions between President Bush and Prime Minister Singh also addressed the issue of non-proliferation of weapons of mass destruction, and President Bush expressed the opinion that 'as a responsible state with advanced nuclear technology, India should acquire the same benefits and advantages as other such states.' He also promised that he would work to achieve full civil nuclear energy co-operation with India as it pursues its goals of promoting nuclear power and achieving energy security. In this context the President gave an undertaking to secure the US Congress's agreement to adjust US laws and policies and also work with 'friends and allies' to 'adjust' international regimes and address the issue of fuel supplies for safeguarded nuclear reactors at Tarapur expeditiously. Co-operation between the two countries is based on the understanding that there will not be any diversion of nuclear fuel and technology away from civilian purposes or to third countries without safeguards. These understandings were to be reflected in a safeguards agreement to be negotiated by India with the International Atomic Energy Agency (IAEA).[6]

The Indian prime minister promised that India would assume the same responsibilities and practices as other countries with advanced nuclear technology, such as the US. These would involve identifying and separating civilian and military nuclear facilities and programs in a phased manner and filing a declaration regarding its civilian facilities with the IAEA. This was considered necessary because the Indian nuclear power program began as an undifferentiated program and the strategic program is an offshoot of this research. However, Indian authorities claim that 'identification of purely civilian facilities and programmes that have no strategic implications poses a particular challenge,' and this has necessitated the drafting of a separation plan by the Indian authorities that will identify the civilian facilities to be offered for safeguards in phases.

The range of undertakings made by the Indian government included taking a decision to place voluntarily its civilian nuclear facilities under IAEA safeguards; signing and adhering to an Additional Protocol with respect to civilian nuclear facilities; continuing India's unilateral moratorium on nuclear testing; working with the United States for the conclusion of a Multilateral Fissile Material Cut Off Treaty; refraining from the transfer of enrichment and reprocessing technologies to states that do not have them and supporting international efforts to limit their spread; and ensuring that necessary steps have been taken to secure nuclear materials and technology through comprehensive export control legislation and through harmonization and adherence to the Missile Technology Control Regime (MTCR) and Nuclear Suppliers Group (NSG) guidelines.

Opposition at home

However, the United Progressive Alliance (UPA) government faced stiff opposition at home. The Left parties, on whose support the UPA government depends, felt that the India–US Joint Statement was a 'continuation of the pro-United States shift' in Indian foreign policy and a deviation from both the policy of non-alignment and the Indian government's Common Minimum Programme. The CPI-M politbureau expressed skepticism about the references to spreading democracy and combating terrorism, and expressed its concerns about making alliances with the US 'at a time when the superpower has become notorious for its unilateralist and anti-democratic activities.' The CPI-M was aggrieved that the government had not discussed its views and proposals with all the parties concerned before deciding on the course of action. The party's leaders felt that the present government was continuing the 'undemocratic practices' of the erstwhile National Democratic Alliance (NDA) regime, which had promoted secret negotiations between Strobe Talbott and Jaswant Singh on security and foreign policy issues. The CPI-M also made it very clear that it was in favor of an independent nuclear policy and pointed out that 'India had always opposed the discriminatory policies of the nuclear haves and have-nots ... [and] was also committed to nuclear disarmament and making the world free of nuclear weapons' adding that the Rajiv Gandhi plan for disarmament was the last major initiative taken in this regard.[7]

The CPI-M was concerned that the US would impose restrictions that would hamper the development of an independent Indian nuclear technology policy for peaceful purposes and research activities for overcoming reliance on imported nuclear fuel. The CPI-M was also unhappy that the US administration had not recognized India as a nuclear weapons power (merely as a state with advanced nuclear technology) and had not supported its claim for a permanent seat in the UN Security Council. It asserted that the NDA regime had accepted a 'junior partnership' with the US and that the much publicized India–US Defence Framework was based on this asymmetrical partnership. It also wanted to know what the US had got in return for offering India civilian nuclear co-operation and urged the government to clarify whether there was an understanding about buying US defense equipment to the tune of billions of dollars. There may well be a grain of truth in these allegations, as India has recently stepped up defense collaboration with the US. It has recently signed 'its biggest-ever military deal' with the US for eight long-range maritime reconnaissance aircraft for the Indian navy for $2.1 billion and there are other plans in the pipeline.[8]

In March 2006, during President Bush's visit to India, another joint statement was released expressing 'satisfaction with the great progress the United States and India have made in advancing our strategic partnership to meet the global challenges of the 21st century' and the intention to 'expand even further the growing ties between [the] two countries.' The joint statement put emphasis on economic prosperity and trade, energy security and a clean environment, and also global safety and security. On the issue of nuclear co-operation the statement 'welcomed the successful completion of discussions on India's separation plan' and looked forward to the full implementation of the commitments made in 2005. It also welcomed the participation of India in the ITER initiative on fusion energy as an important step towards the common goal of full nuclear energy co-operation. But there were several anti-American demonstrations during President Bush's visit, which indicated that some sections of the Indian public did not support American foreign policy and considered that Mr. Bush was not welcome in India. In March 2006 the US government circulated a statement in the NSG proposing to adjust NSG Guidelines with respect to India to enable full civil nuclear co-operation.[9] But there was considerable opposition to the proposed co-operation between the two countries in the US. The nuclear non-proliferation lobby expressed its disapproval of the discussions taking place between the US and India and opposed the legislation that had been introduced in Congress to amend US laws to enable co-operation between the two countries. Critics of the initiative argued that civilian nuclear co-operation with a country that has not signed the NPT would seriously undermine it and the global nuclear non-proliferation regime.[10]

The Indian government defends its policy

In July 2006, the Indian foreign secretary, Shyam Saran, defended the India–US joint statement of 18 July 2005. He said that 'few other joint statements have been dissected in as much detail as this one,' adding, 'what is so special about the July 18 joint statement that it warrants an analysis even a year later? Is it in any way a defining document of our contemporary diplomacy?' But at the same time he also accepted that it departs from India's 'orthodox positions' on important issues.[11] Although Saran did not mention India's traditional policy of non-alignment he admitted that the era of defensive diplomacy was over. 'If India is to become a credible candidate for permanent membership of the Security Council, then we must adjust our traditional positions. Our foreign policy must reflect our national aspirations and express our confidence as an emerging global player.' He pointed out that American strategic assessments of India articulated in the National Security Strategy of March 2006 and the Quadrennial Defense Review Report of February 2006 describe India as a major power shouldering global obligations and as a key actor, along with China and Russia, in determining the international security environment for the 21st century.

It seems that non-alignment is becoming an obsolete concept as the Indian economy expands and economic considerations begin to outweigh all other considerations. Better relations with the US are in India's national interest. The US is India's largest trading partner, an important investor in the Indian economy, and a major source of technology. Improved ties with the US could accelerate India's growth rate and the process of development. For the US, India is currently one of the fastest-growing export markets. Both countries realize that a technological partnership with the US would enormously benefit a country like India whose future is so tied to the knowledge and service industries. The

Americans also have respect for Indian democracy and the two countries have similar stands on terrorism and security threats from non-state actors. In the field of international relations, the Indians consider the US to be 'the pre-eminent power of our times' which can shape global opinion in India's favor. India 'requires adjustments in the international order so that [its] aspirations are accommodated.' Saran believes that 'the challenge to Indian diplomacy ... is to maximise the gains while minimising the costs, and create an international environment that is supportive of [its] developmental goals.' India needs to overcome the factors that are hampering the growth of the Indian economy. These factors include inadequate infrastructure and energy security. The dialogue with the US is addressing these problems. For example, as a result of post-July 18 discussions, India has been able to finalize Indian participation in the FutureGen initiative dealing with clean coal and the Integrated Ocean Drilling Programme dealing with gas hydrates. The joint statement of July 18 has also enabled Indian participation in the ITER fusion energy initiative. India has now joined a select group of countries (the EU, France, Russia, China, Japan and South Korea) to collaborate in an area that will benefit India enormously.[12]

A structurally disadvantaged Indian government feels that technology denial regimes, led by the US and other advanced countries, are in place that need to be dismantled. India's access to nuclear technology and equipment was limited after 1974 on the grounds that most advanced nuclear technologies have dual uses.[13] Apparently, in the 1980s a Cray supercomputer for better weather forecasting was denied to India, since it could conceivably be used in its nuclear program as well. But American scientists and defense specialists have expressed their misgivings about the reversal of previous policies and the burgeoning relations between the US and India. For example, Hoey argues that India's acquisition of dual-use technology could set off an arms race in South Asia and accuses the US government of using India to contain China.[14] From an Indian perspective, while India's nuclear isolation encouraged indigenous innovation and led to outstanding achievements by Indian scientists in the past, an increasingly globalized and competitive world demands a different response today. As the Indian economy matures, and the country moves towards an ever more sophisticated knowledge- and technology-driven society, more co-operation is needed with other countries. This will also create opportunities for Indian scientists and technologists to benefit from regular interaction with their counterparts in the rest of the world. But the Indian government has also made it very clear that it would not agree to any restrictions on India's strategic program, nor does it expect any assistance from its international partners.

While the US government was considering amendments to US laws to enable full civil nuclear energy co-operation with India, the 18 July 2005 Joint Statement and the Separation Plan were tabled in the Indian Parliament by the prime minister on 7 March 2006. The final version of the Separation Plan was presented to Parliament on 11 May 2006. This plan contained a schedule for placing India's nuclear reactors under safeguards beginning from 2007. The Indian prime minister also made a statement in the Rajya Sabha (upper house) on 17 August and in the Lok Sabha (lower house) on 23 August 2006 that emphasized that 'anything that went beyond the parameters of the July 18 Joint Statement would be unacceptable to India' and that 'India will not place its nuclear facilities under safeguards until all restrictions on India are lifted.'[15] In an interview with *India Today*, the prime minister argued that nuclear power is critical to India's energy security '... if we want to be a world power.' He also expressed faith in President Bush who, in his opinion, of all the US presidents has shown the greatest friendliness towards India. Based on a recent foreign policy review, the Indian government has come to the conclusion that in a globalized world relations with the US need to be given the highest importance.[16]

The Hyde Act (2006) and nuclear non-proliferation

Meanwhile, the Henry J. Hyde United States–India Peaceful Atomic Energy Co-operation Act of 2006, better known as the Hyde Act, was passed by both houses of the US Congress in December 2006. Its purpose was to grant the US administration a waiver from Section 123 of the Atomic Energy Act of 1954 to enable the US administration to resume nuclear commerce with India. The text of this Act makes it very clear that it is based on the principle of nuclear non-proliferation. It begins with the statement that 'It is the sense of Congress that ... preventing the proliferation of nuclear weapons, other weapons of mass destruction, the means to produce them, and the means to deliver them are critical objectives for United States foreign policy' and goes on to say that 'sustaining the Nuclear Non-Proliferation Treaty (NPT) and strengthening its implementation ... is the keystone of United States non-proliferation policy.' The Act categorically states that 'any commerce in civil nuclear energy with India by the United States and other countries must be achieved in a manner that minimizes the risk of nuclear proliferation or regional arms races and maximizes India's adherence to international non-proliferation regimes, including, in particular, the guidelines of the Nuclear Suppliers Group (NSG).' Under section 104 of the Act, the US President is required to report to appropriate Congressional committees on the progress made by India in discharging its obligations as identified by the Act. Among other things, the President is asked to provide 'a description of the steps taken to ensure that proposed United States civil nuclear co-operation with India will not in any way assist India's nuclear weapons program.' Most crucially, he must provide 'a description of the steps that India is taking to work with the United States for the conclusion of a multilateral treaty banning the production of fissile material for nuclear weapons,' as well as the steps the US government is taking to encourage India to declare a date by which India would be willing to stop production of fissile material for nuclear weapons unilaterally or pursuant to a multilateral moratorium or treaty.

The nuclear non-proliferation regime is one of the most important regimes in international relations today. The Nuclear Non-Proliferation Treaty of 1968, which prohibits nuclear weapon states from transferring nuclear weapons to non-nuclear weapon states and from assisting or encouraging them to acquire nuclear weapons, is the cornerstone of this international regime. However, India has always maintained that this treaty is discriminatory. The definition of regimes as sets of implicit or explicit 'principles, norms, rules and decision-making procedures around which actor expectations converge in a given issue-area'[17] creates the impression that regimes are based on a consensus. In reality they are often the product of difficult and intense negotiations and bargaining that lead to critical compromises among the negotiating parties.[18] Furthermore, the possibility of challenges to existing regimes cannot be ruled out, as India's stance and more recently Iran's nuclear policy have shown. Ironically, the Act asks the US administration to 'secure India's full and active participation in United States efforts to dissuade, isolate, and if necessary, sanction and contain Iran for its efforts to acquire weapons of mass destruction.' International regimes are not static; they evolve and with the passage of time may become less consistent internally. A critic of regime analysis points out that interests and power relationships are the proximate and not just the ultimate cause of behavior in the international system.[19] This is the reason there has been so much opposition to the nuclear deal between India and the US in Indian political circles.

The 123 Agreement

In mid-2007 an agreement for co-operation between the Indian and US governments concerning the peaceful uses of nuclear energy, also known as the 123 Agreement, was finalized. In the carefully negotiated text the two parties recognize 'the significance of civilian nuclear energy for meeting growing energy demands in a cleaner and more efficient manner.' It emphasizes the importance of achieving energy security 'on a stable, reliable and predictable basis.' While this and strengthening the strategic partnership between the two countries are the main purposes of the agreement, the focus is equally on the prevention of the proliferation of weapons of mass destruction and support for the objectives of the IAEA and the safeguards system. However, the agreement does not 'hinder or otherwise interfere with any other activities involving the use of nuclear material, non-nuclear material, equipment, components, information or technology and military nuclear facilities produced, acquired or developed by them independent of this agreement for their own purposes.'

Indian political elites felt that the 123 Agreement was more favorable to them than the Hyde Act. The main purpose of the agreement was to facilitate nuclear trade between the US and India 'in the mutual interests of their respective industry, utilities and consumers.' The agreement will remain in force for a period of 40 years and can be extended thereafter for additional periods of ten years. Either party has the right to terminate the agreement by giving written notice to the other party and providing reasons for seeking such termination.

The Nuclear Suppliers Group grants a waiver to India

In July 2008 opposition parties attempted to bring Manmohan Singh's government down. All of these parties were completely against the nuclear deal for reasons that will be explained below. The opposition even accused the government of bribing MPs to vote in its favor. After some dramatic scenes in the Lok Sabha, the government won the vote of confidence on 22 July. A triumphant prime minister hit out at his political opponents and accused the BJP supremo, L.K. Advani, of promoting communal violence and the Left parties of trying to exercise a veto over government decision-making. He reiterated that the agreement with the US would end India's isolation and enable it to trade with the US, Russia, France and other countries, but without any external political interference in the nation's strategic nuclear program. Attempting to assuage his political opponents' fears, the PM asserted that India's strategic autonomy will never be compromised. But Prakash Karat, the CPI-M General Secretary, insisted that the nuclear deal was 'against the interest of the country' and vowed that the 'CPI-M will continue the struggle against the India–US nuclear deal.'[20] He said that 'to make India's foreign policy and strategic autonomy hostage to the potential benefits of nuclear energy does not make sense except for the American imperative to bind India to its strategic design in Asia.'[21] However, the prime minister emerged victorious from this fracas and his government proceeded to seek the blessings of the IAEA. On 1 August the 35-member IAEA Board of Governors unanimously approved an India-specific safeguards agreement.[22] Thereafter, following weeks of speculation, nervousness and uncertainty in India, the 45-nation NSG granted a waiver to India on 6 September, allowing it to participate in global nuclear commerce, and ending 34 years of India's nuclear isolation.

The NSG's deliberations had taken longer than anticipated as several countries (China, Austria, Ireland and New Zealand) had expressed reservations. However, while India's External Affairs minister Pranab Mukherjee was trying to convince the NSG that India would continue to observe a voluntary moratorium on nuclear testing, that it had a no-first-use nuclear weapons policy and that 'India has a long-standing and steadfast commitment to universal, non-discriminatory and total elimination of nuclear weapons,' at home the UPA government insisted that India retains sovereign rights to conduct nuclear tests. This was echoed by the US ambassador to India, David Mulford,[23] and also by India's former President Kalam (one of the chief architects of its nuclear and space programs) who asserted, in an interview with NDTV in September 2008, that India will always have the right to test in the supreme national interest. But both the Hyde Act and the 123 Agreement make it very clear that if India did go down this road it might have to pay a heavy price. With a new administration in office in the US, the Indian government can no longer count on their special friendship with George Bush. Moreover, President Obama, who had not initially supported the 123 Agreement and as a senator had attempted to amend the Hyde Act,[24] made it very clear that non-proliferation and the reduction of nuclear weapons would be one of his key aims and that he wanted a deal with Russia to achieve this.[25]

Armstrong *et al.* point out that the success of the non-proliferation regime is dependent on a commitment from the nuclear powers to reduce their nuclear stockpiles and ensure access to peaceful nuclear technology. This commitment is an important part of the bargain between them and the non-nuclear weapon states.[26] This is one of the main factors responsible for the success or failure of the NPT Review conferences. The 2010 conference held in New York in May led to an agreement on 64 recommended actions covering nuclear disarmament, non-proliferation, nuclear energy for non-military purposes, and a conference to facilitate progress on eliminating nuclear, chemical and biological weapons from the Middle East.[27] The Non-Aligned Movement was strongly represented at this conference and together with the New Agenda Coalition (NAC) 'put forward the most concrete and detailed proposals on nuclear disarmament.'[28] But Iran's Ambassador, Ali Soltanieh, argued that the NAM proposals had been watered down and he accused the nuclear weapon states of blocking disarmament steps sought by the majority. Johnson writes that the 'review conference outcome was most disappointing on nuclear disarmament and safeguards, where it proved difficult to make any concrete commitments beyond what had already been agreed to in 2000.'[29] The final document echoed UN Security Council resolutions 1540 (2004) and 1887 (2009) on non-proliferation and nuclear security and had a number of recommendations on nuclear materials' safety and trafficking. It may be recalled that President Obama had a major role in pushing through UNSC resolution 1887.[30] The conference was uneasy about the US–India nuclear deal and felt that the NSG had lost credibility over its failure to follow its own guidelines and that there was no question of extending the deal made with India to Israel or Pakistan. Meanwhile in India on 25 August 2010, the Lok Sabha passed the controversial Civil Liability for Nuclear Damage Bill 2010. This bill had been introduced in the Lok Sabha on 7 May and was crucial for operationalizing India's civil nuclear agreements with various countries, particularly the US. The opposition, mainly the Left parties and the BJP, had accused the government of trying to 'dilute' the provisions of the bill. The CPI-M general secretary, Mr. Prakash Karat, charged that the Bill had been introduced 'at the behest' of the US administration, which wants to sell nuclear reactors to India and ensure that 'its companies should have no liability in case of a nuclear incident.'[31]

In July 2009 President Obama signed an agreement with Russia (subject to ratification by the US Senate) to reduce American and Russian strategic nuclear arsenals by at least one-quarter. This was a significant move as between them they have 95 percent of the world's nuclear weapons.[32] Then in April 2010 the US and Russia signed the New Start Treaty in Prague. Obama emphasized in his speech that it was 'an important milestone for nuclear security and non-proliferation, and for US–Russia relations' and 'fulfils our common objective to negotiate a new Strategic Arms Reduction Treaty.' He pointed out that it cuts delivery vehicles by roughly half and includes a comprehensive verification regime which will build trust between the two countries. He also asserted that nuclear weapons 'threaten the common security of all nations.'[33] In June 2010, at a UN Forum organized by UNA UK, Hans Blix (former UN weapons inspector) said that 'the new atmosphere brought about by the Obama Administration is a major hopeful development coming after more than a decade of American disinterest in and even disdain for disarmament.' However, he admitted that there were several obstacles to nuclear disarmament.[34]

Conclusion

In June 2009, US Secretary of State Hillary Clinton confirmed that the US is committed to the implementation of the US–India deal. President Obama's visit to New Delhi in November 2010 further strengthened relations between the two countries.[35] During this visit he expressed his support for India's bid to secure a permanent seat in the UN Security Council. He also said that he had undertaken the trip to India to strengthen 'one of the defining partnerships of the 21st century,' build on commercial ties and strengthen bilateral co-operation in various fields. With a view to expanding its energy sector, India has recently signed agreements with France and Russia to achieve its objective of building more nuclear reactors. Electricity companies have already started taking advantage of the liberalization of nuclear trade. But the Indian government has also signed an agreement with the IAEA for the Application of Safeguards to Civilian Nuclear Facilities, after several rounds of consultations.[36] As American security expert Lehman says, the agreement between the US and India is 'an opportunity to strengthen a nuclear non-proliferation regime that is suffering from its own internal weaknesses' such as inadequate enforcement and an inability to engage effectively with the non-parties to the NPT. Bringing India into a more comprehensive regime of nuclear non-proliferation would help to reduce the dangers associated with weapons of mass destruction.[37] China, too, was integrated into the non-proliferation regime as a stakeholder when it was admitted into the NSG and was allowed to conduct nuclear commerce under safeguards.[38] But political considerations should not make us lose sight of the fact that the Indian nation needs nuclear power. With a population of over one billion and a rapidly expanding economy, India is struggling to meet its energy demands and cannot afford to ignore the nuclear option.

Notes

1 T.M. Tate, 'Regime building in the non-proliferation system', 1990.
2 *The Statesman* (Kolkata), 12 October 2008.
3 For further information see www.nuclearweaponarchive.org/India/IndiaOrigin.html
4 Available at www.world-nuclear.org/info/inf53.html
5 Available at www.hindu.com/thehindu/nic/indousjoint.htm
6 S. Dutt, 'The future of US–India nuclear co-operation', *New Zealand International Review*, May/June 2009, pp. 17–22.
7 'Indo–US joint statement, Continuation of pro-US shift: Left parties', available at http://US.rediff.com/news/2005/jul/21left.htm
8 *The Statesman* (Kolkata), 6 January 2009.
9 US–India joint statement, available at www.whitehouse.gov/news/releases/2006/03/20060302–5.html
10 BBC News, available at http://news.bbc.co.uk/go/pr/fr/-/1/hi/world/south_asia/5120782.stm

11 'The India–US joint statement of July 18, 2005 – A year later', available at http://meaindia.nic.in/speech/2006/07/14ss01.htm

12 Ibid.

13 The issue of India's quest for dual-use technology is discussed by Matthew Hoey. He argues that India's acquisition of dual-use technology could set off a regional arms race and is not as innocuous as it sounds. See M. Hoey, 'India's quest for dual-use technology', 2009.

14 Ibid.

15 Ibid.

16 *India Today*, 27 August 2007, p. 15.

17 S.D. Krasner, 'Structural causes and regime consequences', 1982.

18 O.R. Young, *International Cooperation*, 1989, p. 22.

19 Krasner, 'Structural causes.'

20 *The Statesman* (Kolkata), 23 July 2008.

21 P. Karat, *Subordinate Ally*, 2007, p. 32.

22 Also see 'India safeguards agreement signed', 2 February 2009, available at www.iaea.org/NewsCenter/News/2009/indiaagreement.html

23 'India has sovereign right to conduct N-tests: Mulford', *The Statesman* (Kolkata), 11 September 2008.

24 A.R. Jerath, 'Letter clue to Obama's India policy', 2008; S. Varadarajan, 'Promise and pitfalls of Obama's South Asia policy', 2009.

25 'President Obama seeks Russia deal to slash nuclear weapons', *Times Online*, 4 February 2009.

26 D. Armstrong, L. Lloyd and J. Redmond, *From Versailles to Maastricht*, 1996, p. 262.

27 R. Johnson, 'Assessing the 2010 NPT Review Conference', July/August 2010.

28 Ibid.

29 Ibid., p. 6.

30 D.E. Sanger, 'Security Council adopts nuclear measure', *New York Times*, 24 September 2009.

31 'Government woos BJP, Left on N-Bill; says it's open to modification', *The Statesman* (Kolkata), 24 August 2010; 'Lok Sabha passes Nuke liability Bill', *The Statesman* (Kolkata), 26 August 2010, p. 1; 'Left, BJP to oppose N-liability dilution', *The Statesman* (Kolkata), 23 August 2010; 'Government makes changes in N-Bill', *The Statesman* (Kolkata), 21 August 2010.

32 C.J. Levy and P. Baker, 'US–Russia nuclear agreement is first step in broad effort', 2009.

33 Barack Obama's Speech in Prague on New START Treaty, April 2010, Council on Foreign Relations, 8 April 2010.

34 H. Blix, 'Multilateral nuclear disarmament and strengthened non-proliferation', 2010.

35 V. Bajaj and H. Timmons, 'Obama to visit India, and both sides hope to expand ties', *New York Times*, 4 November 2010; 'India is a world power, says Obama', Timesnow.tv, 8 November 2010.

36 This agreement is dated 2 February 2009 but will enter into force on the date the IAEA receives from India written notification that its statutory and/or constitutional requirements for entry into force have been met. The IAEA currently applies safeguards to six nuclear reactors in India under safeguards agreements concluded between 1971 and 1994. The new agreement will bring additional reactors under IAEA safeguards. (www.iaea.org/NewsCenter/News.2009/indiaagreement.html

37 Testimony by the honorable Ronald F. Lehman II on US–Indian nuclear energy cooperation: Security and non-proliferation, before the United States Senate Committee on Foreign Relations, Wednesday, 2 November 2005, SD-419.

38 K. Subrahmanyam, 'We're not a rogue state', *The Times of India* (Chennai), 3 September 2008.

Bibliography

Armstrong, D., L. Lloyd and J. Redmond, *From Versailles to Maastricht*, Basingstoke: Macmillan, 1996.

Blix, H., 'Multilateral nuclear disarmament and strengthened non-proliferation', Speech at UN Forum hosted by the United Nations Association of the UK, 12 June 2010, London.

Chadha, V., *Indo-US relations – Divergence to convergence*, New Delhi: Macmillan India Ltd., 2008.

Hoey, M., 'India's quest for dual-use technology', *Bulletin of the Atomic Scientists*, September/October 2009, pp. 43–59.

Jerath, A.R., 'Letter clue to Obama's India policy', *Daily News and Analysis*, 7 November 2008.

Johnson, R., 'Assessing the 2010 NPT Review Conference', *Bulletin of the Atomic Scientists*, July/August 2010.

Karat, P., *Subordinate Ally, The nuclear deal and India–US strategic relations*, New Delhi: Leftword Books, 2007.

Krasner, S.D., 'Structural causes and regime consequences: Regimes as intervening variables', *International Organization*, 36:2, 1982, pp. 185–6.

Levy, C.J. and P. Baker, 'US–Russia nuclear agreement is first step in broad effort', *New York Times*, 7 July 2009, available www.nytimes.com/2009/07/07/world/europe/07proxy.html

Obama, B., Speech in Prague on New START Treaty, April 2010, Council on Foreign Relations, 8 April 2010, online, available www.cfr.org/proliferation/obmas-speech-prague-new-start-treaty-april-2010/p21849

Subrahmanyam, K., 'We're not a rogue state', *The Times of India* (Chennai), 3 September 2008.

Tate, T.M., 'Regime building in the non-proliferation system', *Journal of Peace Research*, 27:4, November 1990, pp. 399–414.

Tripathi, A.K. and R.N. Tripathi, *US policy towards India: A post cold war study*, New Delhi: Reference Press, 2008.

Varadarajan, S., 'Promise and pitfalls of Obama's South Asia policy', *The Hindu*, 27 January 2009.

Young, O.R., *International cooperation: Building regimes for natural resources and the environment*, Cornell University Press, 1989.

15 Multilateral economic co-operation and the emergence of regional organizations in South Asia

An assessment

Mohor Chakraborty

The growth of regionalism and the formation of regional organizations has been a prominent feature of post-World War II politics. They are usually inspired by specific objectives. While some regions and regional groupings may be concerned primarily with maximizing economic welfare and gains from intra-regional trade and investment, others are more interested in defense and security, or the protection of social and cultural traditions.[1] Here it is useful to make a distinction between neo-Realist approaches to international and regional organizations and neo-liberal institutionalism. While the former emphasizes that hegemonic powers will have a major role to play in the creation of such organizations, the latter argues that states normally behave rationally and will enter into co-operative arrangements if they stand to gain from such co-operation.[2]

In the second half of the twentieth century, a number of regional organizations dealing exclusively with strategic and security matters were established by the two major competing powers – the United States of America (USA) and the former Soviet Union – in the context of cold war rivalry and their policy of expanding their spheres of influence. NATO, SEATO, CENTO (of which Pakistan was a member), ANZUS and so on led by the Western bloc, on the one hand, and the Warsaw Pact and COMECON led by the Soviet Union, on the other, were clear examples of multilateral regional military organizations that were created to maintain order in a bipolar world.

The first initiative to establish a regional organization in which economics remained the main determining criterion was taken in the European region, initially known as the European Economic Community (EEC) and later known as the European Union (EU).[3] Influenced by this European model, in Southeast Asia, some countries had undertaken the formation of a similar type of regional economic organization, known as Association of Southeast Asia (1961) and MAPHILINDO (1963), in order to unify some of the states in the region. Unfortunately, these initiatives did not mature due to power struggles among the regional countries. However, the endeavor to form some sort of a cohesive regional economic organization did not lose its momentum and bore fruit when on 8 August 1967, for the first time in the Asian region, the Association of Southeast Asian Nations (ASEAN) was established at Bangkok. The principal objectives of this Association were: promoting the economic, social and cultural development of the region through joint endeavors and active collaboration and mutual assistance; and safeguarding regional peace and stability.[4]

The twenty-first century is Asia's century but cannot and should not be just about Southeast and Northeast Asia. As Indian Prime Minister Manmohan Singh commented at the Thimpu Summit held in April 2010, 'the 21st century cannot be an Asian century unless South Asia marches ahead and marches together.'[5] However, South Asia has a weak sense of regional identity and has even been described as a region without regionalism.[6] Furthermore there is a sense of mistrust and apprehension towards India in the psyche of the neighbors because of its mammoth size relative to theirs and its power potential.[7] Therefore, India has some difficulty in playing its 'natural' role in the region, that of a hegemon, even a benevolent one. In any case India is as self-interested as the rest of the states/powers in the region and its policy makers have to respond to domestic pressures,[8] making it necessary for them to negotiate every step of the way.

The formation of the South Asian Association for Regional Co-operation (SAARC) in 1985, the Bay of Bengal Initiative for Multisectoral Technical and Economic Cooperation (BIMSTEC) in July 1997, the Kunming Initiative[9] (August 1999) and the Mekong–Ganga Cooperation Initiative (MGC) in November 2000 are examples of multilateral diplomacy in the economic sector. The purpose of this chapter is to discuss and assess the evolving system of multilateral economic co-operation and the emergence of regional organizations in South Asia. The paper will also analyze India's role and interest in promoting multilateralism.

SAARC as a regional and geo-economic entity

The idea of establishing a regional organization in South Asia was first mooted by the late Bangladesh President, Zia-ur-Rahman, in 1977–1978 during his sojourn to Nepal, India, Pakistan and Sri Lanka. During the course of this visit, President Zia-ur-Rahman proposed an instrument of collective self-reliance in a common quest for peace and development of the countries concerned. In May 1980, he issued a formal call for regional co-operation, following which, at New Delhi in August 1983, seven Foreign Ministers (from India, Pakistan, Nepal, Bhutan, Bangladesh, Maldives and Sri Lanka) officially proclaimed the South Asian Regional Cooperation (SARC). At this meeting, the participants expressed their consensus to 'strengthen collective self-reliance and to accelerate development through regional cooperation.' In the wake of this declaration, a series of Foreign Ministers' meetings was held. Finally, on 7–8 December 1985, the first Summit of the South Asian countries was held in Dhaka, where SARC was renamed as the South Asian Association for Regional Cooperation (SAARC). At this summit, the seven member countries agreed to co-operate and work towards finding solutions to their common problems in a spirit of friendship, trust and mutual understanding, and towards the creation of an order based on mutual respect, equality and shared benefit.[10]

SAARC's key objectives, enshrined in its Charter, emphasize promoting the welfare of the peoples of the countries, improving the quality of life and accelerating the pace of economic growth, social progress and cultural development. In order to promote regional integration, SAARC has adopted the goal of establishing a South Asian Economic Union by 2020, progressively through the South Asia Preferential Trade Agreement (SAPTA), South Asia Free Trade Agreement[11](SAFTA) and a South Asian Customs Union by 2015.

Progress under SAPTA

The Sixth SAARC Summit, held in Colombo in 1991, initiated deliberations on Preferential Trading Arrangements (PTA) by establishing the Inter-Governmental Group (IGG) to suggest trade liberalization measures, and as a result the Framework Agreement on SAPTA was signed at the Seventh SAARC Summit in Dhaka on 11 April 1993, coming into force on 7 December 1995. The basic principles underlying SAPTA were the following:

- overall reciprocity and mutuality of advantages so as to benefit equitably all Contracting States, taking into account their respective level of economic and industrial development, the pattern of their external trade, and trade and tariff policies and systems;
- negotiation of tariff reform step by step, improved and extended in successive stages through periodic reviews;
- recognition of the special needs of the Least Developed Contracting States and agreement on concrete preferential measures in their favor; and
- inclusion of all products, manufactures and commodities in their raw, semi-processed and processed forms.[12]

The accrued benefits prompted the SAARC countries to emphasize greater economic integration by launching the second round of negotiations at the SAARC Commerce Ministers' Meeting in January 1996, at the end of which SAPTA–II came into force in March 1997. It covered a wider exchange of concessions and extended the range of products to as many as 2,013 products, among which India offered tariff concessions on 902 commodities.[13] While the duty concessions it offered were in the range of 10 to 50 percent, on a reciprocal basis, India received concessions on a range of products as well (see Tables 15.1 and 15.2). According to SAARC sources, four rounds of trade negotiations have been concluded under SAPTA so far, covering over 5,000 commodities.

The early experiences of successful regional trading blocs of the ilk of the EU and ASEAN, within the PTA model, have demonstrated that a region can become vibrant by increasing its output, income and employment, in addition to improving terms of trade and the ability to attract foreign direct investment (FDI). Moreover, the major rationale behind the idea of a PTA was that it is the

Table 15.1 Concessions offered to India on items under SAPTA

Country	Concessions offered to India on items under SAPTA
Pakistan	363
Sri Lanka	95
Bangladesh	226
Bhutan	47
Nepal	223
Maldives	5

Source: For details, see www.saarc-sec.org

Table 15.2 Tariff lines to SAARC members

Country	Tariff lines to all countries of SAARC under SAPTA	Tariff lines to LDCs	Total
India	472	2,082	2,554
Bangladesh	407	144	551
Pakistan	262	229	491
Nepal	328	163	491
Bhutan	109	124	233
Sri Lanka	155	44	199
Maldives	172	06	178

Source: For details, see www.saarc-sec.org

second-best mechanism, within which discriminatory regional trading arrangements, like common market with zero internal tariffs and a common set of external tariffs on non-members, are best devised as a first step towards non-discriminatory free trade in the international realm.[14] Unfortunately, the SAPTA initiative lost its momentum owing to its over-emphasis on trade liberalization programs without adequately scrutinizing the issue of policy barriers to trade and foreign investment in the region. This shortcoming has impeded the generation of additional trade and commercial opportunities on the one hand, and the encouragement of greater intra-regional investment, technology transfer and development of human resources within the broader framework of South-South co-operation, on the other. In this connection, it may be mentioned that an analytical study, conducted in 1993, attributed the weakness of SAARC as a viable regional economic organization to the absence of a majority of important prerequisites: high pre-arrangement tariffs; high level of regional trade before the arrangement; the existence of complementary as opposed to competitive trade and differences in the economic structures of the countries concerned in South Asia.[15] Moreover, the increasing volume of the bilateral trade gaps of the South Asian partners with India and the balance of trade in favor of India could potentially exacerbate the problem of uneven regional development.

Despite its promising principles and rounds of negotiations aimed at augmenting intra-SAARC trade, SAPTA could not live up to expectations, particularly since the number of commodities it covered for tariff reductions was too low to have an overall lasting impact either on the total regional trade or on the total exports and imports of the component countries. Furthermore, there were conflicts of interest between SAARC's member states. For example, Sri Lanka and Bangladesh wanted India to withdraw all import restrictions imposed on Bangladeshi and Sri Lankan goods. But from the Indian point of view, a trade regime that provided unrestricted access to the sprawling Indian market for all goods from Bangladesh and Sri Lanka, would naturally encourage regional and international investors to boost investments in these countries, which, in terms of India's concept of a liberalized economy, was not favorable. This Indian anxiety was amply reflected in an interview with R.S. Ratna, the Director of the Indian Ministry of Commerce and Industry:

> As of now, Bangladesh and Sri Lanka have competitive advantage over India in the textile sector as they have access to cheap manpower as compared to India. So, Indian textile companies are fearing an onslaught of cheap imports from these countries, which will wreck their growth chances here. Our ministry will take necessary steps to safeguard the interest of our domestic industry.[16]

Thus, notwithstanding their commitment to the policy of economic and trade liberalization national protectionist sentiments among the members of SAARC have, time and again, obstructed the smooth functioning of the SAPTA process.

From SAPTA to SAFTA: towards better understanding

The impact of SAPTA on transforming trade patterns in South Asia and promoting regional integration was modest. Records reveal that though the intra-SAARC trade, which accounted for 3 percent of total regional trade for much of the 1980s, increased to 4.1 percent, 4.4 percent and 5 percent in 1995, 1996 and 1998 respectively, there was no discernible rise in the volume of intra-regional trade in the succeeding years, with 4.1 percent in 2000 and 4.7 percent in 2001, under the SAPTA framework. Consequently, the SAARC counterparts prudently realized that 'It is necessary to progress beyond a Preferential Trading Arrangement to move towards higher levels of trade and economic cooperation in the region by removing barriers to cross-border flow of goods' and to accord special and differential treatment to the 'Least Developed Countries in the region commensurate with their development needs.'[17]

The SAARC member states signed the Framework Agreement on SAFTA at the 12th SAARC Summit, held in Islamabad on 6 January 2004. Thereby, the SAFTA created a scaffold providing for the birth of a South Asian free trade area, with zero customs duty on the trade of practically all products by the end of 2016, on a phase-by-phase basis. It was also agreed that India, Pakistan and Sri

Lanka would reduce their duties to 20 percent in the first phase of the two-year period that ended in 2007. It was further decided that, in the subsequent five-year phase ending in 2012, the 20 percent duty would be further brought down to zero in a series of annual cuts, and that the LDCs (least developed regional countries), namely Nepal, Bhutan, Bangladesh, and Maldives would be provided with an additional period of three years to reduce tariffs to zero. The salient clauses of this SAFTA Agreement included:

- reduction of tariffs to between 0 percent and 5 percent for LDCs
- removal of barriers to intra-SAARC investment
- harmonization of standards and simplification of customs procedures
- co-operation through joint ventures
- co-operation among Central Banks
- establishment of a South Asian Development Fund
- strengthening of transport and transit linkages among SAARC countries
- simplification of visa procedures for business.[18]

Following this understanding, India announced the pruning of the negative list from 744 items to around 500 items for the LDC members of SAARC, thereby enlarging the scope of duty-free entry to the export items of these countries. Addressing the Third SAFTA Council Meeting in New Delhi, held in March 2008, the Union Minister of Commerce and Industry (India), Kamal Nath, called for a review of negative lists to expand trade in goods and enlarge the scope for further trade co-operation among SAARC countries and said:

> In keeping with our commitments, we have already notified the advance-ment of the trade liberalization programme in respect of LDCs by one year and with effect from January 1, 2008, the import duty on all items other than those in the negative list has been reduced to zero. In India, we are trying to see that this transformation is least painful both for the producers within the country and those connected with our supply chain outside the country. Various SAARC mechanisms have focused on developing specific short, medium and long-term co-operation projects to deliver direct benefits to the people. Operationalisation of the SAARC Development Fund and full implementation of SAFTA would pave the way for this development.[19]

This meeting finalized the Draft Protocol for the implementation of SAFTA by Afghanistan, thus paving the way for the formal entry of Afghanistan into SAFTA, and recommended that it would be treated on a par with Maldives as far as the Mechanism for Compensation of Revenue Loss (MCRL) was concerned.

It is a fact that, in the realm of liberalization and globalization, SAFTA is an ambitious attempt at engineering economic unity among SAARC member states, notwithstanding the unequal size of the economies, and is 'motivated by the commitment to strengthen intra-SAARC economic co-operation to maximize the realization of the region's potential for trade and development for the benefit of their people.'[20] SAFTA is an instrument for encouraging geographically contiguous countries to operate at low costs of transaction, supported by the proximity of markets, availability of infrastructure across the region, presence of somewhat similar patterns of consumption and the creation of a large market which fosters investment both from within and outside the region.[21] Thus, the SAARC Secretary General, S.K. Sharma, while addressing the Inaugural Session of the Fifteenth SAARC Summit (Colombo) in August 2008, said:

> SAARC has continued to work on policy goals to promote and strengthen regional trade and economic cooperation. Trade under SAFTA has already commenced. The relevant mechanisms are focusing on reducing the size of Sensitive Lists and strengthening trade facilitation measures. Important steps for Harmonizing of Standards are also taken. An Expert Group is expected to commence the negotiations on a Draft Framework Agreement on Trade in Services. The Inter-governmental Group on Financial Issues is also contemplating discussions on identifying specific steps by the Member States towards deeper economic integration.[22]

In summary, the overall performance of SAFTA against the backdrop of the new globalized economic order has not been as impressive as in the case of ASEAN economic co-operation. In fact, India's imports from SAARC countries are still quite low. Taking each member individually in the matter of imports, it is discernible that India's imports from Pakistan and Nepal are just 0.3 percent of its total imports, while it imports a meagre 0.1 percent from Sri Lanka and Bangladesh. India's exports to SAARC nations (ranging from fruits, vegetables, sugar, coffee and paper, to cotton, cotton yarn, cotton fabric, light engineering goods and pharmaceuticals, etc.) make up 2.8 percent of its total exports – its exports to Pakistan, Nepal, Sri Lanka and Bangladesh being 0.2 percent, 0.5 percent, 0.9 percent and 1 percent respectively of its total exports (see Tables 15.3, 15.4 and 15.5). Thus India is in a position to increase its imports from the SAARC region substantially if there is a serious effort on the part of the members to enhance intra-group trade.

Promotion of trans-regional co-operation: harmonizing state interests?

BIMSTEC as a vehicle for making inroads into Southeast Asia

Trans-regional initiatives – like the Bay of Bengal Initiative for Multi-Sectoral Economic and Technical Cooperation (BIMSTEC),[23] Mekong Ganga Cooperation (MGC), and the Kunming Initiative – could act as a bridge between South Asia and Southeast Asia, giving India more access to the regions beyond its eastern borders and creating opportunities for economic and social development.[24] India, in the context of the new world order, has indicated a desire to strengthen its position in the Asia Pacific region, and initiated a greater network

Table 15.3 India's import from SAARC countries from 1996/97 to 2009/10 (values in US$ million)

	Afghanistan	Bangladesh	Bhutan	Maldives	Nepal	Pakistan	Sri Lanka	Total import
1996–1997	3.05	62.23	33.78	0.17	64.07	36.16	42.84	242.31
1997–1998	10.70	50.81	13.44	0.24	95.16	44.45	30.21	245.00
1998–1999	28.14	62.40	6.13	0.05	144.85	214.45	37.68	493.70
1999–2000	21.06	78.15	18.01	0.40	188.63	68.21	44.23	418.70
2000–2001	26.59	80.51	21.09	0.19	255.08	64.03	45.01	492.49
2001–2002	17.52	59.12	23.92	0.40	355.94	64.76	67.38	589.03
2002–2003	18.46	62.05	32.15	0.33	281.76	44.85	90.83	530.43
2003–2004	40.51	77.63	52.37	0.37	286.04	57.65	194.74	709.31
2004–2005	47.01	59.37	71.00	0.61	345.83	94.97	378.40	997.19
2005–2006	58.42	127.03	88.77	1.98	379.85	179.56	577.70	1,413.31
2006–2007	34.37	228.00	142.05	3.05	306.02	323.62	470.33	1,507.45
2007–2008	109.97	257.02	194.72	4.15	628.56	287.97	634.96	2,117.35
2008–2009	126.24	313.11	151.79	3.97	496.04	370.17	356.57	1,817.89
2009–2010 (April–June)	20.31	55.52	30.70	0.60	109.49	58.70	86.43	361.76

Source: Prepared by the author based on Ministry of Commerce, Export–Import Data Bank, Government of India, New Delhi, April 1996 to June 2010.

Table 15.4 India's export to SAARC countries from 1996/97 to 2009/10 (values in US$ million)

	Afghanistan	Bangladesh	Bhutan	Maldives	Nepal	Pakistan	Sri Lanka	Total export
1996–1997	22.74	868.96	21.98	10.36	165.72	157.22	477.41	1,724.39
1997–1998	21.25	786.46	13.33	8.74	170.05	143.15	489.23	1,632.20
1998–1999	12.81	995.64	9.56	8.38	122.41	106.10	437.13	1,692.02
1999–2000	33.20	636.31	7.57	7.30	151.23	92.95	499.27	1,427.83
2000–2001	25.86	935.04	1.08	24.61	140.84	186.83	640.14	1,954.41
2001–2002	24.37	1,002.18	7.60	26.88	214.46	144.01	630.89	2,050.38
2002–2003	60.77	1,176.00	39.05	31.59	350.36	206.16	920.98	2,784.90
2003–2004	145.47	1,740.74	89.49	42.34	669.35	286.94	1,319.20	4,293.52
2004–2005	165.44	1,631.12	84.58	47.61	743.14	521.05	1,413.18	4,606.14
2005–2006	142.67	1,664.36	99.17	67.58	859.97	689.23	2,024.67	5,547.65
2006–2007	182.11	1,629.57	57.66	68.68	927.40	1,350.09	2,258.30	6,473.81
2007–2008	249.21	2,923.72	86.74	89.72	1,507.42	1,950.53	2,830.43	9,637.76
2008–2009	394.23	2,497.87	111.15	127.91	1,570.15	1,570.15	1,570.15	7,841.61
2009–2010 (April–June)	101.09	445.00	19.99	18.64	335.04	403.97	400.18	1,723.91

Source: Prepared by the author based on Ministry of Commerce, Export–Import Data Bank, Government of India, New Delhi, April 1996 to June 2010.

Table 15.5 India's total trade with SAARC countries from 1996/97–2009/10 (values in US$ million)

	Afghanistan	Bangladesh	Bhutan	Maldives	Nepal	Pakistan	Sri Lanka
Total import	562.35	1,573.35	879.92	16.51	3,937.28	1,909.55	3,057.31
Total export	1,581.22	18,932.97	648.95	580.34	7,927.54	7,808.38	15,911.16
Total trade	2,143.57	20,506.32	1,528.87	596.85	11,864.82	9,717.93	18,968.47

Source: Tables 15.3 and 15.4.

of political partnerships, physical connectivity through road and rail links, free trade arrangements and other forms of co-operation among the countries in the region, for which BIMSTEC has been a linking point. In 1994, India and Thailand floated the idea of setting up a regional bloc in the Bay of Bengal basin. Subsequently, a series of deliberations and inter-ministerial consultations formed the backdrop for the establishment of this forum, initially called BIST-EC (Bangladesh, India, Sri Lanka, Thailand[25] Economic Cooperation), on 6 June 1997 at the First Ministerial Meeting in Bangkok. In 1998, Myanmar was included as a new member. However, when the First BIMSTEC Summit was held in Thailand on 31 July 2004, the leaders renamed the grouping as the Bay of Bengal Initiative for Multi-Sectoral Technical and Economic Cooperation (BIMSTEC). At this Inaugural BIMSTEC Summit, the Indian Prime Minister Manmohan Singh said:

> BIMSTEC is a collective and effective forum for giving full expression to widely rediscover the coherence of the region based on the commonality of many linkages around the Bay of Bengal…. We consider our participation in BIMSTEC as a key element of our 'Look East Policy' and long-standing approach of good neighbours towards all other neighbours by land and sea.[26]

With the formation of BIMSTEC, member countries recommended the formulation of a free trade agreement for facilitating trade and investment, and promoting technical co-operation. This vision became a reality when the leaders endorsed the Framework Agreement on the BIMSTEC Free Trade Area (FTA), for promoting free trade in goods, services and investment, at the First BIMSTEC Summit (2004). The major highlights of the Framework Agreement are as follows:

- Trade in goods will be liberalized through progressive elimination of tariffs and non-tariff barriers, in two phases. Products will be identified for (a) Fast Track and (b) Normal Track.
- For the Fast Track products, the non-Least Developed Countries (LDC) will eliminate tariffs for LDC parties by 30 June 2007, but among themselves by 30 June 2009. The LDC parties will do so for non-LDCs by 30 June 2011, but among themselves by 30 June 2009.

• For the Normal Track products, the non-LDCs will eliminate tariffs for LDCs by 30 June 2010, but among themselves by 30 June 2012. The LDCs will eliminate tariffs for non-LDCs by 2017, but among themselves by 30 June, 2015.[27]

This Bangkok Summit was a watershed event in the history of pan-Asian regional and economic co-operation. Thus, by bringing together some members of SAARC on the one hand (India, Bangladesh, Sri Lanka, Nepal and Bhutan) and some members of ASEAN on the other (Thailand and Myanmar), the activities of BIMSTEC could be designed to eventually form a bridge linking these two regions. To augment bilateral trade and promote commercial relations among the BIMSTEC countries and to accelerate the progress of this regional endeavor in line with its destiny, the Export Import (EXIM) Bank of India extended Lines of Credit to Thailand and Sri Lanka and agreed to contribute two Lines of Credit facilities for Myanmar in order to upgrade the Yangon–Mandalay Railway System and finance the development of information and communication technology in Myanmar.[28] The overall trade of the BIMSTEC members with India since its inception is shown in Table 15.6.

It is clear from Table 15.6 that India's trade with BIMSTEC members in the initial years accounted for around 3 percent of India's total global trade. This trade figure increased from US$2,491.48 million in 1997–1998 to US$12,859.57 million in 2008–2009. In spite of this trade figure, BIMSTEC needs more time to make an impact. A number of problems, still unresolved, have time and again affected relations between India and other members of BIMSTEC and blocked the road for better understanding. One of the major impediments in this context is the limited complementarity of the products, especially with reference to textiles, produced by India on the one hand, and Sri Lanka and Bangladesh on the other. Indian textile companies[29] want textiles to be deemed as 'sensitive' items under the provisions of BIMSTEC-FTA agreement, the agreement proposes that textiles should be in the negative list. At the regional level, India wants to keep its textile market closed for the BIMSTEC member countries. The argument that New Delhi has pleaded is that the competitive advantage of Colombo and Dhaka in this sector is due to their access to cheap manpower and this can shatter the growth potential of Indian textile companies due to the blitz of cheap imports. However, during a visit of the Bangladesh Premier Sheikh Hasina to India in January 2010, New Delhi offered to scrutinize favorably Dhaka's demands for duty-free access for its goods on a priority basis, and agreed to sign an FTA by 2011. This willingness on the part of India[30] has given the Bangladeshi apparel exporters some satisfaction and if it materializes within the scheduled time, this process will naturally have a spillover effect in the BIMSTEC mechanism as well. Therefore, by acting as a conduit between the countries of South and Southeast Asia, BIMSTEC has brought India closer to the Southeast Asian region through the Myanmar–Thailand link.

Table 15.6 India's total trade with BIMSTEC countries compared with its global trade from 1997/8 to 2009/10 (values in US$ million)

Year	Bangladesh	Bhutan	Nepal	Sri Lanka	Myanmar	Thailand	Total trade	India's total world trade	India's total trade with BIMSTEC countries as a percentage of its overall world trade
(April–March) 1997–1998	837.27	26.77	265.21	519.44	273.32	569.47	2,491.48	76,269.47	3.26
1998–1999	1,058.04	15.69	267.26	474.81	203.88	594.11	2,613.79	75,607.43	3.45
1999–2000	714.46	25.58	339.86	543.5	205.69	775.61	2,604.7	86,560.55	3.01
2000–2001	1,015.55	22.17	395.92	685.15	234.4	868.04	3,221.23	95,096.74	3.38
2001–2002	1,061.3	31.52	570.4	698.27	435.32	1,056.22	3,853.03	95,240.00	4.04
2002–2003	1,238.05	71.2	632.12	1,011.81	411.11	1,090.2	4,454.49	114,131.57	3.90
2003–2004	1,818.37	141.86	955.39	1,513.94	498.65	1,440.73	6,368.94	141,991.66	4.48
2004–2005	1,690.49	155.58	1,088.97	1,791.58	519.1	1,767.27	7,012.99	195,053.37	3.59
2005–2006	1,791.39	187.94	1,239.82	2,602.37	636.66	2,286.89	8,745.07	252,256.26	3.46
2006–2007	1,857.57	199.71	1,233.42	2,728.63	923.09	3,193.29	10,135.71	312,149.29	3.24
2007–2008	3,180.74	281.46	2,135.98	3,465.39	994.45	4,111.8	14,169.82	414,786.19	3.41
2008–2009	2,810.98	262.94	2,066.19	1,926.72	1,150.61	4,642.13	12,859.57	488,991.67	2.62
2009–2010 (April–June)	500.52	50.69	444.53	486.61	299.12	994.13	2,775.6	98,049.04	2.83

Source: Prepared by the author based on Ministry of Commerce, Export–Import Data Bank, Government of India, New Delhi, April 1997 to June 2010.

Kunming Initiative/BCIM as an instrument of trans-regional co-operation

The Kunming/BCIM (Bangladesh, China, India and Myanmar) Initiative inaugurated on 17 August 1999 explores the prospects of co-operation by integrating parts or the whole of Bangladesh, China, India and Myanmar. The region has two of the fastest growing economies in the world but is also inhabited by some of the poorest people in the Asia-Pacific. The idea behind the launch of this initiative was that member countries would benefit from improved transport and communication links that would also help to overcome the region's underdevelopment.

The Kunming Cooperation Declaration of 2004 was the fruitful outcome of one of the biggest conferences of this grouping. However, a sort of dilemma has prevailed in the psyche of policy-makers, owing to deep concerns about the security issues in the troubled northeastern region and New Delhi's pessimism with respect to opening up borders, fearing that cheap Chinese goods would flood the markets and might hamper the local producers' bread and butter. Moreover, the unsettled border dispute with China, and India's skepticism regarding this issue, has also haunted the Indian policy-makers. Furthermore, conflicting interests among the partners has hampered implementation of this initiative. Wide publicity of the merits of trade, tourism and economic co-operation is imperative to enable different communities to prepare for such opportunities.[31]

Mekong Ganga Cooperation as a conduit of India's 'Look East' policy

Like the Kunming Initiative, the Mekong Ganga Cooperation (MGC) is another trans-regional endeavor which seeks to transcend the geographical borders between South and Southeast Asian countries. It includes India and five other ASEAN members, Cambodia, Laos, Vietnam, Myanmar and Thailand, and was inaugurated on 10 November 2000 at the Laotian capital, Vientiane, identifying tourism, culture, education and transport linkage as the core agenda for future trade and investment collaboration among the member states.[32] Table 15.7 shows that India's trade with the MGC countries has gradually increased but is still less than 2 percent of its overall world trade.

Conclusion

From our analysis of the emergence of multilateral economic organizations as vehicles for delivering economic prosperity in the South Asian region it is clear that the nation-states of South and Southeast Asia in the post-cold war globalized milieu have realized pragmatically that multilateralism would remain an effective instrument of their economic and foreign policy. The collapse of the cold war order and the evolution of a new economic environment has forced the hitherto superpower-dependent countries to follow alternative avenues for their

Table 5.7 India's total trade with MGC countries compared with its global trade from 2000/01 to 2009/10 (values in US$ million)

Year	Cambodia	Vietnam	Laos	Myanmar	Thailand	Total trade	India's total world trade	India's total trade with MGC countries as a percentage of its overall world trade
(April–March) 2000–2001	9.18	238.29	6.24	234.4	868.04	1,356.15	95,096.74	1.42
2001–2002	12.41	237.08	3.2	435.32	1,056.22	1,744.23	95,240.00	1.83
2002–2003	20.45	366.57	1.73	411.11	1,090.2	1,890.06	114,131.57	1.65
2003–2004	18.88	448.64	0.56	498.65	1,440.73	2,407.46	141,991.66	1.70
2004–2005	18.37	642.46	2.7	519.1	1,767.27	2,949.90	195,053.37	1.51
2005–2006	24.97	822.07	5.57	636.66	2,286.89	3,776.16	252,256.26	1.50
2006–2007	53.67	1,153.07	2.74	923.09	3,193.29	5,325.86	312,149.29	1.70
2007–2008	56.4	1,783.77	3.97	994.45	4,111.8	6,950.39	414,786.19	1.67
2008–2009	49.62	2,147.31	9.53	1,150.61	4,642.13	7,999.20	488,991.67	1.63
2009–2010 (April–June)	14.27	433.43	10.27	299.12	994.13	1,751.22	98,049.04	1.78

Source: Prepared by the author based on Ministry of Commerce, Export–Import Data Bank, Government of India, New Delhi, April 2000 to June 2010.

economic survival. The formation of SAARC and the promotion of regional integration is one of them. The experiments with SAPTA and SAFTA have been a learning curve for the South Asian states. Some economists argue that regionalism can improve the chances of freer trade worldwide, over time. However, others argue that RTAs have emerged as an alternative to achieving trade liberalization as multilateral efforts at the international level (e.g., WTO) have faced political and economic obstacles. The research findings presented in this chapter show that the implementation of SAFTA (and SAPTA) has increased intra-regional trade, but not significantly. Between 1995 and 2001 intra-regional trade was on average only 4 percent of the total trade for the region. There are several reasons for this which include time-consuming negotiations and procedures, limited complementarities, sensitive lists, lack of exportable surpluses (as shown by the crisis in December 2010 over the price of onions), restrictive trade policies, political unpalatableness of structural adjustment especially where it leads to unemployment, and inter-state conflict. However, the South Asian states may also be accused of adopting an instrumental approach to multilateralism, i.e., using it as a foreign policy option.[33] This is further exemplified by India's role in BIMSTEC, the Kunming Initiative and Mekong Ganga Co-operation. All three initiatives are meant to further India's 'Look East' policy. Moreover, most of the South Asian states have signed bilateral free trade agreements with each other, giving rise to a 'spaghetti bowl' phenomenon that is not taken into account by SAFTA. Yet the Secretary-General of SAARC, Sheel Kant Sharma, points out that intra-regional trade has increased from $14 million in 2006 to $687 million in 2009, and that

> an Asian Development Bank (ADB) study done in 2008 pegs potential of trade under SAFTA at $85.1 billion. Large volumes of informal trade are also indicative of potential trade under SAFTA. The fact that intra-SAARC trade volumes are far lower compared to other regions is not a critique of SAFTA. I would say it rather reflects on structural problems of industry and infrastructure.[34]

Papers published by some economists argue that although the potential gains from intraregional South Asian trade could be substantial for the smaller economies, partly because of relatively low transport costs, investment in infrastructure and access to larger markets, the larger economies will not benefit to the same extent unless a larger Asian grouping is institutionalized. This could partly explain India's desire to expand eastwards. However, given the present structure of international trade, unilateral trade liberalization by each of the South Asian countries at their own pace may be their best option. Proponents of free trade argue that co-ordinated liberalization in all of South Asia could be extended to the rest of the world on a most-favored-nation principle. Moreover 'it should be viewed as an integral part of extending and deepening the ongoing economic reforms process in South Asia.' Finally, inter-regional trading arrangements with industrialized countries are likely to yield more gains for South Asia. Emulating the EU (or even ASEAN) model may not work for South Asia. However, economic co-operation could be a stepping-stone to better political relations, as functionalists or neo-functionalists might argue.[35] As this volume demonstrates, there are many areas in which the nation-states of South Asia need to co-operate, and regional organizations like SAARC could facilitate intra-regional co-operation, as the resolutions adopted at the Thimpu Summit demonstrate. Furthermore, the interest shown by various countries and regional blocs in obtaining observer status in SAARC could lead to greater economic dynamism and better understanding between them and the South Asian states.

The 16th SAARC Summit held in April 2010 in Thimphu (capital of Bhutan) has gone down as a watershed event in the chronology of India-South Asia ties. This Summit acted as a platform of regional unity, as the leaders of the SAARC countries pledged to enhance co-operation for the holistic development of South Asia, with particular emphasis on trade and investment; resolving social issues like poverty; and facing up to threats to security emanating from cross-border terrorism, environmental degradation, trafficking of human beings and contraband materials, and anti-democratic rhetoric. Towards this end, at the conclusion of this Summit, which also marked 25 years of the existence of SAARC, a 37-point joint declaration – *Towards a Green and Happy South Asia* – was issued by the member countries. The declaration contained the resolutions for making the region a better place to live in, by improving the standards of living of the South Asian population, estimated at 1.5 billion, accounting for about one-fifth of the total population of the world. In a significant measure to combat the perils of climate change, the *Thimphu Statement on Climate Change*, also issued at the end of the Summit, expressed the determination of the leaders to make South Asia a front-runner in the use of low-carbon technologies and renewable energy. Furthermore, underscoring the need to meet the scourge of terrorism and transnational crimes in a concerted manner, the SAARC leaders reaffirmed their commitment to implement the SAARC Regional Convention on Suppression of Terrorism, its Additional Protocol and SAARC Convention on Narcotic Drugs and Psychotropic Substances. In the realm of trade and investment collaboration, while reiterating their commitment to implement SAFTA in letter and spirit, the regional leaders not only welcomed the signing of the SAARC Agreement on Trade in Services, but also called for its early ratification, as it would open up new vistas of trade co-operation and regional integration. Moreover, taking note of the Reports of the Steering Committee of the proposed South Asian University, the SAARC representatives urged the expeditious finalization of mutual recognition of academic and professional degrees and harmonization of educational curriculums in South Asia. Finally, while endorsing the recommendation to declare 2010–2020 as the 'Decade of Intra-regional Connectivity in SAARC,' the leaders of the member states of SAARC called for collaborative efforts to achieve greater intra-regional connectivity.[36] In sum, therefore, though the 16th SAARC Summit has struck the right chord of co-operation among the member countries for working towards an economically prosperous, socially developed and environmentally friendly South Asia, this optimistic vision needs to be translated into reality, for which the right political will and positive mindset of the political establishment is imperative.

Notes

1 F. Butler, 'Regionalism and integration', 1997, p. 410.
2 R. Cupitt, R. Whitlock and L.W. Whitlock, 'The (Im)mortality of International Governmental Organizations', 1984.
3 See Desmond Dinan (ed.), *The origins and evolution of the European Union*, 2006; Martin J. Dedman, *The Origins and Development of the European Union*, 1996.
4 Official website of the ASEAN, available www.aseansec.org accessed on 16 November 2009.
5 http://zeenews.com/news622549.html
6 Citha Maass, 'South Asia', 1999.
7 See for example Shyamali Ghosh, 'Political dynamics in Bangladesh', 1995.
8 K.C. Dash, *Regionalism in South Asia*, 2008.
9 The Kunming Initiative got its name on 17 August 1999, at a conference on regional cooperation and development among China, India, Myanmar and Bangladesh held in Kunming, the capital of Yunnan province in the southwestern region of China.
10 Tridib Chakraborti, 'SAARC Expands its Wings', 2008, p. 202.
11 The Agreement on SAFTA was signed on 6 January 2004 and it entered into force on 1 January 2006.
12 SAARC website, available www.saarc-sec.org, accessed on 21 January 2010.
13 Of the 902 commodities on which India offered tariff concessions, 390 and 512 commodities were offered to all SAARC countries and the Least Developed Countries (LDC) respectively.
14 Charan Wadhva, 'Assessing SAARC Preferential Trading Arrangement', 1996, p. 175.
15 For details, see J. De Mello, A. Panagariya and D. Rodrik, 'The New Regionalism', 1993.
16 Piyush Pandey, 'India Under Cheap Textile Imports Threat', *Business Standard*, 6 May 2005.
17 Agreement on SAFTA, online, available www.saarc-sec.org, accessed on 19 January 2010.
18 Ibid.
19 www.commerce.nic.in/PressRelease/pressrelease_detail.asp?id, accessed on 20 January 2009.
20 Ibid.
21 J.L. Rao, 'Envisioning A South Asian Union: Challenges', in A.S. Raju (ed.), *Reconstructing South Asia – An Agenda*, New Delhi: Gyan Publishing House, 2007, p. 218.
22 Address of SAARC Secretary General, S.K. Sharma, at the Inaugural Session of the Fifteenth SAARC Summit, Colombo, 3 August 2008.
23 Major product categories that are traded among BIMSTEC countries are live bovine animals; fisheries; coffee and tea; spices; fat, fuels and oils; processed food; chemical and pharmaceutical products; fertilizers; tanning or dyeing products; vehicles and parts; machinery and parts; electrical appliances etc.
24 'Future Directions of BIMSTEC: Towards a Bay of Bengal Economic Community', RIS Policy Brief, no. 12, February 2004, p. 1, online, www.ris.org.in/asianstudy20. htm, accessed on 24 February 2005.
25 These four countries were selected on the basis of their proximity and direct access to the Bay of Bengal.
26 *The Hindu*, 1 August 2004.
27 BISTEC, 'Framework Agreement on BIMSTEC Free Trade Area', 2004.

28 'BIMSTEC Initiative: A Study of India's Trade and Investment Potential with Select Asian Countries', Occasional Paper: 100, EXIM Bank, India, online, available www. eximbankindia.com/old/publi-main, accessed on 29 November 2009.

29 Textiles and clothing exports from India to BIMSTEC countries accounted for around 11 percent, while textile and clothing imports to India was pegged at around 10.6 percent.

30 India will import 14 million pieces of duty-free garments annually, as against eight million now, following talks held during Bangladesh Prime Minister Sheikh Hasina's visit to New Delhi.

31 L.R. Singh, 'The Kunming Initiative,' accessed on 30 January 2009.

32 www.mfa.gov.th/web/882.php, accessed on 31 January 2009.

33 See E. Barbé, 'Multilateralism matters more than ever', 2009.

34 See SAARC website at www.saarc-sec.org/

35 See A.J.R. Groom and Paul Taylor (eds), *Functionalism*, 1975.

36 SAARC website, available http://www/saarc-sec.org/userfiles/16thSummitDeclaratio n29April10.pdf; see also www.sixteenthsaarcsummit.bt, accessed on 1 May 2010.

Bibliography

Barbé, E., 'Multilateralism Matters More than Ever', *Global Society*, 23:2, April 2009.

Baylis, J. and S. Smith (eds), *The Globalization of World Politics*, London: Oxford University Press, 1997.

BIMSTEC, 'Framework Agreement on BIMSTEC Free Trade Area', 31 July 2004, online, available www.bimstec.org, accessed on 2 August 2004.

Butler, F., 'Regionalism and Integration' in J. Baylis and S. Smith (eds), *The Globalization of World Politics*, Oxford: Oxford University Press, 1997.

Chakraborti, Tridib, 'SAARC Expands its Wings: Insinuations in the New Global Order', *World Focus*, New Delhi, May 2008, pp. 201–202.

Chakraborti, Tridib, 'India's Look East Policy: Time for Stock-Taking', *World Focus*, New Delhi, November–December 2009.

Chakraborti, Tridib, 'Sheikh Hasina's India Mission: From Distance to Proximity', *World Focus*, New Delhi, January 2010, pp. 35–41.

Cupitt, R., R. Whitlock and L.W. Whitlock, 'The (Im)mortality of International Governmental Organizations' in P. Diehl (ed.), *The Politics of Global Governance*, London and Boulder, CO: Lynne Rienner, 1997.

Dash, K.C., *Regionalism in South Asia*, London: Routledge, 2008.

Dedman, Martin J., *The Origins and Development of the European Union, 1945–95: A History of European Integration*, London: Routledge, 1996.

Delgado, J.D.R., 'SAFTA: Living in a World of Regional Trade Agreements', IMF Working Paper, WP/07/23, 2007.

Dinnan, Desmond (ed.), *The Origins and Evolution of the European Union*, Oxford: Oxford University Press, 2006.

EXIM Bank, 'BIMSTEC Initiative: A Study of India's Trade and Investment Potential with Select Asian Countries', *Occasional Paper: 100*, India: EXIM Bank, online, available www.eximbankindia.com/old/publi-main, accessed on 29 November 2009.

Ghosh, Shyamali, 'Political Dynamics in Bangladesh: Relations Between Bangladesh and India', *International Studies*, 32:3, 1995.

Government of India, Ministry of External Affairs, *Annual Report: 2004–2005*, New Delhi: Government of India, 2005.

Government of India, Ministry of External Affairs, *Annual Report: 2005–2006*, New Delhi: Government of India, 2006.

Government of India, Ministry of External Affairs, *Annual Report: 2008–2009*, New Delhi: Government of India, 2009.

Groom, A.J.R. and P. Taylor (eds), *Functionalism: Theory and Practice in International Relations*, London: University of London Press, 1975.

Kelegama, Saman, 'SAARC – From Association to Community', *South Asian Survey*, 6:2, July–December 1999.

Keohane, R., *After Hegemony: Co-operation and Discord in the World Political Economy*, Princeton: Princeton University Press, 1984.

Maass, Citha, 'South Asia: Drawn Between Cooperation and Conflict' in E. Gonsalves and N. Jetly (eds), *The Dynamics of South Asia: Regional Cooperation and SAARC*, New Delhi: Sage, 1999.

Mann, Baljit, 'Governance in South Asia: Problems and Prospects', in Kulwant Kaur and Baljit Mann (eds), *South Asia: Dynamics of Politics, Economy and Security*, New Delhi: Knowledge World, 2006.

Mello, J. De, A. Panagariya and D. Rodrik, 'The New Regionalism: A Country Perspective', in J. De Mello and A. Panagariya (eds), *New Dimensions in Regional Integration*, Cambridge: Cambridge University Press, 1993.

Paul, T.V., *South Asia's Weak States: Understanding the Regional Insecurity Predicament*, Stanford Security Studies, 2010.

Pigato, M., 'South Asia's Integration into the World Economy', *World Bank Report*, Washington, DC: World Bank, 1997.

Research and Information System for Developing Countries, 'Future Directions of BIMSTEC: Towards A Bay of Bengal Economic Community', *RIS Policy Brief*, India, no. 12, February 2004, online, available www.ris.org.in/asianstudy20.htm, accessed on 24 February 2005.

Research and information system for developing countries, 'Mekong Economic Corridors: Asia's New Lifelines', Mekong *Ganga Policy Brief*, No. 2, October 2007, online, www.ris.org.in/MGPB2.pdf, accessed on 24 February, 2008.

Rao, J.L., 'Envisioning a South Asian Union: Challenges' in A.S. Raju (ed.), *Reconstructing South Asia – An Agenda*, New Delhi: Gyan Publishing House, 2007.

Sharma, S.K. (Secretary General of SAARC), Address at the Inaugural Session of the Fifteenth SAARC Summit, Colombo, 3 August 2008, online, available www.saarcsec.org, accessed on 15 August 2008.

Singh, L.R., 'The Kunming Initiative: Prospects for Sub-regional Cooperation', online, available www.asianscholarship.org/asf/ejourn/articles/rajen_sl.pdf

Srinivasan, T.N., 'Regional Trading Arrangements and Beyond: Exploring Some Options for South Asia', *Report No. 142*, Washington, DC: World Bank, 1994.

Upadhyaya, Shashi, 'Pakistan's Perception of India's Role in SAARC', *South Asian Studies*, 31:1 and 2, January–December 1996.

Wadhva, Charan, 'Assessing SAARC Preferential Trading Arrangement: India's Role', *South Asian Survey*, 6:1, January–June 1996.

Weerakoon, Dushni, 'Economic Cooperation in South Asia: Challenges and Constraints', in A.S. Raju (ed.), *Reconstructing South Asia: An Agenda*, New Delhi: Gyan Publishing House, 2007.

World Bank, 'India–Bangladesh Bilateral Trade and Potential Free Trade Agreement', *Bangladesh Development Series*, Paper No. 13, Dhaka: World Bank Office, December 2006, online, available www.worldbank.org.bd/bds, accessed on 15 February 2010.

Newspapers

Business Standard, India, 6 May 2005.
Daily Star, Dhaka, 4 January 2005.
The Hindu, India, 1 August 2004.

Internet sources

www.aseansec.org
www.bimstec.org
www.commerce.nic.in/PressRelease/pressrelease_detail.asp?id
www.cpd-bangladesh.org/work/dpnational.html
www.eximbankindia.com/old/publi-main
www.mfa.gov.th/web/882.php
www.ris.org.in/asianstudy20.htm
www.saarc-sec.org
www.worldbank.org.bd/bds
http://zeenews.com/news622549.html

Index

For Product Safety Concerns and Information please contact our EU
representative GPSR@taylorandfrancis.com
Taylor & Francis Verlag GmbH, Kaufingerstraße 24, 80331 München, Germany

www.ingramcontent.com/pod-product-compliance
Lightning Source LLC
Chambersburg PA
CBHW060151280326
41932CB00012B/1718